LOOKING AT GAY
AND
LESBIAN LIFE

LOOKING AT GAY
AND
LESBIAN LIFE

Warren J. Blumenfeld
&
Diane Raymond

Beacon Press   Boston

This book is dedicated:
to members of twelve-step programs everywhere whose guiding principles made my participation in this project possible;
W.B.

* * *

to K., who gives me hope for future generations;

D.R.

* * *

and to the memory of all those who were taken from us too soon.

Beacon Press
25 Beacon Street
Boston, Massachusetts 02108-2800

Beacon Press books
are published under the auspices of
the Unitarian Universalist Association of Congregations.

96 95 94 93 92 91 90 89   8 7 6 5 4 3 2

Library of Congress Cataloging-in-Publication Data
Blumenfeld, Warren J.
   Looking at gay and lesbian life / Warren J. Blumenfeld and Diane Raymond.
     p. cm.
   Includes bibliographies and index.
   ISBN 0-8070-7907-3
   1. Homosexuality—United States.   I. Raymond, Diane Christine.
   II. Title.
[HQ76.3.U5B58 1989]
306.76′6′0973—dc20   89-42590

Contents

5

Introduction

In the mid-1980s a new alternative high school opened its doors in New York City. The Harvey Milk Memorial High School—named in honor of the slain gay San Francisco City Supervisor—was launched to help bring gay and lesbian students, many of whom were living on the streets, back into a school system they had left. Fully accredited and receiving partial funding from the public school system, the new school soon became front-page news; television and radio talk shows were quick to provide forums where the merits of this concept could be debated.

On the one hand, some people saw the existence of the school as a positive step toward meeting the needs of lesbian and gay students. Such students, advocates argued, were commonly harassed in school, with little protection from figures of authority. Often they had little recourse but to endure the harassment or leave school. On the other hand, opponents of the school saw it as the establishment of a dangerous precedent where students were segregated from one another and tax dollars were used unwisely. Some even argued that the school's creation reflected a kind of favoritism toward gay and lesbian students.

Regardless of one's position in this debate, however, one point is certain: the Harvey Milk Memorial High School came into being in response to a long-standing problem not limited to New York City. That is, to be gay or lesbian, or even perceived as such, puts one in a very vulnerable position throughout the entire educational process. But in high school in particular, where individuals are dealing with their own emerging sexuality, gay and lesbian students are not simply a minority group, but may even be viewed as threatening. Anyone who remembers back to high school will probably remember how most forms of difference were suspect. But differences associated with sexuality are even more volatile.

11

This treatment is obviously not confined to our school systems. Indeed, there is little question that lesbians and gays have been and continue to be the victims of prejudice and discrimination throughout the society.

> American homosexuals were condemned to death by choking, burning, and drowning; they were executed, jailed, pilloried, fined, court-martialed, prostituted, fired, framed, blackmailed, disinherited, declared insane, driven to insanity, to suicide, murder, and self-hatred, witch-hunted, entrapped, stereotyped, mocked, insulted, isolated, pitied, castigated, and despised. (They were also castrated, lobotomized, shock-treated, and psychoanalyzed.)... External judgments internalized became self-oppression.... When simply working, living, and loving, homosexuals have been condemned to invisibility. (Katz, pp. 17-18.)

Citizens from a country that prides itself on promoting individual liberty and tolerance of diversity may find it difficult to accept the idea that gays and lesbians — who make up a significant percentage of the population — suffer from the effects of prejudice. In the United States alone, that means that the members of this sexual minority number in the millions. Though not all of them are oppressed equally, and though some — because they are also, for example, women, members of racial or ethnic minorities, or elderly — may suffer other sorts of prejudice, all share the fact of their exclusion from mainstream society. This exclusion — or discrimination — is based on prejudice and takes a variety of forms.

Though there is no denying that conditions for gays may be better today than they were one hundred years ago, today's climate is hardly supportive; for example:

- Few states have any legal protections for gay people. One can be denied housing or employment merely because one is gay.

- A study by the National Gay and Lesbian Task Force (1984) found that more than 90 percent of the respondents had experienced some type of victimization because of their sexual orientation and over 33 percent had been threatened with violence. A case in point: in Bangor, Maine, a twenty-three-year-old gay man was beaten and thrown off a bridge into the Kendeskeag Stream. He drowned, and his attackers bragged of their deed. The young men accused in this incident were given a light sentence and placed on probation.

- The United States Supreme Court ruled in 1986 that there is no constitutional guarantee of the right to privacy for the performance of sexual acts commonly associated with gay men.

- There is no legally sanctioned way for same-sex partners to make a public declaration of their commitment to each other.

It is not difficult to come up with other examples. It is likely, though, that as you read the list, some of them did not strike you as forms of prejudice; or you may in fact believe such treatment is justified. This book examines some of the reasons for that view and investigates some of the social and historical circumstances surrounding the treatment of lesbians and gays. But why, you may wonder, is there any value in pursuing these topics?

Why Discuss This Topic?

Even if it is true that there is a significant number of gay and lesbian people, it is also true, nonetheless, that the overwhelming majority of the world's population is heterosexual. Why should anyone want to investigate the topic of homosexuality? Consider the following reasons:

It is no mere coincidence that the black liberation, women's liberation, and gay/lesbian liberation movements flourished in quick succession in the 1960s. Though each movement focused its attention on a different target group, they shared certain beliefs about oppression, and they sought to question many of the assumptions held by the majority about difference and social norms. For example, feminists argued against sex roles and sexist stereotyping. They challenged concepts of "femininity" and "masculinity," maintaining that to channel individuals along gender lines is ultimately restrictive for both males *and* females. Each of us, feminists argued, while of a certain biological sex, has an incredible potential for growth that is unrelated to that biology. To say that certain actions are required or prohibited "because you are a woman (or man)" is to rob us of that potential.

Similarly, gay liberationists argued (as feminists had for sex roles), that rigidly enforcing heterosexuality as a social norm limited both homosexuals *and* heterosexuals. The gay liberation movement insisted that we must acknowledge certain truths: that not everyone will marry or wants to marry; that not all people are attracted to members of the other sex; that few people are exclusively heterosexual or homosexual; that men are not always sexually active and women not always passive. In doing so, they challenged certain social institutions and demanded a new framework in which alternative sexual lifestyles were not only admitted but also approved. This has implications not just for homosexuals but also for heterosexuals, for whom rigid standards of sexual behavior are also unfulfilling.

For some, these kinds of changes in practice and transformations of values are threatening to the social order. They maintain that norms and rules of conduct maintain stability and security, and are essential to the preservation of society. This argument, then, implies that human beings are especially fragile, vulnerable to confusion, and in need of rigid structures and that society is a fragile grouping whose survival is a tenuous one at best. There are many who have disagreed with either or both of these claims. But, however one views them, this position is still debatable, for it assumes that *all* such norms are essential to that goal, and are equally productive. It also assumes that a society which encourages and nurtures diversity cannot survive.

By investigating issues related to sexual preference and by evaluating assumptions about sexual "normalcy," one has the opportunity to make distinctions between those norms which are useful and those which might constitute, in the words of the political theorist Herbert Marcuse (1955), "surplus repression." That is to say, not all rules are necessary; some may be products of another historical period, others may be the result of factual error. Regardless of their origin, though, an excess of rules may be just as disastrous for a society as an absence of them. An excess of rules may lead to stagnation, apathy, and a reduced capacity for creativity. Questioning social norms, on the other hand, can excite all of us to learn new ideas which could change our lives. And, even if we decide to retain all the rules we have, that decision will at least be the result of a process of critical thinking and analysis and not an unexamined acceptance of what we have been taught.

Along these lines, there are those who fear that a serious investigation of value systems may lead to deep personal confusion. Since roles provide a measure of security, how will I know how to be, what to do, how to act if these roles are now put into question? Some have even argued that studying sexuality will encourage students to experiment sexually; others maintain that viewing homosexuality as an alternative lifestyle will confuse those who have not clarified their own sexual identity. These fears, though, seem to be ungrounded. There is no evidence supporting the claim that responsible discussions of sex and sexuality will lead either to experimentation outside the classroom or a confused sexual identity. Rather, it appears that a serious, mature, and open discussion of these issues helps students to sort out fact from myth, increasing the likelihood of responsible decision-making. And, rather than the confusion, an understanding of alternative expressions of sexuality aids in an acceptance of one's own orientation, regardless of what form that might take.

To make these points more concrete: since a significant percentage of the population is gay or lesbian, to examine one's attitudes about homosexuality can help to enrich one's relationships, whether they occur with friends, classmates, co-workers, or family members.

Finally, though all of us share membership in the human species, it is also obvious that each of us is different and unique. In some way, then, all of us deviate from a norm, whether that deviation be physical, social, attitudinal, or behavioral. Each of us, therefore, can benefit from alleviating prejudice. And as prejudice diminishes in society, each of us can feel less threatened by our own uniqueness. If homophobia—fear and hatred of gays, lesbians, and bisexuals—is a form of prejudice, then it has destructive effects not only on gay people but also on those who are homophobic. Just as racism cripples both white people and people of color, so homophobia threatens to undermine all of us.

It is probably apparent at this point that this book is not without assumptions of its own. Indeed, there is no claim made here to neutrality, though each chapter presents a number of competing arguments on the issues in question. This discussion, then, is grounded on four fundamental assumptions:

- That homosexuality is a legitimate life option.

- That being gay or lesbian is more than merely having sex with someone of the same sex.

- That homophobia—like other forms of prejudice—is a devastating and insidious condition which closes off life options and stifles the spirit. It is *not* simply a harmless fear, like a fear of heights.

- That eliminating prejudice is a necessary (though not sufficient) step in human development. Hence, gay and lesbian liberation is an essential part of human liberation.

It is only through dialogue that change is possible, and it is only through careful reasoning that one can begin to acknowledge the *need* to change. As the philosopher Erich Fromm has put it:

> I believe that the only force that can save us from self-destruction is reason; the capacity to recognize the unreality of most of the ideas that man holds, and to penetrate to the reality veiled by the layers and layers of deception and ideologies; reason, not as a body of knowledge, but as a "kind of energy, a force which is fully comprehensible only in its agency and effects..."; a force whose "most important function consists in its power to bind and to dissolve." Violence and arms will not save us; sanity and reason may. (Erich Fromm, p. 179; quote from Ernst Cassirer, p. 13.)

The major sections of this book are summarized:

"A Discussion about Difference: The Left-Hand Analogy" uses the striking similarities between left-handedness and homosexuality as a basis for analogy. In doing so, it introduces many of the concepts which later chapters explore in greater depth.

"Socialization and Gender Roles" explores the ways in which human value systems are developed through the process of socialization, and specifically how this process affects the ways in which societies assign roles according to the biological sex of the individual. This chapter provides a background against which the issue of homosexuality is introduced.

"Sexuality" looks at general attitudes concerning human sexuality and focuses on same-sex relations by analyzing animal and cross-cultural same-sex behavior. This chapter attempts to provide a model for understanding sexuality free from traditional bias.

"What Causes Homosexuality?" examines some of the common explanations that have been put forward for the development of sexual orientation. The discussion exposes the weaknesses inherent in many of these theories.

"Sexuality and the Heritage of Western Religion" explores some of the major similarities and differences in the world-views of the major Western religions. It then suggests how contemporary attitudes toward homosexuality may have emerged from those frameworks.

"Prejudice and Discrimination" looks at the nature of prejudice as a general concept and then places homophobia within that framework.

"History of Lesbian and Gay Movement Politics" traces the development of the gay and lesbian liberation/rights movements, emphasizing the diversity of political strategies involved and showing the mutual influence between this movement and other political trends.

"AIDS: Politics and Precautions" examines the medical, social, and political ramifications of the AIDS epidemic and discusses other forms of sexually transmitted diseases in addition to safer sex precautions.

"Lifestyles and Culture" provides information about the realities of gay and lesbian life and responds to many of the myths and stereotypes about gay people.

"The Homosexual in Literature" surveys the foundations of this genre and provides an extensive bibliography of lesbian and gay literature.

Terminology

Of primary importance to any discussion of lesbians and gays is the issue of identity and the meaning of the term "homosexual." An ongoing and oftentimes heated debate is currently underway among researchers in the social sciences who, though acknowledging the universal existence of homosexual activity throughout time, are in disagreement over when in history some people began to construct their personal lives around same-sex attractions.

There are two major schools of thought on this matter. On the one hand, there are those who argue for the existence of a continuous history and culture for people who could be called, in today's term, "homosexual." This view, often referred to as "essentialism," maintains that gays and lesbians have always and everywhere existed. On the other hand, there are those who argue that definitions of personal identity are culturally based and, except for a few isolated pockets in history, homosexual identity is a relatively modern invention developing in the West around the end of the 19th century. This view, referred to as "constructivism," assumes that a break took place in the 19th century in our thinking about sexual identity, enabling a "homosexual identity" to emerge. More recently, some theorists have suggested the possibility that these competing views are not mutually exclusive. Later chapters will flesh out these views in more detail.

It is important for the reader to be aware of these distinct positions. This book, as one might discern, leans toward a constructivist view of the development of sexual identity. However, some of the cited materials (Boswell, for example) assume an essentialist perspective. Here we use the terms "homosexual," "gay," and "lesbian" for purposes of clarity and simplicity, but do not mean to imply complete agreement with either of the two positions.

Many labels have been given to individuals who were thought to have physical and/or emotional attractions to members of their own sex. Some of these terms have been positive, some negative. In this book we have deliberately opted to use certain terms over others. Therefore, some explanation of our choice of terminology is essential here.

We see the goal of this book as one of broadening our ability to raise key questions, and addressing questions of language is the first step toward that goal. Language provides us with the means to describe and understand the world. But language can also color our perceptions, and lead us to have certain expectations about that world which may or may not be true.

Just as African Americans today reject the term "Negro" in part because it was imposed on them, many gays and lesbians reject the term "homosexual," the term that psychiatrists, lawyers, teachers, and the clergy have historically used for them. In addition, the term "homosexual" reflects a narrow, clinical focus on sexual conduct itself, giving rise to a popular belief that this orientation is only about sex.

Therefore, throughout this book the terms "gay" and "lesbian" are generally used in preference to "homosexual," unless the concept is meant to refer to it as a clinical entity.

Furthermore, we draw special attention to our use of the term "lesbian." As women, lesbians struggle against both homophobia and sexism; in addition, though the word "gay" sometimes includes lesbians (much like, perhaps, the word "man" in its generic sense is said to include women), in practice this use tends to make lesbians more invisible. Further, using the word "gay" to include lesbians and gay males may mask the many real differences that exist between the two groups.

It is important to emphasize that gayness or lesbianism itself is far more than sexual behavior alone, but often includes attitudes, values, and lifestyle choices. To engage in "homosexual sex" is not necessarily equivalent to being a gay male or lesbian—that is, having an affectional preference or orientation for members of one's own sex. "Gay" and "lesbian" are ways of labelling oneself as multi-dimensional. As one author notes:

> A homosexual person is gay [or lesbian] when he [or she] regards himself [or herself] happily gifted with whatever capacity he [or she] has to see people as romantically beautiful. It is to be free of shame, guilt, regret, over the fact that one is homosexual, that the searchlight of one's childhood vision of human beings shined more brilliantly on members of one's own sex than on those of the other. That, for whatever reason, it illuminated those and gave them fascination—and burst then with sexual brilliance when the body learned to crave what it had been pursuing. To be gay [or lesbian] is to view one's sexuality as the healthy heterosexual views his [or hers]. (Weinberg, p. 70.)

Later chapters will also show that these terms have emerged because of the presence of certain social and historical circumstances; one cannot, then, consider these labels in isolation from the prevailing social ideology. Indeed, the terms "lesbian," "gay," "bisexual," "heterosexual," and "homosexual" are all products of history and culture. As such, their meaning can be created and recreated, and all of us can struggle toward more authentic ways of loving. It is to that mission that we dedicate this book.

REFERENCES

Boswell, John. *Christianity, Social Tolerance, and Homosexuality: Gay People in Western Europe from the Beginning of the Christian Era to the Fourteenth Century.* Chicago: University of Chicago Press, 1980.

Cassirer, Ernst. *The Philosophy of the Enlightenment*, trans. F. Koelin and J. Pettegrove, Princeton University Press, 1951.

Fromm, Erich. *Beyond the Chains of Illusion*. From *The Philosophy of Enlightenment*, by E. Cassirer. Boston: Beacon Press, 1955.

Katz, Jonathan. *Gay American History: Lesbian and Gay Men in the U.S.A.* New York: Avon, 1976.

Marcuse, Herbert. *Eros and Civilization: A Philosophical Inquiry into Freud*. Boston: Beacon Press, 1955.

Weinberg, George. *Society and the Healthy Homosexual*. St. Martin's Press, New York, 1972.

Acknowledgments

There were many people who helped in a number of ways in the creation of this book. It would not be possible to thank them all, but several should be singled out for their special assistance. They include: Elizabeth Heron, Cathy Hoffman, R.P. Wasson, Jr., and Thomas Whitaker. In addition, we thank the following groups and individuals for their suggestions and support:

The Chicago Resource Center;
The Haymarket People's Fund;
The Human Rights Committee of Cambridge Rindge and Latin High School, Cambridge, Massachusetts;
Allen Young, writer, community activist;
Linda Hirsch, Gay and Lesbian Speakers Bureau of Boston;
The Reverend Robert Wheatley, Unitarian Universalist Church;
Bret Hinsch, Harvard University, Asian Studies;
John Flanagan, Harvard University, Islamic Studies;
Paul Schalow, University of Massachusetts, Amherst, Japanese Studies;
Rachel Rasmussen, Harvard University, Divinity School;
Sara Wunsch, Chair, Cambridge, Massachusetts Human Rights Commission;
David Scondras, Boston City Council;
Kevin Cathcart, Director, Gay and Lesbian Advocates and Defenders;
Kathleen Marotta, Cambridge, Massachusetts;
Gary Reinhardt, Harvard University Divinity School;
Sukie Magraw, California School of Professional Psychology;
John Mitzel, Glad Day Bookshop, Boston;
William Barnert, Gay and Lesbian Speakers Bureau of Boston;
Kevin Berrill, National Gay and Lesbian Task Force, Washington, D.C.
Mark Steinberg, Family Service Association, Somerville, Massachusetts;
Jim Voltz, Dignity/Boston;
and the Staff of the Department of Music, Harvard University, for moral support and the generous use of their computer.

A Discussion about Differences:
The Left-Hand Analogy

What do left-handedness and homosexuality have in common? This prologue explores some of the similarities which do in fact exist between the two. Though comparing handedness and sexual orientation might seem akin to comparing artichokes and jet planes, as we do so, many striking connections appear. Although this analogy in no way is meant to imply any sort of statistical correlation between left-handedness and homosexuality, it does aim to show how society transforms the meanings of what appear to be value-neutral personal characteristics into morally significant facts.

Every analogy attempts to make a point. Whether one does so successfully depends on how much the items being compared really resemble each other. This one suggests that there are crucial ways in which handedness and sexual orientation are similar. What follows here is a thumbnail sketch of some of those similarities, themes which will be addressed in greater depth throughout this book.

It is estimated that one out of every ten people is left-handed. In fact, this statistic probably holds true for all places and all times. That means there are approximately 25 million left-handed people in the United States alone; and, in a classroom of, say, thirty, at least three people are probably left-handed. Amazingly enough, the statistics are virtually the same for people who act on same-sex attractions.

Left-handed people have existed throughout the ages in all cultures, in all races, in all social classes, and in every country. Even the earliest cave drawings show left-handed figures. Similarly, same-sex acts have proba-

23

bly always existed. Even some of our most ancient literary fragments contain references to love between members of the same sex.

Who is Left-Handed and Lesbian and Gay?

Though it may seem obvious, it is not always easy to determine who is left-handed. Some people, for example, use different hands for different activities. Former President Gerald Ford uses his left hand to write while sitting and his right hand to write on blackboards while standing. Some people can successfully manage with either hand. In fact, it is probably true that most people aren't exclusively right-handed or left-handed. We usually, however, define our handedness in terms of whichever hand we use the most, especially in writing. Nevertheless, people in general exhibit a great variety of hand skills which covers a broad continuum between exclusive left-handedness and exclusive right-handedness.

The same difficulty exists when we try to apply labels referring to sexual orientation. Some people very early in their lives develop an awareness and acceptance of their attractions to members of their own sex. Others, though, may reach this stage later in life. Some people may be attracted to both sexes, defining themselves as "bisexual." In fact, it is probably true that most people aren't exclusively heterosexual or homosexual. Most of us, however, define our sexuality by the sex with which we feel the more comfortable and to which we experience the stronger attraction. Nevertheless, people's sexuality is fairly flexible, covering a broad continuum between exclusive homosexuality and exclusive heterosexuality.

So far, these facts might seem interesting, but not particularly noteworthy. But for those who are left-handed or gay or lesbian, it might be comforting to know that they are not alone. And for the majority, right-handed people and heterosexuals, it might be worth considering that not everyone is the same. What "righties" usually take for granted—cutting with scissors, working with most tools, even writing from left to right—often involves awkward adjustment for "lefties." Similarly, what "straights" usually take for granted—holding hands in public, going to school dances, introducing girlfriends or boyfriends to parents—also often involves awkward adjustments for lesbians and gays.

Prejudice and Discrimination

Though you might not think your friend or mother or classmate is all that weird because she or he is left-handed, such tolerance has not always been the case. In fact, for centuries, left-handed people have been viewed with scorn and even, at times, with fear.

Such scorn was often justified with references to religious texts such as the Bible. Both the Old and New Testaments consider "the left" to be the domain of the Devil, whereas the "right" is the domain of God. For this reason, Jesus told his followers to "not let thy left hand know what thy right hand doeth." (Matthew 6:3.) Jesus also describes God's process for separating good from evil in the Last Judgment: "...the King [shall] say unto them on His right hand, 'Come, ye blessed of my Father, inherit the Kingdom prepared for you from the foundation of the world....' Then shall He say unto them on the left hand, 'Depart from me, ye cursed, into everlasting fire, prepared for the devil and his angels....' " (Matthew 25: 32-41.)

Early Christians applied these categories so strictly that they even held that the saints, while still infants, were so holy that they would not suck from the left breasts of their mothers!

It is not only the Bible that condemns left-handedness. This was also the case in some ancient societies. The ancient Greeks and Romans shared this attitude. For example, the philosopher Pythagoras argued that left-handedness was synonymous with "dissolution" and evil, and Aristotle described good as "what is on the right, above, and in front, and bad what is on the left, below, and behind." (Fincher, p. 33.) The Romans further reinforced these beliefs by standardizing the right-handed handshake, and in Western countries alphabets favor right-handed people in being written from left to right.

Later, in the Middle Ages, left-handed people were sometimes accused of being witches or sorcerers. The present-day wedding custom of joining right hands and placing the gold ring on the third finger of the left hand began with the superstition that doing so would absorb the evil inherent in the left hand.

Though few people today condemn left-handedness, lesbians and gays continue to be feared and excluded. Such treatment is also often justified with references to religious texts such as the Bible. Though there is great disagreement over the interpretations of certain passages in the Bible, it is difficult to find anything positive in passages like the following: "If a man also lie with mankind, as he lieth with a woman, both of them have committed an abomination: they shall surely be put to death; their blood shall be upon them." (Leviticus 20:13.)

Early Christians expanded this to include women when St. Paul condemned women "who did change the natural use into that which is against nature." (Romans 1:26.)

Though homosexual relations were condoned for some males in Classical Greece, the Romans, beginning around the 4th century C.E. (Common Era), prescribed the death penalty for male homosexual behavior. Though sentences were rarely carried out, these laws were later used as the foundation for both Canon Law (the law of the Catholic Church) and many civil laws throughout Europe. During the High Middle Ages, beginning in the late 12th century, a number of governments punished people accused of same-sex eroticism with banishment, mutilation, and death by fire. People discovered engaging in same-sex acts were sometimes accused of being witches or sorcerers. In fact, the present-day term "faggot" is said by many to come from the practice of capturing gay men and tying them together as if they were a bundle (or "faggot") of wood to ignite as kindling over which a woman suspected of being a "witch" would be burned at the stake. Homosexuality was a crime punishable by death in Colonial America, and in England until 1861. Following the American Revolution, Thomas Jefferson proposed that the penalty be reduced from death to castration. In the United States today, the Supreme Court has ruled that laws which prohibit private, consensual, . adult sexual acts commonly associated with homosexuality are constitutional.

Even our terminology often reflects such biases. Words like *sinister* in Latin and *gauche* in French suggest a moral evil or physical awkwardness associated with left-handedness. (Note that their opposites, *dexter* in Latin and *droit* in French, mean "skillful," "artful," "clever," "correct," or "lawful.") In fact, the English word "left" comes from an old Dutch word (*lyft*) meaning "weak" or "broken," whereas "right" derives from an Anglo-Saxon word (*riht*) meaning "straight," "erect," or "just." The word "ambidextrous" literally means "being right-handed on both sides." Phrases like "left-handed compliment" are insults to left-handed people.

Correspondingly, there exists a heterosexual bias in the language we use. There are no common words like "husband" or "wife" that refer to same-sex partners. And words like "bachelor" and "spinster" often inaccurately label gay men and lesbians regardless of their relationship status. If a gay person is involved in a media story, newspapers or the evening news commonly use phrases like "avowed homosexual" or "homosexual affair"; in contrast, no equivalent terminology is used to identify the sexuality of a heterosexual person.

All right, you might respond, but what does this have to do with the treatment of left-handed people and lesbians and gays today? Regarding left-handers, most tools and utensils and most packaging of products are designed for the ease of right-handed people. These include phonograph arms, power saws, corkscrews, sewing machines, and even gum wrappers. Left-handed pilots are not allowed to sit on the right side of the cockpit to reach the controls in the center, even though to do so would make it easier for them.

In the case of lesbians and gays, most laws and ordinances are made to protect the rights of heterosexuals, and, in most states in the United States, these protections do not extend to gays and lesbians. Homosexual relationships do not have legal status. No state recognizes lesbian and gay marriages, people can be denied employment and housing in most areas simply because they happen to be lesbian or gay, and gays and lesbians are often prevented from serving as adoptive and foster parents.

No one really knows why a little more strength in one hand over the other or preference for one sex over the other has been the basis of wide-scale persecution of a minority group of human beings.

How did such social preferences arise? Some people argue that the preference for right-handedness began with the military. If all soldiers were right-handed, they would all pass to the right of their enemy, keeping the enemy on their left side, where they held their shields, and enabling them to maintain a uniform defensive posture. This practice then extended to rules of the road, except in countries such as England, where they drive on the left side of the road. But even there, the practice was established from a right-handed preference. Knights on horseback would keep their opponents to their right with their lances when jousting.

It is possible that the emphasis on heterosexuality began with the early Hebrews, who were under pressure from competing faiths and cultures. Male homosexuality was a religious practice of the holy men of the Canaanite cults and it was an accepted activity in the early years of the Greek empire. In order to insure the survival of the Jewish faith, condemnations of many of the beliefs and practices of their neighbors, including that of homosexuality, were used to emphasize the differences between the Hebrews and their competition. Also, because their numbers were constantly depleted by drought, disease, and warfare with their neighbors, the early Hebrews placed restrictions on homosexual behavior to promote an increase in their birthrate.

Nowadays, we tend to think of these practices as "natural" and to overlook their origin in history and social necessity. Thus, what began as human diversity has been translated into moral pronouncements of all sorts.

Causes: Biology? Environment?

Any difference from the norm gets more attention from researchers. This is certainly the case with left-handedness and homosexuality. Few ask what causes right-handedness or hand orientation in general, or heterosexuality or sexual orientation in general.

Some theorists believe that the cause of left-handedness is biological, citing evidence that left-handed people are dominated by the right side (hemisphere) of the brain. Some researchers, though, dispute this view, arguing that the correlation does not hold true in many cases.

There is also evidence to suggest that left-handedness may be genetic—that it is inherited—since there is a higher statistical probability that two left-handed parents will have a left-handed child. Others maintain that left-handedness is a result of an imbalance in the mother's hormones while the fetus is developing *in utero*. Some theorists have suggested that a distinct preference for one side over the other is shown as early as the second day of life.

Some social scientists argue that left-handedness is environmentally determined and may be a form of mimicking or copying of the behavior of another left-handed family member by the developing child. And some people argue that left-handedness is a choice as opposed to being biologically determined, while others maintain that hand orientation is influenced both by heredity and environment, citing possible genetic factors that are then modified by cultural influences. Still others say that left-handedness is pathological, a result of trauma to the brain or stress to the mother during pregnancy.

Likewise, some believe that the cause of homosexuality is biological, that some people are born with this orientation. Some researchers suggest that homosexuality is genetic, that there is a gay or lesbian gene. Others maintain that homosexuality is the result of an hormonal imbalance in the fetus or the pregnant woman. Some theorists have suggested that sexual orientation toward one's own sex over the other sex is determined as early as the fourth or fifth year of life.

Some researchers posit that homosexuality is environmentally determined as a result of certain family constellations. Some, though, argue that homosexuality is simply a choice a person makes, while others maintain that sexuality is influenced both by heredity and environment, citing possible genetic factors that are then modified by cultural influences. Still others say that homosexuality is a physical defect, perhaps a result of injury to the fetus or stress to the pregnant woman.

The fact remains that no one knows for sure the causal factors in the development of handedness or sexual orientation. The evidence that does exist tends to be inconsistent and often contradictory. It is therefore likely that there is no unitary explanation that applies in every instance.

Stereotypes abound in reference to both left-handed people and people with same-sex attractions. Left-handers are often labeled, for example, as willful and stubborn. Gays and lesbians are termed immature or sexually insatiable. Often, people have the notion that all left-handers are controlled by the right side of the brain, making them more visually oriented and artistic, while being less verbal and less inclined to grasp abstract concepts than right-handed people. In addition, some people even think that lefties are at greater risk of committing criminal offenses. Likewise, some people have the notion that all gay men are overly effeminate and prey on young children, and lesbians are man-haters who secretly want to be men.

Is It Natural?

No one really knows why hand preference or sexual preference occurs. In nature, four-legged creatures do not seem to show a preference for a side. And more animals seem to have developed "bilaterally," meaning that they have matching equal pairs which may be used interchangeably. There seems to be no solid evidence to support the idea of an animal preference of either the right or the left side, except for a few species of animals and plants, and sometimes a few individuals of different species. The honeysuckle is one of the few plants that twines to the left. The morning glory twines to the right, and others twist either way depending on other variables. Gorillas seem to exhibit a slight left-handed bias. But why humans prefer one side over the other remains a mystery even today. And, in the universe overall, there seems to be no common law for inanimate objects in terms of motion and favoring sides.

With respect to sexuality, many varieties of insects and reptiles, almost every species of mammal, and many types of birds engage in some form of homosexual behavior both in the wild and in captivity. Also, in some cultures, homosexual activity not only exists but is often encouraged. For example, the Azande and Mossi people of the Sudan in Africa and various tribes in New Guinea consider same-sex relations to be the norm. Adult lesbian relationships are quite common among the Azande, the Nupe, the Haussa, and the Nyakyusa people of Africa, as are adolescent lesbian activities among the Dahomeyan, the !Kung, and Australian aborigines.

Overall, there seems to be no common law for the attraction of inanimate objects, though some people have postulated that only opposites attract. Though this may hold true for positive and negative electric charges, this theory is contradicted time and time again. For example, in metallurgy, various metals which vary slightly chemically combine with little difficulty to form strong and stable unions. In addition, the concept of opposites is a subjective one, and males and females actually have quite a lot in common.

Why does all this matter anyway? Well, it matters to some who believe that certain kinds of differences are innately unnatural. This attitude has led many theorists to propose strategies for changing an exhibited hand or sexual preference. They have urged parents to encourage young childen to emphasize their right hands, especially in writing. In some schools, teachers have even tied the youngsters' left hands behind their backs or made them sit on their left hands to promote use of the right hand. Even noted baby doctor Benjamin Spock once urged mothers to discourage the use of the left hand in their infants. This treatment often results in emotional outbursts, speech impairments such as stuttering, reading problems, and other learning disabilities. And some "lefties" have tried to conceal their orientation, to "pass" as right-handed in order to fit in with the dominant majority group.

Homosexuals have also been coerced into changing their sexuality. "Experts" have urged parents to encourage young children to manifest behaviors and to engage in activities which are considered to be "appropriate" to their sex. Schools have traditionally withheld teaching about the positive contributions made by lesbians and gays in all areas of society. Most sex education either omits any mention of alternatives to heterosexuality or presents homosexuality only as a form of deviance to be avoided. This often results, for those who are not heterosexual, in self-hatred and isolation. Like lefties, some gays and lesbians have tried to conceal their orientation, hoping to "pass" as heterosexual in order to be accepted by the majority.

These kinds of treatments have prompted some people to question the underlying assumptions of the superiority of the majority group. Some lefties have maintained that they are the same as righties and that there are as many different kinds of left-handed people as there are right. Similarly, some lesbians and gays have maintained that they too are the same as heterosexuals and that there are as many different kinds of homosexual people as there are heterosexuals—but that certain types tend to be more visible because they fit into our expectations.

Others, however, have maintained that "being different" endows its possessors with exceptional qualities such as intuitiveness, creativity, and the like. In actuality, there seem to be some areas in which left-handed people do have an advantage. Neurologists have shown that left-handed people adjust more readily to underwater vision, giving them an advantage in swimming. In the sports of baseball and tennis there is a significantly higher percentage of left-handed players. For instance, 40 percent of the top tennis professionals are left-handed, and 32 percent of all major-league batters, 30 percent of pitchers, and 48 percent of all those who play first base are left-handed. In fact, the term "southpaw" was coined to describe left-handed pitchers. In a typical major-league ballpark they pitch from east to west with their south, or left arm (home plate being located to the west to keep the sun out of the batter's eyes).

Gay and lesbian people also may have certain advantages. For example, they are generally less bound to gender-based role expectations within a relationship, they don't constantly have to worry about birth control, and by not being fully accepted within society, they may be more tolerant of difference and so can objectively critique their cultures.

Politics

In a world which ignores or hinders expressions of diversity, some people are pushing for rights of minority groups. Many political activists reject mere "tolerance," maintaining that such an attribute simply promotes invisibility and continues the discriminatory treatment of these groups. Some activists are demanding that society make more physical accommodations to left-handed people and reject all prejudices that prevent full support for the left-hander. Gay and lesbian activists, in like fashion, are demanding that society grant equality of treatment and an end to oppressive laws that prevent full inclusion of lesbians and gays. An early left hand activist of sorts was Michelangelo, himself a left-hander, who bucked convention in his Sistine Chapel mural by portraying God as granting the gift of life through Adam's left hand. Gay and lesbian rights activities date back to the late 19th century in Germany, with calls for progressive law reform and public education. More recently, some individuals have created organizations such as the National League of Left-handers and the National Gay and Lesbian Task Force to provide resources, support networks, and social settings for others like themselves. Some businesses which cater to the needs of left-handed people and gays and lesbians have come into being.

Minority advocates sometimes cite the examples of famous members of their group throughout history. Famous "lefties" include: Alexander the Great, Judy Garland, Gerald Ford, Marilyn Monroe, Leonardo da Vinci, Betty Grable, Ringo Starr, Casey Stengel, Rock Hudson, Ben Franklin, Harpo Marx, Carol Burnett, Raphael, Paul McCartney, Robert Redford, King George VI, Jimi Hendrix, Michael Landon, Babe Ruth, Charlie Chaplin, Mark Spitz, Ryan O'Neal, Cole Porter, Paul Williams, Cloris Leachman, Pablo Picasso, Michelangelo, Charlemagne, Kim Novak, Peter Fonda, Lou Gehrig, Rex Harrison, Dick Van Dyke, Arnold Palmer, Ted Williams, Stan Musial, Dick Smothers, Lord Nelson, Richard Dreyfuss, Clarence Darrow, Lefty Gomez, Herbert Hoover, Marcel Marceau, Edward R. Murrow, Anthony Newley, Warren Spahn, Henry Wallace, Queen Victoria, Paul Klee, Caroline Kennedy, and Lewis Carroll.

The list of famous people who have had important same-sex relationships through history is also impressive: Socrates, Sappho, Alexander the Great, Julius Caesar, King Richard II, Pope Julius III, Francis Bacon, Queen Christina, Leonardo da Vinci, Gertrude Stein, Alice B. Toklas, King James I, Hans Christian Andersen, Virginia Woolf, Walt Whitman, Dag Hammarskjöld, Bessie Smith, Michelangelo, Herman Melville, Willa Cather,

Colette, Rock Hudson, Janis Joplin, Henry David Thoreau, Margaret
Fuller, Alexander Hamilton, Montezuma II, Pope Sixtus IV, Plato, Natalie
Clifford Barney, W.H. Auden, Bill Tilden, T.E. Lawrence, John Maynard
Keynes, Marcel Proust, Vita Sackville-West, Sophocles, Aristotle, Kate
Millett, King Edward II, Barney Frank, Radclyffe Hall, Leonard Bernstein,
Renee Vivien, and Montgomery Clift. (Bullough; Haeberle; Katz, Klaich;
Walker; Wallechinsky.)

Regardless of the diversity in political views among left-handed people,
and among lesbians and gays, there seems to be agreement that there
must be greater awareness of the needs of these minorities. Authors have
formulated credos to help solidify these political movements. Here are
excerpts from two of these essays. From "A Left-Handed Manifesto":

Be it resolved that all left-thinking citizens, mindful that their Birthleft has
been denied them, shall henceforth stand up for their lefts. We call upon
each one of them to support this Bill of Lefts, and specifically to buy
left—purchase only left-handed products.... Act left—don't knuckle under!
You've made enough adjustments.... Remember! There are at least 25
million left-handers in America. Singly they can do nothing, but united they
can change the world. (DeKay.)

From "A Gay Manifesto":

Where once there was frustration, alienation, and cynicism, there are new
characteristics among us. We are full of love for each other and are showing
it; we are full of anger at what has been done to us. And as we recall all the
self-censorships and repression for so many years, a reservoir of tears pours
out of our eyes. And we are euphoric, high, with the initial flourish of a
movement. (Wittman.)

REFERENCES
(For Left-Handedness)

DeKay, James T. *The Left-Handed Book*. New York: M. Evans and Company, Inc.,
     1966.
DeKay, James T. *The Natural Superiority of the Left-Hander*. New York: M. Evans
     and Company, Inc., 1979.
Fincher, Jack. *Sinister People: The Looking-Glass World of the Left-Hander*. New
     York: G.P. Putnam's Sons, 1977.
Gould, George M. *Right-Handedness and Left-Handedness*. Philadelphia and
     London: L.B. Lippincott Company, 1908.
Wagener, Anthony P. *Popular Associations of Right and Left in Romance Litera-
     ture: A Dissertation*. Baltimore: J.H. Furst Company, 1912.
Wile, Ira S. *Handedness: Right and Left*. Boston: Lee & Shepard Company, 1934.

(For Gays and Lesbians)

Bullough, Vern. *Homosexuality: A History*. New York: New American Library, 1979.

Haeberle, Erwin. *The Sex Atlas: A New Illustrated Guide*. New York: Continuum Publishing Co., 1982.

Katz, Jonathan. *Gay American History: Lesbians & Gay Men in the U.S.A.* New York: Avon Books, 1976.

Klaich, Dolores. *Women & Woman: Attitudes Toward Lesbianism*. New York: Simon & Schuster, 1974.

Walker, Mitch. *Men Loving Men: A Gay Sex Guide and Consciousness Book*. San Francisco: Gay Sunshine Press, 1977.

Wallechinsky, David; Wallace, Irving; and Wallace, Amy. *The People's Almanac Presents The Book of Lists*. New York: William Morrow, 1977.

Wittman, Carl. "A Gay Manifesto." In *Out of the Closets: Voices of Gay Liberation*, edited by Karla Jay and Allen Young. New York: Douglas/Links, 1972.

Chapter 1

Socialization and Gender Roles

Society and Culture

Human beings are a social species. We interact all the time with other people in school, on the job, at home, on the street. We live in *society*, which is a comprehensive social grouping. Often a person's society is defined in terms of the country in which she or he may live, or one may identify with smaller groupings like a person's town or state. At other times, one may define one's society in terms of one's common interests or activities.

Every human society has culture. Yet there is no precise definition of the concept of "culture." In fact, there are over 200 different definitions of culture used by social scientists. Loosely, though, culture in its fullest sense includes all of the learned aspects of human society: those which are taught to new generations of human beings. It involves the symbols, the language, the sets of values, the material items, and the norms of behavior which the members of the social grouping share.

A related social grouping is a "community." It can refer to people living within a specific geographical region such as an extended neighborhood or district like the Beacon Hill area of Boston or the Fillmore district of San Francisco. A community can also include people scattered throughout a larger society, who share common characteristics or interests, share similar institutions, or are linked by a common history. Thus, we might talk of a "medical community," "Asian-American community," "world Catholic community," "artistic community," "community of students." No matter how community is defined, however, certain factors remain constant. Members of a community are united by a common means of communication, share common values and a sense of commitment, and are in some important ways self-contained. An individual can be a member of a number of different communities. As one becomes a part of a community, one feels "at home," supported as an integral part of something larger.

* * *

Culture is the major element which distinguishes humans from other forms of animal life. Unlike human beings, who have to be taught their culture, animals are governed to a much greater extent by fixed, biologically inherited behavior patterns called *instincts*. Birds know by instinct to migrate and to build nests. Chickens and goats sound and act pretty much the same in Kenya as they do in Kansas.

Most social researchers, however, believe that humans are influenced little by strong behavioral instincts. The human infant, of all animal infants, has the longest period of dependency; its very survival is dependent on the caretaking of adult members of its species. If it were left alone, its prospects of survival would be severely limited and it would not learn the characteristics and behavior patterns we tend to take for granted as "human." Thus, our learning occurs in relationship with others. But what if this interaction were somehow interrupted?

Social Isolation

Imagine for a moment what it would be like if, for some reason, after you were born you were immediately placed in a dark and silent room where you had no contact with any other human beings, though your basic bodily needs for food and elimination of waste were taken care of. What if this situation continued for years? What kind of a person do you think you might be? What would your personality, your values, your emotions, your attitudes in general be like?

Behavioral scientists have suggested possible answers to these questions by studying actual cases of children who were discovered after having been in involuntary isolation for extended periods of time. For example, there is documentation of children condemned to circumstances of extreme isolation by cruel, psychopathic, or psychotic parents. One case involves a child (M.S.), who was left alone in a stable for the major part of his first three and one-half years. While asleep in the stable, the child was brought food and no one ever spoke to him. He received little exercise or sensory stimulation.

When he was discovered at the age of three and one-half, M.S. was sent for retraining to a children's home. His height at the time was that of a twenty-month-old boy, he had rickets, and his muscles were extremely weak. He did not speak, could only produce indistinguishable noises, and could not understand spoken language. He could not eat with a spoon, and repeatedly soiled his clothes.

His emotional reactions were severely limited. He did not cry even when he injured himself, and he appeared apathetic and indifferent to any form of human contact.

He improved considerably after a few years of retraining, cooperating with people, learning to dress and feed himself, and developing basic speech. Nevertheless, he suffered from a developmental delay throughout his life. (Langmeier and Matejcek.)

Other examples include the rare and amazing instances of children raised by animals such as goats, bears, wolves, leopards, and wild sows. These are the so-called "feral" children. One story in particular involves two young children who were apparently raised by a pack of wild wolves.

Outside the village of Godamury in India in 1920 there were sightings of two girls, eighteen-month-old Amala and eight-year-old Kamela, running with three large wolves and two cubs. Missionaries in the area approached and captured the children and brought them to an orphanage. At the time of capture, both children exhibited distinct animal behaviors. Kamela used her hands and arms only for locomotion and grasped and caught objects only with her mouth. She had extremely strong muscular shoulders, and there were large callouses on her knees, soles of her feet, her elbows, and her palms. Her hair was matted and when chased she ran quickly on all fours, sometimes outdistancing her pursuers. Both children drank from a bowl like wolves, and Kamela growled and bit when anyone approached her. During the day the children curled up in a corner of their room to sleep. However, by night they prowled and occasionally howled three times in the fashion of a wolf.

Amala died within the first year after she was sent to the orphanage. Kamela progressed extremely slowly. After four years she could only speak six words and after eight years could only speak in short sentences. It took her three years to be able to stand erect and her first independent steps on two feet occurred after six years of retraining. After living in the orphanage for nine years, Kamela died at the age of seventeen. (Gesell; Zingg.)

Though only a limited number of cases of children raised in isolation have been found, those which do exist can shed light on what it is that makes us all humans. Researchers have found in such cases that there is an inverse relationship between isolation and developmental level after retraining: the greater the amount of time in isolation, the less the chance for the child to reach age-appropriate levels of physical and mental development.

Components of Culture

Symbols.   Put simply, a *symbol* is something which stands for something else. To be meaningful and effective it must be understood by a significant portion of the society. Examples of symbols are the green, yellow, and red colors of traffic lights which have no meaning *per se* but only as they represent certain ideas. Another symbol is the gold band worn on the ring finger of the left hand to signify that its wearer is married to a person of the other sex.

Few symbols are universal. The color white, for example, signifies purity and goodness in some societies, and death and mourning in others. Being a bit plump is a sign of prosperity and good health in some places, but is not generally viewed favorably in the United States. Greetings vary from the handshake to a bow.

Language.   One of the most important set of symbols is language: a symbolic means by which people transmit the elements of their culture. Human beings must learn the languages of their cultures as a means of becoming a part of their community. As with symbols, differences in language can reflect differences in the needs and priorities of a given culture. For example, some cultures have no words to describe specific colors, only the words for "light" and "dark." Eskimos have several words for the varying types of "snow," suggesting the importance to that culture's survival of an awareness of subtle differences in snow. The rest of Western culture—with the exception of those who love to ski—has few reasons to be aware of these fine distinctions.

Values.   Values are the beliefs shared by people within a society in terms of what is considered good and bad, right and wrong, desirable and undesirable. (Popenoe.) As with symbols, values also vary depending on the society and historical period. For example, ancient Greeks and Romans justified infanticide under certain circumstances. In Japan, the ritual of *hara-kiri*, which many would censure as a particularly abhorrent form of suicide, was a respectable way to restore honor to one's family's name. Eskimos put their elderly on ice floes to die. Indian women, until very recently, were expected to immolate themselves on their husbands' funeral pyres. Some societies value certain animals as sacred, not to be killed even in times of severe famine. Other societies justify cannibalism.

Consideration of these differences has given rise to a view known as *cultural relativism* which maintains that there are no objective standards for judging particular cultures. Rather, we must put attitudes, values, and norms of behavior in a particular context, evaluating from within: "When in Rome, do as the Romans do." What "works" in one society at a given time may be dysfunctional in some other social setting.

Material Items.   The artifacts, artwork, machines, and the utensils of a group all comprise a culture's material items. The manner in which these items are made often tells something about the nature of the culture, about differences between social classes, attitudes toward females and males, religious observances, and even the uses of leisure time.

Norms.   Norms are prescriptions or rules serving as common guidelines for social behavior. They refer to the expectations of how people are supposed to act, to think, or to feel in specific situations. (Popenoe.) However, norms should not be confused with "normal," which merely signifies being in the majority or being the most common type. It is not normal to have red hair, but it is certainly within the norm because it is accepted and regarded as proper and right.

Norms go by various names depending on their social importance:

a.   *Folkways* are social customs and rules or standards of behavior. Though generally considered important, they often can be ignored without provoking intense reactions or violating some basic taboo. For example, we generally expect someone invited to a birthday party to bring a present. But, if this doesn't happen, although there might be embarrassment or no invitation the following year, nothing extremely serious is likely to occur.

b.   *Mores* are rules of behavior which are weighted more heavily than folkways, and their violation is usually a serious matter. Societies often view their own mores—correctly or incorrectly—as essential to their continued survival; thus, violations of mores often carry serious social sanctions.

c.   *Laws* are codes of social behavior which have been written into legal statutes in order to regulate human conduct. Laws have the power of the community behind them, and their violation entails punishment of some kind.

Assimilation/Pluralism

One can analyze the composition of a society in two ways. A society can be like a melting pot in which different ingredients (cultures) are thrown together to form a goulash; in this process, each ingredient gives up its distinctiveness and takes on the flavor and consistency of the entire pot. As new cultures enter, they may gradually merge, giving up their distinctiveness (such as their language, religion, customs). This process is *assimilation* and either can occur voluntarily or can be forced upon the group.

A related process is that of *acculturation*. It occurs as a minority accepts and takes on the values, language, and societal norms of the dominant group. This can but does not necessarily lead to assimilation.

A society can also be likened to a patchwork quilt, in which diverse segments retain their distinctive patterns and designs to form the whole. When different groups live together, retaining and honoring their respective individual identities and cultures, the result is *cultural pluralism*. A good example of this type of society is Switzerland, which is subdivided primarily into three cultural-linguistic groups—German, French, and Italian—and is characterized by cooperation and political unity.

Most industrial societies today (with notable exceptions such as Japan and Norway) are pluralistic to some extent. However, these societies generally expect that various cultures will assimilate into the dominant culture. (See Chapter 8 for more discussion of culture.)

Subculture

Within a given society there are groups of people which, while sharing some elements in common with the main or dominant culture, also have different styles of living arising from their own cultural traditions. These groups are called *subcultures* and are many times distinguished along ethnic, religious, racial, economic, or age lines. A subculture also arises when members of a certain group exhibit behavior patterns which sufficiently distinguish it from the dominant culture. If a subculture challenges the values and norms of the dominant culture, the subculture is referred to as a *counterculture*. One of the most easily identifiable countercultures was the youth movement of the mid- to late 1960s—labeled by the mainstream media as "hippies"—which questioned dominant cultural values relating to materialism, competition, patriotism, fashion, and work.

An individual can be a member of a number of different subcultures. Some of the numerous subcultures within the United States include Italian-Americans, Jews, Hispanics, welfare mothers, senior citizens, and Vietnam veterans. An individual can even be a member of a subculture while at the same time belonging to the dominant culture.

Socialization

It makes no difference where a child is born—Paris, Atlanta, New Guinea, Moscow—all children undergo the process of socialization.

Formally defined, it is the life-long process through which people acquire personality and learn the values, attitudes, norms, and societal expectations of their culture. Though the content varies from one culture to the next, the process of socialization is very much the same. Through this process people come to understand their culture, begin to develop a sense of who they are, and come to know what is expected of them in terms of their social role. While an acorn will inevitably become an oak tree, humans require socialization to realize their humanity.

A social role is any pattern of behavior which an individual in a specific situation is encouraged to perform. The term comes from the language of the theater, being derived from the French *rôle*, referring to the "roll" of paper containing an actor's part. A role is not the same as the person who is performing it at the moment—just as the role of Macbeth has been played by countless actors over the last 350 years. Macbeth has certain characteristics which, regardless of the particular actor who plays the part, enable the audience to recognize him as "Macbeth." Yet, as a stage role leaves some room for interpretation, so too most social roles involve general guidelines but not exact behaviors.

Individuals play a number of different social roles. One can, for example, play the role of a daughter, a mother, a student, a friend, a patient, and a professional. Each of these roles has a set of expectations associated with it. The role of student, for example, involves coming to class on time, treating teachers respectfully, participating in class discussions, doing homework on time, and so forth. Our understanding of these expectations enables us to recognize "inappropriate" behavior.

Though we have the capacity to reflect on these roles, most of us do not even notice them. There is an old folk saying that "the fish will be the last to discover the ocean"; and, like those fish, most of us are not aware of the pervasiveness of our own "ocean."

Actors are given their roles by the person in charge of casting, instructed by the director, and handed a part to memorize. In learning a social role, however, we have a variety of teachers and models.

For the young child the most important *agents of socialization* are parents or guardians who consciously and unconsciously *model* certain behaviors while *teaching* all sorts of roles: "No, dear, not like that, like this." As roles become more and more sophisticated, people may begin to learn them from others who are already performing them. For example, a college freshman may "learn" to be a college student by observing the sophomores.

When a young child enters school, teachers are not merely the transmitters of knowledge, but they also serve to continue and supplement the process of socialization. It is in these early years of school when the child learns many of the "rules" of behavior and becomes a social being to an ever greater extent. Later, peer relationships play a more significant role in the socialization process.

Social agents whose importance should not be underestimated are the media. From the television tube, the stereo and radio speaker, the movie screen, the pages of newspapers, books, and magazines, and billboards of all conceivable varieties we receive messages that help to formulate or reinforce our attitude and value systems. The media expose people to the latest concepts of style, beauty, morality, and social behavior.

People often learn their roles by playing complementary roles which are then interdependent. Juliet, for example, learns to play her part by taking cues from Romeo and vice versa. Social roles are similar; there cannot be wives without husbands, parents without children, teachers without students, leaders without followers.

Are There Differences between Males and Females?

There are many factors which combine to determine the types of roles which a given individual will eventually play. These factors include age, interests, motivation, intellectual and physical ability, race, socioeconomic level, biological sex, ethnic background, and others. Though all of these factors are extremely important, for purposes of this discussion we will focus on the element of biological sex.

Traditionally it is assumed that since females and males are in some ways physically different, they therefore are "naturally" different also in terms of the ways in which they think, feel, act, and relate to others. This difference some attribute to inborn (or genetic) biological factors.

Those who maintain that there are significant differences between males and females might describe males as rational, emotionally strong, and aggressive and females as intuitive, emotional, and passive. It therefore follows that males and females are best suited for different roles in society.

Nineteenth-century poet Alfred Lord Tennyson, in these lines from his poem "The Princess," supports such a view:

Man for the field and woman for the hearth,
Man for the sword and for the needle she,
Man with the head and woman with the heart,
Man to command and woman to obey,
All else confusion.

These lines not only urge different roles for the sexes, but also suggest that social order and stability depend on the preservation of those roles.

Many people, however, are questioning the assumption that males and females are "naturally" opposites. Instead, they maintain that society reinforces certain differences, emphasizing those traits rather than the many similarities that exist. Thus, this view suggests that the major behavioral differences are due to socialization rather than biology.

Sex and Gender

Of course females and males are in certain aspects different. It is therefore necessary to differentiate here between two terms: *sex* and *gender*. Though the terms are often used interchangeably, *sex* (female or male) is a biological concept referring to chromosomes (XX-female, XY-male), our external genitalia—our gonads (i.e., ovaries or testes), our internal genitalia (e.g., uterus or prostate), our hormonal states, and our secondary sex characteristics (e.g., the development of body hair and breasts on females following puberty).

Gender, however, is not a biological concept, but rather a cultural or psychological trait associated with males and females.

If an extraterrestrial being visited our planet from a distant galaxy, it might derive a number of possible conclusions from its first look at our species, *homo sapiens*. It might, for example, take note of some differences between those called "males" and those called "females." This same extraterrestrial might also conclude that these forms of humanity are simply two varieties of the same species and are extremely similar in many respects. If, for example, our space visitor ventured into a biology laboratory and came into contact with full female and male skeletal displays, it would be hard-pressed to differentiate between the two. Further, in terms of external appearance, males and females are all unique as individuals; but, when taken as a group, are not all that different.

This imaginary scenario raises the question of just how "different" males and females really are. Though there are some studies which suggest that young boys have a slightly higher tendency toward aggressiveness than young girls, and that there may be some small differences in mental abilities between the sexes, the overwhelming conclusion is that there is very little evidence to prove that the psychological differences commonly attributed to each sex are essentially inherent. (Maccoby and Jacklin.)

Some, like the psychologist Carl Jung, for example, believe that all people contain both a feminine aspect (which Jung calls the "anima") and a masculine aspect (the "animus") and that for an individual to be fully adjusted it is important to recognize and integrate both. More recently, studies by gender researchers suggest that the most effective individuals are those who are able to combine traditional masculine and traditionally feminine qualities. (Bem.)

For these reasons, throughout this book the term *other sex* will be used over the term *opposite sex*. In actuality, the concept of opposites is a subjective one and can be misleading. Furthermore, as our extraterrestrial friend would correctly observe, males and females are two forms of the same species.

Gender Roles

The ways in which a society assigns its social roles to each sex reflect concepts of gender. As we have already discussed, a "social role" is any pattern of behavior which an individual in a specific situation is expected to perform. Therefore, a *gender role*, is any social role linked with being female or male.

The first thing a parent asks in the delivery room following a birth is what is the biological sex of the baby. A birth certificate registers whether the infant is male or female. Grafted onto this biological identity are certain *cultural* patterns or assumptions which affect nearly everything the person will do throughout a lifetime.

From birth, infants receive cues about conduct appropriate for each sex. Boys are dressed in blue, girls in pink. Adults bounce boy babies, and coo to girls.

Gender-role expectations affect how we live our lives. From the time we are born, our society assigns different roles and behaviors to the two sexes. Over time these roles are perceived as innate or "natural," while in actuality they are culturally based. Since the Industrial Revolution of the 18th century, it has been supposed that men in our society must be hard-working and should be the ones who support their families financially, should be competitive, and should aim toward success. Women, on the other hand, have been taught to take care of the home and the children, to be nurturing and supportive and not overly concerned with their own needs. Furthermore, both sexes are expected to be attracted very early in their lives to members of the other sex, to eventually marry, and to raise children of their own.

Masculine/Feminine

Our society recognizes essentially only two distinct gender roles. One is the *masculine*: having the qualities or characteristics which a given society attributes to males. The other is the *feminine*: having the qualities or characteristics attributed to females. (There is also a third gender-role option, though it is generally not sanctioned within most Western cultures. It consists of an integration of the other two roles. This is the role of *androgyny*, derived from the Greek words *andros* meaning man and *gyne* meaning woman.)

Stereotypes

> Rosey Grier, a 290-pound professional football player, once "confessed" to the media that he liked to relax by needlepointing. One reporter then asked: "Aren't you afraid people will think you're a sissy?"

Regardless of what is the basis for gender-role development, it is clear that social customs and norms reinforce many shared preconceptions about the sexes. Some of these may be inconsistent or even contradictory, but they share the common element that they are prescribed rules of conduct for us all. These preconceived notions are termed *stereotypes*, which are defined as standardized mental pictures that are held in common by members of a group and which represent oversimplified opinions, affective attitudes, or judgments. (Webster.)

We have already discussed some of the gender-specific role stereotypes as they relate to male and female children. Similarly, stereotypes are imposed onto adults according to sex. Even when men and women both exhibit similar outward behavior, the sex of the person will often determine the societal stereotype affixed to that behavior. For example, what may be seen as "assertive" behavior in a man may be called "pushiness" in a woman. A man may be seen as being "enthusiastic," whereas a woman is accused of being "emotional." Where a man is viewed as "confident" or "firm," a woman, on the other hand, is considered "stubborn" or "bitchy."

Sociologist Robert K. Merton (1957) describes this phenomenon as "the self-fulfilling prophecy," whereby a behavior practiced in the in-group is virtuous, while the very same behavior on the part of an out-group member is wrong. For example, Abe Lincoln may be thrifty, but Abe Cohen is tight with a dollar. This obviously creates a no-win situation for out-group members who may try to emulate the dominant group to gain social acceptance and yet are judged negatively for their attempts. This occurs frequently when women try to compete with men. Cynthia Epstein, for example, points out that women lawyers are seen as abrasive, whereas men behaving in similar ways are dramatic.

Gender Identity

In most cultures, children are raised to take on specific roles associated with their biological sex very early in life. Therefore, in most cases people maintain an identity of themselves in terms of gender. Social researchers list three component parts of gender identity relative to a given society. (Weinrich.)

The first of these is *core gender identity*, which describes the person's innermost concept of self as male or female, as defined by the culture. The second category is *gender role*, which is the set of roles prescribed for females and males. The third is *sexual orientation*, whereby a person is erotosexually attracted to a person of the other sex, of the same sex, or to persons of both sexes.

Each person adheres to or varies from existing definitions of masculine and feminine in each of the three categories. There are those who adhere to all three categories, and those who differ in one, two, or all three. Therefore, the three categories are not necessarily interconnected.

The term "gender transposition" describes the pattern of adherence to or variance from existing definitions of masculinity and femininity. Examples of a gender transposition which follows typical or prescribed patterns include men and women who perceive themselves in terms of their biological sex, who wear the clothing and perform the culturally defined roles according to their sex, and are erotosexually attracted to some members of the other sex. Gender transpositions which vary from typical patterns include transsexuals (people who have changed or want to change their sex surgically) who "transpose" on core gender identity and usually on gender role; transvestites (cross-dressers) who "transpose" on gender role; and gay males, lesbians, and bisexuals who "transpose" on sexual orientation. It would be incorrect to generalize that these groups of people (transsexuals, transvestites, gay males, lesbians, and bisexuals) are transposed on all three categories of sexual identity, though some within each group may be. It is a common misconception that all gay males, for example, enjoy wearing dresses, that all transvestites want to be of the other sex, or that all people who want to change their sex are homosexual.

Gender Identity—Social Implications

Sex researchers have developed terms describing component parts of gender identity as a means of comparison and analysis. Originally value neutral, many of these terms have become morally loaded.

If a person wishes to step outside of the gender role assigned to her or him, she or he may be branded with a label of the other sex. For example, if a woman aims to be a corporate executive or airline pilot, she is sometimes accused of "trying to be like a man" and is considered to be "too masculine," whereas if a man trains to be a ballet dancer, terms like "feminine" or "womanlike" are used to describe him.

Children often confuse sex roles, and make "inappropriate" choices. When a little girl announces that she plans to be a fireman, adults merely smile. They know she doesn't yet have it right, but they're not worried. By the time it matters, she will have learned her sex role so thoroughly that it simply will never occur to her to be a fireman. In the meantime she has other things to learn: there are now dolls to play with and take care of, pretty clothes to try on, shiny black patent-leather shoes, and as a special reward she may help Mommy with housework and stir the batter in the big white bowl. No one ever really tells her to be "domestic" or "esthetic" or "maternal" *but she's learning.*

A little boy, meanwhile, is learning other things. Balls and bats have miraculously appeared to play with, realistic toy pistols, and trains, blocks, and marbles. The shoes he finds in his closet are sturdy enough to take a lot of wear, and just right for running. One day there is an old tire hanging by a rope from a tree in the back yard, just right for swinging. No one ever tells him to be "active" or "aggressive" or "competitive" *but somehow, he's learning.* (David and Brannon, p. 7.)

What's Wrong with Gender Roles?

It is clear that knowing what one's role is in a given situation is comforting; such knowledge provides one with a measure of stability and a framework within which one can predict acceptable and unacceptable behaviors. Whether it be the role of "bridesmaid," or "celebrity," or "salesperson," rules for roles offer parameters to guide our conduct if we wish to be viewed as *good* bridesmaids, or celebrities, or salespersons. Gender roles are no different. They describe how to be good men or good women and they give us a framework for understanding conduct. How can any of this be negative?

In fact, there are costs associated with strict adherence to gender roles. For example, research on masculinity reveals that higher male mortality may be attributed to the stress inherent in the masculine role. (Journard.) For women, it appears that those who score highest on femininity tend to have very low self-esteem. (Bern.) Further, research on depression indicates that it is more frequent and more intense in men and women who adhere most rigidly to gender roles. Also, for women, expressions of helplessness and passivity seem to encourage higher rates of mental illness. (Chester.) Conversely, studies done with college students reveal that the more androgynous the male or female student (that is, the higher one scores on both masculine and feminine traits), the higher one's self-esteem is likely to be. (Spence, Helmreich, Stapp.) These kinds of observations have led some to conclude that our insistence on conformity to gender roles condemns men and women to a "one-sided existence." (Tolson.)

Deviance

Conformity to generally accepted norms is usually rewarded by the society. However, when behavior goes against these norms, this is often defined as *deviance*, and the individual or group of individuals who stray from these norms are said to be exhibiting *deviant behavior*. In terms of gender roles, *inversion* is used in psychiatric and medical circles to describe a reversal of commonly expected gender roles.

Not all behaviors, however, which go against established social norms are devalued. At times certain kinds of differences are accorded positive value and are judged as exceptional. Though it is not clear why some behaviors are valued and others are not, it does appear that all societies value certain behaviors over others and that every society's value system is different.

With respect to sexuality, there is an expectation in most Western societies that people will have physical attractions for and sexual experiences limited to members of the other sex—*heterosexuality*. However, the classification of "deviant" is given to people who desire these experiences with members of both sexes (*bisexuality*) or with members of the same sex (*homosexuality*). (The word "homosexual" has a mixed genesis: *homos* from Greek meaning "same," and *sexus* from Latin meaning sex.)

Other groups are also defined as "deviant." An example of this is the person who prefers to wear clothing commonly associated with members of the other sex. Society calls such people *transvestites* or *cross-dressers* and, aside from theatrical performances or holidays such as Halloween or Mardi Gras, this behavior is generally considered to be a violation of gender-role expectations.

However, this has not always been the case. In many pre-industrialized societies, people who bridged the genders were often accorded positions of honor and esteem. These cross-dressers filled the roles of spiritual leaders, healers, priests, caretakers of the young, social commentators, teachers, and agents of social change. In fact, among the Navajo people, they were known as *nadle*, meaning "changers," and were given high status within the culture. (In South-West Africa they were called *omasenge*, and in Polynesia *mahu*.)

Gender Role Flexibility—The Case of the Berdache

Not every culture divides males and females along strictly masculine and feminine gender lines. Take, for example, many of the native American Indian cultures, particularly before the onset of European cultural influence. These were generally egalitarian cultures in which male and female gender roles were complementary and were given equal status and value. The male role included hunting and warfare duties, while the female role included the gathering of food and care of children. However, in over 130 of these societies, gender roles were set aside for those group members who either would not or could not fit into the roles assigned to their own sex. Called *berdache* by the French and *bardaje* by the Spanish, they were persons (usually male, but sometimes female) who were permitted a gender-blurred or inter-gender status.

Most *berdache* wore many of the articles of clothing, took on tribal duties, and exhibited mannerisms and speech patterns traditionally accorded to members of the other sex. (Greenberg.) In line with their gender-mixing status, male *berdache* were defined as "non-men," rather than as "women," and female *berdache* were defined as "non-women," rather than as "men," by other members of the group.

Though some *berdache* were subject to ridicule, it appears that many held esteemed positions in many societies, often with special roles in tribal rituals and ceremonies. Among the Crows, for example, male *berdache*, known as *bote*, held specific ritual functions. In the Winnebago tribe, they often acted as oracles. The Zuni reportedly had two male *berdache*, known as *Lhamena*, who held high office in the tribe. (Jacobs.) Among the Kutenai of Montana, female *berdache* were esteemed warriors and guides, and among the Mohave, women known as *hwame* were respected as powerful shamans and healers. (Roscoe.) A Lakota man describes his *berdache* experiences; in the language of his people he is called a *winkte*:

> I have always filled a *winkte* role. I was just born this way, ever since I can remember. When I was eight I saw a vision, of a person with long gray hair and with many ornaments on, standing by my bed. I asked if he was female or male, and he said "Both." He said he would walk with me for the rest of my life. His spirit would always be with me. I told my grandfather, who said not to be afraid of spirits, because they have good powers. A year later, the vision appeared again, and told me he would give me great powers. He said his body was man's, but his spirit was woman's. He told me the Great Spirit made people like me to be of help to other people.
>
> I told my grandfather the name of the spirit, and Grandfather said it was a highly respected *winkte* who lived long ago. He explained *winkte* to me and said, "It won't be easy growing up, because you will be different from others. But the spirit will help you, if you pray and do the sweat." The Spirit had continued to contact me throughout my life. If I practice the *winkte* role seriously, then people will respect me. (Williams, p. 198.)

Origins of Sex-Role Differences

Essentialists: Nature Theorists.   There is considerable research exploring the origins of sex-role differences. At this point in time, no one knows for certain what causes people to be "masculine" or "feminine," as the evidence is often conflicting and at times difficult to interpret. However, we might characterize two schools of thought which seem to represent the main perspectives in the debate. On the one hand there are the *essentialists*, who argue that masculinity and femininity are inherent, or inborn, in our nature as males and females. Or, more clearly, that all females and only females are feminine, and that all males and only males are masculine. Some essentialists conclude from this that men and women are different, but equal, while others maintain that one sex is superior to the other. Aristotle, for example, claimed that men are suited by nature to dominate women:

> The male is by nature superior, and the female inferior;
> and the one rules, and the other is ruled;
> and this principle, of necessity, extends to all mankind.

For philosophers like Aristotle, Kant, and Thomas Aquinas, these differences between males and females are inevitable and unchangeable. Sigmund Freud posed the question of whether women's passivity and men's aggressiveness are ultimately rooted in the biological differences in male and female sexuality:

> The male-sex cell is actively mobile and searches out the female one, and the latter, the ovum, is immobile and waits passively. This behavior of the elementary sexual organisms is indeed a model for the conduct of sexual individuals during intercourse. The male pursues the female for the purpose of sexual union, seizes hold of her and penetrates into her. (Freud, p. 101.)

Other essentialists, such as the contemporary sociologist Steven Goldberg, argue that male aggression is universal and immutable, caused by differences in hormones:

> Men are not stronger and more aggressive than women *because* men are trained to be soldiers, nor do women nurture children *because* girls play with dolls. In these cases society is doing more than merely conforming to biological necessity; it is utilizing it. Because the initial masculine and feminine directions are engendered only by sexual differences in capacity and, perhaps, propensity and not by instinct, men and women must learn the specific manner in which their society functions. The male's aggression

advantage and the female's maternal feelings are not social in origin.... Societies conform their institutions and socialization to the sexual directions set by physiological differentiation, first because they must and second in order to function most efficiently. (Goldberg, pp. 117-18.)

There are, however, essentialists—for example, the feminist Shulamith Firestone—who believe that there are innate biological differences between the sexes, but that this is changeable as we develop the technology to alter our biology (e.g., through artificial (alternative)insemination, "test-tube babies," artificial placentas, etc.)

Constructivists: Nurture Theorists.   On the other hand, there are also the *constructivists* (sometime called *nurture theorists*), who, though they do not deny that there are gender differences between the sexes or that these differences require some explanation, argue that the basis for these differences is *social* rather than biological. These theorists refuse to use terms like "masculine" or "feminine" without some reference to a given society, since they argue that these concepts are *not* innate. Thus, they postulate that gender is not preordained, but rather learned.

The psychologist John Money, for example, says that "social learning is the dominant mechanism for the development of gender." (Money, p. 5.) He uses the phrase "neonatal plasticity" to describe the flexibility of the human species to learn new behaviors. To use language as an analogy, we all have the *capacity* to learn language, but some of us will speak Spanish, some Chinese, some English, based on what we are *taught*. For "nurture theorists," then, gender, like language, is "society-relativized."

Another constructivist, Theodore Roszak, argues that the concepts of masculinity and femininity are social constructs and not innate to being human:

> ...the sooner we have done with the treacherous nonsense of believing that the human personality must be forced into masculine and feminine molds the better. No matter how lyrically intoned, the notion that women are innately "feminine" and therefore uniquely responsible for the fate of the softer human virtues is a lethal deception. To think this way is to play dumb to the fact that throughout civilized history men have unloaded the nurturing talents on women for base purposes of manipulation and exploitation. Worst of all: it is to continue giving the men of the world a solid-gold rationale for repressing those talents in themselves and for thus stripping power of its humanitarian discipline. (Roszak, pp. 101-02.)

Gender-Role Socialization: Operational Factors

Two factors are in operation in the process of gender-role socialization: differential treatment and identification with role models. (Popenoe, 1986.)

Differential Treatment.   Quite simply, "differential treatment" means that from the moment of birth, males and females are treated differently.

> Children learn about sex roles very early in life, probably before they are eighteen months old, certainly long before they enter school. They learn these roles through relatively simple patterns that most of us take for granted. We throw boy babies up in the air and roughhouse with them. We coo over girl babies and handle them delicately. We choose sex-related colors and toys for our children from their earliest days. We encourage the energy and physical activity of our sons, just as we expect girls to be more docile. (Howe, p. 397.)

Many parents and guardians, serving as the chief agents of gender-role socialization in the child's formative years, punish boys more severely when they fail to learn their prescribed gender roles; boys grow up with a fear of being called "sissy," or being "like a girl." Boys are strongly discouraged from exhibiting behaviors which are considered to be "feminine," such as crying or lisping or playing with dolls. As one study found:

> Demands that boys conform to social notions of what is manly come much earlier and are enforced with much more vigor than similar attitudes with respect to girls...and at an early age, when they are least able to understand either the reasons for or the nature of the demands. Moreover, these demands are frequently enforced harshly, impressing the small boy with the danger of deviating from them, while he does not quite understand what they are. (Hartley, p. 458.)

This often leads to anxiety on the part of the boy, and also contempt for anything hinting at "femininity."

This differential treatment usually continues once the child ventures out of the home. In school, often, the brighter a boy is, the higher are his teacher's expectations of him. Boys receive more reprimands in school, but they also receive more praise. (Meyer and Thompson.) However, the brighter a girl is, the less she is expected by her teacher to succeed at a given task. (Crandall, *et al.*)

Teachers frequently give subtle cues regarding gender expectations, such as, for example, complimenting girls on the way they dress rather than on their scholastic achievement. Boys are generally judged on what they *do* whereas girls are judged on how they look. (Joffe.)

One student looks back on his early schooling:

Even back in kindergarten, boys were channeled into certain activities such as athletics while girls were channeled along the lines of housekeeping "skills" such as cooking and cleaning up the classroom. This channeling seemed to grow more intense in each consecutive level of grade school.... It was usually the girls who were encouraged by their teachers to take advantage of the field trips to the opera each semester, while the boys were pushed to attend a local big-league baseball game. It was the girls who were allowed to help the teacher mix the paints for art period while the boys were permitted to leave for recess early to get the balls out of the equipment room. (Blumenfeld.)

Identification with Role Models. Identification with role models becomes an important form of socialization as the child grows older. Again, the parent or guardian and teachers are the most powerful role models for the young child.

As discussed, gender roles for males are often more strictly enforced than for females. Some people believe that this is partly a result of girls having greater access to female role models than boys have to male models. Some girls identify with their mothers in the process of spending time with them during the day. Though the situation may be changing, boys may still lack male role models, since fathers are often less available and teachers in the lower grades are often females.

The girl has her same-sex parental model for identification with her more hours per day than the boy has his same-sex model with him. Even when home, the father does not usually participate in as many intimate activities with the child as does the mother, for example, preparation for bed and toileting.... Despite the shortage of male models for direct imitation, a somewhat stereotyped and conventional masculine role is spelled out for the boy, often by his mother, women teachers, and peers in the absence of his father and male models...consequently, males tend to identify with a culturally defined masculine role, whereas females tend to identify with their mothers. (Lynn, p. 466.)

In the early school years the majority of teachers are women who generally receive low monetary rewards and status within the society. Subsequently, students pick up the message that women are less able professionally than men, and this ultimately affects how the female students regard their own abilities. (Fennema.)

The media also serve as a modeling agent of gender-based roles. Again, though change is slowly occurring in the depiction of females and males as social equals, many of the traditional, stereotyped visions of masculinity and femininity remain. The tough, "macho," he-man image continues as the standard of the male ideal, whereas the image of women remains very often that of the "weaker sex."

Sexism

The inequalities in the ways the media portray females and males are simply reflections of a social reality. In operation is the system of *male dominance*, in which males are often accorded greater access than females to the social rewards of power, status, and money.

We have already suggested that the roles assigned to each sex, in all likelihood, do not necessarily arise from significant innate differences among males and females, but are rather culturally defined. Yet, even if there were an inescapable connection between biological sex and gender-role assignments, this alone would not account for the value judgments people make about the bearers of those roles:

> While males do have greater physical strength than females and probably greater biologically based aggressiveness, these factors in themselves do not adequately explain a cultural system that gives higher value and prestige to the particular behaviors involved. (Stockard and Johnson, p. 199.)

To value certain behaviors over others based on the sex of the person in question is the basis of *sexism*: "the highly developed and systematic subordination of women to men, and the creation of particular rules and prohibitions according to one's sex." (Altman, p. 67.)

In Western culture, maleness and definitions of masculinity serve to promote the domination of males over females and to reinforce the identification of maleness with power. For societies where this is the case, the term *patriarchy* is used—as opposed to the term *matriarchy* (the rarer of the two), which denotes a society in which females hold the major positions of power. Within patriarchal societies, males are encouraged to be competitive and value physical courage and toughness, and to devalue qualities considered "feminine," such as gentleness and expressiveness. This social conditioning can take its toll on both boys and girls. By the time most females reach the fourth grade, they believe they have only four occupational options open to them: nurse, secretary, teacher, or mother.

The psychologist E.P. Torrance conducted studies showing what he called the "inhibiting effects" of sex-role conditioning on creativity. He used a Product Improvement Test, requiring children to "make toys more fun to play with." By the fifth grade, it was very difficult to get girls to work with science toys. They frequently protested, "I'm a girl, I'm not supposed to know anything about things like that." Boys were about twice as good as girls at explaining ideas about toys. (Howe.)

In the meantime, while girls are learning to be passive and are preparing for lives in support of males, boys are learning to define their identity in terms of power, and learning that they must compete for it with other males. As one observer of his own socialization notes:

> What I must grow up to be, what it must mean to me to be a male human being, was presented to me as inevitable and unquestionable. Masculinity was defined for me by the social world I was part of as a set of personal characteristics that must become a part of my identity. I, like all male children, was taught that my value as a person depended on my power over others. I was taught that I must compete for personal power, and that to be successful I must conceal feelings of weakness, tenderness, and dependence, and present myself to other men as self-sufficient and insensitive. (Silverstein.)

Thus, though roles may serve to define us and give us a place in our social structure, they can also be confining. As one teacher notes, for example:

> Seven years ago I did not recognize that helping children adjust to traditional sex roles was contradictory to helping them develop their potential. Yet for children to make such an adjustment, they must severely limit their development—literally shut off parts of their personalities and cut themselves off from many physical and intellectual challenges. (Greenleaf, p. 5.)

The novelist Lillian Smith has described the division of people according to race as "the dance that cripples the human spirit." Perhaps one could argue that sex-role divisions also cripple. Today we hear much in the popular media about the difficulties in communication between men and women; perhaps the differences in the ways we are socialized can account for these gaps in mutual understanding.

Language itself may reinforce sexist stereotypes. Indeed, the language we use expresses the way we experience the world around us, and the words people use in talking about men and women reveal social attitudes toward the sexes. Many people argue that sexist language has practical implications in that it reinforces sexist behavior.

For example, the following words, though referring to non-human animals, are sometimes applied to people:

Stud	Kitten	Bitch
Wolf	Bunny	Shrew
Buck	Bird	Cow
Lion-hearted	Chick	Nag
Fox	Lamb	Sow

All but the first four are used in regard to females, and tend to be either negative in tone or else cast females in the role of sexually passive objects. The first four, though, are applied to men to signify bravery or sexual prowess.

Other words, usually used as "masculine" and "feminine" nouns, have subtle yet definite differences in meaning that reflect the values placed on males over females:

Masculine	Feminine
Brave	Squaw
King	Queen
Wizard	Witch
Landlord	Landlady
Patron	Matron
Grandfatherly Advice	Old Wives' Tale
Sir	Madam
Master	Mistress
Host	Hostess

Also, there are some words which seem to apply almost exclusively to women—for example, "hysterical," "gossip," "flirt," "old bag"—which almost always have negative connotations.

Income by Occupation and Education

One of the most important economic and social transformations in this century has been women entering the paid workforce. In 1880 only about 18 percent of all women, as compared to nearly 75 percent of the men, were in the labor force. The percentage of women steadily increased until World War II. During the war, women filled many of the jobs vacated by men who left to serve in the military. At that time, about 38 percent of all women had paying jobs. When the men returned after the war, women were asked to relinquish their jobs, and subsequently there was a brief decline in the number of women working outside the home. Since the postwar era, however, the percentage of women workers has increased. By 1986, they constituted 41.3 percent of the labor force. (Division of Labor Force Statistics.)

On the average, women engaged in full-time year-round employment earn only 69.2 percent of the salary of their male counterparts for equivalent work:

Occupation	Median Weekly Earnings (male)	Median Weekly Earnings (female)	Ratio female/ male earnings in percent	Percent of females to male work-ers by occu-pation
Managerial and Pro-fessional Specialty Occupations	$608.00	$414.00	68.1%	43.6%
Mathematical and Computer Sciences	696.00	521.00	74.9%	36.2%
Health, Diagnosing Occupations	722.00	499.00	69.1%	26.0%
Teachers, College and University	656.00	479.00	73.0%	27.5%
Teachers except Col-lege and University	501.00	411.00	82.0%	71.0%
Social Scientists and Urban Planners	683.00	470.00	68.8%	42.8%
Lawyers and Judges	812.00	609.00	75.0%	24.9%
Writers, Artists, Entertainers, Athletes	504.00	374.00	74.2%	39.8%
Technical and Administrative Sup-port Occupations	437.00	282.00	64.5%	62.7%
Sales Occupations	447.00	239.00	53.5%	40.9%
Service Occupations (Protective and Household)	284.00	191.00	67.3%	50.5%
Service Occupations, (except Protective and Household)	239.00	195.00	81.6%	58.6%
total	$419.00	$290.00	69.2%	41.3%

(Total represents female-to-male weekly earnings ratio in 230 occupa-tions. Source: Division of Labor Force Statistics.)

Other Cultures

By now, we have seen how powerful is the influence of socialization in the development of values and attitudes in general and in gender identity, and the assignment of sex roles in particular. Though we ordinarily take these models for granted, and may even assume that such behavior is the same the world over, the fact is that different cultures have very different concepts of what is appropriate behavior for males and for females. Evidence of diversity among varying societies supports the contention that the assignment of roles is not a result of any intrinsic genetic differences between the sexes, but rather is governed by a multiplicity of social factors.

When we examine sex-based roles in a number of different cultures, it is apparent that some perceive males and females to be innately different in temperament and thus prescribe opposite behaviors for each sex. Other groups, however, see little or no innate difference between the sexes, as far as temperament is concerned. Therefore, such societies tend to foster greater flexibility and equality in roles. Culture, then, exercises great license in selecting those aspects of human behavior which it seeks to encourage or discourage.

> And while every culture has in some way institutionalized the roles of men and women, it has not necessarily been in terms of contrast between the prescribed personalities of the two sexes, nor in terms of dominance or submission. (Mead, p. xi.)

For example, in her famous work *Sex and Temperament*, the anthropologist Margaret Mead compares three separate cultures of New Guinea. One of these, the mountain people called the Arapesh, have a radically different structuring of sex roles from our own. In fact, the Arapesh have no idea that males and females are temperamentally different. Arapesh society tends to be a cooperative one, where women and men "unite in a common adventure that is primarily maternal, cherishing, and oriented away from the self towards the need of the next generation." (Mead, p. 15.) Warfare is virtually unknown among the Arapesh. Men have as much (or even greater) responsibility for the rearing of children as women. The society lacks a hierarchical political structure, and there is little competition among members of the group. As a result, though people may enjoy different roles, there seems to be no judgment of inferiority or superiority attached to them.

Another tribe, known as the Tchambuli, have a very different social organization from the Arapesh. They do have clearly defined sex roles, but they are the opposite of our own. Tchambuli women, in fact, manage all the business affairs of the society, believing men to be lazy and catty. Men wear fancy ornamentation, while the women are unadorned and businesslike. Girls in Tchambuli society are "bright and free," while small boys are "already caught up in the rivalrous, catty, and individually competitive life of the men." (Ibid.)

The third society, the Mundugumor, like the Arapesh, does not distinguish males and females by temperament, but, unlike the Arapesh, supports a highly aggressive, warlike attitude for both sexes. Both men and women are fiercely possessive, and both are rejecting of children. Mead discusses how difficult life is from the earliest years on for children who are nursed only when it becomes absolutely necessary and given no affection or emotional support.

In looking at these three disparate cultures, Mead concludes that social conditioning, rather than biological sex, is the primary factor in the development of gender identity. The human personality, she posits, is extremely malleable and traits which we label as "masculine" and "feminine" are forged by cultural conditions.

Changing Conceptions of Gender Roles

The last hundred years have seen a gradual yet ever-present questioning of restrictive gender roles. A major impetus for this has come out of the women's suffrage movement of the latter part of the 19th century, when women fought for the right to vote in both England and the United States. It was during this time that the feminist movement emerged. In addition, some women were questioning other aspects of patriarchal culture. Though feminists disagreed about policy, strategy, and priorities, feminism itself began as a movement whose purpose was to liberate women. Though there was no consensus among feminists as to what form such liberation would take, all agreed that women were oppressed.

This "first wave of American feminism" began to seek equality for women in politics, education, and employment. In addition, it began to raise questions about traditional role expectations within the family unit. As more women began to work outside the home, there were many changes in society as a whole. Further, during World War II, many women took on traditional male occupations as men were drafted into the military. Though most of these women were forced out of the workplace when the men returned, the seeds of change had been planted.

Advancements in birth-control technology meant that women were not as tied to the reproductive process, thus opening up more options for women. This availability of birth control led to a questioning of the traditional view that the primary function of sex was procreative, and that women's sole purpose was to seek fulfillment through childbearing.

The "second wave of feminism" in the 1960s, commonly referred to as

"The Women's Liberation Movement," pushed for an end to sexism in all spheres of life, the personal as well as the political. Strategies ranged from direct confrontations to electoral political involvement in an attempt to attain social, economic, educational, and political parity between females and males. In addition, many challenged basic societal assumptions about the inevitability of sex roles and prescriptions about sexuality itself.

Many feminists have pointed out that questioning rigid sex roles not only opens up greater possibilities for women to develop to their fullest potential, but also relaxes some of the restrictions which inhibit men in their personal expression. As we have seen, sex roles for men are far more strictly defined and hence, are more limiting. Young girls, for example, may receive less ridicule for being "tomboys" than do young boys for being "sissies." Females can wear a greater variety of clothing than can males. Hence, males can benefit greatly from redefinitions of what it is to be male and what it is to be female.

Homosexuality and Gender Roles

Like heterosexuals, homosexuals are raised in a culture which teaches certain gender-role expectations. And, likewise, homosexuals are influenced by the same social messages and patterns of reinforcement. Many homosexuals whose identities were formed in the days prior to the development of a clearly defined "gay identity" and the questioning of gender roles that accompanied feminism, have spoken of the rigidity of roles even within the underground homosexual community. Many lesbian couples, for example, designated one woman as the "butch" and the other as the "femme." While the former might have dressed in traditionally male clothing, had short hair, and carried herself in imitation of men, the latter would have taken on the mannerisms and styles of traditional femininity. And, just as rigid roles lock heterosexuals into certain patterns and provide for little if any flexibility, so too did these roles restrict homosexuals from fully expressing their potential. But roles can also give one a label and a sense of security in knowing what to expect.

But this is not to suggest that the condition of homosexuality itself is a gender dysfunction. In fact, homosexuality is not the result of any gender confusion, as some people believe, but rather is a sexual and affectional orientation. Homosexuals who took on traditional roles were in fact simply mimicking what mainstream heterosexual society was modeling. With the emergence of the Women's and Gay and Lesbian Liberation Movements in the 1960s, this model was increasingly called into question. Along with this new consciousness, fewer and fewer lesbians and gays, like heterosexuals, now exhibit role-playing behavior within relationships.

Sex researcher Evelyn Hooker, for example, studied a group of gay men in order to determine the relation between homosexuality and gender-role behavior. Though she argued that in society considerable pressure is brought to bear on those who transgress the limitations of traditionally defined gender roles, she nonetheless observed that the gay men she studied suffered no gender confusion.

Homosexuals may, for a variety of reasons, question traditional concepts of masculinity and femininity; but this reevaluation is not the cause of the sexual orientation, though it may be the result of it. Gay men, then, can be just as "masculine," lesbians just as "feminine" as heterosexuals. Also, some "feminine" men and some "masculine" women are heterosexual.

Conclusion

There is a tendency to reject any claims that imply that we are conditioned by forces around us. Most of us assume that we have freely chosen our likes and dislikes: that we believe certain behaviors are right "just because they are" and not because those behaviors receive approval; that we buy the products we buy because they are worthwhile and not because of a media campaign; and that we are attracted to the individuals we are because of their positive qualities and not because they meet social expectations. Somehow, we believe that this freedom makes those choices even more worthy, and we resist any theoretical framework that might hint at a compromise of that freedom.

This chapter does not argue that we are "mere products" of our surroundings, but it does suggest that much of what makes us who we are is the result of a subtle yet pervasive cultural process. This process is not "brainwashing"; nor are we helpless robots programmed to behave in inevitable ways. Rather, it is the very basis of our survival, the means by which one generation transfers to the next information about and understanding of what it means to be a human being. But there are costs as well as benefits associated with that process. Since every culture has its own agenda, there are limitations on each individual's expression of difference. How much variety can a society safely endure?

Because we are not helpless robots, we can consider the socialization we receive. We can evaluate the input our culture transmits to us, and we can decide if whatever limits *are* imposed are oppressive. This chapter begins to raise some of those questions with respect to gender and gender-role expectations. Chapter 2 explores these issues as they concern sexuality itself.

REFERENCES

Altman, Dennis. *Coming Out in the Seventies*. Boston: Alyson Publications, Inc., 1979.

Andersen, Margaret. *Thinking About Women: Sociological and Feminist Perspectives*. New York: Macmillan, 1983.

Aristotle. *Politics*, ch. 5, trans. Benjamin Jowett, Oxford: Clarendon Press, 1985.

Bem, Sandra. "The Measurement of Psychological Androgyny." *Journal of Consulting and Clinical Psychology* (1974) 42: 155-162.

Bern, S. "Psychology Looks at Sex Roles." Paper presented at UCLA Symposium on Women, May 1972.

Blumenfeld, Warren. "School is Not a Gay Place to Be." *Edcentric Magazine*, 1971, Vol. III, No. 5.

Broverman, Inge. "Sex Role Stereotypes and Clinical Judgments of Mental Health." *Journal of Consulting and Clinical Psychology* (1970) 34.

Chester, P. *Women and Madness*. Garden City, N.Y.: Doubleday, 1972.

Crandall, V.J.; Katkovsky, W.; and Preston, A. "Motivational and Ability Determinants of Young Children's Intellectual Achievement Behaviors." *Child Development* (1962) 33: 643-661.

Current Population Reports. "A Statistical Portrait of Women in the United States." Washington, D.C.: Government Printing Office, 1978.

David, Deborah S., and Brannon, Robert. "The Male Sex Role: Our Culture's Blueprint of Manhood and What It's Done for Us Lately." In *The Forty-Nine Percent Majority: The Male Sex Role*, edited by Deborah S. David and Robert Brannon. Reading, Mass: Addison-Wesley, 1976.

Division of Labor Force Statistics, Office of Current Employment Analysis, Bureau of Labor Statistics, 1986.

Fennema, Elizabeth. "Women and Girls in the Public Schools: Defeat or Liberation?" In *Beyond Intellectual Sexism: A New Woman, a New Reality*, by Joan I. Roberts. New York: MacKay, 1976.

Firestone, Shulamith. *The Dialectic of Sex: The Case for Feminist Revolution*. New York: Morrow, 1970.

Freud, Sigmund. *New Introductory Lectures on Psychoanalysis*, trans. and edited by James Strachey. New York: W.W. Norton and Co., 1965.

Gesell, A. *Wolf Children and Human Development*. New York, London: Harper and Brothers, 1940.

Goldberg, Steven. *The Inevitability of Patriarchy*. London: Temple Smith, 1973.

Greenberg, D.F. "Why Was the Berdache Ridiculed?" In *The Many Faces of Homosexuality: Anthropological Approaches to Homosexual Behavior*, edited by Evelyn Blackwood. New York: Harrington Park Press, 1986.

Greenleaf, P.T. *Liberating Young Children from Sex Roles*. Somerville, Mass: New England Free Press, 1972.

Hartley, R.E. "Sex-Role Pressures and the Socialization of the Male Child." *Psychology Reports*, vol. 5, 1959, p. 457.

Hooker, Evelyn. "An Empirical Study of Some Relations between Sexual Patterns and Gender Identity in Male Homosexuals." In *Sex Research: New Developments*, edited by John Money. New York: Holt, Rinehart, & Winston, 1965.

Howe, Florence. "Sexual Stereotypes Start Early." In *Issues in Feminism: A First Course in Women's Studies*, edited by Sheila Ruth. Boston: Houghton Mifflin, 1980.

Jacobs, Sue-Ellen. "Berdache: A Brief Review of the Literature." *Colorado Anthropologist* (1968) 1, pp. 25-40.

Joffe, C. "Sex Role Socialization and the Nursery School: As the Twig Is Bent." *Journal of Marriage and the Family* (1971) 33.

Journard, S.M. "Some Lethal Aspects of the Male Role." In *Men and Masculinity*, edited by J. Pleck and J. Sawyer. Englewood Cliffs, N.J.: Spectrum Books, 1974.

Jung, Carl. *Analytical Psychology: Its Theory and Practice*. New York: Vintage Books, 1968.

Langmeier, J., and Matejcek, A. *Psychological Deprivation in Childhood*. New York: Halsted Press, 1963.

Lynn, David. "The Process of Learning Parental and Sex-Role Identification." *Journal of Marriage and the Family* (1966) 28: 466-470.

Maccoby, Eleanor Emmons, and Jacklin, Carol Nagy. *The Psychology of Sex Differences*. Palo Alto, Calif.: Stanford University Press, 1974.

Mead, Margaret. *Sex and Temperament in Three Primitive Societies*. New York: Morrow Quill, 1935.

Merton, Robert K. *Social Theory and Social Structure*. Glencoe, Ill.; The Free Press, 1957.

Meyer, W.J., and Thompson, G.G. "Sex Differences in the Distribution of Teacher Approval and Disapproval Among Sixth-Grade Children." *Journal of Educational Psychology* (1956) 47.

Money, John. *Love and Love Sickness: The Science of Sex, Gender Difference, and Pair Bonding*. Baltimore: Johns Hopkins University Press, 1980.

Pleck, Joseph. *The Myth of Masculinity*. Cambridge, Mass.: MIT Press, 1982.

Poponoe, David. *Sociology*. 6th edition. Englewood Cliffs, N.J.: Prentice-Hall, 1986.

Roscoe, Will. "Living the Tradition: Gay American Indians." In *Gay Spirit: Myth and Meaning*, ed. Mark Thompson. New York: St. Martin's Press, 1987.

Roszak, Theodore. "The Hard and the Soft: The Force of Feminism in Modern Times." In *Masculine/Feminine: Readings in Sexual Mythology and the Liberation of Women*, edited by Theodore Roszak and Betty Roszak. New York: Harper, 1969.

Silverstein, M. "Power and Sex Roles in Academia." *The Journal of Applied Behavioral Science* (1972) Vol. No. 5.

Spence, J.T., Helmreich, R., and Stapp, J. "Ratings of Self and Peers on Sex Role Attributes and Their Relation to Self-Esteem and Conceptions of Masculinity and Femininity." *Journal of Personality and Social Psychology* (1975) 32.

Stockard, Jean, and Johnson, Miriam M. *Sex Roles*. Englewood Cliffs, N.J.: Prentice-Hall, 1980.

Tolson, A. *The Limits of Masculinity*. New York: Harper and Colophon, 1977.

Torrance, E.P. "Changing Reactions of Preadolescent Girls to Tasks Requiring Creative Scientific Thinking." *Journal of Genetic Psychology* (1963) 102: 271-233.

United States Department of Labor. *Employment and Earnings, 1984.* Wash. D.C.: U.S. Printing Office, 1985.

Webster's Ninth New Collegiate Dictionary. Springfield, Mass.: Merriam-Webster, Inc., 1983.

Williams, Walter L. *The Spirit and the Flesh: Sexual Diversity in American Indian Culture.* Boston: Beacon Press, 1986.

Zingg, R.M. "Feral Men and Extreme Cases of Isolation." *American Journal of Psychology* (1940) 53: 487-517.

Further Readings

de Beauvoir, Simone. *The Second Sex.* N.Y.: Alfred A. Knopf, 1953.

Falk, Ruth. *Woman Loving: A Journey towards Becoming an Indepedent Woman.* N.Y.: Random House, 1975.

Fox, Mary Frank, and Hesse-Biber, Sharlene. *Women at Work.* Palo Alto, Cal.: Mayfield Publishing Company, 1984.

Freeman, Jo, ed. *Women: A Feminist Perspective.* Palo Alto, Cal.: Mayfield Publishing Co., 1984.

Heilbrun, Carolyn G. *Toward a Recognition of Androgyny.* N.Y.: Alfred A. Knopf, 1973.

Millett, Kate. *Sexual Politics.* N.Y.: Doubleday, 1969.

Pleck, Joseph H., and Sawyer, Jack. *Men and Masculinity.* Englewood Cliffs, N.J.: Prentice-Hall, 1974.

Pogrebin, Letty Cottin. *Growing Up Free: Raising Your Child in the '80s.* N.Y.: McGraw-Hill, 1980.

Rice, Allgeier Elizabeth, and McCormick, Naomi B. *Changing Boundaries: Gender Roles and Sexual Behavior.* Palo Alto, Cal.: Mayfield Publishing Co., 1983.

Voydanoff, Patricia, ed. *Work and Family: Changing Roles of Men and Women.* Palo Alto, Cal.: Mayfield Publishing Co., 1984.

Chapter 2

Sexuality

Two graduate students are sharing an apartment as lovers. They made the decision a little over two years ago to live their lives together. One is studying for an advanced degree in history, hoping to be a college professor one day. The other will soon be completing a nursing program. They both took out college loans to defray tuition costs and they have part-time jobs to make ends meet. One tutors high school students in writing skills and the other works at a local neighborhood health clinic.

Each has played a significant role in the other's life since shortly after they were introduced at a party while still undergraduates. Conversation flowed easily from the very beginning, and that invisible quality of physical chemistry helped to send "sparks" flying between them.

Today they share many things together, including their books and records, cleaning the apartment, expenses, their good and bad moods. They also share a bed.

Suppose our description ends here. Even with all these details about the individuals involved, there are still many questions remaining. Who are the two people in the story? Is one a young man and the other a young woman? Are they two woman? Or two men? Are they married? Did they establish a sexual relationship early on or did they wait until they were living together? What was the reaction of their families? Or their friends?

A wide array of answers is possible because styles of relationships and sexual behaviors take many forms and, though sexuality is one of the most universal of all human experiences, it remains something which is both individual and personal.

Forms of sexual relationships also vary. Law in the United States recognizes only marriages with one husband and one wife (*monogamy*); and when sexual activity does not extend beyond two people (married or not) their relationship is said to be *monogamous*. Different cultures, however,

65

accept other models of relationships. For example, some cultures of Africa—and at one time the Mormons here in the United States— practiced *polygamy*, in which more than one wife or more than one husband was permitted as part of a socially sanctioned relationship. More specifically, *polygyny* occurs where multiple wives are married to one man, and *polyandry* (the rarer of these arrangements) involves multiple husbands.

The Purpose of Sex

"Sexuality" refers not only to the basic biological sexual functions of our species, but also to the attitudes, beliefs, values, fantasies, taboos, rituals, and customs which individuals and societies have constructed in connection with those biological functions. We tend to assume that because sex is, to some extent, a biological act, our standards for it must not vary from one society to another. Yet there is an enormous diversity among social groupings on sexual attitudes and sexual practices.

For example, in some cultures, rules about virginity (for men *and* women) are very strictly enforced, while for others it is enforced only for women. In some cultures virginity is believed to be a *deficit* for marriage and is actually discouraged. Though every culture has taboos relating to sexuality, those taboos also vary. In some settings, women are taboo during menstruation. In others, boys and girls may not even see each other. Even kissing is taboo in some societies. Attitudes toward nakedness also differ among different societies, and there is even great variation on what parts of the body a group believes should be covered.

Not only do notions of marriage vary, but so do marriage rituals. For example, in one group, a bride-to-be must have sex the night before the marriage with the father of her husband-to-be. In others, marriages are arranged with no involvement on the part of those to be married. Finally, even *definitions* of certain sexual practices can change, depending on the institutions of a given society.

For example, though incest is almost universally condemned, there is no universally accepted definition of it. The Old Testament instructs men to marry their brothers' widows, but in many cultures, sex with one who has "kinship" connection—even if there is no "blood" relationship—is viewed to be incestuous. This would include not only those we would describe as "step" relations and "in-law" relations, but also at times even members of the same social network. Some cultures allow cousins—even first cousins—to marry, others do not. The early Hawaiians allowed sisters and brothers of their nobility to marry, believing this practice kept the race pure.

We can easily describe the great range in what different people or even different societies think about sex and what they prescribe as part of a sexual repertoire. We can also infer what individuals or groups view as the purpose of sex, that is, what assumptions underlie their sexual practices. These sorts of attitudes about sexual conduct, though, no longer merely describe what people do or think, but rather justify some kinds of sexual practices and condemn others. These views range from the very conservative, which excludes far more than it includes, to the very permissive.

The Conservative View

Conservative views of sexuality narrow the range of permissible sexual practices, thereby condemning virtually all sex except that which leads to procreation within marriage. In this view, the source of the prohibition is generally a religious one, often associated with the Judaeo-Christian tradition. Because sex is a physical act, conservative views often maintain that it severs us from our own spirituality and hence from God. Some conservatives claim that interest in sex makes us no better than non-human animals. Some even stricter views regard sex itself as an evil and recommend *celibacy*—sexual abstinence. Some argue that sexual pleasure itself is an evil. In the New Testament of the Christian Bible, St. Paul advises people to renounce, or abstain, from all sexual activity as he has done. He considers celibacy a high ideal:

> For I would that all men were even as I myself. But every man hath this proper gift of God, one after this manner, and another after that. (I Corinthians 7:7.)

> I say therefore to the unmarried and widows, it is good for them if they abide even as I. (I Corinthians 7:8.)

Marriage is permitted, but only as the lesser of two evils:

> But if they cannot contain, let them marry: for it is better to marry than to burn. (I Corinthians 7:9.)

An example of an entire group of people practicing sexual abstinence is the Shakers, a Protestant sect from New England, who subscribe literally to the Christian doctrine of sex as sin. In order for them to increase their numbers, they adopt children in marriage rather than reproduce.

In the conservative view, "good sex" is that which occurs within the confines of heterosexual marriage sanctified by God for the purpose of procreation. The theologian Thomas Aquinas is quite clear on this point:

...[i]n the human species offspring require not only nourishment for the body, as in the case of other animals, but also education for the soul...children must be instructed by parents who are already experienced people.... Moreover, a long time is needed for this instruction.... Now, a woman is not adequate to this task alone; rather, this demands the work of a husband, in whom reason is more developed for giving instruction and strength is more available for giving punishment. Therefore, in the human species, it is not enough, as in the case of birds, to devote a small amount of time to bringing up offspring, for a long period of time is required. Hence,... it is natural to the human being for the man to establish a lasting association with a designated woman, over no short period of time. Now, we call this *matrimony*. Therefore, matrimony is natural for man, and promiscuous performance of the sexual act, outside matrimony, is contrary to man's good. For this reason, it must be a sin.

And on the topic of male masturbation:

It is evident from this that every emission of semen, in such a way that generation cannot follow, is contrary to the good of man. And if this be done deliberately, it must be a sin.

The conservative view continues to have adherents today:

Let the sexual act be the expression of the conscious desire and decision to become parents, and that act reaches its zenith in human feeling, inspiration, and fulfillment.... Let two persons extend their love for each other into the tender and responsible decision to have and care for children, and they will find the meaning of the sexual experience immeasurably enriched.... Sex without love, love without marriage, and marriage without creative commitments to children (or the equivalent) are in constant danger of vanishing away. Persons disregard the laws of growth and development in human nature only to find that they have forfeited their heritage. (Bertocci.)

People who moderate the conservative view still hold that sexuality should take place only within marriage, but allow it to occur between the partners for physical pleasure and for an enhancement of communication.

The conservative position is not without its difficulties. Who is to say what is God's will? What about differing interpretations of the Bible? Furthermore, even if procreation is a primary purpose of sexual activity, why must it be the only one?

The Liberal View

Obviously, the strict conservative view excludes most sexual practices outside of procreative sex within marriage. The liberal view, on the other hand, maintains that there is nothing necessarily wrong with sex as an end in itself. This view, then, would allow birth control, masturbation, sex for pleasure; in fact, according to this view, any sex between consenting adults is justified. From a legal perspective, liberals usually recommend the elimination of laws that punish people for what are sometimes called "victimless crimes." They often defend this argument on the basis of a "right to privacy."

> Bed is the place to play all the games you have ever wanted to play, at the play-level—if adults could become less self-conscious about such "immature" needs we should have fewer deeply anxious and committed fetishists creating a sense of community to enable them to do their thing without feeling isolated.... There are after all only two "rules" in good sex, apart from the obvious one of not doing things which are silly, antisocial, or dangerous. One is "Don't do anything you don't really enjoy," and the other is "Find out your partner's needs and don't balk at them if you can help it." In other words, a good giving and taking relationship depends on a compromise (so does going to a show—if you both want the same thing, fine; if not, take turns and don't let one partner always dictate).... (Comfort, pp. 287-8.)

The liberal position raises some questions. Is, for example, premarital sex right or wrong? When is one an "adult," that is, ready to engage in sexual activity? Are sexual relations outside of marriage justified, as long as the partners consent? Finally, some people question the entire concept of *consent*: how does one identify when true consent has been given? Who is capable of giving "informed consent"?

The Libertine View

This view, in extreme opposition to the conservative view, maintains that "anything goes" in the sexual realm. In fact, it argues that sexual practices do not belong in the category of ethical judgments. Sexual practices, the libertine maintains, are neither right nor wrong, any more than liking a certain work of art or type of wine or flavor of ice cream could be right or wrong; such judgments, then, are aesthetic rather than prescriptive, and they vary from one person to another. Consequently, whatever is pleasurable is justified. "Good" sex is "whatever feels good." This view holds that sexuality gives human existence its meaning:

> It is only by sacrificing everything to sensual pleasure that this being known as Man, cast into the world in spite of himself, may succeed in sowing a few roses on the thorns of life. (de Sade, p. 135.)

The Marquis de Sade, the paradigmatic representative of the libertine view, urges women as well as men to enjoy sexual emancipation:

If we admit...that all women should submit to our desires, surely we ought also to allow them to fully satisfy their own.... Charming sex, you will be free; just as men do, you shall enjoy all the pleasures that Nature makes your duty, do not withhold yourselves from one. Must the divine part of mankind be kept in chains by the other? Ah, break those bonds; nature wills it. Have no other curb than your tastes, no other laws than those of your own desires, no more morality than that of Nature herself. Languish no more under those barbarous prejudices that wither your charms and imprison the divine impulses of your heart; you are as free as we are and the career of battles of Venus are as open to you as to us. (de Sade, p. 119.)

The libertine view raises a number of issues. In particular, while to some it may appear to have the advantage of divorcing sexuality from moralistic value judgments, one must also keep in mind that acceptance of the libertine view disqualifies one from making moral statements about sexual practices of any kind. Nothing is wrong as long as there is pleasure. Whose pleasure is of concern? Is it all parties involved? How is pleasure defined? Would the libertine view justify sexual exploitation or coercive sex—rape, for example—as long as *someone* desires it? And what about concerns over sexually transmitted diseases, and especially about AIDS?

The Feminist View

Like the liberal view, the feminist position insists on the importance of consent in sexual practices. But this view also requires mutuality and equality in sexual interactions. As a result, exploitative sex, such as prostitution, is condemned.

[C]omplete sex acts preserve a respect for persons. Each person remains conscious and responsible, a "subject" rather than a depersonalized, willless, or manipulated "object." Each actively desires that the other likewise remain a "subject." Respect for persons is a central virtue when matters of justice and obligation are at issue. Insofar as we can speak of respect for persons in complete sex acts, there are different, often contrary requirements of respect. Respect for persons, typically and in sex acts, requires that actual present partners participate, partners whose desires are recognized and endorsed. Respect for persons typically requires taking a distance from both one's own demands and those of others. But in sex acts the demands of desire take over, and equal distance is replaced by mutual responsiveness. Respect typically requires refusing to treat another person merely as a means to fulfilling demands. In sex acts, another person is so clearly a means to satisfaction that she or he is always on the verge of becoming merely a means.... In complete sex acts, instrumentality vanishes only because it is mutual and mutually desired. Respect requires encouraging, or at least protecting, the autonomy of another. In complete sex, autonomy of will is recruited by desire, and freedom from others is replaced by frank dependence on another person's desire. Again the respect consists in the reciprocity of desiring dependence, which bypasses rather than violates autonomy. (Ruddick, p. 118.)

Though it is clear in the feminist view that respect and mutuality are necessary conditions for "good sex," it is not always clear how these concepts translate into actual practices. For example, incest could be wrong, but it is not wrong because of the parties' biological relationship, but rather because of the possible exploitation that occurs, say, between an adult and a child. Hence, there might not be any "absolutes" as far as sexual conduct is concerned. Adultery or incest or casual sex could be right or wrong, depending on the overall context of the relationship between the participants. So this view treats sex as similar to other human activities like friendship, where we hold that certain values should apply. Conservatives might ask what might be the consequences of such a view to the institution of the family? How does one determine what counts as "exploitative"? Is adultery exploitative? Prostitution? Casual sex?

Two Contrasting Cultural Views of Sexuality

There are enormous differences between cultures in terms of sexual practices and sexual attitudes. Two island cultures make this clear.

The Case of Mangaia

Mangaia is one of the Cook Islands within the Polynesian chain. It is a sun-drenched tropical paradise where nudity among young people is quite common and young girls and boys are expected to masturbate from a very early age up to the age of ten or eleven. Between the ages of twelve and fourteen, a young male passes through a puberty ritual where the upper flap of the foreskin of his penis is cut (superincision). This action initiates him into the world of adult sexuality. At this time he is given information about sexual intercourse (*coitus*) and other sexual techniques and told about the importance of helping females to reach orgasm. Within a few weeks he has sexual relations with a sexually experienced older woman.

After this rite he enters a period when he works at sex like a young bull, going from woman to woman, attempting to satisfy her sexually by extending intercourse (fifteen to thirty minutes with a great deal of thrusting), trying to bring her to climax a number of times before a mutual climax at the end. Both partners are active and vigorous during intercourse, with a commitment to mutual pleasure. It is important that the male perform well, since the young woman will discuss his sexual competence with other young women, and will describe to him the sexual prowess of other young men. (Gagnon, pp. 10-11.)

Islanders reside in huts and because the size of the hut is quite small, sexual activity takes place in full view of the young woman's family, who politely ignore the proceedings.

Young women receive advice on sexual matters and are taught and encouraged to have frequent orgasms. The Mangaians especially value intercourse during pregnancy because it is thought to be more enjoyable than sex before conception; some islanders believe that continued intercourse during pregnancy ensures an easier birth. Romantic love is not always an aspect of youthful relationships. Affection and love are thought to develop out of satisfactory sexual relations. After marriage, love often develops as sexual activity begins to decline.

The Case of Inis Beag

Inis Beag is a small island off the coast of Ireland. Populating the island is a fishing and farming community which strictly adheres to the tenets of the Roman Catholic faith.

Matters relating to sexuality are rarely discussed and there is no sexually charged speech, no erotic song or poetry, no sexual joking. Women learn about menstruation and menopause only as they happen, and men believe that the sexual act only drains their bodily energies.

Nudity is strictly discouraged. A man is not even permitted to take off his shoes in front of another man's wife.

During those infrequent occasions when sex does occur between a married couple, the act itself takes the form of a duty:

> ...the husband opens his nightclothes under the covers; the wife raises her nightgown; and they do it as quickly as possible. Women are taught merely to endure the sex act, and the possibility of female orgasm appears to be practically unknown to men and women. (Gagnon, p. 11.)

Men and women in this culture enter into their marriage vows inexperienced and untutored in sexual matters, and women do not seem to experience sexual pleasure of any kind. Sexuality itself is shrouded in both ignorance and guilt.

History of Sexual Attitudes

> The only clear "lesson" of history is that people have created many different designs for arranging human life and putting sexuality into human life. (Gagnon, p. 15.)

We tend to take it for granted that human sexuality is more instinctive, more primordial than the other sorts of activities in which we engage. Hence, we classify sexual behavior separately from other kinds of behavior which are learned, like playing tennis, riding a horse, speaking a language, or understanding mathematics. But in any given culture or society at any particular moment, people are learning to become sexual in the same sorts of ways that they learn to become anything else. They pick up cues—consciously and unconsciously—from their surroundings and from the people around them. This process continues throughout one's life and is so subtle and so pervasive that it seldom receives conscious attention.

All societies developed as the result of compromises, all of which involve costs and benefits. For sex *per se*, the only innate aim is the release of tension, and there are no necessary objects in this drive for release. But societies teach us to attach certain values to certain objects of desire as part of our learning and experience. Societies teach us who may be sexual (e.g., old or young), what we may do (e.g., heterosexual intercourse), when we may do it (e.g., only after marriage), where we may do it (e.g., "in the privacy of one's home"), and why we do it (e.g., to have children, for pleasure, to express affection). And all of these vary from social grouping to social grouping.

Prior to the end of the 18th century, nearly all justifications of sexual practices in Western societies were based on religious values. The "flesh," unlike the "spirit," was thought to be "weak," subject to temptation, and easily corrupted. Since sex was an impulse of the flesh, it came to represent a fall from grace. Sex had only one purpose, namely, procreation. Celibacy, as we have seen, was often held to be an even higher value in Catholic Christianity.

The 19th century saw industrialization and the growth of technology in Western countries such as England and the United States. Victorian England had powerful sexual taboos to the point where piano legs—thought to resemble the naked human leg—were covered so as not to offend anyone. Yet this was a time full of contradictions: though sex was not discussed in "proper" households and "good" Victorian husbands bothered their wives for sex as little as possible, there were 40,000 prostitutes on the streets of London, along with rampant sexual abuse of children. Moreover, the age of consent for girls was thirteen! The double standard, part of Christian tradition as well, was deeply entrenched in this culture, leading to the two models of "femininity": the Virgin Mary—virgin, nurturer, lacking in sexual desire; or Eve—the temptress, seducer, sexually insatiable.

Sigmund Freud (see Chapter 3), toward the end of the 19th century, worked to bring sex "out of the closet." He pointed to the pervasive contradictions about sexuality in his own society. In insisting that even infants were sexual, he tried to break free of the many taboos about sex that served to heighten frustration and neurosis. Though there has been much criticism of Freud from varied quarters, his contribution to our understanding of sexuality and repression represents a radical departure from traditional thinking about sexual behavior.

Today, after the so-called "sexual revolution" of the 1960s, there has been a questioning of many of the assumptions people hold about sex. In addition, the Women's Movement and Gay and Lesbian Liberation Movements have criticized repressive standards of sexual conduct as well as double standards for sexual behavior for males and females. Improvements in birth control, abortion procedures, and biomedical technologies have helped to separate sex and reproduction. During the latter part of the 19th century into the 20th century a distinct sexual *identity* for homosexuals and heterosexuals developed. Though there is still much room today for debate on the costs and benefits of this greater openness about sexuality, there is no doubt that sexual mores have changed radically.

Homosexuality/Bisexuality

Attractions come in a variety of forms. Standard psychology texts refer to "object-choice" to designate the object of a particular sexual attraction. This term is neutral and implies no valuing of particular objects over others. Yet societies give us differing messages about what are appropriate attractions, and it reinforces certain kinds of expressions of those attractions. The terms "heterosexual," "homosexual," and "bisexual" describe certain kinds of preference for certain kinds of object-choices.

Is it a Choice?

To date, there is no unitary theory which adequately explains the acquisition of personal tastes. Why do some people love the color blue while others prefer red over blue? Why do some people feel a meal is incomplete without potatoes while others don't like potatoes?

Concerning sexual tastes, do people have a choice in their attractions or is this something over which they have no control? The answer to this question hinges on the complex issue of sexual development about which there are numerous and contradictory theories (see Chapter 3).

On the one hand, a same-sex attraction for some people may be the result of a conscious decision. For them, these attractions develop after rational consideration of their options. Some eventually come to define themselves as lesbian, gay, or bisexual depending on how comfortable they may feel with their choice.

On the other hand, for the majority of those with same-sex attractions, although the decision to act on their attraction stems from a conscious decision, the attraction itself is the result of a drive over which they have no choice. Some people are aware of this attraction as early as the age of four or five. Others may not identify it until much later in life. Homosexuality, therefore, can be viewed as a positive attraction *toward* members of the same sex, rather than a revulsion *against* members of the other sex.

The terms *sexual preference* and *sexual orientation* are becoming more common to describe people's sexual attractions. (Likewise *affectional preference* and *affectional orientation* are used to denote the object of a person's affectional desires—usually but not exclusively similar to the sexual.) While they are often used interchangeably, "preference" implies that a choice may be involved, whereas "orientation" suggests more of a deep-seated or innate direction to one's sexual desires.

Physical Diversity

It is important to distinguish certain physical conditions from sexual orientation. Though often confused with homosexuality, they are separate and unrelated phenomena.

Transsexuals. Some people confuse *transsexualism* with homosexuality. Transsexuals are people whose core gender identity is other than that of their biological sex. Such individuals frequently report that they somehow had the wrong gender assignment or are "trapped" in the wrong physical body. Sometimes transsexuals undergo surgery to change their external genitalia to fit the other sex (*gender reassignment*). For a man, this involves silicone and hormone injections to enlarge the breasts, removal of body hair through the process of electrolysis, removal of the penis, and the construction of a vagina using the skin of the penis to form the interior walls. For women, it involves removal of the breasts (mastectomy), hormone injections which create male secondary sex characteristics including body hair and the lowering of the voice, and construction of a prosthetic penis. For transsexuals of both sexes, the operation often brings their body image into harmony with their internal identity and sexual orientation. It is important, however, not to confuse homosexuality with transsexualism since most homosexuals feel comfortable with their biological identities and do not want to become the other sex. Furthermore, many transsexuals are heterosexual.

Intersexuals. Intersexuality is a biological condition in which the person has the internal reproductive anatomy of one sex with ambiguous external genitalia. For example, a person might be a biological female in terms of hormones and reproductive system, but may manifest an enlarged clitoris that may resemble an underdeveloped penis. There are cases of intersexuals who have been assigned at birth a gender different from their biological one. In some cases this is a deliberate decision on the part of the parents, while in others it occurred when parents mistook the external appearance for the actual biological sex.

Hermaphrodites. Unlike intersexuals, whose external appearance may confuse or mislead as to their actual biological sex, hermaphrodites possess the reproductive organs of both sexes. For example, a hermaphrodite may have a penis *and* developed breasts or a uterus and no breasts; or they may have an ovary on one side of the body and a testes on the other.

Eunuchs. This condition is the result of social engineering. Eunuchs are intact biological males who, because of accident, disease, choice, or punishment, have their testicles or penis or both removed. Historically, eunuchs were often slaves who were placed in charge of harems because they could be trusted with the women or were the favored sexual partners of royalty—for example, Alexander the Great.

Act versus Identity

Act. Labels are words given by people to add shape and meaning to reality and to identify easily other persons, things, or ideas. Without labels, communication would be strained and time-consuming and ideas would be more difficult to grasp. But at the same time, labels—because they are "shortcuts" to understanding and identifying—may *over*simplify and even mislead.

Language includes a number of terms that serve as labels to denote different expressions of our sexuality. But there is even disagreement over precisely what aspects of sexuality these labels should identify and highlight.

One view maintains that because sexuality implies first and foremost a *behavior*, labels should be given to the behavior in question rather than to the person engaging in the behavior. In this context, heterosexual sex becomes sex that takes place between people of different sexes while homosexual sex is sex that occurs between people of the same sex.

One of the strongest proponents of labeling behavior rather than individuals is sex researcher Alfred Kinsey. He based his discussion on interviews he conducted in the 1940s and 1950s with approximately 20,000 men and women. Kinsey's findings shocked both the scientific community and the general public with the revelation that a great number of men and women had satisfying same-sex sexual experiences at some point in their lives. His purpose, however, was not to shock, but rather to urge a reconsideration of sexual categories then in operation. Not only did the labels "homosexuality" and "heterosexuality" not describe *most* people whose preferences were not exclusive, but they also did not allow for any overlapping behaviors. Partly in an attempt to help alleviate the stigma surrounding same-sex acts, Kinsey argued that homosexuality and heterosexuality are parts of a continuum and that to define people in terms of sexual behavior is difficult if not impossible.

The human mind, argued Kinsey, divides reality into artificial categories. As the animal world is not simply divided between "sheep and goats," in like fashion, people cannot be pigeon-holed into two discrete sexual categories.

Identity. In contrast, there are those who feel that sexuality is more than merely a behavior but is rather an aspect of personal identity which strongly influences the ways people live their lives and view the world at large. The terms "heterosexual," "homosexual," and "bisexual" are, then, labels which refer not only to sexual behaviors, but also to the persons who engage in those behaviors.

Opponents of views like Kinsey's maintain that sexual practices are not irrelevant to a person's sense of self. Though they admit that few people are exclusively homosexual or heterosexual, they argue nonetheless that most people do have a preference which helps to define who one is. Among this group, however, there is disagreement over the origins of a sexual identity. Regarding homosexuality, one camp—the essentialists—maintain that a homosexual identity can be traced back through the ages of antiquity. The other camp—the constructivists—argue that, though homosexual acts have always existed, a personal identity in terms of sexual orientation is period- and culture-specific and is a relatively modern invention dating only from the later 19th century. Therefore, they maintain that it is necessary to be cautious in labelling historic figures and circumstances. For example, we know today that in ancient Greece, among certain members of the elite classes, a homosexual relationship between an older man and an adolescent boy was sanctioned by the culture. Such relationships were integral to a youth's education and promoted intellectual and social communication across the generations. But to label ancient Greeks as "homosexuals" or "gay" would be to employ a modern term to denote historical figures with radically different values and attitudes. What history can show us, however, is that people have created many different plans for organizing human life, including its sexual aspect.

Today, sexual labels to define identity are widely understood and accepted by more and more people. For better or worse, a common word to mean heterosexual is *straight*, from the term "straight arrow" (or "straight as an arrow"), denoting adherence to conventional values or standards of behavior.

Many homosexuals prefer to use terms which suggest an outlook on the world and a lifestyle emphasized by affection and love rather than merely sexual behavior. For males, the term *gay* has gained wide acceptance. Though the derivation of the word is vague, during the 19th century it meant prostitute. During the 20th century homosexual men adopted the term to describe their lifestyle positively and nonclinically. Before non-gays were aware of the term, it was used as a code word to enable people to more easily recognize one another when life for homosexuals was not as open as it is today. The public at large was introduced to the term in the 1938 Hollywood film *Bringing Up Baby* when Cary Grant, clad in .women's attire while his own clothes were drying, joked to Katharine Hepburn that he was "turning gay."

The term *lesbian* for females has a clearer genesis. The Greek island of Lesbos in the 6th century B.C.E. (Before the Common Era) was the setting in which young women shared in the delights of the mind as well as the body, taught by the poet Sappho. As one of Sappho's remaining fragmentary poems states:

> You may forget but
> Let me tell you
> this: someone in
> some future time
> will think of us.

Some people argue that labels denoting sexual orientation or preference should not exist because such labels tend to perpetuate arbitrary divisions—and besides, "We are all just people anyway." Indeed, within those cultures that permit the enormous diversity of consensual sexual expression without censure or condemnation, such labels seem not to exist. Others argue that labels relating to sexual identity exist because of social structures and expectations, and that sexual preference does make a difference in the ways we view ourselves and our world. Some even argue that acceptance of one's homosexual identity is a necessary pre-requisite for a positive sense of self, and is on a fundamental level a *political* act which begins the process of questioning social judgments and expectations. Finally, others argue that each individual should be free of all pressures to identify by sexual preference and instead should decide what (if any) label to apply.

Regardless of what stand one takes, it is obvious that categories relating to sexual orientation do exist. What is not exactly clear is how they came into being. But these labels are social constructs, much like labels relating to race and ethnicity. (See Chapter 5.) In the future such divisions may be viewed as historical curiosities that reflect a time long past, or the divisions may remain without values attached to them.

The Heterosexual-Bisexual-Homosexual Continuum

Alfred C. Kinsey and his colleagues in 1948, in *Sexual Behavior in the Human Male*, and again in 1953, with *Sexual Behavior of the Human Female*, revealed a much greater incidence of homosexual behavior than previously acknowledged. Of the over 12,000 men interviewed, 37 percent had some overt homosexual experience to orgasm between adolescence and old age, 25 percent had had more than incidental homosexual experiences for at least three years, while 4 percent were exclusively homosexual throughout adulthood.

In the similar study for women, of the 8,000 interviewed, 28 percent acknowledged having had erotic responses to other women, 13 percent had experienced orgasm with another woman, and 19 percent had had some sexual contact with other women by the age of forty.

Kinsey countered the myth that homosexual behavior was an unusual and isolated phenomenon. He reported that the incidence of persons with homosexual histories was virtually identical in every geographic region of the country: large cities, small rural communities, and farms. People with these histories were found among every occupation, socio-economic class, and age group. The overwhelming evidence of homosexual behavior "in spite of the severity of the penalties that our Anglo-American culture has placed upon it through the centuries" led Kinsey to conclude that "such activity would appear in the histories of a much larger portion of the population if there were no social restraints." (Kinsey, *et al.*, 1948, pp. 637 and 632.)

Activists have drawn from these statistics the figure of 10 percent as an estimate of the population who could be considered gay, although contradictory studies make an accurate number difficult to obtain.

To chart his findings Kinsey devised a seven-point scale with 0 representing those whose histories were exclusively heterosexual and 6 for those who were exclusively homosexual. Others were placed along the scale depending on the percentage of heterosexual or homosexual sexual acts for males in relation to their overall sexual behavior. (The percentages were slightly lower for females.)

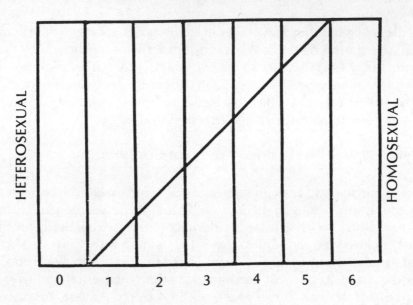

Heterosexual-homosexual rating scales

Based on both psychological reactions and overt experience, individuals rate as follows:

0. Exclusively heterosexual with no homosexual.
1. Predominantly heterosexual, only incidental homosexual.
2. Predominantly heterosexual, but more than incidentally homosexual.
3. Equally heterosexual and homosexual.
4. Predominantly homosexual, but more than incidentally heterosexual.
5. Predominantly homosexual, but incidentally heterosexual.
6. Exclusively homosexual.

The Kinsey studies show that the predominant sexual experience of males and females for a majority of the population occurs with a member of the other sex. However, a little over 18 percent of males and slightly fewer females have at least half of their sexual experiences with a member of the same sex. But what about those who fall within the range of 2-4 on Kinsey's chart, those who experience comparable sexual interest in both sexes? For some of these people, the labels "heterosexual" or "homosexual" may be inappropriate. Therefore, a third term, *bisexual*, is often used.

Sigmund Freud postulated that we are all born with a bisexual potential and that, for unknown reasons, some of us become heterosexual and others homosexual. According to Freud, there are actually three types of homosexuals (whom he calls "inverts"): *absolute*, who are exclusively attracted to members of their own sex and, he believed, biologically predisposed toward homosexuality; *amphigenic*, who could be attracted to either sex; and *contingent*, whose homosexual behavior is dependent on environmental factors and thus may change.

Kinsey's findings and other studies also suggest that some people are bisexual and that sexuality is indeed more fluid and complex than once believed.

Just as there are a variety of heterosexual and homosexual people, so too are bisexuals not a homogeneous group, either in overt behavior or psychological experience. For some, bisexuality can be a stage of transition from exclusive heterosexuality to homosexuality (or vice versa) as newly uncovered feelings begin to emerge. For others, bisexuality represents a genuinely equal attraction to both sexes or attraction to both with a preference for one over the other.

Some researchers suggest that because of the different ways males and females are socialized in this culture, differences may exist in the ways that bisexuality is viewed by society:

> Bisexual behavior on the part of American women is more apt to be tolerated with less stigma attached to female homosexual activity. Women in our society are thus subjected to somewhat less pressure to identify as either homosexual or heterosexual. Many who do eventually arrive at a lesbian identity emphasize the voluntary nature of their commitment. (Humphries.)

One woman tells her story as a bisexual:

> Everybody knows about bisexuals—they're *confused* ("Just a stage you're going through...you'll eventually choose...you're not secure in your mature heterosexuality yet...you're afraid of the other sex and the same sex is less threatening..."); they're *sex maniacs* ("They will do it with *anyone*, anytime..."); they're *shallow* ("They can't commit themselves to any one person or even any one sex for a long-term deep relationship...they're typical 'swingers'...they're fickle...").
>
> Well, having been a self-named bisexual woman for the last seventeen years, let me just relate my experience. *Confused?* I have been deeply in love with men and women. Being in love with women was frowned upon by society, and therefore, harder to live with in terms of the *outside* world, but *inside* was the important part. It was an irreversibly empowering part of my life, and gave me a gentle power and love of my own kind that changed me profoundly with women and men from that point in time onward. It was most definitely not a phase. Spiritually, emotionally, historically, it thrives within me, even if I am now with a man. *Nymphomanic?* For many years, my bisexuality was solely spiritual, emotional, and political. It set the stage for

the physical component, which seemed to follow naturally. Gay, lesbian, straight, and bisexual people all vary widely in terms of individual sexual appetite. *Fickle?* Personally, I've been a one-person gal my whole life—they call it "serial monogamy." Yet I have never aspired to marrying and doing the accepted family patterns if I didn't feel good doing them. I have been in love with a man at times and I have been in love with a woman at other times. Of course I have yearned for additional flings with others (of both sexes, regardless of who I was with) just like any other human being in love. Fidelity is just another individual decision and varies widely for all people.

For me, naming myself as a bisexual feels true and feels fun. There may be others who feel the same way, but simply haven't heard the information that there is a third option in terms of a lifetime sexuality. (Deihl.)

Situational Homosexuality

[M]any people engage in same-sex acts without necessarily identifying as homosexual. Alternatively, a person may not have actually engaged in same-sex sexual acts, although they would define themselves as homosexual. (Richardson & Hart, p. 73.)

Kinsey's study not only suggests the wide range of human sexuality, but it also brings to the surface certain problems of sexual definition. Though at first glance terms like "homosexuality" and "heterosexuality" might seem to have obvious applications, the issue is far more complicated. Engaging in homosexual sex, or for that matter heterosexual sex, is not the same as being a *homosexual* or *heterosexual*. Some people engage in heterosexual sex while mainly desiring to be with someone of their own sex. This is true for people who are either denying their true sexual object choice or for one reason or another cannot act on this. In addition, there are instances when people have sexual relations with others of their own sex even though their true attractions are to the other sex. This condition is referred to as *situational homosexuality* and may be the result of sex segregation in closed institutional settings where individuals are isolated from the other sex. In environments such as prisons, the military, mental hospitals, single-sex schools, and religious orders where there is a mix of people with both homosexual and heterosexual orientations, both short- and long-term homosexual activity may occur.

Prisons.   Same-sex activity in prisons should not be confused with similar activity that occurs outside of prison walls. Generally, prison is an antisexual environment. Some people have sex, others do not. The Institute for Sex Research interviewed 700 male prisoners and their study showed that very few of these men had levels of sexual activity equivalent to even 10 percent of what they experienced on the outside. For male prisoners, though sexually satisfying and loving relationships do exist, often sexual activity that does occur is an expression of dominance rather than affection.

> The problem is not one of orgasms or sex acts, but rather of the meaning of the sex acts. Many heterosexual male prisoners view the sexual world very much as do male prostitutes. That is, the homosexual act in prison is defined as being heterosexual for one person and homosexual for the other. One man is defined as masculine, strong, powerful, and controlling, while the other is feminine, weak, subordinate, and controlled. The stronger inserts his penis into the weaker—the act of penetration parallels the act with women, and assures a symbolic continuity with experiences in the world outside the prison. (Gagnon, p. 267.)

Homosexual activity in prison seems to be slightly less common for women than for men, but it appears to involve more emotional commitment and affection. Women, like men, come into prison with mixed sexual histories:

> The amount of sex in these [prison] relationships is often minimal, out of preference or lack of privacy, but they may be quite emotional and long-term, which produces trauma when one partner is released. (Gagnon, p. 268.)

The Military.   During combat or times of extreme stress, sexual activity within the military is quite rare because mere survival is given top priority. However, when large numbers of individuals are placed together in single-sex military encampments, homosexual activity occurs for soldiers of all sexual orientations. Some of the heterosexual men may have access to females off the military base. At other times they may respond sexually with other men as do homosexual men. Here there is a degree of equality and choice between the partners. Issues of dominance and submission among men in the military exist to a far lesser extent than they do in prisons.

Closed Religious Orders.   As in the case of single-sex boarding schools, homosexual activity also exists for both women and men within religious seminaries, cloisters, and convents, though this is often vehemently denied by religious leaders of all denominations. Within orders which prescribe celibacy, many practitioners do live up to their vows of celibacy. Others are sexually active and some engage in homosexual activity. A task force set up by the Archdiocese of San Francisco issued a report in 1983 that estimated that 30 percent of Roman Catholic priests, nuns, and brothers have homosexual orientations. (DeStefano, p. 43.) Many believe this to be an extremely conservative estimate. In addition, many nuns consider lesbianism to be an integral part of their lives. (Curb.) Sexual activity in closed religious orders, therefore, can either be considered situational homosexuality or it may reflect a true homosexual orientation of the participants. As in other institutional settings where membership is voluntary, sexuality is conducted in secret; otherwise the participants would either be separated from one another or, as in most cases, they face expulsion.

How Do You Know?

The problem of giving definition to sexual orientation does not end with a discussion of situational homosexuality. There is also the instance of homosexual experimentation that is common in the childhood and adolescent experiences of many people, especially males. For some this is a transitory activity leading to a heterosexual or bisexual orientation later in life. For others it is a preparatory development for an eventual gay or lesbian lifestyle. If it is true that a significant number of people have had same-sex relations, how do we know which of these individuals is a lesbian or gay male? Is it the young person who fantasizes about someone of their same sex in their class or on their school's swimming team? Is it the young person who has had a few sexual experiences with someone of the same sex? Is it the man who is married to a woman for years who occasionally has sex with men? Is it the woman who is married but unhappy with her sexual relationship with her husband and who has very close but non-sexual attachments to other women? What about the person who struggles against but never acts on desires for members of the same sex? What about those who feel an occasional sexual attraction to people of the other sex?

There are several possible answers to these questions. One is that one's sexuality is really a matter of personal preference, not just the overt behavior. Thus, one need not be exclusively heterosexual or homosexual all of one's life to assume one label or the other. Indeed, one need not be actively sexual at all; in other words, it is possible to be celibate and still take on a sexual identity. Indeed, much of sexuality revolves around thought, feeling, and desire, none of which necessarily entails action. In addition, the realm of *fantasy* plays an important role in the sexual life of the individual. Few researchers have explored the relation between fantasy and orientation; most focus on sexual acts. But perhaps orientation hinges more on the deep-seated fantasies of the individual than on overt behavior. Fantasies provide a means by which we can transcend social disapprobation and even physical limitations. Thus, exploring our fantasies may give us a clearer picture of who we are.

Though there is often great media attention to sexual activities, sex educators suggest that each individual should decide when she or he is ready and responsible enough to engage in sexual relations, free from social pressure. Further, sexual activity, or the absence of it, has nothing to do with sexual orientation. People can be attracted to persons without acting on it, and this feeling of attraction is what sexual preference is all about. This confusion may result from the popular misconception that homosexuality and sex are one and the same. Rather, it is a matter of orientation, of where one's sexual and affectional, emotional and physical interests primarily lie.

Coming Out

Whatever a person's primary sexual orientation is in adulthood, many social and physical scientists believe that this orientation and sex-role identity are formed by the age of three. Money and Ehrhardt, for example, postulate that the object of a person's attraction is an integral part of gender identity and that sexual orientation is determined to a large extent during the developmental years of late infancy and early childhood.

Most of Western societies are organized around a heterosexual norm. Parents assume that their children will grow up to be attracted to someone of the other sex; popular culture presents heterosexual images and role models; everything from new cars to pizza is advertised by sexy men and women who fall in love with one another right in front of us. But for people who do not fit this norm, this feeling of being different may lead to alienation or isolation. This is exacerbated by the fact that in many instances these individuals are not supported by family members.

> Gay people are for the most part not born into gay families. They suffer oppression individually and alone, without benefit of advice or frequently even emotional support from relatives or friends. This makes their case more comparable in some way to that of the blind or left-handed, who are also dispersed in the general population.... (Boswell, p. 85.)

The reverse is generally the case for other groups whose minority status is more visible, such as ethnic minorities or people of color. As Vern Bullough says, "It is still much easier to hide one's gayness than to proclaim it."

Various options for disclosure exist for lesbians, gay males, and bisexuals. First, they can continue to deny to themselves and to others that they have strong attractions for members of their own sex. This concealment, though, can lead to devastating consequences. Though the author of the following quote was writing about men, it applies equally to women:

> Every time a homosexual denies the validity of his feelings or restrains himself from expressing them, he does a small hurt to himself. He turns his

energies inward and suppresses his own vitality. The effect may be scarcely noticeable: joy may be a little less keen, happiness slightly subdued; he may simply feel a little run-down, a little less tall. Over the years, these tiny denials have a cumulative effect. (Fisher, p. 249.)

Another option is for people to lead double lives by having same-sex contacts in secret and living a public heterosexual life. Most gay people can easily "pass" in straight society. Or they can try to change their sexual fantasies and desires in the therapeutic setting. However, because sexual orientation is such a deep and integral aspect of a person's personality structure, this option has been unsuccessful in the majority of cases. (See Chapter 3.) This sort of conflict may be so intense in some instances that it results in suicide.

The option which a greater percentage of people with same-sex orientations is deciding to take is that of dealing realistically and honestly with their feelings, in a metaphoric sense, "coming out of the closet." Or as some see it, "coming out of the coffin" of silence and fear into the light of day.

Some researchers have concluded that there is a definite "coming-out process" which many bisexuals and homosexuals pass through. It is often a lengthy and ongoing process that can occur at any stage of life. Some people report an awareness of their same-sex attractions and come out at a very early age:

> I remember when I was six or seven years old, there was this other boy, I don't remember his name, who was about the same age or maybe a year younger. He had sandy brown hair and a little turned-up nose, and I was crazy about him. When I was with him on the playground, I was enamored by the way he moved, and I loved to watch his muscles move beneath his shirt. When he wasn't around, his image was constantly in my mind and I sometimes stared out my bedroom window hoping to see him walk by. I knew that boys weren't supposed to feel about other boys the way I felt about him, so I didn't tell anyone. I didn't even talk to him very much because I didn't know how to act around him. But one thing I did understand: I knew by this time what a crush was, and this definitely was one. Since those early days, my attraction for men has grown and today as I am in my forties it remains an important part of my identity. (Mahler.)

Others, though, report an awareness of their attractions much later in life:

> For me, it wasn't until I was sixty-six that I came out—a few years after my husband died and the last of my six children had left the nest. I guess it was a shock to my family when I told them, especially my grandchildren, who couldn't believe their "granny" was a lesbian. But I've had a certain feeling for women for a long time though I never could quite put a name to it. Now

my grandchildren, one in particular, think it's great and tell all their little friends, who think it's great too. I guess it's easier being a lesbian today than in my day; though I've come to realize that this is my day too. (Tucker.)

There are, in fact, varieties of experience which characterize an awareness of one's homosexuality:

I honestly didn't know I was gay when I got married at age twenty—or at least I wasn't aware of it. I was married in the 1960s to my high school sweetheart. In our fifteen years together, we raised two daughters, we had a nice house in the suburbs, I had a great job, I even had a stationwagon—the quintessential American dream—and I was happy and truly loved my wife. But around our twelfth year together I developed feelings I couldn't ignore—desires for men that only became stronger over time. I eventually confided this to my wife and naturally, at first, she was extremely shocked and hurt. I joined a support group with other men in my situation and, shortly thereafter, I moved from my house into a small apartment a few miles away. Not long after that my wife filed for divorce. Over the past year or so she has come to accept and understand my feelings and today we are on the road to becoming friends. We share joint custody of our two teenage daughters, who come over to my place on Wednesdays and Saturdays. It was difficult for them at first, but because of the strong foundation of honesty and openness I set with them, we continue to have a good relationship. They like and trust John, my lover of five years, and they respect me for refusing to live a lie. (Weber.)

I had a few crushes on other girls in high school but it never really went anywhere because I never said anything to them. I guess I was afraid of their reaction and I was afraid it would get back to my parents. So I just sort of loved them from a distance. Then after graduation I went away to college. This was really the first time I was away from home for any length of time. Looking back now, I suppose I chose the college that I did because it was the one farthest away from my family. Though I had a close relationship with them, I needed to be far away to feel safe enough to explore my feelings for women. I was lucky because there was a lesbian and gay student group on my campus. I didn't know what I would find there but one Wednesday night I pulled up my courage and went. I guess I expected all the women to pounce on me, but that didn't happen. I walked into the room and sat way in the back of the meeting. During the break a few people, women and men, introduced themselves. They were really friendly. We went on a picnic on Sunday and it felt good, but somehow weird, to be out in public with openly lesbian and gay people. The following spring, when I was home for Easter, I told my family. (McCormick.)

"Coming-Out" Models

Researchers have developed theoretical models charting the coming-out process. Two models are those of researchers Vivienne Cass and Eli Coleman. Cass and Coleman patterned their concepts after the multistage theoretical models of personality development pioneered by people such as sociologist Charles Horton Cooley, philosopher George Herbert Mead, and psychoanalysts Sigmund Freud and Erik Erikson, who believed that personal identity develops along an interactive process between the individual and his or her environment. Such models may differ in their specific view of human development, but all share the basic assumption that human beings move through life experiences within a particular framework. This framework provides a means by which one can understand the process an individual is experiencing and also to predict what form future stages might take. In addition, an awareness of these stages enables the individual to gauge her or his relation to other individuals who are having or have had similar experiences. These models have been suggested as explanatory frameworks for a variety of human processes. For example, Lawrence Kohlberg describes stages of moral development, Jean Piaget outlines stages of sensory-motor development, and Elisabeth Kübler-Ross charts six stages in the process of coming to terms with death.

Vivienne Cass proposes a "coming-out" model with six interconnecting stages:

Stage 1: Identity Confusion. This is the "Who am I?" stage associated with the feeling that one is different from peers, accompanied by a growing sense of personal alienation. The person begins to be conscious of same-sex feelings or behaviors and to label them as such. It is rare at this stage for the person to disclose inner turmoil to others. Writing about women experiencing this stage, one researcher says:

> Acknowledgment of the sexual element of being different is often accompanied with feelings of denial, shame, anxiety, and ambivalence. This is a time of great dissonance and inner turmoil. A woman faces a conflict between the process of socialization, which teaches her that she will probably marry and have a family, and her feelings, which pull her toward wanting intimacy with other women. (Lewis, p. 465.)

Stage 2: Identity Comparison. This is the rationalization or bargaining stage where the person thinks, "I may be a homosexual, but then again I may be bisexual," "Maybe this is just temporary," or, "My feelings of attraction are simply for just one other person of my own sex and this is a special case." There is a heightened sense of not belonging anywhere with the corresponding feeling that "I am the only one in the world like this."

Stage 3: Identity Tolerance. In this "I probably am a homosexual" stage the person begins to contact other homosexuals to counteract feelings of isolation and alienation, but merely tolerates rather than fully accepts a homosexual identity. The feeling of not belonging with heterosexuals becomes stronger.

Stage 4: Identity Acceptance. There is continued and increased contact with other homosexuals in this stage, where friendships start to form. The individual thus evaluates other homosexuals more positively and accepts rather than tolerates a homosexual self-image. The earlier questions of "Who am I?" and "Where do I belong?" have been answered.

Stage 5: Identity Pride. This is the "These are my people" stage where the individual develops an awareness of the enormous incongruity that exists between the person's own increasingly positive concept of self as lesbian or gay and an awareness of society's rejection of this orientation. The person feels anger at heterosexuals and devalues many of their institutions (e.g., marriage, gender-role structures, etc.). The person discloses her or his identity to more and more people and wishes to be immersed in the gay or lesbian subculture consuming its literature, art, and other forms of culture.

Stage 6: Identity Synthesis. The intense anger at heterosexuals—the "them and us" attitude that existed in stage 5—softens at this stage to reflect a recognition that some heterosexuals are supportive and can be trusted. However, those who are not supportive are further devalued. There remains some anger at the ways that lesbians and gays are treated in the society, but this is less intense. The person retains a deep sense of pride but now comes to perceive less of a dichotomy between the heterosexual and homosexual worlds. A homosexual identity becomes an integral and integrated aspect of the individual's complete personality structure.

Eli Coleman proposes a second model to chart the coming-out process using five stages. Unlike the Cass version, this one focuses in its later stages on the formation of romantic attachments:

Stage 1: Pre-Coming-Out. At this stage, the individual is not conscious of same-sex feelings because of the strong defenses built up to keep such unwanted self-knowledge from reaching a conscious level. The person does feel, however, somehow different from others but does not understand the reasons for this.

Stage 2: Coming-Out. At this stage the person comes to a conscious or semi-conscious acknowledgment of having homosexual thoughts or fantasies. During this period of great personal confusion, the person may disclose feelings to one or a few trusted individuals for external validation. Some people begin to make contacts with other individuals who identify as gay or lesbian and may avoid telling close friends, who are presumably heterosexual, and family members who may reject them.

Stage 3: Exploration.   During this stage, the person interacts more with other lesbians or gay males and "experiments" with a new sexual identity. Here the individual often develops improved interpersonal skills which may result in a more positive self-image. Many people with homosexual orientations enter this period during adolescence. Many others who are not afforded this opportunity during their teenage years because of the social makeup of the culture subsequently undergo a "developmental lag." (Grace.) Therefore, some "homosexual individuals often-times do not enter their true adolescence until their chronological adolescence has long passed." (Coleman, p. 36.)

Stage 4: First Relationship.   Following the period of sexual experimentation of Stage 3, the person may desire a more stable and committed relationship which combines emotional and physical attraction. These relationships often do not last because they are frequently entered into before the basic tasks of coming-out and sexual exploration are completed.

Stage 5: Integration.   This stage, where the public and private identities merge into one unified and integrated self-image, is ongoing and continuous and will last for the rest of the person's life. Relationships are often characterized by greater non-possessiveness, honesty, and mutual trust and can be more successful than first relationships. The person is better equipped to meet the problems and pressures of everyday life.

Studies suggest that the coming-out journey that begins with an early awareness of same-sex feelings to the development of an integrated identity takes between ten and fourteen years. (Kooden et al.) Some people move more quickly than others. And some may become stuck and never progress to the final stages. The reasons why people move from stage to stage, or fail to move, are very complex and difficult to comprehend fully. Theorists have stressed, however, that societal attitudes are important in affecting the development of a person's positive identity.

As one researcher states:

Indeed it would seem that the gay liberation movement over the past decade has facilitated the process of acquiring a positive homosexual identity by providing more in the way of a social support system than previously existed. (Minton, p. 12.)

Also:

The decision to conceal the homosexual identity from significant others may be detrimental to psychological well-being. Is it possible to achieve an integrated personal identity or have authentic relationships while concealing fundamental aspects of the self?... In choosing to hide an essential part of the self, individuals are left with a gnawing feeling that they are really valued for what others expect them to be rather than for who they really are. (Minton and McDonald, p. 102.)

It must be emphasized that these coming-out models merely depict general patterns and each person comes out in different ways under unique circumstances. In addition, some people never truly complete this process, which begins with fear and confusion and leads to an identity integration. Some people become stuck or retreat back into earlier stages of the process.

It is also important to mention that males and females tend to differ slightly at points within the process. Generally women come out and have homosexual experiences at a somewhat later age than their male counterparts. (Gagnon.) The median age at which males are aware of same-sex attractions on a conscious level is between thirteen and fourteen, whereas females reach this awareness at about the median age of eighteen. (Jay and Young.) Males tend to see their homosexual orientation determined at an earlier age than females. (Humphries.) Furthermore, the median age for males having their first same-sex encounter is at age fifteen, and for women this is at about the age of twenty. (Kooden *et al.*) The amount of sexual experimentation also tends to vary between lesbians and gay males, with gay males engaging in more one-time sexual contacts than lesbians, especially during the early stages of the coming-out process. (Nuehring *et al.*)

The Kinsey Institute's 1982 study of sexual preference revealed that 70% of the lesbians interviewed had no homosexual experiences in high school, and 62% of them reported a primarily heterosexual orientation up to age 19. Yet more than half the homosexual men interviewed reported primarily homosexual feelings and behavior. (Bell and Weinberg.)

Finally, various studies confirm that lesbians have more heterosexual experience than gay males. Saghir and Robins found that 79% of the lesbians compared to 52% of male homosexuals had had heterosexual intercourse. Whether these differences result from the differing socialization of men and women or from some inherent biological difference between the sexes is not clear.

During the later stages of the coming-out process, both males and females can and do form stable and strong relationships. This tends to be true, however, more in the case of lesbians than gay males. This probably has more to do with gender-role expectations than sexual orientation:

Women's sexuality seems more intimately connected to relationships than men's, and sex for a woman can be difficult or even unpleasant outside the context of a meaningful relationship. (Schaef, p. 32.)

These apparent differences may say more about the disparity in the attitudes and behaviors of males and females in general than about the differences particular to gay males and lesbians. This can be explained by looking at the disparate ways in which males and females are socialized in this culture: males are encouraged to be competitive and to be concerned about their sexuality at a relatively early age, whereas females are taught to be nurturing and to devalue their sexuality. However, as sex-role and gender-role stereotypes change, many of these differences may eventually fade.

What Do They Do in Bed?

Because of the enormous societal stigma on same-sex relationships, the sexual element is steeped in myth, which tends to deepen this stigmatization. When the topic of homosexuals comes up, many heterosexuals wonder "How do they have sex?" or, put more simply, "What do they do in bed?"

The answer is that lesbians and gays do in bed pretty much what straights do in bed except it is done with a partner of the same sex. However, though sexual acts may be similar, a societal double-standard exists. When heterosexuals engage in anything other than the "missionary position"—man on top, woman on the bottom with the man's penis penetrating the woman's vagina—society tends to label this as mere "sexual variation." But what is seen as sexual variation for heterosexuals is often viewed with disgust and labeled as a "perversion" when performed by same-sex couples.

Much of the prejudice against homosexuals and bisexuals may be a result of a lack of knowledge about the varieties of sexual behavior. But it also seems to be based on a belief that males and females naturally "fit" and hence should be joined together sexually and emotionally. But there is much to suggest that same-sex sexual relations are as pleasurable as heterosexual ones. Researchers Masters and Johnson, in a study of human sexuality, observed that same-sex couples are more communicative with their partners and more sensitive to their partners' needs. In addition, some studies (e.g., Hite) reveal that many women do not achieve orgasm from heterosexual intercourse, and that more direct clitoral stimulation is necessary; for many women, the angle of the penis during coitus does not afford this kind of stimulation. Some feminists have written of this as "the myth of the vaginal orgasm." Finally, it is true that certain activities are more enjoyable for some people, but this does not make clear why we assume that we can only enjoy those activities with a member of the other sex.

In truth, however, there are very few sexual acts that are exclusively heterosexual or exclusively homosexual. Though it is true that a male and a female can experience genuine sexual fulfillment with one another, it is likewise true that two males or two females can experience such fulfillment. Indeed, a female knows a female's body as a male knows a male's body. From this intimate and personal knowledge, when two females or two males make love, each partner can trigger sexual arousal and intense pleasure in the other.

Specific Sexual Acts

As human beings, our sexuality is not something that is limited to our genitals. Rather, many areas of our bodies are capable of receiving and transmitting erotic sensations. Therefore, sexual relations, heterosexual and homosexual, include both a non-genital as well as a genital focus.

The range of sexual activities of gay males and lesbians is not unlike that of heterosexual males and females, with the exception of heterosexual intercourse. Nongenital sexual stimulation includes kissing, hugging, caressing, massaging, and general tactile stimulation of the body.

Genital sexual stimulation includes, for males, oral-penile (fellatio) oral-anal (popularly known as "rimming"), penile-anal penetration (sometimes termed "sodomy"), penile-interfemural (penis of one between thighs of other), penile rubbing of other parts of the body, and hand-penile stimulation (masturbation).

For women, genital stimulation includes oral-genital contact (cunnilingus), oral-anal, vaginal penetration with fingers or hands, and genital stimulation by rubbing (tribadism).

There are many myths about gay sexuality. For years, since women were not viewed as sexual beings, sex between two women was unthinkable. As a result, popular mythology pictured lesbians either as having enlarged clitorises or as incapable of sexual enjoyment without some phallic substitute, without what is termed a "dildo." Though the use of a dildo does occur on occasion in lesbian sex, it is by no means the norm.

There are a variety of positions in which both gays and lesbians enjoy sexual relations. These include lying, standing, sitting; different partners on top or bottom; partners facing each other or front to back, or with both partners engaged in mouth-to-genital contact.

There is a popular notion that in gay and lesbian sex each partner plays a certain role, imitating heterosexuals in the traditional missionary position. In actuality, though individuals certainly may have personal preferences, partners generally enjoy a variety of styles and actions of expression. (See "Safer Sex Precautions," Chapter 7).

What is Natural?

We use the word "natural" in all sorts of contexts; we refer to "natural childbirth," "a natural athlete," "natural foods," "naturally curly hair," "natural fibers," and even a "natural wit." The term also has applications to aspects of sexual behavior. Critics of homosexuality, for example, sometimes maintain that same-sex sexual practices are "unnatural," meaning that such behavior is absent in non-human animal species. Defenders of homosexuality, on the other hand, argue that such behavior is universal among animal species and so is in fact "natural." There is, however, a third view which maintains that what non-human animals do is irrelevant to human considerations. In fact, in medieval times one argument extolling the value of same-sex love commended it precisely because it *was* "unnatural," that is, it separated humans from non-humans. Let's examine each of these positions.

Homosexuality as Unnatural

Some people view homosexuality as a perversity which is contrary to the "natural laws" of the universe. One of the leading proponents of this view has been the Roman Catholic Church. A key factor in the development of orthodox Catholic ethics since the 12th century, the concept of natural law includes standards which the Church has inferred to follow from an ordering of nature. This natural order derives its significance from God's existence, and so is, like God, objective, eternal, and unchanging. In terms of procreation, what is "natural" according to this view is procreative sex. Thus, the Church has concluded that the expression of homosexuality is "intrinsically immoral."

One writer echoes this argument:

Biologically absurd behavior like homosexuality cannot be condoned or accepted as normal without endangering normal development of our young toward their own duty to reproduce. (Cameron.)

The Roman Catholic Church also considers many forms of heterosexual reproduction unnatural. In our technological age, a modern update of this position was articulated by the Vatican in a 1987 document entitled "Instruction on Respect for Human Life in Its Origin and on the Dignity of Procreation: Replies to Certain Questions of the Day." In it

Pope John Paul II opposes all forms of biomedical reproduction, defining as "morally illicit" any form of conception other than those arising from the sexual act of a married couple. The Church specifically condemns embryo transfer, *in vitro*, and all other forms of alternative fertilization, prenatal diagnosis and investigation of the fetus, the collection of sperm through masturbation, genetic research and engineering, and most forms of birth control. In the 1987 document it also restated its opposition to abortion.

Those who hold to the unnaturalness of homosexuality focus on biological studies which view some forms of homosexual behavior within the non-human animal world as a mere form of youthful play in readiness for "mature" heterosexual coitus or as a form of dominance:

> The occasional mounting of male animals by other males—apes in particular—is not true homosexuality but is in part playful and learning behavior in the immature, and in part a way of avoiding violent fighting between two males. The weaker one signifies submissiveness by "presenting" his rear, the stronger signifies dominance by mounting and making a few routine penile thrusts without intromission or ejaculation. (Hunt, p. 299.)

Mountain sheep (*Ovis dalli stonei*) express dominance through homosexual behavior. (Geist.) After a battle between two males, the winner, sporting an erection, mounts the loser. The human equivalent of this behavior might be the prison situation, in which the stronger males often sexually dominate the weaker ones.

Some scientists assert that forms of homosexual behavior may occur in nature because of mistaken identity. Some animals and insects have been observed to make "mistakes" in sexual object choice, confusing a member of the same sex for one of the other sex. For example, in fruit flies (*Drosophila melanogaster*) the scent of newly born males is similar to that of sexually receptive females and young males are sometimes courted by older males. (Tompkins *et al*.) In addition, in some insect species in which the female is larger, some male insects become so disoriented that they have been known to confuse a female of their species with completely inappropriate objects such as twigs, bananas, aluminum cans, and beer bottles.

Homosexuality as Natural

> When animals do something that we like, we call it "natural." When they do something that we don't like, we call it "animalistic." (Weinrich.)

On the other side are those who believe that what is found in the world is natural and, since homosexual behaviors are found both among humans and non-human species, such behavior is natural. Advocates claim that non-procreative sexual behavior occurs widely among animals other than humans. Furthermore, just as homosexuality in humans covers a wide range of behaviors, so too with animals: "there is scarcely any aspect of human homosexuality that does not have at least a moderately close parallel in some animal species." (Weinrich, p. 202.)

Proponents agree that some forms of homosexual behavior in other species are simply designations of social dominance, mistaken identity, or playfulness. They also maintain, however, that homosexuality constitutes an integral and important part of the four billion years of the natural selection process. Same-sex behaviors in many species contain a definite sexual element. Sometimes this includes erections in males and vaginal lubrication in females involving two members of the same sex:

> It seems unreasonable to suppose that these [behaviors] all represent mistakes in development, environmentally induced pathologies, or even genetic diseases, if only because of their wide occurrence and continuity through time. Rather, it is theoretically possible that alternative forms of sexual expression are of positive significance in animal evolution. (Kirsch.)

Kinsey and his associates observed and documented case studies of homosexual contacts both in the barnyard and in the wild. These behaviors were found in species of rats, mice, hamsters, guinea pigs, rabbits, porcupines, marten, cattle, antelope, goats, horses, pigs, lions, sheep, monkeys, dogs, bulls, cows, rams, stallions, donkeys, elephants, hyenas, cats, sows, ewes, raccoons, and porpoises. (Kinsey, 1953, p. 449.) Occasional homosexual copulation has also been observed between adult male green lizards (*Anolis garmani*) in Jamaica (Trivers), and homosexual copulation-like behavior between female tropical gecko lizards (*Lepidodactylus lugubris*) on Oahu Island, Hawaii (Werner.) Researchers have also identified the following male insects that engage in same-sex courtship and copulation attempts: field crickets, cockroaches, fleas, cimicid bugs, pentatomid bugs, corixid bugs, naucorid bugs, coreid bugs, nymphalid butterflies, ichneumonid wasps, chironomid flies, calliphorid flies, drosophilid flies, tephritid flies, muscid flies, syrphid flies, sacrophagid flies, anthophorid bees, chrysopid lacewings, and tortricid moths.

Kinsey determined that sexual contacts between males of various species proceed to the point of orgasm, especially for the male that mounts another male. This is less the case, however, for non-human females. But it is uncertain how often non-human females achieve orgasm in any type of sexual encounter. (Kinsey, 1953, p. 449.) Females of various species of monkeys have, however, exhibited mounting behaviors with mutual genital stimulation that often results in orgasm. (Goldfoot *et al.*)

Homosexual behavior is sometimes a form of affection or sexual "rehearsal" for heterosexual coitus. Male langur monkeys (*Presbytis entellus*) exhibit high levels of sexual excitement, mount, and frequently embrace other males as females sometimes look on. This has been compared to youthful homosexual experimentation among adolescent human males. These behaviors also tend to solidify and strengthen male relationships which are essential in cooperative endeavors. (Hrdy.)

Instances of homosexual behavior have been observed in other species of primates, including chimpanzees and baboons. Writes one observer of two male monkeys:

> Insertion of the penis into the anus was finally made, followed by rapid strokes and kissing of the lips until mild, general, convulsive movements resulted.... The transitory functional paralysis attending a complete orgasm seems to be the ultimate reaction sought for as the erotogenic play advances from one stage to another, and after a period of rest the play begins all over again. (Kempf, pp. 134-5.)

Female homosexual behavior is also common in monkeys and other primates. Partners embrace in coital positions and on occasion show marked interest in one another's genitalia in which one will take the partner's labia and manipulate them gently between the teeth. (Bingham.)

Homosexual behavior also occurs among dolphins. In one study researchers placed dolphins of both sexes in a large tank and observed them for a number of months. They noticed two of the males forming an extremely close attachment to each other. One of these males was taken out of the tank for three weeks and, when reunited with the other, the results were recorded:

> No doubt could exist that the two recognized each other and for several hours they swam side by side rushing frenziedly through the water, and on several occasions they leaped completely out of the water. For several days, the two males were inseparable and neither paid any attention to the female. This was in courting season, and at other times the two males seemed bent only on preventing the other's copulation with the female. (McBride *et al.*, p. 121.)

One of the most striking parallels of homosexuality in animals to that of humans is found in five species of gulls, and most commonly in Western gulls (*Larus occidentalis*). (Hunt and Hunt.) These pairs court each other, defend a territory, and alternate sitting on a nest as do male-female couples. A few perform mounting and attempt copulation.

Most species of mammals are not monogamous; however, over 90 percent of bird species are at least as monogomous as humans. (Weinrich.) These female-male gull couples generally form long-term relationships, staying together over successive seasons. Between 8 and 14 percent of the mated couples cooperating in the incubation of eggs laid in a nest are two females. The couples are presumed to be lesbian because they are attending a clutch of eggs (five to six), which is more than generally found in the nest of a female-male couple. Between 10 and 20 percent of these eggs are fertile, which indicates that at least one member of the couple is copulating with a male, and some of the eggs hatch. In instances in which chicks are born, the females raise the young together and, in a sense, become lesbian mothers! If, on the other hand, the mothers were not paired with another female, the chicks most likely would not survive.

Critiques of "Natural"

The two approaches discussed above, though they end with differing conclusions, share a belief that empirical investigations of non-human animals can help us to make determinations about human conduct. While they may interpret the evidence in different ways, they nonetheless insist that there is some relevance in these kinds of studies. There is, however, a third view, which rejects this assumption and instead examines the notion of "naturalness" itself.

If the term "natural" means "whatever appears in nature," then, this third view maintains, we are left with a circular argument. It is obvious that same-sex behavior occurs in nature (at the very least among humans), so this would legitimize homosexuality. But this is clearly not what is intended in these views.

Suppose the word "natural" means "whatever non-human animals do." If one accepts this analysis, some rather odd consequences follow. Must we commit ourselves to whatever patterns of behavior we observe in other species? Should we, then, be polygamous, eat our young, go without clothing, defecate in public, give up medical technology? Don't we often value what is human precisely because it is unique to our species?

In addition, we must wonder which species are relevant in our investigation of non-human behavior. Since there is no one form of behavior universal to all species, we are forced to select some for comparison. Which do we choose? Wouldn't any choice have to be somewhat arbitrary and imply some prejudgment of the issue? And even other primates, though closest to us in terms of biological development, are still different in significant ways. In terms of sexual behavior in particular, the human ability to separate sex and procreation appears to be a significant difference from other species.

Finally, this critical position argues that, even if the word "natural" has some coherent meaning (which it doubts), the label is still merely *descriptive*. That is, to call something "natural" is merely to assert that some behavior occurs somewhere else in nature. Why, then, do the other two views assume that a value judgment follows from this description?

Defenders of homosexuality want to find similar behaviors in non-human animals, critics seek to dismiss such connections; each view, though, sees this task as an important one because each view implies that rightness or wrongness follows from "naturalness" or "unnaturalness." It is this point that the third position challenges.

What if we could determine that aggression is "natural"? Would it follow that we should encourage humans to be as aggressive as they can be? What happens to the uniquely human abilities to reason, to act without compulsion from "instinct"? In fact, we usually refer to the activities of non-human species as "behavior," to distinguish it from human "conduct"; the latter implies an element of volition which we tend to assume is absent in non-human animal behavior. We are the only species, for example, which reads and writes; why is it that no one suggests that these activities are "unnatural"? Perhaps, as the third view suggests, the term "natural" is a loaded one, what logicians call a "persuasive definition"; that is, might it be that we call "natural" that which we commend and "unnatural" that which we condemn? If this argument is correct, then it would follow that human *ethics* (including sexual ethics) would have to depend on considerations other than the purely empirical—or even than what behaviors are most common, either in our own species or others.

Cross-Cultural Analysis

If you were to pick up a telephone and randomly dial a number to any part of the world, to be able to communicate successfully with the person on the other end of the line, you would have to know approximately 10,000 different languages and dialects. Most of us, though, hardly feel competent with our own language, and we generally consider it a phenomenal accomplishment when someone knows more than two or three different languages fluently.

This example suggests that most of us know very little about the languages, customs, and values of other peoples. We tend to assume, in fact, that our own values are objectively correct and universally accepted. We often describe those who differ from us as "backward," "primitive," "pagan," or even "barbaric." This attitude is sometimes called *ethnocentrism*: the belief that one's own cultural values are the right ones, and are superior to all others.

Though this attitude may serve the purpose of unifying a group, thereby aiding in its ultimate survival, it also has the effect of creating divisions and suspicions between groups and their members.

Much of the research of recent anthropologists indicates the tremendous diversity among different societies. Researchers like Margaret Mead and Ruth Benedict developed a new breed of anthropology which was considered radical for its time in its attempt to understand different cultural norms and values without judging them from a Western perspective. Rejecting ethnocentrism, they urged anthropologists to cultivate a respect for other cultures by learning the languages and values of the society and by describing rather than evaluating the phenomena which occurred within them.

Mead and Benedict emphasized that if anthropological data are to be evaluated accurately, one must not look simply at the overt behaviors in question, but also at the social institutions which influence them; further, they maintained that anthropologists and historians should avoid projecting their own values onto other cultures, as this hinders serious understanding.

Ideas about sex and sexuality play a major role in every culture. From marriage customs to attitudes about early childhood sexuality to beliefs about the roles of males and females—all of these ideas shape people's behavior in a given social setting. But many cross-cultural studies conclude that the criteria for socially sanctioned sexual behavior within various cultures are extremely arbitrary. "There is little agreement among diverse cultures as to what is acceptable and what is unacceptable sexual behavior." (Churchill.)

Additionally, many of the assumptions about sex can be traced back to the beginnings of written language, when people in developing cultures lacked knowledge of anatomy and physiology and even the most basic information about the reproductive process. And each generation passes these ideas on to the next, often with little questioning of the assumptions implied. Finally, much of the research which has dealt with these issues has occurred within a context which is already loaded with its own assumptions about sex.

Every society prescribes a set of rules which shape and structure the expression of sexuality; sexual behavior is never totally free from social constraints. People everywhere are trained from infancy throughout life to adhere to the rules of their culture by a system of rewards and punishments.

The poet Goethe once wrote that homosexuality is as old as humanity itself and can therefore be considered natural. Though this behavior is prevalent everywhere and at all times, homosexuality is disapproved of for females and males in some societies, including our own, and its expression is suppressed. In these societies, homosexual behavior is unacceptable for all members of the community under any circumstance. Anthropologists sometimes use the terms *homoerotophobic* or *sex negative* to describe such societies. (Churchill.) These groups often view sex as threatening to the social structure and place many restrictions on its expression.

On the other hand, a larger number of societies condone or even encourage homosexual behavior for at least some of their members under certain circumstances. These societies are *homoerotophilic* or *sex positive*. (Churchill.) Such cultures tend to appreciate the complexities of human sexuality, and remove sexual practices from the sphere of valuing. Simply stated, a behavior that is considered aberrant or deviant in one place may be the norm in another.

There seems to be no one inherent reason why a society approves or disapproves of homosexuality. Some have suggested declining population as reason for disapproval, so sex for procreation is given a higher value. Others emphasize the value placed on the male role and condemnation of anything which does not adhere to it. Others have cited social factors such as the low status and lack of power of women (male homosexuality may be extolled or in many cases lesbian behavior severely restricted), or economic factors (men who are too poor to acquire a wife substitute male lovers until they can marry). But no one explanation seems to work in all cases.

Anthropologists and social historians have long looked at a variety of world cultures as the basis for comparative studies. Until recently, however, little unbiased information had been collected on the topic of homosexual behavior. Margaret Mead has discussed some of the reasons why the absence of data on homosexuality in other cultures may not be reliable. She points out that language barriers, unbreakable cultural taboos, needs for personal privacy, and distrust of Caucasian investigators may hinder the gathering of data. In addition, the biases of the researchers may affect the results. Some investigators, she notes, fail to report what they do see, some are concerned only with acknowledged homosexual behavior (not what occurs secretly), and some don't identify behaviors different from those more commonly observed in our own society. What some investigators identify as condemnations or attempts to suppress homosexuality are really simply forms of regulation. Finally, in some pre-industrial societies, "conventions of courtesy demand telling a questioner what he presumably wants." (Churchill, p. 71.)

In an attempt to remedy these problems, the American Anthropological Association passed a resolution at its 1970 annual national convention:

Be it resolved that the American Anthropological Association recognizes the legitimacy and immediate importance of such research and training and urges the active development of both.

Pre-Industrial Societies That Disapprove

There are societies other than Western that attempt to suppress homosexual behavior. There are probably two reasons for this. First, virtually every one of these societies is sparsely populated and homosexuality is discouraged as one means of stabilizing or increasing the size of the group. Second, though at an earlier period in history some of these cultures accepted same-sex relations, the influence of Judaeo-Christian teachings through colonial domination changed this more tolerant view.

The classic study by researchers C.S. Ford and F.A. Beach lists twenty-eight world cultures of the seventy-six for which information was available in which homosexual activities are condemned: Alorese, Balinese, Chiricahua, Cuna, Goajiro, Haitians, Ifugao, Klamath, Kurtatchi, Kwaki-utl, Kwoma, Lakher, Lepcha, Manus, Marshallese, Mbundu, Ojibwa, Pima, Ramkokamekra, Rwala, Sanpoil, Sinkaietk, Siriono, Tikopia, Tongans, Trobrianders, Trukese, Tswana [males only], Yaruro. Penalties for violating anti-homosexual rules range from mild sanctions, such as ridicule, to the threat of death. However, even within many of these cultures, same-sex behaviors are quite prevalent and conducted in secret.

Societies That Approve

History records a number of ancient cultures that were homoerotophilic. Some of these include the Celts, Scandinavians, Egyptians, Etruscans, Cretans, Carthaginians, and Sumerians. Ancient Greek society is well-known for its acceptance of male homosexuality, particularly those same-sex relationships that developed between older teachers and their younger students. (See Chapter 4.) The Old Testament adds the Canaanites and Chaldeans to the list of cultures which sanctioned forms of homosexuality. In addition, homosexuality enjoyed approval in Roman culture until the third century C.E. (Churchill.)

The Greek historian Timaeus described the erotic life among an elite class of male Etruscans of ancient Italy:

When they are with friends or relatives their custom is the following. When they have stopped drinking and are going to bed, servants bring them courtesans, beautiful boys, or women, while the lamps are still burning. When they have enjoyed themselves sufficiently with these, they fetch young men in their prime, and let them enjoy themselves with these courtesans, boys or women. They pay homage to love.... They are very fond of women, but find more pleasure with boys and young men. (Licht.)

Homosexuality has also enjoyed acceptance among the peoples of the Mediterranean area, North Africa, China, and Japan from ancient times to the present, especially for males.

In ancient China, it appears that bisexuality was the norm for men within marriage, with the man having extramarital affairs with younger men or men of lower social rank, as in Greece at around the same time. (Hinsch.) A case can also be made for the existence of a homosexual identity appearing in ancient China. There are writings in which men viewed themselves as primarily homosexual in orientation and gained a degree of social approval.

When Pan Zhang was young he had a handsome bearing. At that time people desired him. King Zhong Xian of the state of Chu heard of his fame and came to request his writings. Thereafter he wanted to study together with him. They fell in love with one another at first sight. Their feelings were like those of man and wife. They shared the same coverlet and pillow. They were intimate without limits. Afterwards they died together and everyone mourned them. They were buried together at Lofus Mountain. Suddenly a tree grew on the peak. The branches were long and the twigs had leaves. All embraced one another.... Its name was the "Shared Pillow Tree." (*Duanxiu pian*, pp. 38-39.)

And there is the story of Chinese Emperor Ai (reigned 6 B.C.E.-1 C.E.) who "in his nature did not care for women." (Ban Gu Pan Ku.)

Emperor Ai was sleeping in the daytime, and Dong Xian [his male lover] was laying on his sleeve. The emperor wanted to get up but Dong Xian was asleep. The emperor did not want to disturb him so he cut off his own sleeve and got up. His love and thoughtfulness went this far. (Wang Shunu.)

Men having similar "natures" as the Emperor were afterwards referred to as "the men of the cut sleeves."

In the case of 17th-century Japan, an argument can also be made for the existence of a homosexual identity among men. The book *Nanshoku Okagami (The Great Mirror of Manly Love)* by Ihara Saikaku was published in Kyoto and Osaka in 1687 (subtitled *Honcho Waka Fuzoku, The Ways of Young Men in Our Land*). In the book, the author gives definitions to male sexuality as *joshoku* (the love of women) and *nanshoku* (the love of men). Both were considered normal categories and were not mutually exclusive. A third category of men, however, also existed. The *onna girai* (so-called "women-haters") preferred male love exclusively.

> In the case of Japan, the acceptance—indeed, the celebration—of homosexual love seems to have reached a pinnacle during the feudal period of that country. At that time homosexual love was considered more manly for the knight than heterosexual love.... Since the Americanization of Japan, homosexuality is less flagrant there, although the [Asian] attitude toward this subject remains permissive in spite of Western pressure. (Churchill, p. 78.)

It is extremely likely that lesbianism also existed in many of these cultures. However, little source material exists on this topic. Besides, most material that does remain gives a picture of sexuality from only a male perspective.

When we review cross-cultural histories of same-sex relations, it is apparent that its acceptance or rejection is not related to the evolutionary level of any given culture. Some people contend that homosexuality is more in evidence as cultures are in decline, inferring that the behavior is itself a sign of, or cause of, moral and social decadence. In truth, however, same-sex relations have been approved or even encouraged when cultures are heading toward their zenith as well as in times of deterioration and decay. The same holds true for societies that condemn such behaviors. For example, the Persian empire had strong anti-homosexual taboos while it was in decline. In ancient Greek and Roman society, homosexuality flourished while the cultures were moving forward, but restrictions appeared during their ebb. Homosexuality thrived during the height of Renaissance Italy and Medieval Japan. And in certain African and native American Indian tribes, the acceptance or non-acceptance of same-sex behaviors has nothing whatever to do with cultural rise or decline.

Ford and Beach found that, in forty-nine (64 percent) of the seventy-six societies other than our own, "homosexual activities of one sort or another are considered normal and socially acceptable for certain members of the community": Aranda, Aymara, Azande, Chamorro, Chukchee, Creek, Crow, Dahomeans, Easter Islanders, Hidatsa, Hopi, Ila, Karaki, Kwai, Koniag, Koryak, Lango, Mandan, Maricopa, Menomini, Nama, Naskapi, Natchez, Navajo, Omaha, Oto, Palauans, Papago, Ponca, Pukapukans, Quinault, Reddi, Samoans, Seminole, Siwans, Tanala, Thonga, Tinguians, Tswana [females only], Tubatulabal, Tupinamba, Witoto, Wogeo, Wolof, Yakut, Yuma, Yungar, Yurok, Zuni.

Within virtually every known world culture, procreation and marriage in one form or another are prescribed for most men and women. So, in these cultures where homosexual behavior is accepted, it is not intended as a replacement for heterosexual relationships for the majority of people. However, for some, it may turn out to be an acceptable alternative.

Very often male and female same-sex behaviors are culturally defined in different ways. Most societies accord males higher status than females and social roles are constructed differently. In addition, a dissimilar set of regulations are imposed on males and females in the expression of homosexuality. Therefore, when examining same-sex relations cross-culturally, it is clear that these behaviors are different for each sex and have different social meanings as well.

Males.   The expression of homosexual behavior varies for males in many pre-industrial societies. It can be viewed as taking three essential forms: the trans-gender model, the ancient model, and the Melanesian model. (Adam.)

Some societies have created a third gender role for males and females who do not or cannot fit their prescribed gender-roles. This third, or trans-gender, role combines behaviors which are thought to constitute both the masculine and feminine roles. Often the primary sexual activity for men who occupy this role is homosexual. For example, the male Native American *berdache* (see Chapter 1) usually had sex with other males of the tribe, though not with other male *berdache*. Often they married male braves, forming stable and long-term unions which frequently lasted until the death of a partner.

In contemporary Tahiti, males who adopt this trans-gender role are accepted in their same-sex orientation and are even granted a semi-institutionalized position of esteem. (Davenport.)

The ancient model refers to the patterns and forms of sexual expression usually associated with the Greeks at the time of Socrates and Plato. Sex transcended generational lines where an older and usually married man took a young male lover. This was an accepted second stage of parenting, with the older man transmitting knowledge to the youth. As the young man matured, he most likely married a woman and fostered his own young male lover. In addition, sex was very common between Greek men of different generations and also of the same generation in the military. Often on the evening before engaging the enemy, soldiers made love on the field. The Greeks believed that a soldier would fight all the more fiercely on the battlefield so as not to embarrass himself before his beloved. Hence, today we have the saying that "an army of lovers cannot lose."

Major aspects of this model of inter-generational male sexuality are evident among the Samurai of Feudal Japan and the Mossi and Azande civilizations of the African Sudan. (Adam.) In addition, up to approximately 1950, the Siwans of the Libyan desert followed this model. Though they adhered to the doctrine of Islam, which condemns some forms of homosexuality, their cultural and linguistic roots stem from the ancient Berber culture, which was homoerotophilic. Young Siwan males engage in sexual relations with older men:

> All men and boys engage in anal intercourse...and males are singled out as peculiar if they do not indulge in homosexual activities. Prominent Siwan men lend their sons to each other, and they talk about their masculine love affairs as openly as they discuss their love of women. Both married and unmarried males are expected to have both homosexual and heterosexual affairs. (Ford and Beach, pp. 131-2.)

When the youth reaches marrying age, he takes a wife and acquires a young male lover of his own.

The society of Melanesia, a group of Pacific islands north and east of Australia, maintains strict rules dictating avoidance between males and females. At early puberty, young males go through secret initiation rites where they are separated from all females for an extended period of time, sometimes for a number of years. Older bachelors train young novices to the ways of the male group, and homosexual relations are essential to this process. The Western belief that homosexual behavior results in the feminization of males is directly contradicted by the Melanesian (and ancient) models, in which such behavior is not only condoned, but is thought to be essential for a boy's entry into manhood. In Melanesia, semen is considered an important and necessary component of growth and strength for males and insemination of young boys is obligatory for the male line to survive. Following the puberty ceremonies, males are expected to marry women and are encouraged to end homosexual activity.

For the Karaki of New Guinea:

> Bachelors...universally practice sodomy and in the course of his puberty rites each boy is initiated into anal intercourse by the older males. After his first year of playing the passive role he spends the rest of his bachelorhood sodomizing the newly initiated. This practice is believed by the natives to be necessary for the growing boy. (Ford and Beach, p. 132.)

Some societies place less emphasis on anal intercourse and instead focus on oral-genital contact.

Many pre-industrial societies do not adhere strictly to either the ancient or the Melanesian models of homosexual behavior. Rather, they may adopt a mixture of elements from both of these models. For example, among the Marind of Irian Jaya, youths live in forest lodges during the day with other bachelors. At night the young men sleep with older married men and are taught the ways of hunting and gardening by the man and his wife.

Females. Because most societies structure the roles of females differently from those of males, the expression and meaning of homosexuality for women often differs. By and large, there has been a greater accumulation of knowledge of male homosexuality because it is usually more visible and because most cultures place more emphasis and value on male sexuality in general. In addition, most anthropologists have traditionally been men.

Ford and Beach reported lesbian activity in only seventeen out of the seventy-six cultures they surveyed. A more recent study, however, found ninety-five cultures where lesbian and female cross-gender behavior existed. (Blackwood, 1984.)

Though female homosexuality is understood to exist in virtually every society, it seems to be less formalized and less visible than its male counterpart. For example, ritual male insemination as observed in the Melanesian model appears to have no analogy in female homosexuality, since females were thought to contain inherent femininity and reproductive capacities precluding sexual contact with other females.

Despite powerful constraints on female activities, the expression of lesbian behavior has been documented cross-culturally. The anthropologist Evelyn Blackwood groups this behavior into two categories: informal relations and formal relations. The form this behavior takes is contingent on the degree of independence—economic and social—that females have over their lives. Blackwood summarizes:

> ...where women have more control over their productive activities and status, both formal and informal relations may occur. Where women lack power, particularly in class societies, they maintain only informal lesbian ties or build institutions outside the dominant culture. (Blackwood, 1986, p. 10.)

According to Blackwood, formal lesbian relations are "part of a network or social structure extending beyond a pair or immediate love relationship, and occur within such social relationships as bond friendships, sisterhoods, initiation schools, the cross-gender role, or woman marriage." (Ibid.)

The female cross- or trans-gender role parallels that of males in the case of the North American *berdache*. Within these essentially egalitarian cultures in which gender-roles are complementary, female *berdache* often performed hunting duties, fought in battles, and wore traditional male clothing. Many of them married other women and set up households in which they often raised children.

Within the Azande society of Africa, after a woman fulfilled her duties as a wife, some established formal lesbian relationships. These relationships were often with another of her husband's wives, and sometimes even included maintaining their own residence.

An example of a sisterhood arrangement was evident in Hong Kong from approximately 1865 to 1935 in three districts of the Pearl River Delta. (Sankar.) At its height, an estimated 100,000 women, having no interest in marrying men, formed a marriage-resistance movement. Members were called "*sou hei*" ("self-combers"), owing to the fact that they combed their own hair in the style of married women rather than having it combed for them in the marriage ceremony.

The *sou heis* moved away from their parents and formed sisterhood bonds in a series of houses. Each residence contained five to six women and at times sexual relations formed between two or three of the "sisters."

Informal relations among women are non-institutionalized and do not extend outside the immediate social setting. (Blackwood, 1986.) These include adolescent sex play and experimentation, plus affairs and relationships of women in harems or other polygynous household arrangements. They are usually secretive and private in nature and constitute the most common lesbian relationships in societies in which female sexuality is rigidly repressed, as in the case of Near Eastern women. However, informal relations also exist in societies which are more egalitarian. Among the !Kung of Southern Africa, adolescent females often engage in sexual play with other girls (Shostak), and the same is true in Australian aboriginal cultures among female cross-cousins. (Roheim.)

Conclusion

When it is realized that 100 percent of the males in certain societies engage in homosexual as well as heterosexual alliances, and when it is understood that many men and women in our society are equally capable of relations with partners of the same or opposite sex, and finally, when it is recognized that this same situation obtains in many species of subhuman primates, then it should be clear that one cannot classify homosexual and heterosexual tendencies as being mutually exclusive or even opposed to each other. (Ford and Beach, p. 236.)

This chapter opened with what happened to be a simple description of two people involved in a sexual relationship. What has emerged, however, is an awareness that human sexuality is far more complicated than one might at first suspect. Though it is obvious that there are certain technical—that is, biological—aspects to sexual practices, what is also true is that what the human species does sexually depends far more on one's social context than on one's biology.

The two people in our description, for example, could be in any one of a variety of relationships. They could be legally married, or not. They might be monogamous or polygamous. They might be homosexual, heterosexual, or bisexual.

Further, these characters could have a number of differing relationships to the society of which they are a part. Their behavior might or might not be consistent with social norms. And, if what they are doing is not what the majority of society is doing, they might have to keep their involvement secret or face social disapproval.

In addition, we have seen that the issue of sexual identity is a complicated one, that sexual practices are not necessarily synonymous with sexual identity. Further, this chapter makes clear that there are ethical views which judge sexual practices as moral or immoral, depending on certain philosophical assumptions. Depending on these views, the actions of our couple may be seen as justifiable or unjustifiable, regardless of the social norms that exist at the time.

Human beings, as Chapter 1 has shown, are almost infinitely flexible. Our species is not compelled by instincts, programmed toward inevitable patterns of behavior. Though we have obvious physical and psychological limitations, humans are also able to make choices, to defer satisfaction, to take responsibility for behavior. This is true in sexual practices as much as other aspects of human experience.

Our ability to separate sex and procreation has been condemned by some and celebrated by others. These beliefs shape our sexual practices as well as our attitudes. Successive chapters in this text examine the more specific impact of these views on homosexuality.

REFERENCES

Adam, Barry D. "Age, Structure, and Sexuality: Reflections on the Anthropological Evidence on Homosexual Relations." In *The Many Faces of Homosexuality: Anthropological Approaches to Homosexual Behavior*. Edited by Evelyn Blackwood. New York: Harrington Park Press, Inc., 1986.

Aquinas, Thomas. *On the Truth of the Catholic Faith, Summa Contra Gentiles*. Book III: Providence, Part II. Translated by Vernon J. Bourke. New York: Doubleday & Co., 1956.

Ban Gu Pan Ku. *The History of the Former Han Dynasty*. Vol. 3. Translated by Homer H. Dubs and P'an Lo-chi. Baltimore: 1955.

Bell, A.P., Weinberg, M.S., and Hammersmith, S.K. *Sexual Preference*. Bloomington, Indiana: Indiana University Press, 1981.

Benedict, R. *Patterns of Culture*. Boston: Houghton-Mifflin, 1959.

Bertocci, Peter A. "The Human Venture in Sex, Love, and Marriage." In *Social Ethics*. Edited by Thomas Mappes and Jane Zembaty. New York: McGraw-Hill, 1977.

Bingham, H.C. "Sex Development in Apes." *Comparative Psychology Monograph*. Vol. V. 1928.

Blackwood, Evelyn. "Breaking the Mirror: The Construction of Lesbianism and the Anthropological Discourse on Homosexuality." In *The Many Faces of Homosexuality: Anthropological Approaches to Homosexual Behavior*, edited by Evelyn Blackwood. New York: Harrington Park Press, Inc., 1986.

Boswell, John. *Christianity, Social Tolerance, and Homosexuality: Gay People in Western Europe from the Beginning of the Christian Era to the Fourteenth Century*. Chicago: University of Chicago Press, 1980.

Bullough, Vern L. *Homosexuality: A History*. New York: New American Library, 1979.

Cameron, P.A. "Case Against Homosexuality." *Human Life Review* (1978) 4 (3), 17-49.

Cass, Vivienne. "Homosexual Identity Formation: A Theoretical Model." *Journal of Homosexuality* (1979) 4. New York: Hawthorn Press.

Churchill, Wainright. *Homosexual Behavior in Males: A Cross-Cultural and Cross-Species Investigation*. Englewood Cliffs, N.J.: Prentice-Hall, Inc., 1967.

Coleman, Eli. "Developmental Stages of the Coming Out Process." *Journal of Homosexuality* (1981-2) 7(2/3). New York: Hawthorn Press.

Comfort, Alex. "On Advanced Lovemaking." In *Feminist Frameworks*, edited by Alison M. Jaggar and Paula Rothenberg Struhl. New York: McGraw-Hill, 1978.

Curb, Rosemary and Manahan, Mary, eds. *Lesbian Nuns: Breaking Silence*. New York: Warner Books, 1985.

Davenport, W. "Sexual Patterns and Their Regulation in a Society of the Southwest Pacific." In *Sex and Behavior*. New York: John Wiley, 1965.

Deihl, Marcia. Original statement solicited for this text.

DeStefano, George. "The Hypocrisy of the Catholic Church." In *The Advocate*, Feb. 4, 1986. Los Angeles: Liberation Publications, Inc.

Duanxiu pian (Records of the Cut Sleeves) in *Xiangyan congshu (Collected writings on Fragrant Elegance)*. Vol. 9, p. 2A. Shanghai: 1909-1911. Taken from *Chengzhai zaji (Miscellany of the Sincerity Studio)* by Lin Zaiquing.

Fisher, Peter. *The Gay Mystique: The Myth and Reality of Male Homosexuality*. New York: Stein and Day, 1972.

Ford, C.S., and Beach, F.A. *Patterns of Sexual Behavior*. New York: Harper and Brothers, 1951.

Gagnon, John H. *Human Sexualities*. Glenview, Ill.: Scott Foresman, 1977.

Geist, V. *Mountain Sheep: A Study in Behavior and Evolution*. Chicago: University of Chicago Press, 1971.

Goldfoot, D.A., Westerborg-van Loon, H., Groeneveld, W., and Slob, A.D. "Behavioral and Psychological Evidence of Sexual Climax in Female Stump-Tailed Macaque, Macaca arctoides." *Science* (1980) 205; 1477-1479.

Grace, J. "Gay Despair and the Loss of Adolescence: a New Perspective on Same-Sex Preference and Self-Esteem." A paper presented at the Fifth Biennial Professional Symposium of the National Association of Social Workers, San Diego, 1977.

Hinsch, Bret. "Reflections in the Bronze Mirror: Male Homosexual Identity in Ancient China." Harvard University, unpublished manuscript, 1987.

Hite, Shere. *The Hite Report: A Nationwide Study of Female Sexuality.* New York: Dell Books, 1981.

Hrdy, S.B. *Male and Female Strategies of Reproduction Among the Langurs of Abu.* Unpublished Ph.D. Thesis, Harvard University, 1975.

Humphries, Laud. "Exodus and Identity: The Emerging Gay Culture." In *Gay Men: The Sociology of Male Homosexuality,* edited by M.P. Levine. New York: Harper and Row, 1979.

Hunt, G.L., and Hunt, M.W. "Female-Female Pairing in Western Gulls, *Larus occidentalis.*" *Science* (1977) 196; 1466-1467.

Hunt, M. *Sexual Behavior in the 1970s.* Chicago: Playboy Press, 1974.

Jay, Karla, and Young, Allen, eds. *The Gay Report: Lesbians and Gay Men Speak Out about Sexual Experiences and Lifestyles.* New York: Simon and Schuster, 1979.

Kempf, E.J. "The Social and Sexual Behavior of Infrahuman Primates with Some Comparable Facts in Human Behavior," *Psychoanalytical Review* (1917) 4.

Kinsey, A., Pomeroy, W.B., Martin, C.E., and Gebhard, R.H. *Sexual Behavior in the Human Female.* Philadelphia: W.B. Saunders, 1953.

Kinsey, A., Pomeroy, W.B., and Martin, C.E. *Sexual Behavior in the Human Male.* Philadelphia: W.B. Saunders, 1948.

Kirsch, John A.W. "There are Many Natural Forms of Sexual Expression." In *Human Sexuality,* edited by Harold Feldman and Andrea Parrot. Beverly Hills: Sage Publications, 1984.

Kohlberg, Lawrence. *Psychology of Moral Development.* New York: Harper & Row, 1983.

Kooden, J.D., Morin, S.F., Riddle, D.F., Rogers, M., Sang, B.E., and Strassburger, F. *Removing the Stigma: Final Report, Task Force on the Status of Lesbian and Gay Male Psychologists.* The American Psychological Association, 1979.

Kübler-Ross, Elisabeth. *On Death and Dying.* New York: Macmillan, 1970.

Lewis, Lou Ann. "The Coming-Out Process for Lesbians: Integrating a Stable Identity." *Journal of the National Association of Social Workers* (1984) 29:5.

Licht, Hans. *Sexual Life in Ancient Greece.* New York: Barnes and Noble, 1932.

Mahler, Jay, original statement solicited for this text (pseudonym).

Masters, William H., and Johnson, Virginia E. *Human Sexual Response,* Boston: Little, Brown, 1966.

McBride, A.F., and Hebb, D.O. "Behavior of the Captive Bottle-Nose Dolphin, Tursiops truncatus." *Journal of Comp. Physiol. Psychol.* (1948) 41.

McCormick, Janice. Original statement solicited for this text (pseudonym).

Mead, Margaret. *Sex and Temperament in Three Primitive Societies.* New York: Morrow Quill Paperbacks, 1935.

Minton, Henry L. "Homosexual Identity Formation: A Dialectical Perspective." A paper presented at the meeting of the Canadian Psychological Association, Calgary, Canada, 1980.

Minton, Henry L., and McDonald, Gary J. "Homosexual Identity Formation as a Developmental Process." In *Origins of Sexuality and Homosexuality*, edited by John P. DeCecco and Michael G. Shively. New York: Harrington Park Press, 1984.

Money, John, and Ehrhardt, A.A. *Man and Woman, Boy and Girl: Differentiation and Dimorphism of Gender Identity from Conception to Maturity*. Baltimore: Johns Hopkins Press, 1972.

Nuehring, E., Fern, S.G., and Tyler, M. "The Gay College Student: Perspectives for Mental Health Professionals." *The Counselling Psychologist* (1974) 4: 64-72.

Piaget, Jean. *The Essential Piaget*, edited by Howard E. Gruber and J. Jacques Voneche. London: Routledge and K. Paul, 1977.

Richardson, D., and Hart, J. "The Development and Maintenance of a Homosexual Identity." In *The Theory and Practice of Homosexuality*, edited by J. Hart and D. Richardson. London: Routledge and K. Paul, 1981.

Roheim, G. "Women and Their Life in Central Australia." *Journal of the Royal Anthropological Institute of Great Britain and Ireland* (1933) 63: 207-265.

Ruddick, Sara. "Better Sex." In *Philosophy and Women*, edited by Sharon Bishop and Marjorie Weinzweig. Belmont, Calif.: Wadsworth, 1979.

de Sade, Marquis. *The Sadian Woman and the Ideology of Pornography*, edited by Angela Carter. New York: Harper Colophon Books, 1978.

Saghir, M., and Robins, E., "Clinical Aspects of Female Homosexuality." In *Homosexual Behavior*, edited by Judd Marmor. New York: Basic Books, 1980, p. 292.

Sankar, Andrea. "Sisters and Brothers, Lovers and Enemies: Marriage Resistance in Southern Kwangtung." In *The Many Faces of Homosexuality: Anthropological Approaches to Homosexual Behavior*, edited by Evelyn Blackwood. New York: Harrington Park Press, Inc., 1986.

Sappho. *Sappho: A New Translation*, edited by Mary Barnard. Berkeley, Calif.: University of California Press, 1958.

Schaef, Ann Wilson. *Women's Reality*. Minneapolis: Winston Press, 1981.

Shostak, M. *Nisa, the Life and Words of a !Kung Woman*. Cambridge, Mass.: Harvard University Press, 1981.

Thompkins, L., Hall, J.C., and Hall, L.M. "Courtship-Stimulating Volatile Compounds from Normal and Mutant *Drosophila*." *Journal of Insect Physiology* (1980) 26: 689-97.

Trivers, Robert. *Social Evolution*. Menlo Park, Calif.: Benjamin/Cummings Publishing Co., Inc., 1976.

Tucker, Rosie. Original statement solicited for this text (pseudonym).

Wang Shunu. *Zhongguo changji shi (A History of Chinese Prostitution)*. Shanghai, 1936.

Weber, Douglas. Original statement solicited for this text (pseudonym).

Weinrich, James D. "Is Homosexuality Biologically Natural?" In *Homosexuality:*

Social, Psychological, and Biological Issues, edited by W. Paul, J.D. Weinrich, J.C. Gonsiorek, and M.E. Hotvedt. Beverly Hills, Calif.: Sage Publications, 1982.

Werner, Yehudah L. "Apparent Homosexual Behavior in an All-Female Population of Lizards, *Lepidodactylus lugubris*, and its Probable Interpretation." Jerusalem: Hebrew University of Jerusalem, 1980.

Further Readings

Adair, Nancy, and Adair, Casey. *Word Is Out: Stories of Some of Our Lives*, San Francisco: New Glide Publications, 1978.

Aldrich, Ann. *We Too Must Love*. New York: Fossett, 1958.

Alyson, Sasha, ed. *Young, Gay, and Proud*. Boston: Alyson Publications, 1980.

Back, Gloria. *Are You Still My Mother? Are You Still My Family?* New York: Warner Books, 1985.

Baetz, Ruth. *Lesbian Crossroads: Personal Stories of Lesbian Struggles and Triumphs*. New York: William Morrow, 1980.

Barbach, Lonnie Garfield. *For Yourself: The Fulfillment of Female Sexuality*. New York: Doubleday, 1976.

Boston Women's Health Collective. *Our Bodies, Ourselves: A Book by and for Women*. New York: Simon and Schuster, 1971.

Bell, Alan, and Weinberg, Martin. *Homosexualities*. New York: Simon and Schuster, 1978.

Benjamin, Harry. *The Transsexual Phenomenon*. New York: Julian Press, 1966.

Bode, Janet. *View from Another Closet: Exploring Bisexuality in Women*. New York: Hawthorn, 1976.

Burhek, Mary. *My Son Eric*. New York: Pilgrim Press, 1979.

Califia, Pat. *Sapphistry: The Book of Lesbian Sexuality*. Tallahassee, Fla.: Naiad Press, 1980.

Clark, Don. *Loving Someone Gay*. New York: New American Library, 1978.

Clarke, Lige, and Nichols, Jack. *I Have More Fun with You than Anybody*. New York: St. Martin's Press, 1972.

Constantine, Larry, and Martinson, Floyd. *Children and Sex: New Findings, New Perspectives*. Boston: Little, Brown and Co., 1981.

Diamond, Liz. *The Lesbian Primer*. Somerville, Mass.: Women's Educational Media, Inc., 1973.

Fairchild, Betty, and Hayward, Nancy. *Now That You Know: What Every Parent Should Know about Homosexuality*. New York: Harvest/Harcourt Brace Jovanovich, 1979.

Fricke, Aaron. *Reflections of a Rock Lobster: A Story about Growing Up Gay*. Boston: Alyson Publications, 1981.

Hanckel, Frances, and Cunningham, John. *A Way of Love, a Way of Life: A Young Person's Introduction to What It Means to Be Gay*. New York: Lothrop, Lee, and Shepard Book, 1979.

Heron, Ann, ed. *One Teenager in Ten: Writings by Gay and Lesbian Youth*. Boston: Alyson Publications, 1983.

Hocquenghem, Guy. *Homosexual Desire*. London: Allison & Busby, 1978.

Humphreys, Laud. *Tearoom Trade*. Aldine-Atherton, 1975.

Jay, Karla, and Young, Allen, eds. *After You're Out: Personal Experiences of Gay Men and Lesbian Women*. New York: Pyramid Books, Harcourt Brace Jovanovich, 1975.

Jones, Clinton. *Understanding Gay Relatives and Friends*. New York: Seaberry Press, 1978.

Klaich, Dolores. *Women + Women: Attitudes toward Lesbianism*. New York: Simon & Schuster, 1974.

Klein, Fred. *The Bisexual Option: A Concept of One Hundred Percent Intimacy*. New York: Arbor House, 1978.

Kohn, Barry, and Matusow, Alice. *Barry and Alice: Portrait of a Bisexual Marriage*. Englewood Ciffs, N.J.: Prentice-Hall, 1980.

Masters, William, and Johnson, Virginia. *Homosexuality in Perspective*. Boston: Little, Brown, 1979.

Miller, Merle. *On Being Different: What It Means to Be a Homosexual*. New York: Random House, 1971.

Muchmore, Wes, and Hanson, William. *Coming Out Right: A Handbook for the Gay Male*. Boston: Alyson Publications, 1982.

Reid, John. *The Best Little Boy in the World: The True and Moving Story of Coming to Terms with Being Gay*. New York: Ballantine, 1973.

Sergent, Bernard. *Homosexuality in Greek Myth*. Boston: Beacon Press, 1984.

Silverstein, Charles. *A Family Matter: A Parents' Guide to Homosexuality*. New York: McGraw-Hill, 1977.

Spada, James. *The Spada Report: The Newest Survey of Gay Male Sexuality*. New York: Signet, New American Library, 1979.

Switzer, David, and Switzer, Shirley. *Parents of the Homosexual*. Philadelphia: Westminster Press, 1980.

Vida, Ginny, ed. *Our Right to Love*. Englewood Cliffs, N.J.: Prentice-Hall, 1978.

Weinrich, James D. *Sexual Landscapes: Why We Are What We Are, Why We Love Whom We Love*. New York: Charles Scribner's Sons, 1987.

Wolff, Charlotte. *Bisexuality: A Study*. London: Quartet Books, 1979.

Wolff, Charlotte. *Love between Women*. New York: Harper Colophon, 1972.

Wysor, Bettie. *Lesbian Myth*. New York: Random House, 1974.

Chapter 3

What Causes Homosexuality?

"All gay males have a distant father and a domineering mother."
"Lesbians have distant mothers and identify with their fathers."
"Gay males have a surplus of female hormones and lesbians have a surplus
of male hormones."
"Psychotherapy can help to convert a gay person to heterosexuality."

Homosexuality is different from the norm. And what is different in
some way or another from the mainstream is usually puzzling to
observers. Often, our curiosity leads us to want to know *why*, to find the
cause. As homosexuality has been identified as a sexual orientation and
has become an increasingly more visible phenomenon, many experts
from a variety of disciplines have offered a range of theories to account
for its existence. From biological theories about genes and hormones; to
psychological theories about family constellations; to behavioral theories
about reinforcing experiences—these classic views and many others have
been proposed and tested to ascertain whether any provides a reasonable
causal explanation for the phenomenon. Some theories have long since
been discounted; others still continue to have their adherents.

It is not possible to present here even a brief overview of all of the
competing theories; instead, we will offer some representative theories
as a way to provide a conceptual basis for consideration of explanations of
homosexuality. Further, this chapter does not assume that homosexuality
alone requires explanation. Instead, it looks at some of the possible
causes of sexual orientation, whatever form—heterosexuality, homosexuality, or bisexuality—it might take.

Science and Methodology

Science—Then and Now

The word "science" is derived from the Latin word *scire* meaning "to know." And the scientific enterprise seeks to gain knowledge of the workings of the natural order. Science is not simply about observation, but about finding the order and meaning in those observations. Such ordering is often a result of a leap of imagination probably not unlike that which occurs in artistic creation.

The tools of science provide a means by which we organize our world and explain events within it. Yet science itself has undergone many changes through history. Thomas Kuhn in *The Structure of Scientific Revolutions* has written of what he calls *paradigms* or models for science. He argues that scientific inquiry is a product of a given frame of reference that tends to incorporate data into it and subsume it under some general theory. It is only when there is a significant body of contradictory data that a paradigm changes.

Early science was grounded in the paradigm that the world was orderly, divinely inspired, and purposeful. Human beings were seen as God's special creation, and the Earth was viewed to be the center of the universe. Indeed, the earliest scientists were not really scientists by today's standards. We would probably be more likely to describe them as philosophers or metaphysicians, since much of what they did was to speculate about the workings of the universe. Pervasive was a belief that there had to be a *purpose* to whatever occurred, that no event could be random or without meaning. Current religious beliefs influenced much of what science studied. "Do angels know the future?" was considered, for instance, as a legitimate question for scientific inquiry. Appeals to faith or authority were considered sufficient to rebut a scientific challenge. Indeed, so sure were medieval theologians that the earth was the center of the universe that they told Galileo they had no need to look through his telescope.

This kind of theorizing flourished under the ancient Greeks who viewed contemplation as the highest form of human endeavor. Manual labor was held in low regard, so scientific theorizing did not include experimentation. Early scientists such as Aristotle viewed the world as a closed system, in which truth could be derived deductively from basic "self-evident" axioms. There is a story that Aristotle wrote a treatise on the number of teeth in a horse's mouth without even considering the possibility of checking his thesis on an actual horse!

The "scientific revolution" of the 1500s signalled a radical departure from this way of viewing the world. Copernicus's thesis that the earth moves around the sun appeared in print for the first time in 1543. Rather than focusing on purposes, these modern scientists asked about *causes*. Rather than seeing the universe as governed by some divinely inspired plan, they saw it as an enormous machine which could be taken apart and analyzed. In place of appeals to divine authority or scripture, the scientific revolution substituted testing and retesting to verify hypotheses.

The state of science at a given time is influenced by, and influences, the prevailing ideology of a given culture. Views about homosexuality in particular have been affected by ongoing scientific inquiry. In earlier days, when homosexual practices were first being considered scientifically, they were often viewed as evidence of possession by the Devil and were thus severely punished. Later, as scientific investigation began to focus on the idea of causal explanations, there were many theories which attempted to explain the origins of homosexuality. But science is not "value-free," and much of the methodology of those investigations was grounded on the assumption that homosexuality (and not heterosexuality) needed explanation.

Exploring Biases

In the late 1940s social psychologist Stanley Schachter identified a phenomenon concerning the typical reactions of people in a group to nonconformity. These findings have been substantiated over and over again by other psychologists, anthropologists, and sociologists. His research might be summarized into three basic claims:

Firstly, in any human grouping, the majority tends to conform to a set of accepted beliefs and tends to notice more any *deviance* from those social standards. For example, in societies where eating certain foods is strictly forbidden, those who deviate from the norm receive more attention than those who do not. Similarly, if you were to walk down a busy city sidewalk wearing only your underwear, you would undoubtedly receive more than your share of notice! And, if the standard involves deep-seated emotions, this attention will be even more pronounced. For instance, we seldom notice left-handedness, though people in other societies (where, say, left-handedness is considered to be a sign of the Devil) might have intense reactions to the phenomenon. In our society, homosexual behavior, as it is less common, is attended to more than the same behavior occurring between heterosexuals. Indeed, homosexuals are frequently accused of "flaunting" their sexual preference when what is probably the case is that we just notice the behavior more because it doesn't fit the norm.

Secondly, often, the group perceives those who fail to conform not only as different (a description, but not a value judgment), but also in more negative ways—as sick, unhappy, misinformed, dangerous, rebellious, infantile, mentally disturbed, etc. Indeed, as we saw in Chapter 1, people often confuse the term "deviance" with a negative moral judgment such as "immoral." Judgments about homosexuality clearly fit this description.

Thirdly, it is frequently the case that the conformers will try to "convert" the deviants to the accepted social behavior. They may do so in any of a number of ways, ranging from incentives to conform (indeed, acceptance itself is often the reward) to stricter punishments or social disapproval. For example, those who dress differently may not get desirable jobs; Mormons were ejected from many communities because of their belief in polygamy; interracial couples in this country were frequently harassed or even jailed.

These points begin to provide a basis for understanding the dynamic involved in prejudice. (See Chapter 5.) But here this framework makes a different point. Though we may have no trouble accepting that prejudice exists among "ordinary" people in social settings, we tend to assume that scientists—psychologists, researchers, psychotherapists, etc.—have found ways to transcend their emotions, to make science "neutral." But it is important to keep in mind that Schachter's framework applies all too well to scientific research in general, and to research on homosexuality in particular. With few exceptions, most scientists studying homosexuality behave exactly as Schachter's analysis would predict. First, there is a significant body of research on the origins of homosexuality, especially on how to discover "homosexual tendencies" in people. Yet scientists have not done a correspondingly large amount of research on heterosexuality and its possible causes. To fail to do so is to assume that there is a clear-cut and unambiguous distinction between homosexuality and heterosexuality (see Chapter 2 for further discussion of this claim); and that heterosexuality occurs "naturally" and so needs no explanation.

Second, much of the research done in this area is filled with value judgments in the guise of "neutral" scientific inquiry. Even after the American Psychological Association's change in nomenclature (as discussed later in this chapter) researchers continued to use terms like "distorted," "psychopathology," "disturbed," "sodomite," "invert," "perversion," "abnormal," and "degenerate" to describe homosexuality. These terms might sound fancier than labels like "fag," "faggot," "fairy," "lezzie," and "dyke," but their effect is the same. And scientific terminology may be even more harmful, as it is allegedly unbiased and hence has claim to greater legitimacy.

Finally, the purpose of such research has often been to change homosexual behavior and/or to enable parents, teachers, and other figures of authority to detect such "tendencies" early in young children. Techniques like castration, lobotomy, electroshock, psychotherapy, behavioral modification, and drug therapies have been recommended and adopted to try to change sexual orientation. Clearly, this behavior is grounded in the assumption that homosexual behavior is problematic and therefore has to be changed.

What Is Scientific Research?

Because this chapter will be examining a good deal of the scientific research on the issue of homosexuality, it is important at the outset to clarify what science is, as distinct from other disciplines and other ways of thinking about the world.

Scientific research must meet specific criteria in order for it to have legitimacy. John Dewey identified five factors in problem-solving or the scientific method:

- There must be a "felt difficulty" or problem to be addressed.
- There must be a location and definition of the felt difficulty.
- One must suggest solutions (hypotheses) to the problem.
- Using deductive reasoning, one must predict the consequences of the various suggested solutions.
- One must test the hypothesis in action.

Scientific research, once it has gone through this process, must also be *reproducible*, meaning that the results of an experiment cannot be unique but rather must be able to be shown a number of times; and confirmable, meaning other scientists from other laboratories—no matter what their political, religious, or emotional predispositions—should be able to derive the same results from the same experimental situation. Stage 4 of Dewey's analysis involves assuming the truth of the hypothesis in question, and making predictions based on its assumed truth. If these predictions are realized, we can take this "success" to confirm to some extent the reliability of the original claim. For example, if I hypothesize that people become gay because of some early childhood exposure to gay people, then I must deduce that a significant number of children who have had contact with a gay person will become gay. Though the success of the predictions does not guarantee the truth of the belief (that is, there may be other hypotheses which would yield the same results), it does give some assurance that I can be reasonably safe if I begin to act on it.

Further, a scientific hypothesis must be, at least in theory, *testable*. That is, even if I now lack the technology to determine whether there is life in another galaxy, I can certainly imagine without difficulty an experiment that would do this. But if an hypothesis is untestable *in principle*, then it is unscientific. For example, the claim "When it thunders, God is angry" is untestable. Ironically, this means that if nothing counts as a falsification of a theory, then the theory is unscientific. For example, "Cars with dead batteries can't start" is testable and falsifiable if I can find one car with a dead battery that starts. But "Cars won't start if a demon has hexed them" provides no possible way to test or to falsify. And, in testing an hypothesis, a researcher must make certain that the evidence warrants the conclusion. The stronger or more general a conclusion is, the stronger the evidence must be. If all I want to prove, for example, is that there is at least one white swan in the world, then I need only a sample of one for the truth of my claim. If, however, I want to maintain that most swans are white, I need a bigger sample to warrant my conclusion. There are times when evidence is significant, but may be used to generalize far beyond what is warranted. For example, there is a significant body of evidence to suggest that children who are abused may as adults abuse *their* children; but it would be a mistake to generalize from this evidence that this is true of *all* abused children. And if a theory leads to conclusions which are clearly falsified by the data, then the theory must be discarded.

These points become especially important in considering homosexuality scientifically, since the existence of homophobia (see Chapter 5) makes it difficult to be sure that one has a random sampling of gay people. Since it is probably true that most gay and lesbian people are not open about their sexual orientation, it is possible that scientists are not studying the "average" gay person. For instance, often the subjects who were used to test hypotheses of earlier researchers were patients who were either unhappy with their sexual orientation and wanted to change, were emotionally disturbed, or were in institutions. Thus, any results from these experiments must be suspect. Indeed, one factor which may bias a theory of homosexuality is the sexual orientation of the observer. Finally, it is important to make sure that the evidence really does support the conclusion in question and not some entirely different conclusion. For instance, the fact that some women feel guilty after having an abortion may not prove the wrongness of abortion, but perhaps only the need for better counselling beforehand. And if we are out to prove a causal connection, then we must show more than just the conjunction of two events; rather, we must prove that one event *necessarily* leads to the other, that is, that the later event *would not have occurred* without the earlier.

The criteria for scientific research ensure that, insofar as it is possible in any human venture, it is not prejudice or faith alone that provides us with our beliefs. These criteria enable us to make well-founded generalizations about uniformities in and characteristics of the world around us. In using the scientific method successfully, one can predict events or behavior patterns without depending helplessly on popular beliefs or "intuition." And, finally, it provides one with a basis for discriminating the strength of one belief from another rather than indiscriminately agreeing with all positions or arbitrarily selecting one.

By way of summary, the following questions may be helpful in considering the research on homosexuality to be discussed in this chapter:

- Is there *real* evidence for the hypothesis in question?
- Is there *sufficient* evidence to warrant the hypothesis?
- Has a random sample been used to collect data?
- Does the evidence justify any other alternative hypotheses?
- Does the hypothesis have real predictive capability?
- Have the experimental results been *confirmed* by other researchers in *repeated* experimental trials?
- What assumptions—proven or unproven—underlie the hypothesis being tested?
- Has the experimenter biased the results? If so, in what ways? Could this bias have been avoided?
- Have all irrelevant variables been controlled? Is it possible?

Theories

The ancient Greek philosopher Plato tells the story of how sexual orientation originated. In his *Symposium,* he recounts a myth of creation which began with three sexes—male (descended from the Sun), female (descended from the Earth), and a third "hermaphrodite," which was half male and half female. These beings had "rounded backs and sides, four arms and four legs, and two faces, both the same, on a cylindrical neck, and one head, with one face on one side and one on the other...." (p. 542.) But all of these beings became overly arrogant and tried to "scale the heights of heaven and set upon the gods." (p. 543.) Zeus, the king of all the gods, wanted to weaken them without actually destroying them (since that would also put an end to the offerings they gave to the gods), so he came up with the idea of splitting all of them in two. But each half-being began to pine for its other half, arousing Zeus's pity for them. So he rearranged their "private parts" so that the males and females could copulate with each other. And those women who are attracted to other women and those men who are attracted to other men are "naturally" seeking their other halves. The latter, he said, possess the "most virile constitution." (p. 544.)

A very different sort of explanation of homosexuality comes from the other side of the world. The Lepchas in the Sikkim Himalayas explained homosexuality as the result of eating the flesh of an uncastrated pig.

Though these myths have few adherents today, many other theories have been proposed to account for homosexuality.

Biological Theories

Biological explanations seek to find some *physical* explanation for the effect in question. Though these theories do not discount the importance of environmental and experiential factors, they all share the view that biology is the *primary* determinant of sexual orientation.

Virtually everyone agrees that environment and genetic makeup interact. We know, for example, that even most "fixed action patterns" (what are sometimes called "instincts") require learning; and we know that the most advanced learned traits require a certain evolutionary process to develop them. Many "environmentalists" are willing to consider the biological constraints that limit human behavior; many "essentialists" emphasize the role of the environment in shaping patterns of conduct. But for the former, the connection between genes and environment is largely arbitrary, not determined by biological factors. The latter, on the other hand, tend to focus on the "nonarbitrary," biologically/genetically determined connections between environment and behavior.

Genetic.   The earliest search of the causes of homosexuality focused on the genes. Genes are the biological building blocks which transmit inheritable characteristics (e.g., height, eye color, etc.) from generation to generation.

If the genetic hypothesis is correct, then it would make sense to study twins who share a genetic makeup. There are two kinds of sets of twins: *monozygotic* (identical twins), who share the same genotype, and *dizygotic* (fraternal twins), who do not and are thus no more closely related than individual siblings. If there is a significant divergence in the differences between identical twins and the differences between fraternal twins, then the truth of the genetic hypothesis would seem likely, since all sets were raised in the same environment.

In one experiment (Kallman), eighty-five pairs of male fraternal and identical twins were followed, where at least one member was known to be homosexual. It turned out that both members of the fraternal twins were homosexual in fewer than fifty percent of the cases; but in the case of the identical twins, both were in all cases.

Though these results appear conclusive, in fact there are many problems in this study which made its results scientifically suspect. First, there is no evidence that the twins were reared apart, thus failing to address the question of the influence of environmental conditions. In addition, there is some question whether the researcher's sample was representative, since the majority were socially and emotionally maladjusted. It is also unclear how Kallman determined which twins were identical and which fraternal, there being as much as a thirty percent margin of error. Finally, how can the genetic thesis be true if there was no evidence of homosexuality in the fathers of these pairs? In fact, one year after the study Kallman himself rejected the genetic hypothesis, since the twins had been reared together; he concluded instead that homosexuality results from an interplay of genetic and environmental factors.

Heston and Shields studied only five identical and seven fraternal pairs. But these pairs were all reared together and constitute far too small a sample size to demonstrate anything at all. In addition, other studies that have tried to replicate Kallman's have failed to yield the same results. One study in particular (Rainer *et al.*) found cases of monozygotic twins with different sexual orientations. There is also some evidence that, within each pair, the twins were treated differently, with the later-to-be-homosexual twins given more mothering.

There continues to be interest in this genetic hypothesis. For example, a recent study at the Boston University School of Medicine found that gay men are more likely than heterosexual men to have a gay brother. Of the fifty gay men studied, twenty percent had a gay brother, compared to only four percent of the fifty-one heterosexual men. They did not find any higher incidence of lesbian sisters among the gay men.

Another study tried to determine "familial aspects" of lesbianism. The principal investigator for the study stated:

> What we have found in this study [of lesbians] is compatible with a genetic component to male homosexuality. A closer look must now be taken to determine the association of sexual orientation with genetics and early social environment. (Pillard, p. 2.)

It is very difficult to prove a genetic cause of sexual orientation. This is not to suggest that heredity has nothing to do with sexual orientation, only that it seems not to be sufficient to account for it. In fact, there may be a basic theoretical difficulty in all genetic research. Since the only acceptable evidence for a genetic basis to homosexuality would have to come from studies of relatives, to argue for transmission within families it makes sense to study the family members (especially twins); but families share not only genes but also a wide range of environmental factors: parental attitudes, religion, friends, school environments, and so forth. To demonstrate the connection one would have to separate the genetic components of behavior from the non-genetic, and this is almost impossible to do.

An experimental situation of growing interest to genetic researchers, especially those concerned with issues such as sexual orientation and IQ, for example, is provided by the phenomenon of adoption. If we could trace the biological parents of adopted children and determine if there is a statistically significant correlation between the sexuality of the child and biological parents, then the genetic hypothesis would appear to have support. This type of experimental research, if demonstrating such a correlation, mitigates the criticism of similar environments, since the children are not reared by their biological parents. And certainly many homosexual men and women have reproduced, and some have probably given up those children for adoption. But such studies are problematic for a number of reasons. For one, it would be difficult to obtain a sizeable enough number of study subjects. Difficulties in tracing parental lineage exist from a practical perspective and ethical issues arise with respect to rights to privacy and confidentiality. Also, would subjects—either children or parents—be honest about their sexual orientation? What about teenage pregnancies, where sexual orientation may not be obvious or may appear to change? Would the biological mother's information about the biological father, if he cannot be found, be reliable? Finally, it is often the case that adoption agencies try to place children in similar households; so perhaps the environmental hypothesis cannot ever be completely nullified.

Although heritability is an easy concept to define, it can be very difficult to handle on a practical level. And because human beings are not experimental organisms, a controlled situation is never possible. When we search for a genetic factor, it is sometimes relatively easy to search back into a family's lineage to determine the inheritability of the trait; because of the complexity of homosexuality and the secrecy surrounding it, this is not really likely.

> In the case of some rare and clear-cut defect, like a missing finger, the mere observation of several instances in the same family affords good evidence of a hereditary factor. But homosexuality is so common that the discovery of a number of cases in the same family would have no significance. Even if investigation revealed some families with an unusually high proportion of homosexuals in several successive generations, this still would not amount to proof of hereditary causation. (West.)

There may be many different ways in which genetics and environment interact to affect eventual sexual orientation. Some forms, for example, may be genetically determined, whereas others might have a genetic basis but require a certain kind of environmental input. There may be other kinds of homosexuality which are less directly controlled by the genes. And to assert that sexual orientation has a genetic component is a fairly modest claim, since all human behavior has a genetic component of some sort.

Sociobiological. The sociobiological theory of human behavior attempts to show the connection between the social behavior of a species and its biological makeup. It begins by attempting to identify those traits that are common to people in all cultures and higher-order species, assuming, of course, that such universal traits exist. The universality of that trait is then deemed to be an argument for its biological basis. Understanding our sociobiological nature will, the biologist E.O. Wilson hopes, "help us learn what we really are and not just what we hope we are." And what we are is controlled by our genes:

> ...(our genes) swarm in huge colonies, safe inside gigantic, lumbering robots, sealed off from the outside world, communicating with it by tortuous indirect routes.... They created us body and mind; and their preservation is the ultimate rationale for our existence. (Dawkins, p. 21.)

Territoriality, xenophobia (fear of strangers or foreigners), and waging war are all cited as universal traits. Thus, sociobiologists make use of Charles Darwin's theory of natural selection ("survival of the fittest") as a guide to human conduct rather than abstract concepts such as "natural law" or religion. Thus, genes are "selfish" in that they seek their own continued biological survival. Even sex-related behavioral traits are given a biological basis. So, any unselfish (altruistic) behavior not clearly self-regarding would require an explanation.

E.O. Wilson, in his classic treatise on sociobiology *On Human Nature*, devotes considerable attention to the phenomenon of homosexuality. Since the sociobiological perspective maintains that all human behavior is rooted in biology and the principle of natural selection, then it is necessary for Wilson to come to terms with the phenomenon of homosexuality. Indeed, homosexuality presents the sociobiologist with an interesting dilemma: if biology "programs" us toward survival and adaptation and if biological "fitness" involves reproduction, how can homosexuality be "natural"? Ironically, Wilson's eventual answer to this question is one that is highly supportive of homosexuality. He maintains, in fact, that homosexuals may serve a twofold natural biological function: 1) as built-in inhibitors of excessive population growth, homosexuals—as non-procreators—provide an important service for human and non-human societies; and 2) as caretakers and nurturers for other members of societies, homosexuals, Wilson argues, hold the key positions in traditional social groupings as well as contemporary technological society. Some sociobiologists go even further to argue that moves to restrict homosexuals from entering "helping professions" such as teaching, day-care, etc., are contrary to nature. Biology, they maintain, need not be approached simplistically, and

> if insemination were the sole biological function of sex, it could be achieved far more economically in a few seconds of mounting and insertion. (Wilson, p. 146.)

Since homosexuality appears in other species, perhaps homosexuals are actually the "genetic carrier of some of mankind's rare altruistic impulses." (Wilson, p. 149.) How do homosexuals keep their genes in the "gene pool" to prevent their gradual extinction? Well, Wilson argues, the genes of homosexuals could proliferate through "collateral lines of descent" (e.g., nieces and nephew). (Wilson, p. 151.) Thus, Wilson and others are not arguing—like, for example, Kallman—that homosexuals and heterosexuals have different genes, but rather that we all have genes which specifically program either homosexuality or heterosexuality, depending on which behavior is more adaptive for the individual. For example, another sociobiologist, James D. Weinrich, suggests that it might be appropriate to become homosexual if one's physical condition precluded the likelihood of one's becoming a successful parent.

Sociobiology has received much criticism from many sources. First, some critics have argued that Wilson's thesis is unscientific since it is untestable. His hypothesis for the existence of an "altruistic gene" tends to be in the form of assertions backed seldom by research and more often than not by analogies to non-human animal behavior. There are many problems in such an approach. In particular, though, Wilson gives no method for proving that genetic makeup programs people toward certain paths of development (rather than, say, simply *permitting* the possibility). Indeed, Wilson's view gives no predictive power whatsoever: if a person turns out to be gay, that person was genetically programmed to do so, but the same is true for a heterosexual, and one has no way at all to tell which is likely. Such a methodology smacks of hindsight or "Monday-morning quarterbacking." Though Wilson insists, "Human nature is stubborn and cannot be forced without a cost" (p. 153), he gives us little in the way of an understanding of the demands of stubborn "human nature."

Second, there is little evidence to support these conclusions about homosexuals in particular. Wilson may be right in arguing that "homosexuality is above all a form of bonding" (p. 150), but isn't heterosexuality as well? And is it true that homosexuals more often than heterosexuals, because of their alleged "caretaking" nature, work in service-oriented professions? There is simply no way of knowing. And, even if it were true, this could be because such professions are safer for gays than others and not because gays are genetically predetermined to pursue them. In addition, what about those gays and lesbians who come out *after* they have had children or the increasing numbers of such people who choose to have children either through adoption or alternative insemination? This goes against the sociobiological notion that homosexuality serves a "population-inhibiting" function. Are those homosexuals who choose to have children unnatural? Or is the "population control" gene at war with the "nurturing, caretaking gene"? What does one do, then, to explain cases which do not fit within the theoretical framework? It would seem that either one must judge them to be unnatural "aberrations" or show what biological purpose they serve; either strategy, though, seems to beg the question.

Finally, even if the sociobiological perspective removes homosexuality from the realm of the "unnatural" (and Wilson certainly maintains that it does), this may be a Trojan horse for homosexuals seeking social acceptance. Such a claim seems in fact to be circular, since all human behavior would end up having a biological explanation. Wilson argues for this greater acceptance of homosexuality:

> All that we can surmise of humankind's genetic history argues for a more liberal sexual morality, in which sexual practices are to be regarded first as bonding devices and only second as means for procreation. (Wilson, p. 14.)

Yet what is "natural" is not necessarily what is right or what we might want to recommend or encourage. For instance, we might argue that aggression is natural to all species; does that justify war or violence directed against another person? How can we even know what is natural for humans when little if any of our behavior is instinctive? Some writers have suggested that there may be no behavior "natural" to humans since much of what we do changes nature.

Wilson also uses this framework to "prove" that women are "naturally" submissive, men are "naturally" aggressive, and racism is a "natural" fear of others different from us. Are we, though, limited to "nature"? Can't one choose to reinforce certain behaviors depending on a value framework that is not simply biological? And, if it were shown that homosexuality was *not* biologically based, Wilson's "gay rights" argument would evaporate.

Hormonal.   Hormones are excretions of the endocrine glands, distributed in the bloodstream or in bodily fluids, which stimulate certain specific functions which occur in another part of the body. Some theorists have hypothesized that homosexuality is caused by hormonal differences between homosexuals and heterosexuals.

The major hormones in question are androgen, testosterone, and estrogen. And though it has been a relatively common practice to label these hormones as male and female hormones, both types occur in each sex and are chemically so similar that they can even transform into each other.

The sex hormones are produced by the gonads (ovaries in women, testes in men) and the adrenal glands, near the kidneys. A woman's adrenals manufacture as much testosterone as a man's, her ovaries produce estrogen and progesterone (required for reproduction), and some testosterone. A man's testes produce ten times more testosterone than his adrenals. Author Barbara Fried explains the similarities between the two hormones in the following way:

> The only wide divergence is the elevated estrogen level in women during ovulation. The average level of androgen is somewhat higher in males than females; the average level of estrogen (excluding the dramatic increase at the time of ovulation) is slightly higher in females than males, until the age of fifty-five. But the average differences are rather small if we consider the ratio of the two numbers, and what effect those relative differences might have on individual behavior is purely speculative. The relationship of hormones to behavior is not well understood; and further, one would expect their impact on an individual to depend not on the absolute amount of hormones present, but on their relationship to the size of the individual and to the internal chemical environment of which they are only a part. Furthermore, within those average differences, there are wide variations that make it *not* uncommon to find women with higher androgen levels than those of the "average" man, and men with higher estrogen levels than the "average" (non-ovulating) woman. (Fried *et al.*)

It would seem that to determine whether there is a hormonal cause to homosexuality, the following questions need responses:

- Do male homosexuals have lower rates of "masculinizing hormones" (such as testosterone and androgen) than male heterosexuals?
- Do lesbians have higher levels of "masculinity hormones" than heterosexual women?
- Do excesses or deficiencies of hormones in the developing fetus (for example, resulting from some stress to the mother during pregnancy) lead to homosexual behavior in adulthood?

The early sexologist Havelock Ellis believed that homosexuality (which he referred to as "inversion") was hormonal in origin, an "anomaly" like color-blindness. He maintained that there were male and female "elements" present in everyone, but that the "male invert is a person with an unusual proportion of female elements (i.e., hormones), the female invert a person with an unusual proportion of male elements." (Ellis, p. 228.)

He meant to suggest through this hypothesis that the condition was not a result of choice; in one case study of a male homosexual, for example, he noted that it "clearly showed that the case was congenital and not acquired, so that it could not be termed a vice." (Ellis, p. 222.) Elsewhere he pleaded for a more sympathetic scientific treatment of homosexuality; yet he nonetheless asserted the inferiority of homosexuality:

> The inverted person may be as healthy as a color-blind person. Congenital sexual inversion is thus akin to a biological variation. It is a variation doubtless due to *imperfect sexual differentiation*, but often having no traceable connection with any morbid condition in the individual himself. (Ellis, pp. 228-29, emphasis added.)

More sophisticated research on hormones has been going on since the 1930s when it became possible to measure hormonal levels. But, until recently, measurement techniques were crude, and they used hormonal levels in urine to estimate levels in the blood. (Different hormones have the same metabolites as testosterone when tested in urine.) Today, new methods to test directly from the blood have increased the accuracy of the measurement, though plasma and urinary testosterone levels are highly sensitive to a number of variables such as diet, sexual activity, cigarette smoking, and emotional stress.

Recent hormonal research on homosexuality has focused on levels of testosterone in gay males. Very little research on hormone measurements has been done on lesbians.

Several studies (including Glass and Johnston), grounded on the hypothesis that gay males suffered from a deficiency in testosterone, injected study groups of men with large amounts of that and other masculinizing hormones. The result in all cases was *not*, as expected, a change in sexual orientation or any effect on the *quality* of sexual response, but an increase in sexual drive. Similarly, estrogen was found to *decrease* male libido, but not sexual orientation.

Other studies tested the testosterone-deficiency theory on castrated men. Investigators (such as Meyer-Bahlburg) found that castration (whether hormonal or surgical) did not increase the incidence of male homosexuality. Similarly, hypogonadal males (who suffer from a deficiency of sex hormone production in the body) do not seem to have a higher incidence of homosexuality.

In 1971, one study (Kolodny) reported significantly lower testosterone levels in predominantly homosexual male subjects. There were, however, some methodological problems with this study. In particular, many of the homosexuals in the study group were heavy marijuana users, and marijuana use lowers testosterone levels. Since that particular study, many others on male homosexuals and a few on lesbians have been conducted to test testosterone levels. In general, the investigators were not able to repeat Kolodny's results. The majority of the studies revealed no differences between the homosexual and heterosexual groups. In two of the studies, the mean level of testosterone was significantly *higher* in the male homosexuals, while two other studies found significantly lower levels of testosterone in the male homosexuals. It appears that the great majority of homosexuals, males and females, had normal testosterone levels.

One must be cautious about assuming that a correlation implies causality. The ancient Egyptians, for example, used to believe that the ibis (their sacred bird) caused the Nile River to overflow its banks simply because the bird's migratory pattern correlated with the time of year when the Nile overflowed. When investigating homosexuality, often (especially among men) sexual orientation occurs before puberty, whereas hormonal changes would be occurring after puberty; thus, hormonal factors could be an index (or result of) rather than a *cause* of homosexuality. One study, for instance (Loraine *et al.*), found that testosterone levels were affected by stress. This fact has led some leading researchers to suggest that any difference among homosexuals might be the *result* of stress stemming from social disapproval. Indeed, changes in hormone levels have been known to be caused by changes in mood, sleep patterns, diet, physical activity, sexual activity, and drug use. There is some question as to whether there was adequate screening for many who were tested. For instance, in much of the research on hormones, the homosexual subjects were selected from groups of prison populations and psychiatric patients. In another study (Griffiths *et al.*) the sample included two women who were taking oral contraceptives. Were other variables, then, properly controlled in these experiments? Finally, only one study (Parks) utilized more than three blood samples. This study used six heterosexuals and six homosexuals, matched for age. All were put on the same daily regimen, and twenty-eight different determinations were made. Researchers discovered no significant differences between the two groups, though great variation in the day-to-day levels of both groups were found. Indeed, testosterone and gonadotropin levels varied by six to twenty-two percent over one month. In the future, such studies might be more reliable if they used control and study groups carefully matched for variables, if they used more precise definitions of sexual orientation (instead of the Kinsey scale, which is not very exact), and if standard laboratory testing were utilized.

Some theorists have hypothesized that prenatal excesses or deficiencies of certain sex hormones predispose individuals to eventual homosexual orientation. This implies that there are critical periods in fetal development when sexual orientation is determined. Karl Ulrich, himself homosexual, argued in the late 1800s that homosexuality was a result of an aberration in the differentiation of the part of the brain responsible for the sex drive. Today, the studies which have attempted to confirm this hypothesis have used two approaches: to search for evidence of prenatal hormone abnormalities in the makeup of adult homosexuals, or to follow the development of infants with suspected sex hormone abnormalities. Dorner and others, using the former strategy, studied the effects of estrogen on adult male homosexuals and heterosexuals. Money and his co-workers studied the effects of prenatal testosterone deficiency on adult male sexual orientation. Dorner found that homosexual males responded to the estrogen in ways that seemed more characteristic of females; from this, he hypothesized that homosexual males experienced a deficiency of testosterone at some time prior to birth. Yet Dorner's data have not been replicated by any other researchers. And his study provides no information about other relevant characteristics of his homosexual or heterosexual study groups. Finally, some homosexual men did not show this response, and some heterosexual men did.

In Money's study, androgen-deficient males who suffered from a chemical abnormality, though *physically* resembling biological females in many ways, still were found to be exclusively heterosexual in erotic imagery and behavior. He also studied women who experienced excess production of testosterone. In that group, he found an eighteen percent incidence of lesbian experience, slightly higher than one would predict from Kinsey's estimates. But most reported no lesbian experiences.

One assumption underlying all of these hormonal studies seems to be that sexual orientation *is* a purely biological phenomenon, and that "homosexuality" and "heterosexuality" are homogenous, unitary categories. But both represent wide ranges of lifestyles and expressions. And romantic attraction and sexual orientation seem to have powerful psychological and emotional components which these theories cannot take into account. How researchers define who is homosexual and who is heterosexual is also problematic. Is a Kinsey 6 the only "true homosexual?" What about a 5? A 4? How does one know? Some of the studies included homosexuals who were also having heterosexual sex, while the "heterosexual" groups included some "bisexuals."

Another assumption of this research is that male and female constitute two opposing, non-overlapping categories, both in terms of biological and behavioral traits; and that these traits are connected solely to male and female hormones. This assumption is presently being challenged by many scientists who find that biological characteristics overlap the sexes.

Recent research has revealed that many biological differences may be the result of societal pressures to conform to sex-role differentiated levels of activity and behavior. Studies have shown, for example, that the constraints placed on female activity from childhood on may cause some of the differences in height, strength, and hormonal secretions. Thus, even the differences we generally take for granted between men and women may be the *result* of differences in treatment rather than, as many people argue, the *cause* (and justification) for it. This research suggests how difficult it is to pinpoint biology as the cause of *anything*, much less anything as complicated as sexual orientation, and it suggests that the role of hormones in human behavior is still uncertain.

Some experimenters have used research on animals to try to bolster their theories of homosexuality. The most famous of these are the Dorner studies. Dorner studied the function of the hypothalamus and pituitary gland in rats and used the information to study the relationship of hormonal secretions to sexual orientation in humans. Yet, in fact, rat and human hypothalamus glands do not function in the same way at all and the analogy in this situation seems problematic.

Chapter 2 describes at length the many animal species that exhibit what appears to be homosexual activity. This evidence would no doubt make clear that those who argue that homosexuality is "unnatural" (if that definition is based on correlation with other animal species) are ignoring the facts. But it is dangerous to overgeneralize from these analogies about behavior to arguments about hormonal causes of homosexuality. Further, one can always ask what species (since there is no one universal pattern of behavior) one should select as a basis for comparison. Much of the research on animals regarding the correlation of hormones and behavior seems to assume that human behavior is instinctive like that of lower animal species, and as such is rigid and codifiable. In fact, though, the diversity of human sexual practices (within our own culture as well as among differing cultures) as revealed by many sex studies suggests that human behavior is more flexible and more varied than the behavior of non-human species. So, even if one can cite hormonal causes for non-human behavior, to do so with humans seems problematic.

Biological theories are highly controversial because of the many assumptions they make about the role biology plays in directing human behavior. And, as we saw in Chapter 1, human behavior is highly malleable, and seems to depend little if at all on instincts or biological programming. Homosexuality in particular is not simply a behavior like scratching or yawning. Nor is it merely a physical characteristic like tallness or having curly hair, since it includes sexual, affectional, and emotional components. It is a complex phenomenon which takes many diverse forms not easily explained from a biological perspective.

Psychoanalytic Theory

[T]he exclusive sexual interest felt by men for women is also a problem that needs elucidating and is not a self-evident fact based upon a chemical ⁓nature. (Freud, 1905, pp. 146-48.)

Sigmund Freud (1856-1939) was the Austrian physician who founded *psychoanalysis*: a method of studying and treating emotional problems by probing the unconscious. One might wonder why psychoanalysis appears at all in a chapter on causation, or why it appears when other psychological theories might not. But one cannot underemphasize the impact of this tradition on modern thinking:

[Psychoanalysis] is probably the only psychological system of thought that can fairly claim to constitute a significant cultural and intellectual force and tradition in the twentieth century in the Western world. (Barratt, p. 443.)

Freud believed that human beings have certain drives—in particular sexual and aggressive drives—which are often repressed because of the demands of civilization. This repression may lead to frustration and neurosis, but civilization's continuing stability requires that people sublimate some of those instincts. Therefore, "culture" protects us against nature and helps to adjust our relations with others, but it also paradoxically forces us to suppress certain drives. Though we may not consciously remember much of our early experience, according to Freud, those experiences become a part of who we are and affect our future personality. Much of psychoanalytic therapy is devoted to drawing out from the patient those early feelings and memories.

Freud placed tremendous importance on the sexual drive. He believed that, at one and the same time, humans are more sexual than animals because humans are not limited to reproduction, yet humans have the unique capacity to *sublimate* that drive—that is, to exchange sexual energy for a different but related sort of energy. For example, sexual energy can be channeled or "sublimated" into non-sexual activities such as work, art, or other endeavors. Though *some* degree of sexual satisfaction seems to be essential for almost everyone, Freud says, some sublimate better than others. And:

...frustration of this variable individual need is avenged by manifestations which, on account of their injurious effect on functional activity and of their subjectively painful character, we must regard as illness. (Freud, 1963 (a), p. 26)

Freud referred to such mental illness at times as *pathology* and at times as *neurosis*. Thus, there is a struggle between the human desire for uncontrolled sexuality and society's need for family and a stable system of reproduction. Neurotics may succeed in suppressing the *outward* expression of those sexual instincts, but this requires a great deal of energy in "trying to cooperate with civilization," and these instincts are inevitably expressed in some other way.

Freud's observations about repression were especially timely in his own day, when attitudes toward sex were very rigid and little was known about the development of sexuality. Indeed, Freud shocked the Victorian world with his claims that infantile sexuality was as much a biological drive as the need to eat. This drive, he added, motivates the infant to seek all kinds of physical gratification, which he termed "polymorphous perversity." Freud identified three distinct zones through which the infant gains pleasure: the oral, the anal, and the genital. As the child develops, this polymorphous sexuality becomes focused on one of these specific zones, beginning with the oral. At about one year, the child begins to focus its attention on the anal; at three or four the genitals become the primary sexual fixation. The object of sexual arousal, however, remains unspecific. The child is interested more in the physical pleasure itself than in what is the source of that pleasure.

What then determines sexual orientation? Freud himself suggests that civilization forces the child's sexuality into cultural norms, sublimating it into culturally acceptable forms of creative energy for some non-sexual task. Thus, the culture at large benefits from sexual repression.

The Oedipal Complex and the Development of Heterosexuality. According to Freud, at age three or four, both males and females become preoccupied with their genitals and begin to recognize that their biological sex is either male or female. For the male, the discovery that he, like his father, has a penis places him in a position of rivalry with the father for the mother's attentions. However, in normal development, the child realizes that he can't have the mother and finds his own female substitute. The male child realizes he is anatomically different and is thereby able to become physically separate.

The female child, however, discovers that she does not have a penis, and, for Freud, this is the moment when she discovers that she is anatomically inferior to the male. She becomes angry at the mother (since she too is an inferior being) and transfers her affections to her father. The girl's lifelong pursuit of her missing penis ultimately leads her, if the development is "healthy," into a heterosexual marriage and the production of a male child.

Thus, for Freud, much of healthy sexuality revolves around reproduction. In fact, he assumed that there is a biological compulsion to reproduce and that, therefore, heterosexuality is the *normal* outcome of sexual development. And, even at its most basic level, biology tells us that the female is passive, the male active. The sperm, Freud tells us, is aggressive and mobile, whereas the egg must wait passively to be fertilized. Women, he says, are also more easily influenced by external factors, since women's sexuality is always "in-relation-to" something else. For Freud, males develop heterosexually as the natural outgrowth of their affection for their mother. Although they suffer castration fears, these disappear as the boy matures. For girls, heterosexual development is quite different. She too would have the mother as a lover but quickly realizes that her body is inadequately equipped to fulfill this desire. Therefore, she turns to the father. It is important to realize here that, according to the Freudian model, she turns to him not because she is sexually attracted to him as a male, but rather because she figures that he is the source of the penis. He can give her one. When she realizes this is impossible, she settles for less and chooses him as a lover.

Heterosexuality for females then is interpreted as the lifelong struggle to compensate for the lack of a penis. For males, it is the natural outcome of the fact that they have a penis. It is an extension of the mother's love, simply redirected:

> As characteristics of the infantile sexuality, we have hitherto emphasized the fact that it is essentially autoerotic (he finds his object in his own body), and that the individual partial impulses, which on the whole are unconnected and independent of one another, are striving for the acquisition of pleasure. *The goal of this development forms the so-called normal sexual life of the adult in whom the acquisition of pleasure has been put into the service of the function of propagation.* The partial impulses, which are then under the primacy of one single erogenous zone, form a firm organization for the attainment of the sexual aim in a strange sexual object. (Freud, 1938, p. 597.)

Freud, however, though he viewed heterosexuality as "normal," did not see homosexuality as unnatural or degenerate. He frequently cited the significant contribution of homosexuals—such as Leonardo da Vinci, whom he profiled in a book—as well as the persistent presence of homosexuality in all cultures. And he criticized any work that assumed that a homosexual object-choice was synonymous with gender confusion. But Freud himself did not claim to discover the cause of homosexuality, nor did he claim that there is *one* cause. For example, he does not explain why identical family dynamics lead to different sexual development; nor does he make clear why some resolve the Oedipal complex by homosexuality, some by heterosexuality.

Freud was convinced that there exists "a very considerable measure of latent or unconscious homosexuality...in all normal people." (Freud,

1963, p. 158.) Male homosexuality, he suggested, might be a fixation on the mother, seeking a lover "in whom he can re-discover himself, and whom he wishes to love as his mother loved him." (Freud, "Certain Neurotic Mechanisms," p. 167.) The choice of homosexuality allows the son to remain true to his mother, his first love-object. Or, Freud hypothe-sized, perhaps male homosexuality is a kind of narcissism in which such a high value is placed on the penis that it leads to an inability to tolerate its absence in the love-object. Or it may be a result of an avoidance of rivalry with the father, or even a product of jealousy toward a (usually older) brother, involving what psychoanalysts term *reaction-formation* against repressed aggressive impulses. A reaction-formation is a behavior pattern which contradicts an underlying feeling. For example, I shower with gifts someone I hate intensely.

Regardless of the ultimate cause, Freud rejected *moral* labels:

It is assuredly no advantage, but it is nothing to be ashamed of, no vice, no degradation; it cannot be classified as an illness; we consider it to be a variation of the sexual function, produced by a certain arrest of sexual development. (For a complete citation, see Chapter 8, Freud, 1951.)

And he consistently emphasized the "costs" to individuals who had to sacrifice their desires to strict sexual codes. This was true not only for homosexuals, he maintained, but also for heterosexuals who expe-rienced impotence or rigidity in marriage, "perverts" whose fixations prevented them from entering into fulfilling sexual relations, and child-ren who were punished for their normal sexual curiosity.

It is one of the obvious injustices of social life that the standards of culture should demand the same behavior in sexual life from everyone.... (Freud, 1963 (a), p. 29.) (See also Freud's letter to an American mother, Chapter 8.)

Disciples of Freud.   Freud himself was very clear that it was not the task of psychoanalysis to "solve the problem of homosexuality," only to point out the determinants of object-choice. (*Ibid.*, p. 158.) But many of Freud's colleagues did not make the same distinction between the concepts of normal and natural and treated the development of homosexuality as "unnatural" as well as abnormal. Consequently, much of the post-Freudian work on homosexuality (e.g., Deutsch, Bieber, Erikson) specifi-cally focused on discovering the roots of this assumedly psychological disease.

Helene Deutsch, a disciple of Freud, tried to explain lesbianism. She argued that there were two causes of lesbianism, one biological, the other *psychogenic* (meaning that some psychological complication has occurred which prevents "normal" development). She cites narcissism as well as

"arrested development" (whereby the girl never outgrows her friendships with other girls), and the "mother-relationship theory" (whereby
the woman, realizing that she cannot have her mother, does not transfer
her affections to her father but instead to other women). Take, for
example, this passage from Deutsch:

> While we ascribe a primary character to this mother tie and support the
> view that in a large percentage of homosexual women the urge to union
> with the mother is predominant, analytic experience teaches us that this
> primary tie must be strengthened by other elements in order to infringe so
> powerfully and directly upon the adult woman's life.... These additional
> elements gain their decisive strength during puberty. In the triangular
> situation, the mother's attraction and the girl's longing for her must prove
> stronger than the biologic demand of heterosexuality.... (p. 353.)

Deutsch is not alone. Most of the post-Freudian theoretical work, right
up until 1973, discusses homosexuality as a psychological disease. More
clinical research took the form of case studies of clients who were miserable and who were encouraged by the psychological profession to be
miserable in an effort to motivate them toward a cure. Other students of
Freud have explained it as a "fixation" from one of the earlier stages of
childhood development. Some have described homosexuality as a kind
of narcissism, since the homosexual is attracted to members of her or his
own sex. Others, though, have maintained that homosexuality is a result
of a "castration complex," whereby the male homosexual sees women as
too threatening and so engages exclusively in sex with other men. Or in
another variation, one psychoanalyst (Fenichel) maintains that male
homosexuals are terrified by the sight of a partner who has no penis
because of castration anxiety; as a result, he said, gay males are attracted
to girlish males as a kind of compromise.

One should note here that all these researchers seem to assume not
only that heterosexuality needs no explanation but also that homosexuality is unnatural. But it is also important to keep in mind that none of the
standard psychological explanations serves to explain homosexuality.
Since homosexuality was viewed without question as a pathology, these
psychoanalysts went about trying to "cure" it. Such researchers believed
so strongly in the "natural" predisposition to heterosexuality that they
assume it can only be subverted by a severe disturbance.

Irving Bieber, for example, terms homosexuality a "hidden but inca-
pacitating fear of the opposite sex," a way to get love and acceptance
from men that homosexuals could not get from their fathers. He based
this conclusion on the results of a questionnaire he distributed to homosexuals and heterosexuals undergoing psychoanalysis. But his methodology has been seriously questioned; the same group of psychiatrists devel-

oped the questionnaire, designed the study, served as raters, developed the hypothesis, interpreted the results, served as analysts for the subjects, and concluded that their hypothesis was confirmed! Bieber himself acknowledged the "bias" of this research:

> The questions asked were not the conventional "objective" ones, and they did not seek to eliminate the observer by pinpointing some specific bit of behavior.... It must be recognized that the questionnaires were not filled out by naive observers but by the patient's own psychoanalysts—well-trained psychiatrists with experience in making value judgments based on clinical impressions and interpretations.

Bieber claimed that he could cure homosexuality. In a study of 106 male homosexuals, 29 (27 percent) showed a significant shift to heterosexual behavior after 150-350 hours of therapy; but most of those who were predominantly homosexual showed little or no change. Furthermore, the populations of gays and lesbians studied were usually from prisons and mental institutions and not from a cross-section of mainstream society. In fact, it was not until 1948 that gay and lesbian people were studied as they existed in the population at large. And the research that has gone on since then appears to refute the popular stereotypes of homosexuals. Today, even the most confident therapists think only 25 to 30 percent of highly motivated homosexuals can change their sexual preference for any period of time.

It was in 1973 that the American Psychiatric Association and the American Psychological Association removed homosexuality from their lists of psychological disorders. They maintained that homosexuality *per se* does not meet the two criteria of a mental disorder: namely, that it involves severe subjective distress and an inability to function in society. The World Health Organization, however, still classifies homosexuality as a disease, and there remains a policy among many psychiatrists that one should try to change a homosexual sexual orientation. As late as 1980, for example, Lillian Robinson cited much of the recent work in the field which still insisted that the homosexual can be "cured," and that the best time to cure the homosexual adolescent, for example, is "while anxiety and guilt about homosexual tendencies are still present." (Robinson, p. 428.)

Feminism and Psychoanalysis.   In the 1970s, feminists began to challenge this psychoanalytic conceptual framework, claiming it to be too narrow and too exclusively male in perspective. Feminist theorists like Alice Miller, Nancy Chodorow, and Carol Gilligan pointed out that the majority of research on human development was done on male subjects.

Conclusions derived from these studies were extrapolated to include women, when in fact they had not been studied at all. In the process of questioning the fundamental male superiority native to traditional psychology, it was a natural step to question the dogma of heterosexuality as well.

Nancy Chodorow, in her book *The Reproduction of Mothering*, grappled with psychoanalytic theory and questioned the fundamental superiority of male development. She also re-examined the conceptual framework which assumed that heterosexuality is the only natural outcome for the child. Boys, in her analysis, separate from their primary identification with the mother with a struggle. Chodorow maintains that their primary task is "personal masculine identification with their father and a sense of secure masculine self achieved through super ego formation and disparagement of women." (p. 165.) She suggests that their gender identity development is the primary focus of their sexuality and their relations with women are focused on domination and/or conquest in order to reinforce their male identity.

Girls, she claims, have a different task. They must learn to be heterosexual. Like boys, their primary identification and first love object is the mother. Unlike boys, their gender identity is not weakened by a transfer of identification from mother to father. Instead, as Chodorow points out, the traditional task of women according to psychoanalytic theory has been to become heterosexual. Women have to transfer their sexual/ emotional attachment from mother to father. But Chodorow claims that "a girl never gives up her mother as an internal or external love object, even if she does become heterosexual." That is, even if she does become sexually attracted to men—specifically her father—it is likely that this attraction develops in addition to the primary homosexual attraction rather than as a replacement. Chodorow suggests that women are basically bisexual.

Men, due to society's strict sex-role stereotypes, cannot afford this sexual liability for their very identity rests on the rejection and domination of all things female. To include in their sexuality the capacity for loving men would be a transgression of the heterosexually stereotyped sex-role functions of the society which forced them to separate from women at the outset. In other words, men have a more fragile grasp on their sexual identity, which they must bolster with strict sex-role behavior and a rejection of anything which falls outside their concept of masculinity. Therefore, they reject their innate bisexuality. Women may have a stronger hold on their gender identity and can allow for their sexuality to express itself either in emotional and/or sexual bonding with other women.

This reinterpretation of psychoanalytic theory suggests that sexual orientation is a psychosocial developmental process. Exclusive hetero-sexuality may be the product of rigid sex-role stereotyping in which sexual orientation and gender identity are confused. Women may have a greater capacity to be bisexual because their sexuality is not as strictly tied to gender role as male sexuality.

Obviously this version of sexual development is as theoretical and as difficult to prove as the traditional psychoanalytic version. But it may make just as good an argument for its interpretation as the other. Further-more, Chodorow remains conscious that she works only within the con-text of Western technological culture—a fact which much of the psycho-logical literature ignores. She includes a sociological analysis in her the-ory pointing out that the society acts as the matrix for the psychological processes she describes. She does not then assume a universality for her theory.

Partly as a result of these feminist critiques, more recent research has begun to investigate homosexuals in their everyday lives. From these studies a new picture emerges of the gay person as emotionally as well adjusted as heterosexual peers—or even better. They have the same needs and developmental traits as heterosexuals. Studies of actual sexual practices indicate that the physiology of orgasm is the same for gay and lesbian, bisexual, and heterosexual people. In fact, apparently sex-role stereotyping affects sexuality more than sexual orientation. The differ-ences that do exist between homosexuals and heterosexuals may be due more to social pressure on gay people than any innate biological differ-ences between the groups.

The American Psychological Association, though it eliminated homo-sexuality from its list of psychiatric disorders, did add one disease called "ego dystonic homosexuality," in which one desires to be a heterosexual and rejects intensely her or his homosexuality. But this does not take into account the sociological factors that could induce such self-hatred, and suggests once again that homosexuality rather than social prejudice is the problem which needs to be "cured."

Environmental/Behavioral Theories

There are some theories that homosexuality may be caused by envi-ronmental factors. For example, perhaps the homosexual had an acciden-tal but pleasurable same-sex incident in childhood, or was segregated by sex for a long period of time in his/her youth (say, in a boarding school). Scientists once even believed that homosexuality was caused by excessive masturbation. There are many popular beliefs that may emerge from an environmental perspective. There are some who believe homosexuals try to recruit children to be homosexuals, that homosexuality is a result of contact with homosexuals, that same-sex orientation is a result of an unhappy heterosexual experience. But there is no evidence to support any of theses contentions.

Regarding homosexuality, most social scientists reject the notion that people simply decide to be attracted to their own sex out of a desire to follow a fad, to rebel against authority, or because of information they are given in a school sex-education class. With the enormous pressure placed on the individual to conform to a heterosexual standard and the stigma placed upon homosexuality, it seems unlikely that this is the case.

Some people also subscribe to the "seduction theory of homosexuality." As this theory goes, same-sex orientations are "caused" by older people (usually men) who "recruit" otherwise "healthy" heterosexuals into a life of sexual depravity or that young people somehow "catch" homosexuality from exposure to another person as if it were a contagious disease like a cold or the flu:

> Like heterosexuality, homosexuality is something that one is usually aware of long before he [or she] ever has any overt sexual experience with it. It is just about as sensible to blame seduction for homosexuality as it is to blame seduction for heterosexuality, yet this is one of the more common theories about the origins of homosexuality. Who has not heard the familiar fairy tale of the ominous stranger, dressed in a trench coat, pockets filled with candy, lurking around the playground, luring small boys to moral disaster from which they never recover? This myth persists, in spite of the fact that the vast majority of cases of child molestation involve heterosexuals and are often incestuous. (Fischer. See Chapter 8 for further discussion of the seduction theory of homosexuality.)

Others hypothesize that certain family constellations may account for the phenomenon. For example, Bieber, in a a study of homosexual men undergoing psychoanalysis, discovered that they tended to have absent or distant fathers and domineering mothers. This evidence suggests an interpretation that, because the father is so "tough" and distant, the son is never able to form a bond with him, and so does not learn the "masculine" role in life. As a result, he may develop an excessive attachment to his mother. Charlotte Wolff discovered that lesbians (not in psychoanalysis) had a distant father *and* mother. But recent studies (e.g., Freund and Blanchard) suggest that parental distance, rather than causing homosexuality, may actually be a response to atypical gender behavior on the part of the child(ren) in the family. Dr. Richard Green, sex researcher and professor of psychiatry, law, and human sexuality at the University of California at Los Angeles, conducted a fifteen-year study of forty-four "extremely feminine boys." He discovered that three-fourths of them matured to be homosexual or bisexual, whereas only one man in his "masculine" control group did. He found some common factors in the families of those boys: parental desire (especially from the father) that the child be a girl; encouragement of cross-gender dressing; less time with the father; and frequent illnesses on the child's part. It is unclear at this time what are the implications of such research, and to date no other researcher has replicated his results. More recently though there are not enough data to suggest a hypothesis, there is some evidence that birth order is also relevant to homosexuality, and that (for male homosexuality) the age of the father is also relevant (the older the parents, the higher the incidence of homosexuality).

Saghir and Robins studied the childhoods of adult male homosexuals. They found that 72 percent of them, compared with a 12 percent control group of heterosexuals, had lost one or both parents before the age of fifteen. Further, 50 percent of the gays but only 17 percent of the hetero-sexuals reported severe marital problems between their parents. Another study (Whitman) found "childhood indicators" of later adult male homo-sexuality, including interest in dolls, cross-dressing, preference for the company of girls rather than boys in games, preference for the company of older women rather than men, assessment by other boys as a "sissy," and sexual interest in other boys rather than girls during childhood sex play. But these "gender-crossing" patterns may be a sign of, not causally related to, homosexuality.

Some suggest that strong sexual taboos in families, leading to intense guilt, may account for later homosexuality, that same-sex preferences may be a reaction to poor models of heterosexuality learned or observed in the home. Or that perhaps parents wanted a child of the other sex, leading them unconsciously to direct the child toward identification with the other gender.

Others argue that there may be environmental factors other than family that might account for later same-sex orientation. For example, Gagnon and Simon maintain that a negative initial sexual experience with someone of the other sex (or a positive initial experience with someone of the same sex) can lead one to opt for homosexuality. Or perhaps an extremely sensitive girl turns to lesbianism after she has been rejected by a boy she loves. These kinds of possibilities have led some behavioral scientists to conjecture that homosexuality is always associated with an unconscious fear of heterosexual relationships.

These environmental theories are fraught with many problems. For one, they have little predictive value—heterosexuals too, for example, come from similar kinds of families as those Bieber describes in his theory. Notice in the following quote how Bieber himself covers all the bases:

The child who becomes homosexual is usually overprotected and preferred by his mother. In other cases he may be under-protected and rejected. (Quoted in Weinberg, p. 96.)

Indeed, if these theories were correct, how could siblings have different sexual orientations, since they come from the same environmental surroundings? The fact is that gay males and lesbians come from an enormous variety of familial constellations. Hatterer, in fact, found over fifty variables in the backgrounds of his male homosexual patients. Some are raised in homes with a hostile/distant father or a hostile/distant mother. But, many come from homes with two loving and caring parents, a single loving parent, extended family homes where other relatives reside, and communal living arrangements where a number of adults take on child-rearing duties.

Also, regarding the theory that fear of the other sex accounts for homosexuality, in truth many homosexuals have had satisfying heterosexual experiences at some point in their lives. Indeed, if one took this theory to its logical conclusion, one could argue that, in fact, heterosexuality is a product of fear of members of the same sex! In addition, given the large number of gays in the population, virtually everyone has had, at some point in his or her life, a gay teacher or minister or friend or relative; not all of those contacts led to a homosexual orientation. This seems to undermine the "contagion" theory of homosexuality. Further, to point in retrospect to some homosexual contact or person as a reason for a homosexual's sexual preference may be to put the cart before the horse. Thus the presence of a homosexual desire may lead one to explore or be responsive to homosexual contact. It appears, then, that it is very likely that such contact occurred, but this does not prove a causal connection. Thus, no one variable is specific for homosexuality in the way that, say, the tubercle bacillus is specific for tuberculosis.

Finally, the behaviors that scientists cite as causative factors of homosexuality may in fact confuse cause and effect; does, for example, an unsatisfying sexual experience cause homosexuality; or is it unsatisfying because of an already existing yet unconscious sexual orientation? These theories may, then, be untestable. Though it may be tempting to cite experiences or behaviors as determinants of homosexuality, in fact none of the behavioral theories suggested to date has provided sufficient evidence to warrant its acceptance.

Does It Matter?

I do not see any great interest on the part of the B'nai B'rith Anti-

Defamation League in the possibility of solving problems of anti-Semitism by converting Jews to Christians.... We are interested in obtaining rights for our respective minorities *as* Negroes, *as* Jews, and *as* homosexuals. Why we are Negroes, Jews, or homosexuals is totally irrelevant, and whether we can be changed to whites, Christians, or heterosexuals is equally irrelevant. (Kameny, p. 153.)

Scientists, as we have seen, are as much part of their cultures as anyone else. And many, as noted throughout this chapter, have begun with the assumption that homosexuality is "unnatural" and so requires an explanation. Few seek the causes of sexual orientation in general. Some critics of these approaches have argued that these "illness" or "aberration" theories are just disguises for the more old-fashioned terminology of "sin" or "evil": "(T)he psychiatric perspective on homosexuality is but a thinly disguised replica of the religious perspective which it displaced." (Szasz, p. 170.)

Indeed, some scientists may have a hidden agenda, since, if it were possible to find determining conditions for homosexuality, then perhaps we could "cure" it. Electroshock, hypnosis, aversion therapy, balanced diet, acupuncture, psychoanalysis, brain alterations, sexual abstinence, prayer, and hundreds of other proposals have been tried to eliminate "homosexual tendencies." Yet clearly to assume a cure is required is to presuppose that a problem exists.

Does it make a difference to know what causes homosexuality in particular or sexual orientation in general? It seems to be more than simple scientific curiosity which motivates researchers working in this area. Certainly, this is not to deny that these are questions worth exploring, but it is important to note that any researcher is selecting one area of interest over another, and the ways in which the questions are formulated often reveal the bias. For example, might there be other sorts of questions which are of value to scientific research? Note how different the following questions sound:

- Do lesbians find that most women are more loving than most men?
- How do gay males manage to avoid all the pressures to conform?
- Considering the extent of social disapproval, what does a gay lifestyle offer that others may or may not?
- Is sex more pleasurable between members of the same sex?
- Is heterosexuality the result of a fear of intimacy with members of one's own sex?
- Is heterosexuality caused by unpleasant early experiences with members of one's own sex?
- Is heterosexuality caused by an excess of hormones of one's own sex?

There is nothing intrinsically unscientific about the questions above, yet they probably seem peculiar to most of us. Few scientists, though, frame the questions in this way, even those who are more "sympathetic." Masters and Johnson, for example, despite their insistence that homosexuality is not a disease, said that they could "cure" it in two weeks!

Does it matter what causes homosexuality? Let's for a moment assume that tomorrow the most esteemed members of the scientific community discover—beyond a shadow of a doubt—what determines sexual orientation. What difference would it make? Let's suppose, assuming we accept the explanation, that the basis is a biological one. What would that mean in terms of the normative implications that might follow? To assume that the explanation is biological is to maintain that the condition is innate. This would also mean that homosexuality is not "contagious" in any way (unless perhaps it is transmitted genetically), so one could not "catch it" from a homosexual. It might make homosexuality akin to skin color or left-handedness—that is, an aspect of human diversity which does not seem to warrant a loss of rights or a difference in treatment. We might argue, by analogy, that just being black or left-handed is in no way problematic except in terms of society's treatment, so homosexuality might be seen as ethically (and biologically) "neutral."

Or suppose the explanation is a psychoanalytic or environmental one—certain infantile experiences or family constellations "cause" homosexuality. This too seems of little relevance to social policy unless we presuppose that there is something wrong with the condition. We are hardly responsible for what we do or is done to us at an early age, especially if, as Freud claims, some of this is universal for all of us as human beings. Also, many positive character traits—kindness, curiosity, etc.— are probably the result of early training and reinforcement. Why might not homosexuality be another such example? Why do we assume that a pathology is involved when the outcome is homosexuality?

Finally, suppose that there is choice involved, why might we not construe homosexuality as analogous to freedom of religious expression? Though most people are born into the religion of their family, they have a choice to remain within that religion, change their religious beliefs to suit themselves, or abandon religion entirely. Just as in any society there might be a majority (in-group) and a minority (out-group) religion, in which a belief in pluralism dictates acceptance of varying views, why might such not be the case with differing sexual practices? Perhaps, some day we will puzzle over why this was *not* society's attitude, just as we now feel morally superior to those who persecute members of minority religious sects.

Homosexuality is not the norm, that much is true. It is, without doubt, unconventional behavior in that it is only practiced by a numerical minority of the population. But, at the same time it is a lifestyle for at least a significant percentage of our society, a significant number of individuals. And Masters and Johnson report that almost all of the individuals they studied — homosexuals and heterosexuals alike — reported fantasies involving members of the same sex. Thus, as has been shown in this and other chapters, homosexuality and heterosexuality are not mutually exclusive categories. But to label homosexuality a result of a "genetic aberration" or a biological "mistake" or a mental "disorder" or "willfulness" or a "breakdown in the normal family" or a hormonal "imbalance" is to cease to describe the phenomenon and instead to make a value judgment. Such values must be defended, not simply asserted as if they were obviously true. And when such values become the basis for research, it is inevitable that the research will fail to provide an adequate and accurate picture of the world.

Conclusion

Theories dealing with the causation of homosexuality appear to reflect the attitudes of the society of the time. Aristotle maintained that it was a result of some bodily defect. In the Dark Ages and medieval period, people engaging in same-sex activity were believed to be possessed by the Devil. Albertus Magnus (1206-1280) viewed it as the result of a burning frenzy (the origin of which was not explained) that could be spread from one person to another. The cure was alleged to be exorcism or, if that failed, burning at the stake. For many years, sexual misbehavior was not treated separately from religious nonorthodoxy; political enemies were labeled sexual criminals as a way to eliminate them as threats to those in power.

A hundred years ago, homosexuality was judged as a vice attributable to individual depravity, linked with insanity, delinquency, and crime. Often excessive masturbation ("self-abuse") was held to be the cause of homosexuality. Its cure was "public censure and private penance." (Churchill, p. 89.)

In the 19th century, when homosexuality first came to be seen as a specific entity and the homosexual as having a particular identity, it was absorbed into a medical framework. At this time homosexuality came to be viewed as a *condition* rather than a *behavior*. With biological explanations from both defenders and detractors, "the true invert" became a character who was blamed as a social degenerate by opponents of homosexuality and viewed as deserving of pity by sympathetic researchers like Havelock Ellis. The French neurologist Jean Martin Charcot (1825-1893) tried to cure cases of homosexuality with hypnosis, but, after modest "success," concluded that it was hereditary.

With the popularization of Charles Darwin's evolutionary theories, commentators described homosexuality as maladaptive, evolutionarily regressive, a threat to society and the human species. The French physician Paul Moreau, for example, termed homosexuality a hereditary degeneracy, the only solution of which was institutionalization. Cesare Lombroso, measuring human skulls, claimed to have proven that homosexuals were at a lower evolutionary stage. Appeals to society's needs and individual health led researchers to distinguish between degenerative and species-enhancing behaviors, with homosexuality classified as the former.

During the early part of the 20th century, when endocrinology became the rage, homosexuality was thought to be glandular. Some argued that it could be cured by hormone therapies. Dorner described homosexuality as an "inborn error of metabolism," and suggested that pregnant women be given injections of steroid hormones.

Today, psychiatric explanations appear to be in vogue, so we hear all sorts of psychoanalytic explanations for homosexuality. All different types of techniques and therapies have been recommended and employed to eradicate a person's "homosexual tendencies." Yet all appear to be unsuccessful, except as temporary measures. And such "therapies" define "success" in terms of eliminating homosexual behavior, without taking into account orientation, fantasy life, attitude, and so forth.

Extraordinary explanations of homosexuality do not seem to account for the frequency of it or its occurrences in varied cultures and even other species. Nor do these explanations make sense of the different ratings on Kinsey's sexual continuum. Yet perhaps it is only because homosexuality is viewed as extraordinary that extraordinary causal explanations are sought. Its prevalence in other species and other societies, its appearance in virtually all settings despite social pressure to the contrary—this evidence suggests that homosexuality is not in fact rare.

Perhaps the dynamic of sexual preference is the same for heterosexuals and homosexuals, involving some combination of many factors which it may not be possible to isolate. Why do any of us like what we like? Why do some of us prefer chocolate ice cream, while others savor mocha chip? Why are some of us drawn to people who are more like us, while others find that "opposites attract"? Why are some of us romantically attracted to people who are blond, brunette, or to people with little or no hair at all? Why don't we usually ask these questions? At this time (and maybe forever), the source(s) of sexual orientation remain(s) a mystery. "At present there is no theory that can account rigorously for why some people engage primarily in homosexual behavior and others do not." (Berman and Davidson, p. 228.)

There is an ancient tale about six blind men and an elephant. They are placed at various spots around the elephant and asked to identify what is the object in question. The one who feels the trunk asserts, "This must be a tree." Another, touching the tail, feels assured that he is holding a snake. The blind man who holds the ears decides that he has the wings of a great bird. Yet it is clear that none of these experiences individually gives us an accurate picture of the reality in question. Instead, we need all of the perspectives before we really have the elephant. Likewise, perhaps our understanding of sexual orientation has to include *all* of the aspects of human experience which serve to make us who we are—the physical, the social, the emotional, the psychological, and the environmental—in order for us to get a complete picture. But any by itself falls short of our demand, for human behavior is perhaps too complex and rich and flexible to be explained so easily and so casually. And this would be true of heterosexuality as well as homosexuality.

This approach will obviously not satisfy those who insist on clear and distinct categories with their accompanying moral judgments of praise and blame. Like each blind person in our story, these individuals feel certain that they have *the* truth. But to do so appears to opt arbitrarily for one explanation over another; instead, taking all perspectives into account seems to respect the scientific data we have while acknowledging the enormous diversity of human sexual practices. Then we can say truly: "Here is the elephant."

REFERENCES

Barratt, B.B. "Freud's Psychology as Interpretation." *Psychoanalysis and Contemporary Science* (1976) 5:443-478.

Bieber, Irving. *Homosexuality: A Psychoanalytic Study*. New York: Basic Books, 1962.

Birke, Lynda. "Is Homosexuality Hormonally Determined?" *Journal of Homosexuality* (1981) 6, 4:35-48.

Birke, L. "From Sin to Sickness: Hormonal Theories of Lesbianism." In *Biological Woman: The Convenient Myth*. Cambridge, Mass.: Schenkman Publishing Co. 1982.

Bleier, Ruth. *Science and Gender: A Critique of Biology and Its Theories of Women*. Elmsford, New York: Pergamon, 1984.

Chodorow, Nancy. *The Reproduction of Mothering: Psychoanalysis and the Sociology of Gender*. Berkeley, Calif.: University of California Press, 1978.

Churchill, Wainwright. *Homosexuality in Males: A Cross-Cultural and Cross-*

Species Investigation. Englewood Cliffs, N.J.: Prentice-Hall, 1967.

Dawkins, R. *The Selfish Gene*. New York: Oxford University Press, 1977.

Deutsch, Helene. *Psychology of Women*. New York: Grune and Stratton, 1945.

Dewey, John. *How We Think*. Boston: D.C. Heath, 1910.

Dorner, G. *Hormones and Brain Differentiation*. Amsterdam: Elsevier, 1976.

Dorner, G. et al., "A Neuroendocrine Predisposition for Homosexuality in Men." *Archives of Sexual Behavior* (1975) 4 (1): 1-8.

Ellis, Havelock. *Sexual Inversion: Studies in the Psychology of Sex*. New York: Random House, 1936.

Fenichel, O. *The Psychoanalytic Theory of Neurosis*. New York: W.W. Norton, 1945.

Fisher, Peter. *The Gay Mystique: The Myth and Reality of Male Homosexuality*. New York: Stein & Day, 1972.

Freud, Sigmund. "Infantile Sexuality." In *The Basic Writings of Sigmund Freud*, trans. A.A. Brell. New York: Modern Library, 1938, pp. 580-603.

Freud, Sigmund. "Historical Notes: A Letter from Freud." *American Journal of Psychiatry*, Vol. 107, April 1951, pp. 286-287.

Freud, Sigmund. "A Case of Homosexuality in a Woman." In *Sexuality and the Psychology of Love*. New York: Collier, 1963.

Freud, Sigmund. "Certain Neurotic Mechanism." In *Sexuality and the Psychology of Love*. New York: Collier, 1963.

Freud, Sigmund. "Sexual Morality and Modern Nervousness." In *Sexuality and the Psychology of Love*. New York: Collier, 1963 (a).

Freud, Sigmund. *Freud's Letters*, edited by E.L. Freud, translated by J. & T. Stern. New York: Basic Books, 1969.

Freund, Kurt, and Blanchard, Ray. "Is the Distant Relationship of Fathers and Homosexual Sons Related to the Sons' Erotic Preference for Male Partners, or to the Sons' Atypical Gender Identity, or to Both." In *Homosexuality and Social Sex Roles*. New York: Haworth Press, 1983.

Fried, Barbara, Hubbard, Ruth, and Henifin, Mary Sue, eds. *Biological Woman—The Convenient Myth: A Collection of Feminist Essays and a Comprehensive Bibliography*. Cambridge, Mass.: Schenkman Publishing Co., 1982.

Gagnon, J.H., and Simon, W. *Sexual Conduct: The Social Sources of Human Sexuality*. Chicago: Aldine, 1973.

Gartrell, N.K. "Hormones and Homosexuality." In *Homosexuality: Social, Psychological, and Biological Issues*, edited by W. Paul, J.D. Weinrich, J.C. Gonsiorek, and M.E. Hotsedt. Beverly Hills, Calif.: Sage Publications, 1982.

Gilligan, Carol. *In a Different Voice: Psychological Theory and Women's Development*. Cambridge, Mass.: Harvard University Press, 1982.

Glass, S.J., and Johnson, R.W. "Limitations and Complications of Organotherapy in Male Homosexuality." *Journal of Clinical Endocrinology* (1944) 4:540-544.

Green, Richard. *The "Sissy Boy Syndrome" and the Development of Homosexuality*. New Haven: Yale University Press, 1987.

Griffiths, P.D. et al. "Homosexual Women: An Endocrine and Psychological Study." *Journal of Endocrinology* (1974) 63:549-556.

Hatterer, L. *Changing Homosexuality in the Male*. New York: McGraw-Hill, 1970.

Kallman, F.J. "Comparative-Twin Study on the Genetic Aspects of Male Homosexuality." *Journal of Nervous and Mental Disease* (1952) 115:283-298.

Kameny, Frank. "Speech to the New York Mattachine Society." July 1964. Quoted in *Sexual Politics, Sexual Communities: The Making of a Homosexual Minority in the United States, 1940-1970* by John D'Emilio. Chicago: University of Chicago Press, 1983.

Kolodny, R.C. *et al.* "Plasma Testosterone and Semen Analysis in Male Homosexuals." *New England Journal of Medicine* (1971) 285 (21):1170-74.

Kuhn, T. *The Structure of Scientific Revolutions*. Chicago: University of Chicago Press, 1970.

Loraine, J.A. *et al.* "Patterns of Hormonal Secretion in Male and Female Homosexuals." *Nature* (1970) 234, 552-554.

Lowe, Marian. "The Dialectic of Biology and Culture." In *Women's Nature*. New York: Pergamon Press, 1983.

Marmor, Judd, ed. *Homosexual Behavior: A Modern Reappraisal*. New York: Basic Books, 1980.

Masters, William H., and Johnson, Virginia E. *Human Sexual Response*. Boston: Little, Brown, 1966.

Meyer-Bahlburg, H.F.L. "Sex Hormones and Male Homosexuality in Comparative Perspective." *Archives of Sexual Behavior*. (1977) 6 (4):297-325.

Miller, Alice. *Thou Shalt Not Be Aware: Society's Betrayal of the Child*. New York: Farrar, Straus, and Giroux, 1984.

Money, John, and Ogunro, D. "Behavioral Sexology: Ten Cases of Genetic Male Intersexuality with Implied Prenatal and Pubertal Androgenization." *Archives of Sexual Behavior* (1974) 3 (3):181-205.

Parks, G.A. *et al.* "Variation in Pituitary-Gonadal Function in Adolescent Male Homosexuals and Heterosexuals." *Journal of Clinical Endocrine Metabolism* (1974) 39 (4):796-801.

Pillard, Richard, and Weinrich, James. "Evidence of Familial Nature of Male Homosexuality." *Archives of General Psychiatry* (1986) 43:808-812.

Plato. *The Symposium*. In *The Collected Dialogues*, translated by Edith Hamilton and Huntington Cairns. Princeton, N.J.: Princeton University Press, 1978.

Rainer, J.D., Mesnikoff, A., Kolb, L.C., and Carr, A. "Homosexuality and Heterosexuality in Identical Twins." *Psychosomatic Medicine* (1960) 22.

Robinson, Lillian H. "Adolescent Homosexual Patterns: Psychodynamics and Therapy." *Adolescent Psychiatry Vol. VIII*, editors Sherman Feinstein, Peter Grovacchini, John Looney, Allan Schwartzberg, and Arthur Sorosky. Chicago: University of Chicago Press, 1980.

Ruse, Michael. "Are There Gay Genes?" *Journal of Homosexuality* (1981) 6 (4). New York: Haworth Press, 1981.

Saghir, Marcel T., and Robins, Eli. *Male and Female Homosexuality: A Comprehensive Investigation*. Baltimore: Williams and Wilkins, 1973.

Sartre, Jean Paul. *Saint Genet: Actor and Martyr*, trans. by Bernard Freschtman. New York: Braziller, 1963, p. 587.

Schachter, Stanley. *Psychology of Affiliation: Experimental Studies of the Sources of Gregariousness*. Stanford, Calif.: Stanford University Press, 1959.

Shields, J.J. "Homosexuality in Twins: A Family Study and a Registry Study." *Archives of General Psychiatry* (1968) (2):149-160.

Szasz, Thomas. *The Manufacture of Madness.* New York: Dell Publishing Co., 1970.

Tauber, E.S. "Effects of Castration Upon the Sexuality of the Adult Male." *Psychosomatic Medicine* (1940) 2: 74-87.

Weinberg, George. *Society and the Healthy Homosexual.* New York: St. Martin's Press, 1972.

Weinrich, James D. "A New Sociobiological Theory of Homosexuality Applicable to Societies with Universal Marriage." *Ethnology and Sociobiology* (1986) 8: 1-9.

West, Donald James. *Homosexuality.* Chicago: Aldine Publishing Co., 1968.

Wilson, E.O. *On Human Nature.* New York: Bantam Books, 1979.

Whitman, F.L. "Childhood Indicators of Male Homosexuality." In *Archives of Sexual Behavior* (1977) 6.

Wolff, Charlotte. *Love Between Women.* London: Duckworth, 1971.

Chapter 4

Sexuality and the Heritage of Western Religion

At least as long as we could articulate such concerns, our species has wondered about the workings of the universe and the significance of our existence. We wonder about how our world came into being, and if it will have an end. We raise questions about the processes of the natural world and whether what occurs has some larger purpose. We marvel at the enormity of the universe and at times feel that our own individual lives are insignificant and perhaps even irrelevant. We face tragedies global and personal and ask "why bad things happen to good people." And though we know that each of us will die, we cannot help but speculate about some other form of existence after the death of the physical body.

There is good reason to feel awestruck at the tremendous complexity and richness of the universe. We now know more about the natural world than did our ancestors who imagined gods of rain and pictured the earth resting on the back of an enormous turtle. We have the electron microscope and a telescope that can photograph the moons around Jupiter. Yet we still experience the mystery of "Being"—we still wonder why we are here and what will happen to us after we die. Religion provides a framework in which one can explain some of those concerns.

By definition a *religion* is a particular system of rites and observances based on faith in and worship of a higher being or beings. Religion's emphasis is on the sacred and the divine.

> The anxiety of meaninglessness is anxiety about the loss of an ultimate concern, of a meaning which gives meaning to all meanings. This anxiety is aroused by the loss of a spiritual center, of an answer, however symbolic and indirect, to the question of the meaning of existence. (Tillich, p. 47.)

And just as different people in different societies grow up learning different languages, so too they learn different sets of religious beliefs. And

152

with those different sets of beliefs frequently come explicit or implicit moral codes to guide human conduct.

Contrasting Visions of the Divine

Few of us know much about religions other than our own. Yet, on examining various world religions, it becomes clear that there are striking differences as well as similarities. All religions, for example, are organized around a belief in a superior force outside of and more powerful than the individual. This force is believed to have some control over the ordering of the universe and the activities of humans. Additionally, all religious faiths have developed systems of rites and rituals which they prescribe for their followers. These systems offer basic moral guidelines for how practitioners should live their lives. Often, there are corollary rewards and punishments which are thought to follow from conformity to or transgression of these codes. Rules about sexual behavior are often a significant aspect of religious doctrines.

Yet, even with these similarities, there are fundamental differences among the many world religions. In particular, they may differ in their beliefs about the creation of the universe and the ways in which it is ordered. But most significant are the differences in the concept of a higher power. These differences can be more easily understood if we think of them as falling roughly into two major groupings. One group includes those religions which are ordered around a belief in several deities (or gods), while the other believes in the existence of only one Supreme Being. Religions which are based on the belief in a number of gods are *polytheistic*, whereas those based on a belief in a single God are *monotheistic*. Some theorists conclude that this distinction may help to account for, at least in part, a religion's attitude toward sexuality.

Polytheism

Many ancient and non-Western cultures—including, for example, the Hindu, most Native American, and the pre-Columbian, such as the Mayan and Incan cultures—are based on polytheistic religions. In general, these polytheistic views seem to attribute similar characteristics to their gods. Particularly significant is the belief that the gods are actually created, and that they age, give birth, and engage in sex themselves. Some of these gods even have sexual relations with mortals. The universe is seen as continuous, ever-changing, and fluid. These religious views are often lacking in rigid categories, and this is particularly true of gender categories, which become mixed and ambiguous. For example, some male gods may give birth, some female gods have considerable power, and at times even the gods themselves engage in homosexual practices. And, in many of the cultures, emerged from these polytheistic views, homosexuality is viewed as one of many natural expressions of human sexuality. Rigid sexual labeling is uncommon; gender roles are often blurred. Even when there are transgressions of norms, penalties are often not strictly enforced.

Monotheism

In contrast, monotheistic religions generally view the Supreme Being as without origin. Such a deity is not born and does not die—that is, the deity has always existed and will always exist without qualitative change. This Being, viewed as a perfect spiritual Being, has an existence completely independent of human beings and transcendent from the natural world. In part, this means that such a Being has no sexual desire, for sexual desire, as a kind of need, is incompatible with this concept of perfection. This accounts for the strict separation between the Creator and the created which is so characteristic of monotheism. This Deity may be described at times in human characteristics, but never acts in a sexual way; instead, creation occurs through the thoughts and will of the Creator. Just as the Creator is distinct from this creation, so too are divisions between the sexes in the form of gender roles strictly defined. This provides practitioners with a clear sense of their roles in society: the guidelines they should follow in relation to their God and to other human beings. In general, spirituality is valued and sexuality comes to be viewed as acceptable only in narrowly defined contexts. Hence, homosexuality is generally condemned and homosexual practices carry severe penalties. Indeed, many sexual practices may be punishable by death, and sex itself is viewed as something akin to a necessary evil the purpose of which is the creation of new generations.

Our emphasis in this chapter, then, is on the dynamic between religious practice and religious belief, rather than on the spiritual aspects of religious views. Further, our focus in this chapter is on Western religious thought, beginning with the polytheism of the early Greeks and Romans. These world views provide the foundation for the eventual development of the monotheistic religions of Judaism, Christianity, and Islam.

The Greeks and Romans

By the very fact that we breathe our love into beautiful boys, we keep them away from avarice, increase their enjoyment of work, trouble, and dangers, and strengthen their modesty and self-control. (Xenophon.)

The Greeks

The ancient Greek world view was based on polytheism. The Greek gods were immortals who in their lives on Mount Olympus and in their frequent descents to earth acted much like mortals. The Greek conception of the cosmos was very much a sexual one. Creation myths are full of sexual intrigue and violence; creation was an *act* of gods, in contrast to the later Christian view of creation as a result of the will of a single God. The Greeks, unlike, for example, the Egyptians, made their gods in their own image, making heaven a pleasantly familiar place. Further, these myths tended to serve more as explanations of natural occurrences rather than rigid codes of right and wrong.

The Greeks considered their gods imperfect. The king of the gods—Zeus—was feared because he was so very powerful, but he was frequently a figure of fun as well. Zeus was neither omniscient nor omnipotent. He could, for example, be deceived. Other deities were attractive in human terms; they appeared in the forms of lovely youths and maidens who peopled woodlands, forests, rivers, and the sea. The Greeks believed that it was important not to anger the gods, as they were often jealous and even fickle. To maintain good relations between mortals and immortals, they developed a set of rituals, some of which involved animal sacrifices or certain cleansing practices. But it is not uncommon in Greek mythology for innocent people to suffer at the hands of gods, angry because some mortal has unknowingly overstepped certain bounds or even because the mortal has caught the attention of some rival god. Indeed, Zeus frequently punished members of the entire line of a family because one ancestor earned his disfavor.

It has been said that the Greeks were the first people in the world to *play*. (Hamilton, 1942, p. 31.) Wealthier Athenian citizens had considerable leisure time, and ancient Greek society glorified the arts in the form of sculpture, architecture, and literature. There were many festivals and athletic competitions which reflected Greek pride in the physical form, especially that of the male. Similarly, the Greek attitude toward sex was, for the most part, value-neutral. The Greeks considered menstruation normal, and regarded masturbation as a natural substitute for sex with another person. Premarital sex was tolerated, at least for men. And, though exclusive homosexuality was probably discouraged as a threat to the family, it was widely tolerated both for older men who had had children and for younger men prior to marriage.

The Greek attitude toward sexuality was based on the concept of *hedone*. As it is translated, *hedone* was "the cheerful enjoyment of life, especially of the joys of love." (Churchill.) Though nowadays we associate the term "hedonism" with lust or decadence, its original meaning was more positive for the ancient Greeks, connoting enjoyment of finer pleasures and a life of nobility.

The behavior of the Greek gods reflected the attitudes and lifestyles of their mortal counterparts. They were, in particular, very sexual. Not only did they engage in sexual activity with gods and mortals, but they competed over which of them was lovelier, and which favorite mortal of theirs was fairer or wiser or stronger.

Like their gods, Greek citizens took great delight in the physical form, feeling no shame in the public display of the naked body. For the Greeks, the body was the dwelling place of the spirit. Hence, there could be no shame in the body, for that would amount to shame in the temple of the spirit. The ideal of beauty was a masculine one.

> "What do you think of the young man, Socrates?" asked Khairephon. "Doesn't he have a handsome face?"
> "Marvelously so!" I said.
> "Well," he said, "if he'll only take his cloak off, you'll forget he has a face at all, he's so overwhelmingly beautiful to look at." (Plato, *Charmides*, 54 cd.)

Numerous works of art, including vases and sculpture, portray not only the naked form but even various sexual activities, including homosexuality.

There is, for example, a famous story about Zeus and his abduction of Ganymede, a young Trojan prince. Innumerable works of Greek art depict this event with Zeus disguised as an eagle to sweep away his beloved. Zeus' original attraction to Ganymede was a uniquely physical one, for Ganymede was supposedly the most beautiful youth alive. And Zeus, though he had numerous affairs with gods and mortals while married to the goddess Hera, selected Ganymede to be his cupbearer and hence become immortal. Homosexual themes appear in the stories of other gods as well. Poseidon (the god of the sea) had his own male lover—Pelops; Apollo (the god of healing) had his Hyacinthus; and Pan (the god of flocks and shepherds) had his Cyparissus. Indeed, love and lust—heterosexual as well as homosexual—are frequent motives for Olympian gods and goddesses.

The Greeks explained many natural phenomena by love affairs between the gods. Hades' abduction of Persephone, for example, is the explanation for the changing of the seasons. A love affair between Hermes and Aphrodite produced a boy, Hermaphrodites. When the handsome youth did not return the love of the fountain nymph Salamacis, the gods answered her prayers and her body was fused with his, thereby making him of both sexes. Hesiod described Eros, the god of love, as capable of subduing both gods and mortals.

Greek cosmology abounds with stories of the love and loyalty men feel for each other: Damon and Pythias, Theseus and Pirithous, Orestes and Pylades, Talos and Rhadamanthus, Harmodius and Aristogiton. In the city of Thebes, male homosexuality was regarded as an expression of "comradeship of arms" among noble warriors. Heracles (Hercules) was said to have numerous male lovers.

> The son of Amphitryon [Hercules], with heart of bronze, he that stopped the wild beast's onset, loved a lad, beautiful Hylas—Hylas of the braided locks, and he taught him all things as a father teaches a child, all whereby he himself became a wealthy man and renowned in minstrelsy. Never was he apart from Hylas—and all this that the lad might be fashioned to his mind, and might drive a straight furrow, and come to the true measure of man. (Theocritus, *Hylas*.)

The most famous of all these stories was that of Achilles and Patroclus. Patroclus was killed by Hector in the Trojan War and Achilles was completely grief-stricken at his death, "sobbing out his noble heart." "I will kill the destroyer of him I loved, then I will accept death when it comes." "O dearest of friends, for want of you I cannot eat, I cannot drink." (Homer, *Iliad*, Book 24, 31-45, and Book 18, 78-126.)

Sexual and affectional practices of the gods were reflected in Greek culture. Sexual relationships between men, often older and younger, were common in this period. In fact, any young boy who did not have a lover was disgraced. This relationship was a crucial part of the younger man's maturation process. To be loved was honorable, for it implied that one was worthy to die for in battle. A similar pattern existed at this time in the city of Sparta, where the lover was called the "Inspirer" and the beloved the "Hearer." The lover taught, the hearer learned. In this way, traditions were handed down and preserved. These relationships were strengthened by daily association and were tolerated as long as they did not threaten the family. Gradually, the younger men would be initiated into the social activities of the older man: the club, the gymnasium, and the banquet.

It is fairly well known that homosexuality was common in ancient Greece. Indeed, we know that it was widespread by the early sixth century B.C.E. (Before the Common Era.) We have many varied kinds of evidence for such a conclusion, including:

> ...primitive graffiti on the rocks of Thera, a wall-painting in a tomb at Paestum, scurrilous political jokes and slanders, Plato's formulation of an ideal philosophical education, and the products of ancient research into the institutions of Crete. (Dover, p. 2.)

Though the laws relating to homosexuality are somewhat ambiguous, we have evidence to infer that ancient Greece was an erotophilic (sex-positive) culture (at least for free *males*) which viewed both homosexuality and heterosexuality as appropriate and equally satisfying forms of sexual expression. Greek authors seem to suggest that sexual desires are flexible, that homosexual and heterosexual attractions are equally tempting. Plato's *Laws*, for example, speaks of an Olympian hero who "never touched a woman, nor a boy either, in the whole period when he was at the peak of his training" (840a). Indeed, many maintained that male homosexual love was the highest form of all relationships.

These tendencies were furthered by the ancient Greek educational system, which emphasized the bond between the older male teacher and the younger male. Girls were excluded from this system, as its sole purpose was to develop and promote the qualities of maleness desirable for citizenship. The admiration and respect of the younger partner for the older, coupled with the older's desire to gain the reverence and affection of the younger, were seen as the best stimulus to learning. The family was virtually ignored in this process; fathers paid little attention to their children, and mothers were responsible only for the care of babies and girl-children. Many of Plato's dialogues about Socrates unabashedly refer to romantic relationships between older philosophers and their younger students. This sort of love

> ...springs from the heavenly goddess, who firstly has had no share of the female, but only of the male; next, she is the elder, and has no violence in her; consequently, those inspired by this love turn to the male, because they feel affection rather for what is stronger and has more mind. (Plato, 1952, p. 79.)

Similarly, Plato was lover to his student Alexis, and Aristotle to his pupil Hermias.

Nonetheless, it would be a mistake to assume that this was the only expression of homosexuality which occurred in ancient Greece. Vase paintings, for example, depict what appear to be sexual liaisons between men of approximately the same age. Since there was no word at that time for the homosexual or homosexuality, today's translations must interpret the sometimes poetic, often fragmentary, information we do have. And some commentators now think that the word for "boy," once assumed to refer to a much younger man, might simply be an affectionate term for "beloved" without any necessary relation to age.

Though it was common for a boy to engage in sexual relations with his teacher and even for soldiers to be lovers, one should not assume that ancient Greek society gave wholehearted approval to all expressions of same-sex attraction. After the age of nineteen or so, the young man was expected to marry and establish a family. Those who did not, or who continued to engage in homosexual relations exclusively, were subject to ridicule or worse. In addition, exclusive sexual passivity in men was met with criticism and at times treated severely. Men who practiced passive homosexual sex exclusively were, for example, thrown out of the army, since such behavior was seen as a reflection of a lack of virility (behaving like a woman?). Finally, rape of a free boy/young man (no such sanctions existed for conduct with slaves) was harshly punished, and male prostitution (again, by citizens) was condemned severely. Gifts were permissible, but they had to be given in a spirit of generosity and not for purchase of sexual favors. Any citizen who sold himself for sex was banned from the exercise of his civil rights:

> ...because the legislator considered that one who had been a vendor of his own body for others to treat as they pleased would have no hesitation in selling the interests of the community as a whole. (Dover, p. 20.)

But this should not be taken to be a condemnation of homosexuality *per se*:

> To be in love with those who are beautiful and chaste I define as an emotion experienced by a soul which is affectionate and sympathetic; but gross misbehavior for monetary payment is the act of a *hubristes* and uneducated man. And in my view it is honorable to be the object of eros without being corrupted, but disgraceful to have prostituted oneself through greed for payment. (Quoted in Dover, p. 47.)

Some scholars have suggested that Greek attitudes toward homosexuality may be related to that society's treatment of women. In Greek mythology, for example, it is Pandora—the Greek equivalent of Eve—who unleashes suffering and death onto the world. In Homer's day (850? B.C.E.) a woman had considerable social freedom within the home, but her position depended upon her husband's success as a warrior and on his ability to maintain his position. The consequences of his failure were slavery or starvation or both. During the 5th and 6th centuries B.C.E., some of the aristocracy's freedom to acquire wives and concubines was restricted. Following Athens' defeat by Sparta in the Peloponnesian War (431-404 B.C.E.) and a plague, both of which took the lives of many Athenian citizens, a "committee of thirty" from the conquering city of Sparta took control of the Athenian government. This dictatorship was ousted after three years of rule, and the emerging democracy of Athens anxiously sought to restore stability and moral order. It became important that not a breath of suspicion fall upon young women and wives, and they were secluded from even male members of the family.

The separation of the sexes was spatially emphasized. While men spent most of their day in public areas such as the marketplace and the gymnasium, respectable women remained at home. In contrast to the admired public buildings, mostly frequented by men, the residential quarters of Classical Athens were dark, squalid, and unsanitary.

Women stayed at home not only because their work did not allow them much chance to get out but because of the influence of public opinion. (Pomeroy, pp.79-80.)

Even the architecture of the home reinforced the separate spheres of men and women.

Women usually inhabited the more remote rooms, away from the street and from the public areas of the house. If the house had two stories, the wife along with female slaves lived upstairs. The sexes were separated to restrain the household slaves from breeding without the master's permission. (Ibid.)

Generally, women were viewed to be intellectually and morally inferior to men, useful for having children but not suitable to be men's companions. As Greek writer Xenophon put it:

Surely you do not suppose that lust provokes men to beget children, when the streets are full of people who will satisfy the appetites, as are the brothels? No, it is clear that we select for wives the women who will bear us the best children, and then we marry them to raise a family. (Xenophon, II, 2, 4.)

Women were married off as early as the age of fourteen, and there was often a considerable age gap between husband and wife. As a result of this as well as the segregation of the sexes, spouses usually had little in common. Indeed, the Greek philosopher Aristotle, in discussing the various types of friendship, does not even mention husbands and wives. Though Plato, in his picture of the ideal city-state in The Republic, urges equal education for women and men, that view was very much the exception in his day. Aristotle, for example, puts women in the same ethical category as children and barbarians, arguing that women, though they have the potential to think rationally, lack the will to act on reason. Any love for a woman that extended past lust was considered madness. What we now call romantic love was believed by the Greeks to be reserved to the male sex. Indeed, the idea of behaving too passionately toward one's wife was shocking to the Greeks. Sex with one's wife was a debt, not an act based on love. Ironically, some philosophers condemned heterosexual sex precisely because it was "natural"—that is, the path taken by non-human animals who do nothing but pursue bodily plea-sures and procreate the species.

Little is known about lesbianism in this period. Plutarch observed that female homosexuality was common at this time, at least in Sparta; but there are few literary references to lesbianism, probably because there were almost no women writers during this period. Sappho, the earliest and most famous of the few female Greek poets, extolled the virtues of love between women. Though only one complete poem of hers survives, the fragments of her works glorify sensual pleasure and love between women. Indeed, the word "lesbian" derives from the fact that Sappho was a native of the city of Mytilene on the island of Lesbos.

The Break with Hedonism.   Not all of Greek thought was as sex-positive as the philosophy of *hedone*. Another current in Greek thought is now referred to as *dualism*, the view that the world is divided into two opposing forces: the spiritual and the material. This duality is also reflected within each male and female between the higher and the lower nature. The higher nature (the soul) is imprisoned within the lower nature (the flesh). The goal of humanity is salvation, and this salvation occurs by allowing the soul to escape from the domination of the flesh. Dualism often viewed sex negatively for this reason. In fact, Socrates characterized the body as a "prison"; death is liberation from that prison, and philosophy is a preparation for death.

A major representative of this dualistic world-view was Pythagoras, a near-mythological figure who allegedly lived during the 6th century B.C.E. The Pythagoreans were members of a minority cult who believed that the universe was divided into two opposing principles: Unlimited Breadth and the Limit. All phenomena fit into one of these two catego-ries, as, for example:

The Limit	Unlimited Breadth
light	dark
odd	even
one	many
right	left
male	female
resting	moving
straight	curved
good	bad
square	oblong
better	worse
superior	inferior

This grouping of male with "right," "good," "better," and "superior" versus female with "dark," "bad," "worse," and "inferior" had a great impact on Western civilization's view of both women and sex.

The Pythagoreans, like other dualists, believed that the soul was imprisoned in the body; one's purpose was to keep the soul pure. The Pythagoreans further developed and refined dualistic thought: the body was governed by evil passions called the "Furies"; salvation of the soul could only be achieved through *katharsis*—a purification that brings about spiritual renewal or release through tension—which required observance of certain taboos so that practitioners could improve and save their souls. Celibacy was encouraged as part of this process of purification, with marriage and procreation viewed as lesser duties.

Empedocles (5th century B.C.E.) carried Pythagorean ideas to their logical extreme and condemned any and all sexual intercourse. Another Pythagorean, Democritus (5th century B.C.E.), condemned men who were "masters of cities but slaves to women."

Plato (420?-347 B.C.E.), a pupil of Socrates (470?-399 B.C.E.), one of the most well-known of the dualists, argued that the senses were always inaccurate, and that the body could not be trusted. "True" reality could not be discovered through the senses, but only through the mind and soul. Learning, for Plato, is simply a process of recalling knowledge which the soul has retained from past lives and experiences but forgotten after birth.

Plato also viewed love in dualistic terms: the high, lofty, ideal, and sacred love on the one hand and the profane, physical, and sensual love on the other. Yet, unlike the Pythagoreans, Plato did not argue that the ideal had to be pursued to the exclusion of the physical. Instead, Plato likened sacred love and profane love to two winged steeds, driving a chariot, one aiming ever upward toward the heavens and the other to the basic elements of life here below. The perfect charioteer would control these opposing forces in such a way that they would work in harmony with one another. In the *Symposium*, for example, Plato states that a male youth has no greater blessing than a virtuous older male lover and that the strongest army in the world should be made up of male youths and their male lovers. But he rejects sexual interest in young boys, as it is not clear how they "will turn out" in terms of virtues and vices. He adds that the relationship between a male youth and an older male is made good by the fact that the love between the two is real (the dualistic belief in sacred love) and not the product of an older man frightened over the loss of money, wealth, or political power, or of a younger man willing to sleep with anyone in order to achieve money, wealth, or political power. Plato acknowledges that in some parts of Greece homosexual relations were prohibited, and that even in Athens, depending on the view of the family involved, a homosexual relationship might be extolled or be something that should be stamped out. Finally, he admits that often youths who prefer homosexual relations marry and beget children only because of the compulsion of law.

Zeno (340-265 B.C.E.), the founder of Stoicism, refined and modified dualistic Pythagoreanism. The Stoics acknowledged that people do in fact live in the real world and not that of the Ideal, and that instincts and emotions were not necessarily antagonistic to right living provided they were kept in submission to a ruling principle. The Stoic watchwords were "nature, virtue, decorum, and freedom from excess." Sex to the Stoics was not bad in itself, since reproduction represented not just a perpetuation of the body but also of the soul. Nevertheless, anything that threatened reason—and this included sex—was suspect. Vigilance was necessary because immoderation in bodily activities made males and females slaves to their bodies and distracted them from philosophic contemplation. It was these minority views, in particular Dualism and Stoicism, that would ultimately be incorporated into the emerging Judaic and Christian world views.

The Romans

The early Romans borrowed much of Greek civilization, including much of Greek culture and religion and many of its attitudes toward sexuality. Like the Greeks, they viewed sexuality as a source of great pleasure, with apparently little moral judgment attached. There is a common misconception that the "fall of Rome" was a result of the prevalence and acceptance of homosexuality. In fact, the toleration of homosexuality was widespread during the early days of the Republic and continued through the height of the Roman Empire. It was only in the final stage of the Empire that repressive laws on homosexuality were enacted:

> ...some [claim] that it was homosexuality and general immorality which *caused* the decline of Rome, others that such sexual license was a concomitant of imperial decadence.... This picture is at variance with the facts. Indeed, insofar as it is due to a projection of the personal standards of imperial writers, it suggests, if anything, a tightening of morality under the Empire. (Boswell, p. 71.)

The Romans borrowed a good deal of their cosmology from their Greek counterparts. Even the Roman gods were virtually identical to the Greek gods, with the only change being their Latin names. Zeus, for example, became Jupiter, Hera became Juno, Poseidon became Neptune. And the Romans seemed also to share with the Greeks a love of art for art's sake as well as an admiration for the male physical form. But there were some differences between the two cultures, including their educational systems and the position of women in society.

Roman attitudes toward sexual matters tended to be more concerned with protecting property rather than promoting certain moral principles. That is, male Romans sought to ensure that their rights over their wives and children were not violated, that their "legitimate" children married into situations that would increase their wealth or prestige, and that they themselves avoided any overt violation of the rights of other male Roman citizens. Marriage, at least for women, was arranged by their fathers and could be dissolved by them; amicable divorce was common. The concept of fidelity applied only to married and marriageable women since it was only in their case that the male's proprietary interest in legitimate succession was of concern. The extensive and pervasive system of slavery and the widespread and legal system of female and male prostitution meant that male Romans had many sexual outlets available to them. What was important for Romans was to respect married women, virgins, and freeborn men.

The Roman system of education had different goals and was organized differently from that in ancient Greece. Rome saw education as a means of transmitting facts and customs from generation to generation rather than a dynamic questioning of facts and values. It was also seen as a means of control in that children were to be taught respect for their ancestors and how to develop the skills to become good citizens. In ancient Greece, the influence of the mother over her male children was low, education took place outside of the home, and fathers abdicated their role as educator to the teacher. In Rome, it was felt that the best education took place in the home. Even at the height of the empire when the custom of educating children at school was well-established, debate still continued over the merits of home education. Mother, as opposed to a slave or others, was to take major responsibility for early childhood education. Thus, her influence over male and female education lasted a lifetime. Father, as opposed to an outsider, was viewed as the male child's true teacher, and fathers took this responsibility as a duty. Furthermore, the outside teacher was expected to behave as if he were the child's father, not lover. These differences probably resulted in differing attitudes toward homosexuality.

Nonetheless, evidence of toleration of homosexuality during the Republic and early Empire is widespread. Polybius (205?-125? B.C.E.), for example, writing during the heyday of the Republic, criticized the lack of moderation in sexual matters of young men in Rome, since nearly all of them were having affairs with courtesans or other young men; but disapproval based on gender was not implied. Rather, Polybius criticized the fiscal extravagance of the "many men who have spent a talent [equivalent to approximately $2,500] for a male lover or 300 drachmas for a jar of caviar from the Black Sea." (Boswell, p. 72.) In addition, Catullus (84?-54? B.C.E.) and other writers of erotic literature treated homosexual love with absolute candor and complete moral indifference. Latin poets made a point of writing hymns to *both* sorts of love; in fact, a favorite theme of light literature was to describe and compare the pleasures of the two. Marriage contracts frequently specified that the husband would have "neither concubine nor catamite [male lover]" (Veyne, p. 29), implying that both attractions were equally tempting and equally wrong.

Under the reign of the emperor Augustus (27 B.C.E.-14 C.E.), Virgil, Tibullus, Horace, and Ovid all wrote of erotic love (or physical acts) between men and men, and women and women without the slightest hint that such might be suspect. Ovid (43 B.C.E.-18 C.E.) mentions two girls, Iphis and Ianthe, who loved each other and were even engaged to marry (*Metamorphoses*, 12:171-535). The god Isis later changed Iphis into a man. The epigrammatist Martial (40?-102 C.E.) mentions by name numerous prominent citizens who had engaged in homosexual affairs, often listing their partners, and mentions having engaged in such affairs himself. In addition, he tells of a woman, Bassa, who was always surrounded by women and whose "monstrous lust imitates a man." (*Epigrammata* 7:67, 70.) Ptolemy refers to "tribates" who even designated their patrons as lawful wives. (*Tetrabiblos* 3.14, 4.5.) During Augustus' reign the government taxed homosexual prostitution and even accorded boy prostitutes a legal holiday. And Gibbon observed in his *History of the Decline and Fall of the Roman Empire* that, of the first fifteen emperors, Claudius was the only one whose taste in love was entirely heterosexual.

It is probably a mistake, though, to suggest that the ancient Romans (and Greeks) were indulgent toward homosexuality. Rather, they did not treat it as a separate problem. Those who were contemptuous of passion urged fellow citizens to repudiate the appeal of boys and women but they did not doubt that such natural attractions existed. When the Romans used the word "unnatural," what they usually referred to was a lack of self-discipline or overly contrived conduct. What they *did*, however, distinguish was not heterosexuality and homosexuality, but activity and passivity in sexual relations as well as the social status of the participants. The writer Artemidorus, for example, accepts "relations that conform with normal behavior," which include relations with one's wife, mistress, or male or female slave; but "to let oneself be buggered by one's own slave is not right. It is an assault on one's person and leads to one being despised by one's slave." (*Onirocritica*, pp. 89-89.) The *Lex scantinia* (149 B.C.E.) made no mention of homosexuality or heterosexuality, but rather protected virgins and free-born youths alike from coercive sex. It was considered disgraceful for a Roman citizen to be the passive agent of someone else's pleasure. This attitude is not so unlike that toward homosexuality in many European and Latin American countries (and in prisons as well), where one is not even considered a homosexual so long as one plays the active role.

After the 1st century C.E. the Roman army became made up primarily of non-Romans, and after the 2nd century it became predominantly non-Italian. The Roman elite became exhausted by the 2nd century, and by the 3rd and 4th centuries, as a result of political instability, economic change, and a lower birthrate, a large number of Rome's noble families were essentially wiped out. Increasingly, even the Roman emperors themselves were from the non-Italian parts of the Empire. By the middle of the 3rd century, a majority of officers in the Roman army were German, and the army ceased to be Roman in all respects except name.

The provincials who came to Rome during this period brought many of their beliefs with them, some of which related to homosexuality. The beginnings of Roman intolerance toward homosexuality and a growing sexual conservatism may be traced to the 3rd century C.E., when a series of laws were enacted regulating various aspects of homosexual relations ranging from statutory rape of a minor to male prostitution to same-sex marriage. Homosexual acts not covered by these laws remained legal until the 6th century C.E., when homosexual relations were categorically prohibited by Roman law for the first time. The influence of Christianity, combined with social and political instability around this time, worked toward a growing intolerance of same-sex sexual practices. By the 4th century C.E. there were reduced freedoms for Romans, and many citizens could no longer choose their religion, occupation, or place of residence. The Catholic Church, as the one organized institution to survive Rome's decay, incorporated these increasingly restrictive policies—including those related to sexual practices—into its doctrine. It is not completely clear why such changes occurred, but many more writers during this time criticized the hedonism of the Greeks and the Romans and began to classify certain forms of sexual practices as morally objectionable.

For example, Philo (1st century C.E.), a Stoic and Alexandrian Jew, went so far as to say that married couples who engaged in sex without a desire to procreate were like "pigs or goats" in quest of sexual enjoyment. Similarly, men who mated with barren women were condemned. Predictably, all kinds of non-procreative sex—including homosexuality—were condemned. Philo argued that the original sin of Adam and Eve was the result of sexual desire, and that such pleasure was "the beginning of wrongs and violation of the law," and that for the sake of sex, man had exchanged a life of immortality and bliss for one of mortality and wretchedness. Since Philo associated the fall of man with sex, and since males usually equated sex with women, Philo could logically and easily blame women for all of mankind's misfortune. Philo, in conformity with dualistic thought, saw women as embodiments of sense perception and passivity which man had to give up to achieve salvation. He particularly condemned male homosexuality because such actions enslaved the person to irrational passion and infected them with the female disease.

> In former days the very mention of it was a great disgrace, but now it is a matter of boasting not only to the active but to the passive partners, who habituate themselves to endure the disease of effemination, let both body and soul run to waste, and leave no member of their male sex-nature to smoulder.... These persons are rightly judged worthy of death by those who obey the law, which ordains that the man-woman who debases the sterling coin of nature should perish unavenged.... And the lover of such may be assured that he is the subject of the same penalty. (Quoted in Bullough, p. 169.)

One of Philo's objections was that homosexual sex was a violation of nature, in which the male homosexual lets

> ...the deep-soiled and fruitful fields lie sterile, by taking steps to keep them from bearing, while he spends his labor night and day on soil from which no growth at all can be expected. (*Ibid.*)

These views were to have a great impact on Christianity in general, and the thought of St. Paul in particular.

The Early Greeks and Romans: A Final Note

Though early Greek and Roman civilizations are often cited as being more open and accepting of great diversity in sexual practices, they were not entirely sex-positive cultures. Indeed, many of their writers viewed sex as dangerous, debilitating, and possibly fatal. Women held an inferior position to men in most cases, and women's sexuality was hardly considered at all. We know very little about lesbianism, other than the fragments we have of Sappho.

Yet Greek and Roman civilization did appear to judge heterosexuality and homosexuality in similar ways. Those writers who extolled the pleasures of love and sensuality seem not to distinguish the pleasures of same-sex from heterosexual love; indeed, there was an ongoing, somewhat playful debate over which was superior. Similarly, those writers who disdain the pleasures "of the flesh" are as critical of heterosexual as homosexual sex; yet such writers never doubt the appeal or the commonness of same-sex attractions.

Finally, the Greek slogan "nothing to excess" probably served to caution against sexual immoderation of all sorts. We still have no definite idea why the ancient Greeks and Romans tolerated homosexuality to the extent that they did, or why that eventually changed.

It is important, though, to recognize that the writings we have from this period are almost exclusively authored by males who were all aristocratic and highly educated. Hence, they represent a very small minority of the culture. As a result, these works do not reflect a full range of the thinking of the time. And, even given that, they are very difficult to interpret and at times even contradictory. How do we read these writings? Are they descriptions of how male aristocrats lived? How male aristocrats thought they should live? Would like to live? Would like to imagine people might live? What we *do* know is that the developing Christian Church adopted many of their ideas about sexual practices from the later Greek and Roman period. Thus, these views were to have a major impact on Western civilization.

Judaism

Hear, O Israel; the Lord our God is one: And thou shalt love the Lord thy God with all thy heart, and with all thy soul, and with all thy might. (Deut. 6: 4-5.)

Today, there are about 14 million Jews in the world, tracing their history back at least 4000 years. They live in all parts of the world, though about a quarter now reside in Israel. Judaism is one of the oldest of the great world religions, and many of the teachings of Christianity and Islam come directly from Judaism.

Unlike many great religions, Judaism has no one towering founding figure despite the importance of certain individuals to the faith. Abraham, though, who led the first Hebrews from the land between the Tigris and the Euphrates Rivers into Canaan, is considered the "father of the Hebrew people."

The Jews were a nomadic people whose lives could not be dependent on place; as a result, they gave great emphasis to portable forms of creative expression—in particular, their beliefs, ideas, and religious rituals. To the Jewish people, Abraham is the "man of faith," the first patriarch whose belief in one Supreme Being became the basis for Judaism. Such a belief was controversial for its time; indeed, we are told that Abraham's father was an idol-maker by profession, and that one day as a youth, Abraham, in his father's absence, smashed all the idols.

Later, Moses—the "law-giver"—led the Israelites out of slavery from Egypt, organizing these semi-nomadic tribes into the worship of one God. After a few centuries in Israel, this land was conquered and they were dispersed. But, by then, the tribal deity had become a cosmic deity, a God who transcended nature. Unlike the gods of, for example, the Egyptians, who were portrayed as animals, the God of the Hebrew people was considered to be unrepresentable. In contrast to the Greeks, who valued reason and sensuality, Judaism has as its basis an emphasis on reason and revelation. Indeed, the cardinal principle of Judaism is the affirmation, or prayer:

Hear, O Israel, the Lord our God is one....

It is called the *Sh'ma*, from its first word, meaning "Hear!"

The basic principles of Judaism are found in the *Torah*, or "Law." Originally, Torah referred to the Ten Commandments, and later to the five "Books of Moses" (Pentateuch). Now, it includes all of the Old Testament, and the whole of the sacred tradition from Biblical times to the present. This includes the *Talmud*, which is the interpretation of Biblical commandments and also deals with many fields of knowledge. Torah contains 613 *Mitzvot*, or Commandments (248 positive and 365 negative) to guide the Jewish people through life.

In order to understand the principles of Judaism, in particular those in reference to sexual practices, it is essential to know something of the historical context in which those principles evolved. Such an approach is not meant to discount the significance of those beliefs, but only to suggest that their origin is, at least in part, dependent on social circumstances. As Albert Einstein has put it:

Concepts that have proved useful in the constitution of an order of things readily win such authority over us that we forget their earthly origins and take them to be changeless data. (Einstein, quoted in Schlipp.)

In particular, it is noteworthy that Judaism was in a struggle to distinguish itself from other cultures and religions—in particular, Greek, Roman, Canaanite, and Egyptian. One way to insist on the distinction was to reject the polytheism of competing world views, with their accompanying idol-worship. Another was to adopt a distinct set of ethical principles which served to remind followers of their "special calling."

Faced with disease, death, and scarcity all around them, the Israelites had an overwhelming need to propagate in order for them to survive. Yet they denounced the "unnatural lusts" and immodest behavior of their pagan neighbors. The ancient Hebrew peoples rejected the Greek idea of sexuality as an end in itself, and instead linked sex with procreation. In addition, they denounced the nudity so common in Greek and Roman culture, maintaining that nakedness is shameful and the functions of the sexual organs obscene. The story of Adam and Eve addresses mythically this issue of shame, and the "forbidden fruit" from the tree of knowledge may be said to represent sexual pleasure or knowledge of sexual behavior.

The Israelites viewed themselves as God's chosen children, and urged a separation from all pagans, based on sanctity and holiness. Circumcision, for example, is said to be a symbolic act representing a covenant between the Hebrews and God. Exodus 19.6 describes the Israelites as a nation of priests, in which every member must live as if he or she has a sacred trust. To make this more concrete for each member, a number of regulations guide daily practices, including restrictions on dress, length and style of hair, dietary habits, marriage laws, even toilet functions. Distinctions, then, are of paramount importance; any ambiguity, as it directly threatens group cohesiveness, is rejected. Fields cannot be sown with two types of seeds, yokes cannot be harnessed with two kinds of animals, and clothes are not to be made with cloth composed of two kinds of thread. Similar regulations occur regarding other practices. Transvestitism, for example, which blurs the distinction between males and females, is condemned. (Deut. 22:5.)

In addition, there are clear and distinct rules for men and women. Women are to be subservient to their husbands. Only sexual intercourse in the "missionary position" (man on top, facing woman) is acceptable. The woman's role in conception was not understood, and it was believed that male sperm was, in fact, human life, only to be incubated within the woman. So bestiality, masturbation, oral sex, and *coitus interruptus* were considered akin to murder. The Canaanites, it was argued, were expelled from their lands because of their forbidden sexual acts.

> You shall not make yourselves unclean in any of these ways; for in these ways the heathen, whom I am driving out before you, made themselves unclean. This is how the land became unclean, and I punished it for its iniquity so that it spewed out its inhabitants. (Leviticus 18: 24-26.)

> Jewish sexual mores were not always this strict.

> There were such extremes as male and female sacred prostitution (fees donated to the Temple as a means of absolution), the introduction of young men to the sexual religious exaltations of orgasm within the Temple, and ceremonial mouth-genital contacts between priests and worshippers. (Tripp, p. 5.)

No one knows why all this changed, but it is likely that more severe restrictions were imposed in an attempt to distinguish Judaism from neighboring views.

With these considerations in mind, it is not surprising to find condemnations of same-sex sexual relations in the Old Testament. Yet, in fact, there are very few references to homosexuality there. Indeed, the Bible says nothing about homosexuality *per se* as a sexual orientation, but refers only to certain kinds of acts. Three specific references from the Old Testament are usually cited in relation to homosexuality:

Thou shalt not lie with mankind, as with womankind: it is an abomination. (Leviticus 18: 22.)

If a man also lie with mankind, as he lieth with a woman, both of them have committed an abomination: they shall surely be put to death; their blood shall be upon them. (Leviticus 20: 13.)

And the remnant of the Sodomites which remained in the days of his father Asa, he took out of the land. (I Kings 22: 46.)

Though one might interpret these statements as clear-cut condemnations of homosexuality, there is still some disagreement about their real significance. Some commentators point out that the word "homosexuality" is never used in the Bible; in fact, the word "homosexual" did not appear in any translation until 1946; the words "invert" and "intersexual" were commonly used for "homosexual" before that time, yet they were never used in any early translation. Indeed, homosexuality is hardly a major concern of the Bible. The earliest codes of the Old Testament, including the Ten Commandments, make no mention of it. The prophets never refer to it. Even when the subject is considered, the references are short, twice interrelated, and contextually subordinate to other Biblical themes. And, whatever same-sex acts are mentioned, they appear in very negative contexts—for example, with allusions to adultery, violence, and promiscuity. So, some argue, it may be homosexual rape, infidelity, promiscuity, or prostitution that is condemned and not homosexuality *per se*.

The story of the destruction of Sodom is the Biblical passage most frequently cited to justify condemnations of homosexuality. Indeed, the word "Sodomite" is sometimes used interchangeably with the word "homosexual."

But before they lay down, the men of the city, the men of Sodom, both young and old, all the people to the last man, surrounded the house; and they called to Lot, "Where are the men who came to you tonight? Bring them out to us, that we may know them." Lot went out of the door to the men, shut the door after him, and said, "I beg you, my brothers, do not act so wickedly. Behold, I have two daughters who have not known man; let me bring them out to you, and do to them as you please, only do nothing to these men, for they have come under the shelter of my roof." But they said, "Stand back!" And they said, "This fellow came to sojourn, and he would play the judge! Now we will deal worse with you than with them." Then they pressed hard against the man Lot, and drew near to break the door. But the rnen put forth their hands and brought Lot into the house to them, and shut the door. And they struck with blindness the men who were at the door of the house, both small and great, so that they wearied themselves groping for the door. (Genesis 19: 4-11.)

But there are many problems in interpreting this story as an argument for a divine proscription of homosexuality:

- Many early Jews and Christians interpret the sin of Sodom to be that of inhospitality. The Hebrew verb yada ("to know"), for example, is not always used to mean "sexual knowledge of," but may mean "being acquainted with." Indeed, in the Old Testament, out of 943 uses of the word, only 10 refer to the sexual sense. To the modern reader "inhospitality" may not seem to warrant the severity of the punishment meted out by God on Sodom. But, if one recalls that this was an era in which travelers depended for their very survival on strangers' hospitality, the story of Sodom may begin to make more sense.

- Most references to the story of Sodom which appear in later books of the Bible seem to support the view that the sin of Sodom was inhospitality, *not* homosexuality. The following passage from the prophet Ezekiel, for example, seems quite clear on this issue:

This is the very word of the Lord God. Did you not commit all these obscenities, as well as your other abominations? Dealers in proverbs will say of you, "Like mother, like daughter." You are a true daughter of a mother who loathed her husband and children. You are a true sister of your sisters who loathed their husbands and children. You are all daughters of a Hittite mother and an Amorite father. Your elder sister was Samaria, who lived with her daughters to the north of you. Your younger sister, who lived with her daughters to the south of you, was Sodom. Did you not behave as they did, and commit the same abominations? As I live, says the Lord.... This was the iniquity of your sister Sodom: she and her daughters had *pride of wealth and food in plenty, comfort and ease, and yet she never helped the poor and wretched*. They grew haughty and wretched and did deeds abominable in my sight, and I made away with them, as you have seen. (Ezekiel 16: 44-52.) (emphasis added)

- Some have argued that Old Testament condemnations of homosexuality were in fact referring to homosexual temple prostitution, a phenomenon which was apparently common among the Greeks,

Canaanites, and other neighboring groups. These pagan practices frequently involved the depositing of sperm into the ground as part of a fertility ritual, giving seed to the goddess of the earth. But this is no more a condemnation of homosexuality than is criticism of adultery or rape a condemnation of heterosexuality. As one Bible scholar notes:

Let's face it, the Old Covenant religious leader, the priest of the Hebrews, could not possibly conceive of healthy normal, God-centered same-sex relationships—why? These priests had only been exposed to same-sex acts as practiced by their pagan neighbors and that always in association with idolatrous religious worship. To the Jew, and to us as well, such practices were blasphemy. To the Jews, homosexual sexual practices were always associated with temple prostitution and that in extremely perverted forms; hence the only logical conclusion that could be arrived at was that all homosexuality was evil, false, pagan, and against nature and God! (Pattison.)

The story of Sodom specifically, even if one argues that it was about homosexuality, could have been about homosexual rape rather than about homosexuality *per se.*

- Many people have forgotten that, in the story of Sodom, God tells Abraham that he will not destroy the city if Abraham is able to find *ten good men.* If the destruction of Sodom was a result of rampant homosexuality, does this mean that there were fewer than ten non-homosexuals in the entire city?

- Finally, there is an odd incongruity in the standard interpretation of this story. Why is Lot offering to give his virgin daughters to the mob if the mob is made up of homosexual men?

- No other mention of Sodom in the Bible appears in the context of discussions of homosexuality. Jesus himself, in referring to the story of Sodom in the New Testament, supports the view that inhospitality was Sodom's chief vice:

If anyone will not receive you, or listen to what you say, then as you leave that house or that town, shake the dust of it off your feet. I tell you this: on the day of judgment it will be more bearable for the land of Sodom and Gomorrah than for that town. (Matt. 10: 14-15; cf. Luke 10: 10-12.)

Indeed, most current Biblical scholarship acknowledges that Sodom's sin was in being stiff-necked and inhospitable and was unrelated to sex.
Not only do many scholars reject the anti-homosexuality interpretation of the story of Sodom, but some even suggested that the stories of Ruth

and Naomi, and David and Jonathan actually have homosexual sub-themes. Indeed, the words now recited as part of many wedding vows were in fact said by Ruth to Naomi:

> Where you go, I will go, and where you stay, I will stay. Your people shall be my people, and your God my God. Where you die, I will die, and there I will be buried. I swear a solemn oath before the Lord your God: nothing but death shall divide us. (Ruth 1: 16-18.)

And David cries out at Jonathan's death:

> I grieve for you, my brother Jonathan, you were most dear to me, your love was wonderful to me, more than the love of woman. (Samuel II: 1: 26.)

Finally, even if such condemnations of homosexuality exist in the Old Testament, negative attitudes toward homosexuality are not necessarily justified. There is much that is part of the Old Testament that we now disregard due to changes in knowledge, technology, and moral climate. Indeed, if one defends one's anti-homosexuality from a Scriptural perspective, then, to be consistent, one must adopt certain practices and abjure others:

- *Food*: Do not eat the fat of ox, sheep, or goats, (Lev. 7: 23.) All meats must be cooked until well done since it is an abomination to eat the blood of any animal, fish or fowl or beast. (Lev. 7: 26.) Do not eat rabbit and ham, bacon, pork chops, ribs, and other pork products. (Lev. 11: 6-7; Deut. 14: 7-8.) Do not eat lobster, crab, scallops, or shrimp. (Lev. 11: 10, 12; Deut. 14: 19-20.)

- *Hygiene*: Male babies must be circumcised on the eighth day after birth. (Lev. 12: 3.) Women are unclean during menstruation and for seven days thereafter, as is everything they touch, and following the birth of children. (Lev. 12: 6-8, 15: 19.) Semen is unclean, as is everything that it touches, and after a discharge (voluntary or involuntary) a man shall wash himself as well as his clothing and be unclean until the evening of that day. (Lev. 15: 2-12, 16-18.) Hybridization of animals or of crops is condemned (Lev. 19: 19; Deut. 22: 9), as well as wearing garments of cloth made of two kinds of material. (Lev. 19: 19; Deut. 22: 11.) It is an abomination to trim the hair on one's temples or to trim one's beard. (Lev. 19: 28.)

- *Observances*: The Sabbath is to be kept holy, no work is allowed, and this extends not only to the faithful, but to their servants as well. (Lev. 23: 3; Deut. 5: 12.) Those who use the name of God in vain are to be put to death. (Lev. 24: 16.) Land is to lie fallow once every seven years. (Lev. 25: 3-5.)

- *On other faiths*: The faithful are authorized to destroy the temples, altars, and graven images of other gods. (Deut. 12: 2-3.) And if a relative attempts to convert you to serve another god, "you shall not yield to him or listen to him nor shall your eye pity him, nor shall you spare him, nor shall you conceal him; but you shall kill him; your hand shall be first against him to put him to death and afterwards the hand of all the people." (Deut. 13: 8-10.) The faithful are admonished not to turn to wizards or mediums. (Lev. 19: 31; Deut. 18: 10-12.) Furthermore, the faithful are authorized to stone wizards and mediums to death. (Lev. 20: 27.)

- *Charity*: Creditors "at the end of every seven years...shall grant a release. And this is the manner of the release: every creditor shall release what he has lent to his neighbor; he shall not exact it of his neighbor, his brother, because the Lord's release has been proclaimed." (Deut. 15: 1-2.) And the faithful are to maintain the poor and to feed them at no cost. "If there is among you a poor man, one of your brethren, in any of your towns within your land which the Lord your God gives you, you shall not harden your heart or shut your hand against your poor brother, but you shall open your hand to him, and lend him sufficient for his need, whatever it may be." (Deut. 15: 7.) And we should give such freely and not grudgingly. (Deut. 15: 10; Lev. 25: 35-37.)

- *Punishment and war*: The Old Testament does not permit an alternative to capital punishment when an offender kills with premeditation, but (Deut. 19: 11-13) there must be more than one witness to the crime. (Deut. 19: 15.) "A stubborn and rebellious son shall be brought to the authorities and stoned to death." (Deut. 21: 18-21.) The citizens of cities which surrendered during wartime are to be made slaves. (Deut. 20: 10-11.) If a city refuses to surrender and must be captured, then all the males therein are to be put to death without exception. The women, children, and property of captured cities are to be taken as the spoils of war. (Deut. 20: 12-14.) Additionally, a soldier may take a beautiful female captive as a wife and "she shall bewail her father and her mother a full month; after that you may go into her as her husband." (Deut. 21: 13.)

- *Women*: The sons of Jacob kill Shechem for raping their sister, Dinah, but Jacob condemns them for it. (Gen. 34: 1-31.) If a man marries a woman and discovers that she is not a virgin, then "they shall bring out the young woman to the door of her father's house and the men of the city shall stone her to death with stones, because she has wrought folly in Israel by playing the harlot in her father's house, so you shall purge the evil from the midst of you." (Deut. 22: 13-21.) Fornication and adultery are condemned, yet adultery is permitted for married men. (Lev. 20: 10.) An unmarried man who sleeps with an unbetrothed virgin must marry her. (Deut. 22: 28-29.) As for children born out of wedlock: "No bastard shall enter the assembly of the Lord; even to the tenth generation none of his descendants shall enter the assembly of the Lord."

Judaism and Sexuality Today

The early history of Judaism is the history of the survival of very small tribes struggling against external challenges. As the group felt itself to be more threatened, restrictions became even more repressive. Assimilation came to be seen as a threat, so rigid barriers were erected between believers and nonbelievers. For that reason, there was a strong procreative emphasis as well as a denigration of the sex-for-pleasure attitude that was linked with competing views such as those of the Canaanites. The institution of marriage was a crucial one in Judaism. There was no place in society for single people; in fact, a man who continued to put off marriage had to explain himself to the elders of the community. Widows and widowers remarried quickly. Within marriage, though, there was some sexual freedom. The Talmud, for instance, allows sexual intercourse even when the woman is unable to bear children. And it cautions men not to have more than four wives so that they can satisfy them all! In addition, male sperm was viewed to contain the whole of nascent life, leading to condemnations of "wasted seed." Finally, this early society held women in very low regard; for a man to "act like a woman" (sexually or otherwise) was a degradation. Stories in the Old Testament repeatedly reinforce the view that the nature of women is a problematic one. Eve and Delilah are examples of temptresses who bring on man's downfall. Lot's daughters plied him with liquor and then went to bed with him so they could have children. Potiphar's wife, despairing of ever seducing Joseph, accused him of rape. All of this should not be dismissed in considering the widespread condemnations of homosexuality today.

Today, there are many different interpretations within Judaism of the proper attitude toward sexuality. These differences may reflect more general differences within Judaism as to interpretations of the *Torah*.

There are three primary branches to Judaism: Orthodox, Conservative, and Reform. Each differs some in its interpretation of specific laws and practices.

- *Orthodox* Jews advocate strict observance of traditional rituals and customs.
- *Reform* Jews stress the prophetic ideas of the Bible rather than the Law, and have abandoned certain traditional practices which they believe are unsuited to modern life.
- *Conservative* Jews take a middle position between Orthodox and Reform.

Each of these branches has a position on sexual morality in general and homosexuality in particular.

Orthodox Jews generally condemn homosexuality as a sin and a violation of nature. Robert Gordis, for example, likens homosexuality to alcoholism. Though he rejects criminal penalties for homosexuality, he also rejects more liberal pleas for tolerance. Hershel Matt, on the other hand, argues for a more liberal interpretation of the Torah. He suggests that, though the Torah condemns homosexuality, the prohibitions cited there all are related to *choice*. Transgressions may not be punished so severely if there are mitigating circumstances, such as drunkenness, financial duress, threat of torture, physical illness, accident, or insanity.

Though interpretations may differ about the degree of responsibility, all judge the offender more leniently. Real sin, then, involves free choice:

> For one thing, a truly Torah approach, taking seriously the injunction of the Torah tradition not to judge another person until one stands in his place, would acknowledge that no human being is able to know the exact degree of another's freedom; that God alone has the knowledge; that God alone, therefore, has the ability and the right to judge a person's culpability; and that none of us humans, therefore, ought to presume to judge a homosexual or automatically regard a homosexual as a sinner—since, as already implied, sin involves not only overt action but also intention, decision, and responsibility. (Matt., p. 118.)

Homosexuality, for Matt, is not a real choice, and so the Torah may have less stringent application: *"for very many homosexuals the prospects of change to heterosexuality are almost nil."* (Matt, his emphasis, p. 118.) Thus, he urges compassion:

> Furthermore, a Torah approach would look with deep compassion upon the plight of many homosexuals in our society. It would share the anguish of a human being who for years—perhaps since early adolescence—has had to live with a growing sense of being different and "queer"; in constant

fear of being discovered; knowing that, if discovered, he might well be looked down upon as perverted, loathsome, dangerous; with the consequent fear of being mistreated, humiliated, and ridiculed, perhaps blackmailed, excluded or expelled from many types of employment, and denied acceptance and friendship. ("The Lord seeks the pursued" and we should imitate Him in this regard.) (p. 119.)

To do this, our actions must reflect this compassion; he cites as examples of what sorts of actions we might undertake that "we must make a genuine effort to dispel the popular myths and repeal the legal disabilities that have made the life of many homosexuals into a living hell." (Ibid.) Further, he argues that "we should, as Jews, vigorously oppose any legal penalties for such homosexual behavior [between consenting adults]." (Ibid.)

Others urge that faith in Judaism allows for homosexuality, even if it is freely chosen, and that homosexuals need not be "Jewish outcasts":

You may say that there is no room in Judaism for the expression of homophile feelings, that the Torah and rabbis and chochmei Talmud [sages] through the ages have condemned it, if they dealt with it at all. But who among us practices halacha [Jewish law] in all its rulings? Who among us abides by all of our tradition's historic precedents? Who among us does not justify for ourselves our own departures from halacha? Are some departures worse than others? Is an expression of love, if not within a narrow definition, really among the worst of departures? (Anon.)

These three views—that homosexuality is sinful; that homosexuality is "imperfect," yet not freely chosen; and that homosexuality should be judged by the quality of its relationships—find defenders within modern-day Christianity as well.

Islam

By the noonday brightness, and by the night when it darkeneth, thy Lord hath not forsaken thee, neither hath He been displeased. Surely the future shall be better for thee than the past; and in the end He shall be bounteous to thee, and thou shalt be satisfied. Did He not find thee an orphan, and give thee a home; erring, and guided thee; needy, and enriched thee? (Koran, xciii.)

Islam is a religion difficult for those reared in the Judaeo-Christian tradition; though Islam is the West's closest neighbor conceptually as well as geographically, this proximity has not aided in understanding.

Islam is the world's fastest-growing religion. At its height, it stretched from India to western Spain; today it has a powerful presence in Africa, the Middle East, Indonesia, and even North America, where there are more than 6 million Muslims. Mecca, Medina, and Jerusalem are the three holiest Muslim cities. Today, a practicing Muslim expects to make a pilgrimage to Mecca at least once in his or her lifetime; for Muslims, Mecca is the *omphalos* (navel) where the world was born, and hence the holiest spot in creation.

Islam denies the divinity of Jesus, though the Koran, the sacred book of Islam, recognizes him as a prophet. In addition, Islam does not accept the Trinity as usually understood:

> The Quran is the tissue out of which the life of a Muslim is woven; its sentences are like threads from which the substance of his soul is knit.... [It] is the revelation of God and the book in which His message to man is contained. It is the Word of God revealed to the Prophet through the archangel Gabriel. (Nasr, p. 42.)

The prophet of Islam, Muhammed (570-632 C.E.), is revered, but the religion itself is not based on the personality of the founder. Indeed, orthodox Islam has rejected all attempts to exalt Muhammed above humanity. He is viewed as an ordinary person whom God singled out to receive revelations:

> The Prophet is the channel through whom man received a message pertaining to the nature of the Absolute and subsequently the relative, a message which contains a doctrine and a method. Therefore, it is Allah himself who is the central reality of the religion, and the role of the Prophet in Islam and Christ in Christianity are thereby quite different at the same time that naturally as "messengers of God" they also bear similarities to each other. (Nasr, p. 17.)

The guiding principle for Islam is to serve God as though one saw him in front of one. To do this, Islamic religion combines three elements: intelligence, will, and speech, all of which humans have "borrowed" from God. Intelligence for Islam is that which is able to realize that there is only one Absolute Reality (Allah) and that all else is relative. The will is able to choose freely between the true and false, the Absolute and the Relative. There is a common misconception that Islam is a fatalistic religion, but the truth is that free will is just as important to Islam as it is to other major religions. Though only God is absolutely free, humans share in this freedom and bear the responsibility of making choices; but, without this freedom, religious faith is not possible. Finally, speech is "in a sense the external form of what we are inwardly" (Nasr, p. 20), making prayer a central part of Islamic rites.

Unlike Christianity, which in its early days was a minority religion often suppressed by those in power, Islam was a powerful world force even in Muhammed's own time. Indeed, at Muhammed's death in 632, most of Arabia had accepted Islam. One century later, there was Muslim rule in most of Northern Africa, Afghanistan, Iraq, Iran, and eastern India. Often these were the results of military conquests by powerful Muslim armies. Many Jews and Christians welcomed those conquests, as Muslim rule was often more just than Byzantine rule. Muslims also tolerated some other religious views, including Judaism, Christianity, and Zoroastrianism, whose advocates were considered "peoples of the book." As a result, Islamic law often varied from place to place, many times leaving intact the already existing traditional civil and religious rites.

In the early years during and after the conquests, there were regional "schools" of law. Only in the ninth century as a result of the great variation in interpretations of code was any attempt made to synthesize general principles of interpretation. Yet even after this attempt there was never anything resembling, strictly speaking, a code. While members of a particular "school" might generally agree on certain points of law, and while a particular judge's decision in a particular case might be said to be binding, the judgment applied only to that case. Such decisions could set precedents for other cases but would not necessarily.

Thus, it is difficult to pinpoint precisely the Islamic code on a given issue. In addition, like other religions, Islam has various sects which disagree on the interpretation of key religious and secular issues. The *Sunni* sect (today the majority sect compromising approximately 91% of Muslims worldwide) emphasizes strict dogma and practice while believing in the separation of politics and religion. Community as a whole is considered more important than a single leader.

Another Muslim sect, *Shiite*, follows Alī ibn abī Tālib (600-661 C.E.) son-in-law of Muhammed. In contrast to the Sunnis, the Shiite views religion and politics as one. A charismatic leader is venerated. Martyrdom for a political cause is justified as a means to paradise. Today in Iran, Shiites control the government.

The *Sufis* are Islamic mystics and can belong to either sect rather than constituting a separate sect. They reject the "worldliness" of much of the Islamic tradition and focus instead on withdrawal from the world as a means to spiritual purity and piety. The Sufis maintain that riches and prestige are obstacles to real spirituality; further, they seek direct communion of the individual with God, rather than on learned interpretations of religious books.

Despite differences in interpretation, Islam does have a powerful legal tradition. A fundamental concern of Islam is guidance, and the *sharia* (law) is considered the best expression of Qur'anic faith. *Sharia* is viewed in Islam as the pre-eternal divine law from which the law (*figh*) is, derived.

Fiqh is in a sense a reflection of the *sharia* which would only be known, in its entirety and perfection to God. The goal of Islamic lawyers is to provide comprehensive guidance for all life, much as the rabbis' goal is to interpret the Torah for practitioners of Judaism.

This code was separated into two parts: obligations to God and obligations to other human beings. Thus, proper observances of faith and prayer fell into the first category, while precepts of individual and social morality formed the basis of the second.

For Muslims, a dichotomy between secular life and religious life makes no sense. Muhammed, though he frequently left civil society to meditate and pray alone, was very much a member of community and an active participant in it. He was, for example, married (to a fairly wealthy older woman) and had six children. Today, Muslims emphasize the importance of community in a practical, economic sense as well as a spiritual sense. For instance, there is a belief that all people should contribute to the support of the poor (usually widows and orphans), and often Muslims spend one-fortieth of their annual income on almsgiving. This is taken as more than an act of charity; rather it is an act of social responsibility, reminding all that they are members of one family.

Muslims have elaborated five cardinal duties, called "pillars" of the true faith. They are:

- witnessing to faith (proclaiming the creed),
- ritual prayer (*dhikr*: remembrance),
- fasting during the lunar month of Ramadan,
- almsgiving,
- pilgrimage to Mecca.

As Islamic lawyers refined their analysis, they distinguished five types of human actions and objects, which different Islamic sects use in different ways to classify actions.

- those which are obligatory,
- those which are meritorious or recommended,
- those which are forbidden,
- those which are reprehensible,
- those which are indifferent.

Unlike Christianity, the Islamic view of human nature is not based on the notion of sin. Islam does not consider humans "fallen," nor is the error of Adam and Eve believed to have been passed on to future generations. Instead of sin, which implies a deep alienation of humans from God, Islam tends to stress human forgetfulness and weakness, not irrationality. We as humans are prone to a kind of religious amnesia, but the Islamic tradition does not require a concept of redemption in the way that Christianity does. Prayer is the means by which we "remember" God's goodness.

Thus, like other major religions, Islam has specific teachings which prescribe patterns for individual life and create a sense of a single community. The *Sharia* contains general teachings as well as concrete ones, giving "a religious significance to what may appear as the most mundane of activities." (Nasr, p. 94.) The guidelines provide the believer with what in Islam is referred to as the "Straight Path," knowledge of right and wrong; and with free will humans have the capacity to choose right or wrong.

Unlike Christianity, which values celibacy as the paradigmatic expression of spiritual devotion, Islam is opposed to it. Marriage is incumbent upon all who are able to marry. Indeed, the Koran focuses far less on sacrifice and abstinence than does the Bible. Even the creation stories are strikingly different: for the Judaeo-Christian tradition, Adam and Eve's creation is asexual—that is, they come into being through the will of God; the Koran, in contrast, states that human beings were created by God with semen and blood.

The teachings of the *Sharia* emphasize the role of the family as the unity of society, with the father functioning as the *imam* who upholds the tenets of the religion and whose authority symbolizes that of God in the world. Islam, then, is a patriarchal religion.

Where, for Christianity, marriage is preferable only to damnation, Islam allows men up to four wives. Their support is completely his responsibility. Further, differences between men and women are emphasized in Islam:

> Man and woman are not the same; each has particular features and characteristics. Women are not equal to men. But then neither are men equal to women. Islam envisages their roles in society not as competing but as complementary. Each has certain duties and functions in accordance with his or her nature and constitution. (Nasr, p. 112.)

Thus, the asceticism that is central to the early Christian tradition is largely absent in Islam (except for *Sufism*). This may be due, at least in part, to Islam's joining of the sacred and the secular. Allah, according to Islamic tradition, is as near as the pulse at one's throat; everything lives by the will and touch of Allah. Hence, there is no rejection of the secular, even of worldly pleasures. It is interesting to note in this context that the Islamic picture of heaven is not that of an ethereal, wholly spiritual realm, but rather a place full of pleasures, including food, drink, and sex. There are details in the Koran of "maidens restraining their glances, untouched before them by any man or jinn." (55: 55.)

Yet the possibilities for sexual pleasure are not so loudly or clearly expressed for women in Islamic tradition. Though both men and women have the ability to enter Paradise, for example, "men have priority over women, by virtue of what God has endowed to them and by what they spend on women of their wealth." (4: 34.) Women have the right to refuse a proposal of marriage and receive some inheritance rights, but men have more rights than women in divorce. The wife is obliged to obey her husband, who is justified in punishing her if she does not submit to his rule. If, for instance, a husband kills his wife and her lover in the act, he is not punishable. The Koran does not even consider the possibility that women might assume leadership roles in the community or receive an equal education or practice polygamy. A woman's testimony is worth only half a man's in court, since she is not considered reliable. Her main duty is to her husband, on which her entrance into heaven depends; even today, failure to obey her husband can result in her death.

Thus, the Muslim woman lacks the power her male counterpart possesses. The institutions of *purdah* (seclusion and veiling), concubinage, and the harem—probably only fully realized during the Ottoman period—represent powerful restrictions on women's freedom. Women are thought to be less capable of prayer and fasting, critical facets of Muslim worship, since menstruation interferes with concentration.

> It were best for a girl not to come into existence, but being born she had better be married or buried. (Iskander, p. 125.)

In the heavenly garden, every man, in addition to his earthly wife, can expect seventy women who would never be sick, bad-tempered, jealous, menstruating, or pregnant (unless he wished).

For Islam, sex is a joy, a blessing from Allah. Though the primary purpose of marriage is to have children, it is expected that both sexes should enjoy sex.

Traditionally, Islamic scholars regard all heterosexual intercourse between persons not legally married as a sin. But Muslim men may have four wives, and some have even more; many have concubines, who are slaves who cannot legally marry but are used for sexual purposes. And adultery is difficult to prove as a charge; someone accusing another of adultery has to provide four witnesses to the act. If the accuser fails to provide the witnesses then she or he is liable to receive eighty lashes.

The Koran seems not to condemn particular actions. Rather, the chief virtue in Islam appears to be to avoid excess, whether it is in terms of sexual indulgence, charitable contributions, kindness to widows and orphans, or obedience to authority.

Much of traditional Christianity's hostility toward Islam has been in reaction to Islamic sexual attitudes. Anti-Muslim attacks often focused on charges of homosexuality, increasing antagonism toward both the group *and* the sexual practice. In fact, both sides, as might be expected, leveled the same charges at each other. Yet the Koran is ambiguous with respect to homosexuality *per se*.

Koran References to Homosexuality

By Muhammed's day the transgressions which were believed to have brought about the destruction of the city of Sodom, as discussed in the Judaeo-Christian Bible, were widely interpreted as being sexual in nature: in this instance male-male rape. In the Koran Mohammed warns against repeating such transgressions:

> Your Lord is the Mighty One, the Merciful. Lot's people, too, disbelieved their apostles. Their compatriot Lot said to them: "Will you not have fear of Allah? I am indeed your true apostle. Fear Allah then and follow me. I demand of you no recompense for this; none can reward me except the Lord of the Creation. Will you fornicate with males and leave your wives, whom Allah has created for you? Surely you are great transgressors."
> " Lot," they replied, "desist or you shall be banished."
> He said: "I abhor your ways. Lord, preserve me and my kinsfolk from their evil doings."
> We delivered Lot and all his kinsfolk, save for one old woman who stayed behind, and the rest We utterly destroyed. We pelted them with rain, and evil was the rain which fell on those who had been warned.
> Surely in that there was a sign. Yet most of them do not believe. (26:161.)

> And tell of Lot. He said to his people: "Are our blind that you should commit indecency, lustfully seeking men instead of women? Surely you are an ignorant people."
> Yet this was their reply: "Banish the house of Lot from your city. They are men who would keep chaste."
> So We delivered him and all his tribe, except his wife, whom We caused to stay behind, pelting the others with rain; and evil was the rain which fell on those who had been warned. (27:54.)

> And We sent forth Lot to his people. He said to them: "You commit indecent acts which no other nation has committed before you. You lust after men and assault them on your highways. You turn your very gatherings into orgies."
> But his people's only reply was: "Bring down Allah's scourge upon us, if what you say be true."

"Lord," said he, "deliver me from these degenerate men."
And when Our messengers brought Abraham the good news they said: "We are about to destroy the people of this town, for they are wicked men." (29:28.)

Lot, too, was an apostle. We delivered him and all his kinsfolk, except for an old woman who stayed behind, and utterly destroyed the others. You pass by their ruins morning and evening: will you not take heed? (37:133.)

The people of Lot disbelieved Our warning. We let loose on them a stone-charged whirlwind which destroyed them all, except the house of Lot, whom We saved at dawn through Our mercy. Thus We reward the thankful.
Lot had warned them of Our vengeance, but they doubted his warnings. They demanded his guests of him. But We put out their sight and said: "Taste My punishment, now that you have heard My warning." And at daybreak a heavy scourge overtook them. "Taste My punishment, now that you have heard My warning!" (54:33.)

Though Muhammed warns against the *abuse* of sexuality, the Koran does not condemn homosexuality *per se* and does not recommend specific punishments for it. Indeed, the references to the story of Sodom seem to be an illustration of God's power rather than a condemnation of homosexuality. Some Islamic interpreters of the Koran view sodomy as a transgression, but in the Islamic tradition a transgression is a fairly minor violation like not observing certain religious rituals. Among the Sunni sect, for example, the practice of homosexuality was fairly widespread, especially among mystic orders in North Africa.

Islamic Shiite fundamentalists, including Iran's Ayatollah Khomeini, on the other hand, have used the Koran to justify harsh penalties against people engaging in consensual homosexual acts. Such penalties have included torture and death. And there have been many individual cases in Islamic history wherein homosexuality is condemned. The judgments, however, are ordinarily not based upon natural law (as in Christianity) as applied to the act itself. Rather, the judgment was often based on the functioning of the participants. Hence, in such a case, the dominant partner was not on trial, but the receptive partner was condemned. Often the penalty was death.

Yet, in general, Islam has been far more tolerant of homosexuality than Christianity has. Anal intercourse is accepted in Islam, the only restriction being that married women must give permission to their husbands. Women are held to be entitled to sexual satisfaction, and since anal intercourse may fail in this regard, their consent is required. In a society in which women were secluded from men and women could not participate equally with men in everyday affairs, it may be that men's social lives revolved around other men. And, with polygamy and concubinage, there may not have been enough women for men. Extramarital sex was severely disapproved of, yet there had to be powerful evidence to prove such a charge. Boswell suggests that homosexual practices were tolerated in Islam so long as the participants had heirs and did not "succumb to excess." In fact, one can find positive references to homosexual love in the Islamic tradition:

> The least of him is the being free from monthly courses and pregnancy.
> (Abu Nawas, quoted in Bullough, p. 228.)

Further, in Islamic Sufi literature homosexual eroticism was a major metaphorical expression of the spiritual relationship between man and God, and much Persian fiction and poetry used same-sex relationships as examples of moral love.

There are few references to lesbianism in the Islamic tradition, but those that do exist appear to be harsher in judgment than the references to males.

The Arabic language contains a huge vocabulary of gay erotic terms, with dozens of terms just to describe male prostitutes. There is an entire genre of Arabic literature in which debates over the merits of male homosexual love are debated. And almost all of the authors wrote standard religious treatises as well as homosexual love poetry. (Boswell, p. 197.)

Islam and Sexual Practice

It is, of course, impossible to know precisely to what extent practice reflects theory, particularly when we are speaking of an era hundreds of years past. Further, it is difficult to assess how reliable reports about a given culture might be, particularly when those reports emerge from hostile ethnic and religious groups. Finally, one should be aware that Islam is not a homogeneous philosophy or religion or set of practices. Rather, it has varied and continues to vary greatly, depending on its cultural milieu. There are, though, several points about Islam that one can make with some degree of confidence.

For one, Islam, because it represents a secular as well as religious law, has enormous power, cultural as well as military. For Islam, the way to realize oneself is to follow community law. And, perhaps because the rule of Islam is that of a dominant rather than minority religious view, there is some room within that doctrine for tolerance, even of other religions such as Judaism and Christianity.

In addition, Islamic faith placed far less emphasis on sin than did either Christianity or Judaism. There were no lost souls in Islam, for there was always some possibility of repentance. And, while waiting for Paradise, one might work the land, trade, fight, and enjoy the many pleasures of the senses, as long as one was not diverted from worship of God.

Every religion has regulations for its practitioners, rules which provide guidance for religious worship and daily life. The Islamic faith is no different. But it is, unlike some of the major world religions, a view which can be characterized as *erotophilic*. Though it by no means treats the sexes equally, it views expressions of sexuality as gifts from Allah. And the segregation of the sexes coupled with women's inferior status may lead to a greater tolerance of homosexuality. This is a characteristic unusual in other monotheistic views.

Christianity

Do not conform to the standards of the world around you, but *change your attitudes* through a *complete renewal of mind,* that you may discern the will of God and know what is good, desirable, and right.... Just as there are numerous parts in the human body, all with different functions, so too we—though many—form one body in Christ and belong individually as members to each other and yet have *different personal attributes* according to the favor God has bestowed on us.... Love each other with the affection of sisters and brothers, and have a profound respect for one another.... Treat all people in equal consideration; never be haughty, but go about with humble folk; and under no circumstances allow yourself to become self-satisfied.... Do whatever possible, on your part, to live at peace with everybody.... (Romans 12:2, 4-6, 10, 16, 18.)

For what is a man profited, if he shall gain the whole world, and lose his own soul? (Matthew 16: 26.)

Christianity began as a Jewish sect. It developed from the life and work of Jesus of Nazareth, whom Christianity views as the Messiah: a new beginning for the human race.

The New Testament, the written basis for Christianity, presents Jesus as both the consummation and the transformation of the Torah. The New Testament's Christianity emphasizes *faith* as well as works; further, membership came to all those who would base their lives on Jesus. Unlike traditional Judaism, one did not have to be born into Christianity. Because it was believed that God fulfilled in Jesus the intent of Mosaic Law, the law's many prescriptions were unnecessary. It was not, then, adherence to an external code that would make one righteous; only by opening oneself to God's love was salvation possible. And though many early Christians maintained Jewish dietary and personal laws, many others maintained that such observances were unnecessary. This was not inconsistent with the message of Jesus, who said:

> Do not suppose that I have come to abolish the Law and the prophets; I did not come to abolish, but to complete. I tell you this: so long as heaven and earth endure, not a letter, not a stroke, will disappear from the Law until all that must happen has happened. (Matthew 5: 17-19.)

The morality of the Sermon on the Mount probably best reflects the message of the New Testament for Christians:

> How blest are these who know their need of God; the kingdom
>   of Heaven is theirs.
> How blest are the sorrowful;
>   they shall find consolation.
> How blest are those of a gentle spirit;
>   they shall have the earth for their possession.
> How blest are those who hunger and thirst to see right
>   prevail; they shall be satisfied.
> How blest are those who show mercy;
>   mercy shall be shown to them.
> How blest are those whose hearts are pure;
>   they shall see God.
> How blest are the peacemakers;
>   God shall call them his sons.
> How blest are those who have suffered persecution for the
>   cause of right; the Kingdom of Heaven is theirs.
> How blest you are, when you suffer insults and persecution
>   and every kind of calumny for my sake. Accept it with
>   gladness and exultation, for you have a rich reward in
>   heaven; in the same way they persecuted the prophets before
>   you. (Matthew 5: 3-12.)

For the early Christians, the message of Jesus was one of forgiveness and salvation:

> God loved the world so much that he gave his only Son, that everyone who has faith in him may not die but have eternal life. It was not to judge the world that God sent his Son into the world, but that through him the world might be saved. (John 3: 16-17.)

And this possibility of salvation was open to anyone, especially those humbled by life circumstances:

> Come unto me, all ye that labor and are heavy laden, and I will give you rest. Take my yoke upon you, and learn of me; for I am meek and lowly in heart; and ye shall find rest unto your soul. For my yoke is easy, and my burden is light. (Matthew 11: 28-30.)

And:

> Many that are first shall be last; and the last shall be first. (Matthew 19: 30.)

There were two factors in the early development of Christianity which were to have a major impact on that view. For one, Christianity was a minority religion. It came out of the rich intellectual and spiritual tradition of Judaism, which included Jewish Palestine as well as Jews living in the Roman Empire. But at first its structural organization was a fluid one, and it was New Testament writers such as Paul and John whose interpretation of Jesus' teachings was a key to early Christianity. Moreover, theologians such as Tertullian wrote extensively to articulate a coherent worldview from the parables and aphorisms of Jesus. By the end of the first century C.E., the Church had a variety of theologies, the majority of which were an extension of Jewish religion with Jesus added as the Messiah; in addition, it borrowed much of Stoicism and the dualism of the Greeks. It took the Apostolic Age the first three centuries to elaborate Jesus' message and to create an organizational structure for the Church; during this period authority was a central concern, as the Christian Church struggled not only internally but also against Roman persecution and with rival movements like, for example, Gnosticism.

Another decisive factor in the development of the early Christian Church was the belief that the future was to be a short one, that Jesus, soon after his crucifixion, would return to consummate his work. Later, when this did not occur, Christian teachers instructed the faithful that they would have to wait patiently. But the fact that these early Christians expected a second coming in their own lifetimes had important implications for many of their prescriptions for daily living and personal relationships.

> I mean, brethren, the appointed time has grown very short; from now on, let those who have wives live as though they had none, and those who mourn as though they had nothing to mourn, and those who buy as though they had no goods, and those who deal with the world as though they had no dealings with it. For the form of this world is passing away. (I Corinthians 7: 29-31.)

Thus, early Christians had to formulate an ethic suitable for this "intertime." One major feature of that ethic was its position on sexual abstinence.

Christianity and Sexuality

Christianity, unlike Islam, is a dualist view, borrowing perhaps from the Platonic and Pythagorean traditions of ancient Greece. For this view, the spirit is constantly at war with the flesh, the flesh being the source of human weakness.

> You must act against nature or rather above nature if you are to forswear your natural functions, to cut off your own root, to cull no fruit but that of virginity, to abjure the marriage bed, to shun intercourse with men, and while in the body, to live as though out of it. (Jerome, Ep. to Demetrias, 130, 10.)

Augustine (354-430 C.E.), for example, believed that prior to their expulsion from the Garden of Eden, Adam and Eve had not had sexual intercourse. Others argued that sex between Adam and Eve was rational, without passion, occurring "the way the farmer sows his seed." (Reuther, p. 162.)

Paul argued that celibacy was ideal, but recognized that not all were capable of it:

> It is a good thing for a man to have nothing to do with women; but because there is so much immorality, let each man have his own wife and each woman her own husband. (I Corinthians 7: 2-3.)

For Paul, then, celibacy was not a requirement, but rather a gift. This was consistent with Jesus' teachings:

> That [celibacy] is something which not everyone can accept, but only those for whom God has appointed it. For while some are incapable of marriage because they were born so, or were made so by men, there are others who have themselves renounced marriage for the sake of the Kingdom of Heaven. Let those accept it who can. (Matthew 19: 11-12.)

Further, Paul insisted that sex within marriage was preferable to being distracted by sexual temptation:

> Do not deny yourselves [husbands and wives] to one another, except when you agree upon a temporary abstinence in order to devote yourselves to prayer; afterwards you may come together again; otherwise, for lack of self-control, you may be tempted by Satan. (I Corinthians 7: 5-6.)

Yet Paul also acknowledges in his letter to the Corinthians that he views this position as a compromise, for his preference is that "you all...be as I am myself" (i.e., unmarried and celibate). (I Corinthians 7:7.) But he is adamant that those who are already married should not divorce, and those who are unmarried might consider remaining in that state.

> To the unmarried and to widows I say this: it is a good thing if they stay as I am myself; but if they cannot control themselves, they should marry. Better be married than burn with vain desire.

> To the married I give this ruling, which is not mine but the Lord's: a wife

must not separate from her husband; if she does, she must either remain unmarried or be reconciled to her husband; and the husband must not divorce his wife. (I Corinthians 7: 8-11.)

Paul's teachings on this subject are directed to both men and women. And, on the surface, a principle which idealizes celibacy would not appear to have any particular repercussions for women as opposed to both men and women. Yet, in practice, this element of the early Christian church had very different implications for women. In principle, Christianity was a democratic philosophy, maintaining that both men and women could enter the kingdom of heaven. Yet there were many aspects of Christianity which were also consistent with a misogynistic world view.

Christianity's treatment of the story of Adam and Eve put the blame for humanity's downfall squarely on Eve. She was the temptress, the seductress whose wiles caused Adam's fall. Mary, the mother of Jesus, is flawless, yet she also is without sexual desire, the eternal virgin whose mission is to bring forth a savior into the world. These two extremes represented for much of Christianity the archetypes of the feminine character; but they also reflect a tension in Christianity itself in its attitudes toward women.

There are occasional references in the Old Testament to women with a certain degree of power; Deborah (Judges 4: 4), for example, is a prophetess and one of Israel's leaders. But, in general, women were expected to marry, bear children, and serve their families. Thus, the idea of celibacy was probably a very radical one for its time. And, for women, it provided the possibility for an identity independent of childbirth (which could often lead to death), sex, and motherhood.

Many women flocked to convert to Christianity in its early days and to devote their lives to spirituality free of earthly concerns; many even abandoned their families. Women were martyred in equal numbers with men. Not only had celibacy never been an option for Jewish women at this time, but Roman law prohibited women from being single and made it mandatory for women who were divorced or widowed to remarry. Thus, Paul's ideas about celibacy were truly revolutionary for their time.

Yet, these changes were occurring at a time in Rome when Roman women (unlike their Jewish counterparts) were increasingly visible in public life. Many were educated; there is even a record of a woman engineer at this time! Roman philosophers such as Epictetus and Seneca emphasized equality in relationships, though many also continued to defend separate spheres for the sexes. But there were many popular writers who feared a loss of family ties and a weakening of social control with women's increasing independence. And Jews followed the laws of the Roman Empire for public life, but kept to their own particular codes for family life, including rules relating to women. The Old Testament books of Esther and Judith extol the virtues of women who saved their people from paganism; but, for the most part, Jewish law expected women to remain passive, relegated to the domestic world.

The early Christian Church drew on both of these traditions, as the first followers of Jesus were both Jews and Gentiles. Women were seen as co-heirs with men of the Kingdom of God, and as possessing the capacity of single-minded devotion to the perfection of the spirit. Paul even said that in Christ there is "neither male nor female." (Gal. 3: 28.) His major concern was that Christians free themselves from worldly cares; to that extent, he preferred celibacy to marriage; yet he also recognized that either an overly zealous focus on celibacy or a lack of sexual control can be far worse than sex within marriage. And there are records of many men and women who were celibate pairs, who together—married and unmarried—devoted themselves to the Church and did not engage in sexual relations. Yet this was hardly a "sex-positive" attitude for either men or women. Fornication, along with idolatry and homicide, was one of the three capital sins of the early Church. And sex with the purpose of pleasure is consistently condemned by virtually all the early Christian writers.

What happens to women in all this? For many Christians, women were the *source* of that temptation which distracted the devout from their observances. Early Christianity viewed the soul as at war with the flesh, and woman came to be equated with "flesh." Some males even interpreted Jesus' injunction to be "eunuchs for the Kingdom of Heaven's sake" as requiring castration. In fact, this was such a widespread practice that in the 4th century the Church Councils forbade self-mutilation. Much of early Christianity settled for marriage as a concession to the inordinate desires of fallen humanity, not as a joyous affirmation of the possibilities of human relationships.

The early Christian Church also most likely borrowed from the sex-negative writings of the later Roman Empire. For example, Plotinus (204-270 C.E.), clearly influenced by Plato's and Aristotle's reverence for the contemplative life, maintained that reason must master all desire. The rational soul does not desire "erotic delights" and eats and drinks only what is necessary to keep the body alive. "It desires evidently nothing that is shameful," and would finally "be in itself free of all passion." (*Enneads*, 5, p. 115.) Porphyry (232-304), a student of Plotinus, condemned *any* kind of pleasure as sinful, including horse racing, dancing, eating meat, theatergoing, and sexual intercourse under any conditions. (I 45; IV, 8, 20.) Tertullian (160-230 C.E.), one of the early Church fathers, blamed women for the downfall of humanity.

You are the Devil's gateway. *You* are the unsealer of that forbidden tree. *You* are the first deserter of the Divine Law. *You* are she who persuaded him whom the Devil was not valiant enough to attack. *You* destroyed so easily God's image man. On account of *your* desert, that is death, even the Son of God had to die. (De Cultu Fem. 1.1.)

Augustine, whose writings have "exerted an incredibly great influence on the mentality, culture, and religious attitudes" of Western life (Bourke, p. 11), who, in particular, "more than any other single writer determined the sexual attitudes of the Christian West" (Boswell, p. 161), rejected erotic love between husband and wife. He too links the downfall of humanity to Eve, stressing her bodily and spiritual inferiority to Adam. Thus, he maintains that woman must be subordinate to man as body is to spirit. Yet he also acknowledges that woman has a rational nature which allows for the possibility of salvation.

A good Christian is found in one and the same woman to love the creature of God whom he desires to be transformed and renewed, but to hate in her the corruptible and mortal conjugal connection, sexual intercourse, and all that pertains to her as a wife. (Augustine, *Sermon on the Mount*, Vol. 11.)

Marriage becomes a way of transforming intercourse from the satisfaction of lust to a necessary duty.

We ought not to condemn marriage because of the evil of lust, nor must we praise lust because of the good of marriage. (Augustine, *Treatise on Marriage*, Vol. 27.)

Augustine even compares the relation of Christian husbands to their wives as akin to Christ's precept to love one's enemies.
The New Testament appears to authorize the subjugation of women:

Wives, be subject to your husbands, as to the Lord. For the husband is the head of the wife as Christ is the head of the Church, his body, and is himself its savior. As the Church is subject to Christ, so let wives also be subject in everything to their husbands. (Eph. 5: 22-24.)

Also:

Likewise you wives be submissive to your husbands, so that some, though they do not obey the word, may be won without a word, by the behavior of their wives when they see your reverent and chaste behavior. (I Peter 3: 1-2.)

Finally, the New Testament is unequivocal in prohibiting divorce in all cases save adultery:

Everyone who divorces his wife except on the ground of unchastity makes her an adulteress and whoever marries a divorced woman commits adultery. (Matthew 5: 31-32.)

I [Jesus] say to you: whoever divorces his wife, except for unchastity, and marries another, commits adultery. (Matthew 19: 9.)

Whoever divorces his wife and marries another commits adultery against her; and if she divorces her husband and marries another, she commits adultery. (Mark 10: 11-12.)

Where does homosexuality fit in such a framework? Early Christian authors condemned any form of sexual activity whose purpose was pleasure; it was only the procreative aspect of sex that made it acceptable. Women's sexuality was not acknowledged except insofar as femininity was a distraction from spirituality. So there was little or no attention to lesbianism. Further, women's role in the productive process was not understood, with women viewed merely as incubators for the developing fetus. Finally, semen itself was considered a source of contamination:

And if a man's seed of copulation go out from him, then he shall wash all his flesh in water, and be unclean until the evening. And every garment, and every skin, whereupon is the seed of copulation, shall be washed with water, and be unclean until the evening. (Leviticus 15: 16-18.)

Some historians have maintained that Christianity hardened its attitude toward homosexuality as a result of its vying for members with other developing world views. For Paul, for example, holiness meant staying separate, in particular from the Romans. Another competitor was Manicheanism. The Manicheans divided people into three classes: 1) the Adept, a small elite, who renounced private property, were celibate and strict vegetarians, and did not engage in trade—they would go directly to heaven upon their deaths; 2) Auditors, men and women of good will who could, nonetheless, not discipline themselves sufficiently to achieve the status of the Adept—therefore, they had to earn money, own property, and marry; after their deaths they would have to spend time in purgatory in order to earn their way into heaven; 3) the sensual members of society totally lost in wickedness. Because the Manicheans believed that semen represented "light" (a good) but were opposed to procreation, they were charged with engaging in homosexual activities and other sexual acts without procreative purpose by Christians. Further, the Manicheans believed that procreation perpetuated human confinement to the material world. The increasingly acrid and vehement debate between the Christians and the Manicheans strengthened the already present anti-homosexual attitudes in Christianity.

St. John Chrysostom (died 407 C.E.), for example, wrote in response to the Manicheanism. He condemned all non-procreative sexual acts and specifically mentioned fellatio (oral penile stimulation). He particularly condemned homosexuality because it was allegedly an unpardonable insult to nature, because it deflected the sexual organs from their primary purpose—procreation, and because it allegedly sowed discord between men and women (thereby threatening the Christian community). For Chrysostom and other writers of this period, male homosexuality posed a great threat since it requires that one allow one's body to be used "as that of a woman" and thus blurs gender roles. He finally argued that "the passions in fact are all dishonorable." (PG, 60: 415 ff., *In Epistolam ad Romanos* homily, 4.)

Interestingly, Jesus himself never condemns same-sex sexual relations. Where one might interpret such condemnations, the source is almost always one of his disciples, Paul in particular. Jesus seemed less concerned with relationships of any sort and more with universal love, humility, and good deeds. In all four gospels of the New Testament, there is no mention by Jesus of homosexuality. As Boswell puts it:

> That early Christian writers did not feel called upon to comment explicitly on such [homosexual] relationships is no more surprising than their failure to mention household pets and is at least comparable to, if not subsumed under, the complete absence from their literature of reference to the type of romantic passion which is the basis for marriage in all industrialized societies. (p. 116.)

Indeed, the word for romantic love, common in Greek thought, never appears in the New Testament. In fact, Jesus appears disturbed by hypocrisy and narrow-mindedness more than sexual irregularity. When he is asked, for example, what commandments are the cornerstones of the law, he replies that they are simply two: to love God with "all thy heart" and to "love thy neighbor as thyself." (Matthew 23:36-40.) Concerning the woman caught in adultery, he urged: "He that is without sin among you, let him first cast a stone at her." (John 8:7.)

There are five references to Sodom in the New Testament: Matthew 10:15; Luke 17:29; Romans 9:29; II Peter 2:6; Jude 7. But none of them, like the passages in the Old Testament, explains or refers in even oblique terms to homosexuality. For example, Matthew 10:15:

> If anyone will not receive you or listen to what you say, then as you leave that house or that town shake the dust of it off your feet. I tell you this: on the day of judgment it will be more bearable for the land of Sodom and Gomorrah than for that town.

This passage seems to support the interpretation that Sodom's sin was inhospitality.

There are four passages in the New Testament in particular that have been interpreted as condemnations of homosexuality:

For this cause God gave them up unto vile affections; for even their women did change the natural use into that which is against nature. (Romans 1:26.)

And likewise also the men, leaving the natural use of the women, burned in their lust one toward another, men with men working that which is unseemly, and receiving in themselves that recompense of their error which was meet. (Romans 1:27.)

For whoremongers, for them that defile themselves with mankind, for menstealers, for liars, for perjured persons, and if there be any other thing that is contrary to sound doctrine. (Timothy 1:10.)

Know ye not that the unrighteous shall not inherit the kingdom of God? Be not deceived; neither fornicators, nor idolaters, nor adulterers, nor effeminate, nor abusers of themselves with mankind. (I Corinthians 6:9.)

These passages may seem to leave no room for differing interpretations. Yet the case is not "open-and-shut," for a number of reasons. Take, for example, the last passage quoted from Corinthians. The following gives the formulations of this statement as they have appeared in succeeding editions of the New Testament:

Year	Bible	Translation	Comment
1525	Tyndale	Be not deceaved for nether fornicators nether worshippers of images, nether whoremongers, nor weaklings, nether abusers of themselves with the mankynde.	In this case, *malakois* is translated as "weakling" and *arsenokoites* as "abusers."
1539	Great Bible	For nether fornicatours, nether worshyppers of ymages, nether advouterers, nether weaklynges, nether abusers of themselves with mankynde.	
1560	Geneva Bible	Nether fornicatours, nor idolators, nor adulterers, nor wantons, nor bouggerers, nor thieves, nor covetous,...	Here the word *malakois* becomes "wantons" and *arsenokoites* becomes "bouggerers."
1568	Bishops Bible	Neither fornicatours, nor idolators, nor adulterers, nor effeminate, nor abusers of themselves with mankinde.	

Year	Bible	Translation	Comment
1582	Rheims Bible	Do not erre. Neither fornicatours, nor servors of idols, nor advouterers, nor the effeminate nor the liers with mankinde.	
1611	King James	Neither fornicators, nor idolators, nor adulterers, nor effeminate, nor abusers of themselves with mankind.	Ironically, there *were* words in Greek for same-sex sexual activities, yet they never appear in the Greek Bible.
1811	Revised Version	Neither fornicators, nor idolaters, nor adulterers, nor effeminate nor abusers of themselves with men.	
1901	American Standard	Neither fornicators, nor idolators, nor adulterers, nor effeminate, nor abusers of themselves with men.	
1946	Revised Standard	Neither the immoral, nor idolaters, nor adulterers, nor sexual perverts...	Here what was "fornicators" now translates as "immoral." Note how vague this term is. Also, "sexual perverts" substitutes for "effeminate" and "abusers of themselves with mankind."
1958	Phillips Translation	Neither the impure, the idolater, nor the adulterer, neither the effeminate, the pervert.	"Pervert" could mean any kind of deviation from a norm, sexual or otherwise.
1958	Interlinear Greek New Testament	Not fornicators, idolaters, adulterers, nor voluptuous persons, nor sodomites.	The translations of "fornicators," "idolaters," and "adulterers" remain fairly constant, but the word "voluptuous" is new. The word "sodomites" throughout Scripture referred to male prostitution until well into the 4th century C.E. It was only later that it was used to label any disapproved sexual activity, and even later that it came

Year	Bible	Translation	Comment
			to refer to homosexuality. In this case, the two words are combined to form one label: "homosexual perversion." Yet this too is unclear. Does it apply to all homosexuals or only "homosexual perversion"?
1961	New English Bible	No fornicators, or idolators, none who are guilty of adultery or of homosexual perversion.	
1966	Today's English Version	People who are immoral, or worship idols, or worship idols, or are adulterers, or homosexual perverts.	
1966	Jerusalem Bible	Of immoral lives, idolators, adulterers, Catamites and Sodomites	*Malakois* is translated "Catamites" (young boys kept and used by men through adolescence). *Arsenokoites* is translated as "Sodomites" (temple prostitutes).
1971	Living Bible (Paraphrased)	Those who live immoral lives who are idol worshippers, adulterers or homosexuals.	
1973	New International Version	Neither the sexually immoral nor idolators, nor adulterers nor male prostitutes nor homosexual offenders.	This has kept true to two different words, but *malakois* refers to the prostitutes, where the Jerusalem Bible has the second word as prostitutes.

The other Biblical passages can all be treated in this way, to suggest both their vagueness and the differing possibilities for interpretation. In fact, originally it was the unanimous tradition of the Church through the Reformation of the 1500s, and of Roman Catholicism until well into the 20th century, to interpret I Corinthians as referring to masturbators and not to homosexuals. The word in Greek, Latinized as *mollitia*, was understood as applying solely to masturbators by both the Greek writers of the early Middle Ages and by the very theologians of those days most vigorous in their condemnation of homosexuality. It may simply be that, as more recent attitudes softened toward masturbation, translations of these passages were reinterpreted to apply to homosexuality.

It is likely that early Christianity paid little attention to the issue of homosexuality. At a time when individual Christians had to face such urgent problems as the possibility of martyrdom at imperial hands, the authority of the Church, and the nature of Jesus, there was little leisure time to formulate a sophisticated code of sexual ethics. Further, there was no consistent body of authority, but rather competing views from Greek dualism, Judaism, Stoicism, and extreme ascetic views like Manicheanism. The preachings of Jesus and his followers seem to respond to situations requiring immediate answers, without necessarily implying a generalization from those answers.

Eventually, though, early Christian writers, as we have seen, condemned sex whose purpose was not procreation. Stoics argued for moderation in all activities, meaning doing only what is necessary; in sexual conduct, this was taken to mean sex for procreative purposes. Paul may have borrowed from these views. This position creates a tension in Christianity, for it would make celibacy a sin as well.

Later, homosexuality came to be associated with paganism and hedonism. Certain unpopular practices such as incest were associated with particular groups such as Jews, barbarians, and homosexuals, increasing popular dislike of both the group *and* the practice. Objections to oral and anal sex were more common, becoming more virulent as homosexuals became an increasingly unpopular minority. Popular works like the *Physiologus*, described by historian E.P. Evans as the most widely read book (except for the Bible) of any sort prior to the 17th century, compared homosexuals to weasels and hyenas, who allegedly also engaged in same-sex activity. But most important in its impact on the thinking of this time were the writings of St. Thomas Aquinas.

The writings of Thomas Aquinas (died 1274) have had a powerful effect on the Christian Church's views on sexuality. In fact, it is Aquinas who represents the final synthesis of medieval moral theology. Aquinas' goal was, at least in part, to construct a framework in which homosexual acts were worse than comparable heterosexual ones. Unlike previous moralists who condemned sexual *excesses* rather than particular sexual practices, Aquinas maintained that there were "vices against nature" and "right reason" which violate the will of God. For Aquinas, such sins fit into three categories, with bestiality (sex with animals) the worst, followed by sodomy and masturbation; rape, adultery, and fornication were the least of these sins. All had in common the fact that sperm was not being intended for procreation; in fact, this explains why, for Aquinas, homosexuality is worse than rape or adultery, since in the latter cases there is at least the possibility of conception.

Though Aquinas did not deny that homosexuality might be natural for an individual, he insisted nonetheless that it was a sin against nature and represented a defect in the person. Such acts, he said, provoke moral repugnance in much the same way as does cannibalism. Aquinas' views are especially important, as they occurred at a time of the solidification of orthodoxy within the Catholic Church. This was a period when the Church began to insist on the acceptance of statements of orthodox theologians like Aquinas. Indeed, between 1250 and 1300, homosexual activity went from being completely legal in most of Europe to meriting the death penalty in all but a few legal documents. This change was frequently used by those in power against their political rivals. It was quite common at this time to lump together "traitors, heretics, and sodomites."

Yet, even if the New Testament clearly condemns homosexuality, it also condemns other practices we today tolerate and even approve. For example, the New Testament is consistently critical of greed and the pursuit of material gain.

> And I say to you, it is easier for a camel to get through the eye of a needle than for a rich man to get into heaven. (Matthew 19:24-25.)

Further, when a man asked Jesus, "What must I do to gain eternal life?" Jesus' answer was:

> If you wish to go the whole way, go, sell your possessions, and give to the poor, and then you will have riches in heaven.... (Matthew 19:21-22.)

And:

> The love of money is the root of all evil things. (I Timothy 6:10.)

Early Christian teachings consistently eschew attachments to worldly goods:

> Instruct those who are rich in this world's goods not to be proud, and not to fix their hopes on so uncertain a thing as money, but upon God, who endows us richly with all things to enjoy. Tell them to do good and to grow rich in noble actions, to be ready to give away and to share, and so acquire a treasure which will form a good foundation for the future. (I Timothy 6:17-19.)

Why have we not insisted on such practices for Christians today, particularly when the message is so much clearer than what has been stated about *sexual* practice? Why have we not created a hated minority of the rich in the way that we have done with gay people?

To understand how moral condemnations change over time, let's look at the issue of usury:

> Unlike homosexuality, usury had been condemned almost unanimously by philosophers of the ancient world as uncharitable, demeaning, and

contrary to "nature," both because it violated the kindness which humans ought to extend to each other in times of need and because it represented an "unnatural" growth of money (the usurer did nothing to earn the increase which accrued to him, and the money therefore increased "unnaturally"). Because they were thought to exploit the poor, who were most in need of loans and least able to afford interest, usurers were looked upon everywhere with disgust. Cicero mentions them in the same breath with child molesters. Early theologians universally regarded Jesus's command to "lend hoping for nothing again" (Luke 6:35) as an extension of Levitical prohibitions of usury among Jews to the entire Christian community.

The ethical case against usury was considerably stronger than that against homosexuality. Many more biblical passages could be claimed to relate to it, including, with only a little stretching, Jesus's constant condemnations of the rich. "Natural law" forbade it. The fathers of the church forbade it. The very same theologians influential in condemning homosexuality forbade absolutely and in no uncertain terms lending money at interest: Peter Cantor, Albertus Magnus, and Saint Thomas Aquinas. Many more church councils had condemned it, beginning with Nicaea, the most famous of all, and including dozens of others before the steady and severe proscriptions of the First, Third, and Fourth Laterans.

By the 14th century usury incurred more severe penalties in church law than "sodomy" did and was derogated in exactly the same terms. The most famous of the commentators on canon law, Panormitanus, equated it explicitly with "unnatural" sexuality: "Whenever humans sin against nature, whether in sexual intercourse, worshipping idols, or any other unnatural act, the church may always exercise its jurisdiction.... For by such sins God Himself is offended, since He is the author of nature. This is why Jean Lemoine felt...that the church could prosecute usurers and not thieves or robbers, because usurers violate nature by making money grow which would not increase naturally."

Because usurers were almost necessarily well-to-do, they were at first even more eagerly prosecuted under civil law than gay people. The same thirteenth-century laws which penalized gay people—the Coutumes of Touraine-Anjou, the Etablissements, etc.—stipulated that the property of anyone who had practiced usury within a year of his death was to be confiscated to the king automatically. Many local statutes empowered nobles to exact the same lucrative penalty. Less judicious proceedings were also employed: the crusade against the Albigensians named usurers as well as heretics as the objects of its enmity. The former were presumably even more tempting to northern nobles short of cash.

But theology, ethics, law, and even crusades were powerless against a practice which increasingly met the needs of the age, and soon ceased to derive support from widespread popular antipathy. As long as most usurers were Jews, prejudice provided a visceral impetus to prosecution for usury, but by the fourteenth century interest banking more and more frequently involved the Christian majority as well, and the emotional basis of opposition to the practice was steadily eroded by its manifest utility and increased familiarity. As a part of the everyday life of the majority culture, its erstwhile objectionableness eventually came to seem so distant that the ethical tradition against it was sidestepped altogether by the ingenious expedient of declaring ancient prohibitions against it to apply only to the demanding of excessive interest. (Boswell, pp. 130-32.)

Another example is the issue of slavery. Unlike usury, slavery was once defended with the Bible:

Such slaves as you have, male or female, shall come from the nations round about you; from them you may buy slaves.... These may become your property, and you may leave them to your sons after you; you may use them as slaves permanently. (Leviticus 25:44-45.)

All who wear the yoke of slavery must count their own masters worthy of all respect, so that the name of God and the Christian teaching are not brought into disrepute. (I Timothy 6:1-2.)

Servants, accept the authority of your masters with all due submission, not only when they are kind and considerate, but even when they are perverse. For it is a fine thing if a man endure a pain of undeserved suffering because God is in his thoughts. What credit is there in fortitude when you have done wrong and are beaten for it? But when you have behaved well and suffer for it, your fortitude is a fine thing in the sight of God. (I Peter 2:18-21.)

Slaves, obey your earthly masters with fear and trembling, single-mindedly, as serving Christ.... For you know that whatever good each man may do, slave or free, will be repaid him by the Lord. (Ephesians 6:5-8.)

Every man should remain in the condition in which he was called. Were you a slave when you were called? Do not let that trouble you.... (I Corinthians 7:20-22.)

John Henry Hopkins, bishop of the Diocese of Vermont, wrote extensive criticisms of the abolitionist position in the mid-19th century. Most of his arguments in defense of slavery were based on scriptural references like those cited above. And he quotes approvingly the analysis of St. John Chrysostom of I Corinthians 7:21:

Let every one of you remain in that vocation wherein you are called. Art thou called, having an unbelieving wife? Remain with her, and do not put her away on account of the faith. Art thou called, being a slave? Care not for it; continue serving. Art thou called, being uncircumcised? Remain uncircumcised. Hast thou believed, being circumcised? Remain circumcised. For even as circumcision profiteth nothing, and uncircumcision hurteth nothing, so neither does slavery or liberty. And in order that he [the Apostle] might teach this yet more plainly, he saith: "But if thou mayest be made free, use it rather." That is, served rather. But why does he command him that might be free to remain a slave? Because he desires to show that slavery does not hurt, but even profits. We are not ignorant, indeed, that some interpret the words "use it rather" as referring to liberty, saying: "If thou mayest be freed, be free." But this is very contrary to the meaning of

Paul. For his design being to console the slave by showing that his condition was no injury, he would not have ordered him to become free. For some, perhaps, might say, "If I cannot [be free] I suffer injury, and have received damage." He does not therefore say this, but as I have said, desiring to show that he who is made free gains no advantage, he saith: "Although it may be in thy power to be manumitted and made free, remain rather in servitude." And then he adds the reason: "For he who is called in the Lord, being a bondman, is the freedman of Christ. In like manner also, he who is called, being free, is the bondman of Christ." For in those things which are according to Christ, both are equal. But how is it that he who is a bondman is free? Because He has freed thee not only from sin, but even from external slavery, though remaining a slave. And how is it that he who is a slave is free, remaining a slave? When he has been freed from the passions and afflictions of the mind. When he has learned to despise money, anger, and the other perturbations of the soul. "You are bought with a price, be not the servants of men." This is said not only to slaves but also to freemen. For it is possible that while he is a slave, he is not a slave, and while he is free, he may be a slave notwithstanding. But how, when he is a slave, can it be true that he is not a slave? When he does everything for the sake of God, when he is neither a deceiver, nor a hypocrite, not an eyeservant: this is to be the slave of men, and yet free. And how, again, does any freeman become a slave? When he performs any action which works evil to men, or works in the service of gluttony, or covetousness, or ambition. For he who is of this sort is a worse slave than all others, although he be a freeman. But consider these things. Joseph was a slave, but not the servant of men, for even in his slavery he was freer than they all. He certainly did not yield to the mistress who owned him, in those acts which she desired. Again, she was free, yet she was a greater slave than all, because she besought her slave, and implored and provoked him, but did not persuade the freeman to do what she desired.... (Hopkins quoted pp. 105-06; from *In Ep. ad. Corin.* C. vii Hom. xix. Ed. Paris, 1636. T.v., p. 196-98.)

Hopkins also responds to the charge that the practice of slavery as it existed in the South was cruel, often involving severe physical punishment:

But the Southern slaves are subject to the lash of the overseer, if they are insubordinate! Suppose they are, no man doubts that some kind of discipline is necessary for those who are idle and refractory; and the only question is whether the summary punishment of twelve stripes is more cruel than the substitute of imprisonment, which modern philanthropy prefers, on the ground of this greater humanity. I confess that I am more than doubtful of the assumption that the wisdom of our age has made any improvement on the practice of former times in this matter. The Mosaic Law, which was divine, ordered forty stripes even for the free Israelite; and children were to be corrected by the rod, as a necessary element in their moral and religious training.... (p. 301.)

He then quotes from Deuteronomy 25:1-3.

If there be a controversy between men, and they come unto judgment, that the judges may judge them, then they shall justify the righteous, and condemn the wicked, and if the wicked man be worthy to be beaten, the judge shall cause him to lie down, and to be beaten before his face, according to his fault, by a certain number. Forty stripes he may give him and not exceed, lest if he should exceed, and beat him with many stripes, then thy brother should seem vile unto thee.

Thus, one may ask how it is that we are willing to discard some parts of the Bible as no longer appropriate for modern life, while we adhere to others? Does the New Testament demand condemnations of homosexuality, or does our animosity toward homosexuality lead us to interpret certain passages in that work as consistent with that animosity?

Finally the Bible is a signpost, not a hitching post. It points beyond itself, saying, "Pay attention to God, not me." And if, as the Bible claims, "God is love, and [the one] who abides in love abides in God, and God abides in him," then revelation is in the relationship. That is why I say the integrity of love is more important than the purity of dogma. In all of Scripture there is no injunction more fundamental than that contained in these simple words: "Love one another." (Coffin.)

The Modern Christian Church and Attitudes toward Homosexuality

As with Judaism, there is no one Christian position on the issue of homosexuality. Here we present samples of representative Christian perspectives on homosexuality. Though there exists a variety of positions on this issue, to simplify we offer three general moral stances:

Homosexuality Is Sinful and Unnatural. This is inherited directly from the writings of Thomas Aquinas. It maintains not only that same-sex sexual practices are immoral, but also that their authors will be punished by God. Karl Barth (1886-1968) summarizes this position:

This [homosexuality] is the physical, psychological, and social sickness, the phenomenon of perversion, decadence, and decay, which can emerge when man refuses to admit the validity of the divine command in the sense in which we are now considering it. (Barth, p. 49.)

And:

The command of God shows him [the homosexual] irrefutably—in clear contradiction to his own theories—that as a man he can only be genuinely human with woman, or as a woman with man. (p. 51.)

For this conservative view, homosexuality is unnatural and degrading to human dignity:

We can only affirm that there are ways of hurting people which break no bones and may even provide the victim with a moment of pleasure. And there seems to have been a clear consensus among Christian thinkers over the ages that genital homosexuality assaults human dignity in some such subtle fashion. (Muehl, p. 75.)

Yet most (with the exception of the so-called "Moral Majority") agree that the more extreme forms of oppression against gay people are not justified by the Christian perspective:

The gay relationship is one form of sexual irresponsibility among many and no more reprehensible than most. Those involved in it have as much place in the pews as all the rest of us sinners. And as long as they recognize it as a problem and are prepared to seek help in dealing with it, there should be no arbitrary limits placed upon their full participation as leaders in the Christian fellowship. (Muehl, p. 78.)

This view does, however, urge celibacy for the homosexual by sublimating sexual desire into good deeds. One is not blameworthy for one's sexual orientation, only for actions:

Only *free* human actions are the proper subject of moral analysis. For this reason the church passes no judgment on the psychological complexities of the homosexual condition, which are often unknown or controversial, but only on *freely* willed actions. It is significant that the sources of Holy Scripture do not speak about the *condition* of homosexuality, but only concerning the immorality of homosexual *actions*. (Knights of Columbus.)

This view continues to be the position of many major Christian churches:

SOUTHERN BAPTIST CONVENTION, *Resolution on Homosexuality*, 1976.

Whereas, homosexuality has become an open lifestyle for increasing numbers of persons, and
Whereas, attention has focused on the religious and moral dimensions of homosexuality, and
Whereas, it is the task of the Christian community to bring all moral questions and issues into the light of biblical truth;
Now therefore, be it resolved that the members of the Southern Baptist convention...affirm our commitment to the biblical truth regarding the practice of homosexuality and sin.
Be it further resolved, that this Convention, while acknowledging the autonomy of the local church to ordain ministers, urges churches and agencies not to afford the practice of homosexuality any degree of approval through ordination, employment, or other designations of normal lifestyle.
Be it further resolved, that we affirm our Christian concern that all persons be saved from the penalty and power of sin through our Lord Jesus Christ, whatever their present individual lifestyle.

And:

GREEK ORTHODOX CHURCH, *Biennial Clergy-Laity Congress*, 1976.

The Orthodox church condemns unreservedly all expressions of personal sexual experience which prove contrary to the definite and unalterable function ascribed to sex by God's ordinance and expressed in man's experience as a law of nature.

Thus the function of the sexual organs of a man and a woman and their biochemical generating forces in glands and glandular secretions are ordained by nature to serve one particular purpose, the procreation of the human kind.

Therefore, any and all uses of the human sex organs for purposes other than those ordained by creation run contrary to the nature of things as decreed by God....

The Orthodox Church believes that homosexuality should be treated by society as an immoral and dangerous perversion and by religion as a sinful failure. In both cases, correction is called for. Homosexuals should be accorded the confidential medical and psychiatric facilities by which they can be helped to restore themselves to a self-respecting sexual identity that belongs to them by God's ordinance.

The following excerpts come from the "Letter to the Bishops of the Catholic Church on the Pastoral Care of Homosexual Persons." The letter was issued by the Vatican theological watchdog, the Congregation for the Doctrine of the Faith. It was dated October 1, 1986, and made public at the Vatican on October 30, 1986. Headings have been added:

On Homosexuality

Although the particular inclination of the homosexual person is not a sin, it is a more or less strong tendency ordered toward an intrinsic moral evil, and thus the inclination itself must be seen as an objective disorder....

It is only in the marital relationship that the use of the sexual faculty can be morally good. A person engaging in homosexual behavior therefore acts immorally.... Homosexual activity is not a complementary union, able to transmit life, and so it thwarts the call to a life to that form of self-giving which the Gospel says is the essence of Christian living. This does not mean that homosexual persons are not often generous and giving of themselves, but when they engage in homosexual activity they confirm within themselves a disordered sexual inclination which is essentially self-indulgent.

As in every moral disorder, homosexual activity prevents one's own fulfillment and happiness by acting contrary to the creative wisdom of God. The Church, in rejecting erroneous opinions regarding homosexuality, does not limit but rather defends personal freedom and dignity realistically and authentically understood....

Just as the cross was central to the expression of God's redemptive love for us in Jesus, so the conformity of the self-denial of homosexual men and women with the sacrifice of the Lord will constitute for them a source of self-giving which will save them from a way of life which constantly threatens to destroy them.

Christians who are homosexual are called, as all of us are, to a chaste life....

On Gay and Lesbian Liberation

Increasing numbers of people today, even within the Church, are bringing enormous pressure to bear on the Church to accept the homosexual condition as though it was not disordered and to condone homosexual activity. Those within the Church who argue in this fashion often have close ties with those with similar views outside it. These latter groups are guided by a vision opposed to the truth about the human person, which is fully disclosed in the mystery of Christ. They reflect, even if not entirely consciously, a materialistic ideology which denies the transcendent nature of the human person as well as the supernatural vocation of every individual.

There is an effort in some countries to manipulate the Church by gaining the often well-intentioned support of her pastors with a view to changing civil statutes and laws. This is done in order to conform to these pressure groups' concept that homosexuality is at least a completely harmless, if not an entirely good, thing. Even when the practice of homosexuality may seriously threaten the lives and well-being of a large number of people [an implied reference to AIDS], its advocates remain undeterred and refuse to consider the magnitude of the risk involved.

The Church can never be so callous.

On Violence against Lesbians and Gay Men

It is deplorable that homosexual persons have been and are the object of violent malice in speech and action. Such treatment deserves condemnation from the Church's pastors wherever it occurs....

But the proper reaction to crimes committed against homosexual persons should not be to claim that the homosexual condition is not disordered. When such a claim is made and when homosexual activity is consequently condoned, or when civil legislation is introduced to protect behavior to which no one has any conceivable right, neither the Church nor society at large should be surprised when other distorted notions and practices gain ground, and irrational and violent reactions increase.

Homosexuality Is Essentially "Imperfect."   This view suggests a "principle of compromise" which, while affirming that heterosexual marriage is the ideal, maintains that the homosexual is not responsible for his/her condition. Therapy does not work in most cases, and celibacy is not always possible.

Celibacy cannot be used as a counterargument because celibacy is based upon a special calling and, moreover, is an act of free will. (Theilicke, p. 102.)

Both the heterosexual and the homosexual are sinners; yet, rather than drive the homosexual to renounce the church, one must seek to incorporate him/her into the church's membership. Such unions are still preferable to promiscuity, though the homosexual is still "sexually handicapped" and the homosexual liaison "cannot be recognized as meeting the standards of Christian marriage." (Jones, pp. 112, 113.)

> Homosexuality can never become an ideal. Attempts should be made to overcome this condition if possible; however, at times one may reluctantly accept homosexual unions as the only way in which some people can find a satisfying degree of humanity in their lives. (Curran, p. 94.)

This is *not* to say that such individuals should be ordained or that homosexual unions should be sanctified by the church. It is to say that homosexuals are not necessarily lost souls.

THE UNITED METHODIST CHURCH, *The Quadrennial Conference*, 1976.

> Homosexuals no less than heterosexuals are persons of sacred worth, who need the ministry and guidance of the church in their struggles for human fulfillment, as well as the spiritual and emotional care of a fellowship which enables reconciling relationships with God, with others, and with self. Further, we insist that all persons are entitled to have their human and civil rights ensured, though we do not condone the practice of homosexuality and consider this practice incompatible with Christian teaching.

LUTHERAN CHURCH IN AMERICA, *Biennial Convention*, 1970.

> Human sexuality is a gift of God for the expression of love and the generation of life. As with every good gift, it is subject to abuses which cause suffering and debasement. In the expression of man's sexuality, it is the integrity of his relationships which determines the meaning of his actions. Man does not merely have sexual relations; he demonstrates his true humanity in personal relationships, the most intimate of which are sexual.
>
> Scientific research has not been able to provide conclusive evidence regarding the causes of homosexuality. Nevertheless, homosexuality is viewed biblically as a departure from the heterosexual structure of God's creation. Persons who engage in homosexual behavior are sinners only as are all other persons—alienated from God and neighbor. However, they are often the special and undeserving victims of prejudice and discrimination in law, law enforcement, cultural mores, and congregational life. In relation to his area of concern, the sexual behavior of freely consenting adults in private is not an appropriate subject for legislation or police action. It is essential to see such persons as entitled to understanding justice in church and community.

Homosexuality Is Natural and Good.   According to this view, the real message of Jesus is tolerance and love. Judgments of sin, it is claimed, must include attention to the inner spirit of the person and the agent's intention. Thus, nothing is "bad in itself" (*malum in se*), but only good or bad depending on its context or end. While this position may condemn selfishness, promiscuity, and the use of coercion, it does so equally for heterosexual as well as homosexual relationships.

This view criticizes the literal interpretations of Scripture characteristic of more conservative positions, and it recommends placing biblical injunctions against certain sexual practices in an historical context. Thus, it argues, since we no longer condemn all non-procreative sex, there is no longer any justification for condemnations of homosexuality. The emphasis is on the ability to *love*; and, though social circumstances may make it more difficult for homosexuals to love, there is nothing inherent in that sexual orientation that precludes the possibility of genuine love:

> The proper ethical stance is to permit a full range of sexuality, based on *love*: such an ethic always asks about the meaning of any particular sexual act in the total context of the person involved, in the context of their society, and in the context of that direction which God desires for human life. It is an ethic equally appropriate for both homosexual and heterosexual Christians—there is no double standard. (Nelson, p. 4.)

And:

> Heterosexual partners by no means possess a monopoly upon sacrificial love and it was far from clear to the Commission [of the Episcopal Diocese of Michigan] that a homosexual relationship is in and of itself incapable of expressing sacrificial love. (Commission of the Episcopal Diocese of Michigan, quoted in Batchelor, p. 128.)

Like the two other views, this more radical theological position condemns repressive laws against homosexuals; unlike these views, however, this third position urges that all offices and ministries should be open even to openly gay people and that the use of church property for gatherings of gay organizations should be permitted. Some who follow this view would even allow ceremonies to unite gay couples; though such services have no legal validity, they do bring to these relationships a "community of support":

> There seems to be a special joy experienced by the clergy who have performed these services. This may be due to the sense of appreciation demonstrated by the couple involved, at finding someone who believes in them and their capacity to love deeply, over time into the unknown future.

That acceptance and belief is generally absent in society at large, which does not readily assume that lesbian and gay couples can be serious in their relationships. To be affirmed and supported at one of life's most precious times of decision is very gratifying. (Wheatly.)

Rev. Troy Perry, founder of the Metropolitan Community Church, a church for gay and lesbian people, has written of his reasons for creating a new church:

> I am not a creature from the outer darkness as you seem to believe. I am a homosexual, and like most of the members of your churches, a man of flesh and blood. I am a member of the church...and an integral part of its people!...
>
> Because of my sexual orientation, you try to condemn me. For two thousand years I have watched you try to destroy my brothers and sisters....
>
> You have watched as we were placed on the rack, thrown to the flames, banished from the midst of society, and you have never said a word!...
>
> I am thankful that I still have a God. You cannot take Him away from me! He is the Author and Finisher of my faith. His name is spelled Love!!!!...
>
> If you will not let me worship Him in your temples, I will worship him in the cathedral of my heart, and build for Him a temple where others can worship with me. (Perry, quoted in Bullough, ch. 2.)

The following churches have taken this third position on homosexuality:

FRIENDS (Quakers), *Philadelphia Yearly Meeting of Friends*, 1973.

> We should be aware that there is a great diversity in the relationships that people develop with one another. Although we neither approve nor disapprove of homosexuality, the same standards under the law which we apply to heterosexual activities should also be applied to homosexual activities. As persons who engage in homosexual activities suffer serious discrimination in employment, housing, and the right to worship, we believe that civil rights laws should protect them. In particular we advocate the revision of all legislation imposing disabilities and penalties upon homosexual activities.

UNITED CHURCH OF CHRIST CONGREGATIONS, *Massachusetts Conference*, 1984.

> We know, with Paul, that, as Christians, we are many members, but we are one body in Christ, and members of one another. With Jesus, we affirm that we are called to love our neighbors as ourselves and that we are called to act as agents of reconciliation and wholeness within the world and within the church itself.
>
> We know that lesbian, gay, and bisexual persons are often scorned by the church and devalued and discriminated against both in the church and in society. We wish to witness to our caring and concern for our gay, lesbian,

and bisexually oriented brothers and sisters in Christ by affirming the following:

- That we believe that gay, lesbian, and bisexually oriented people share with all others the worth that comes from being unique individuals created by God;
- That gay, lesbian, and bisexual persons are welcome as members and participants in this congregation through the same affirmation of membership as is made by all other members of this church;
- That we expect to celebrate and use the gifts, talents, and resources of our gay, lesbian, and bisexual members as we use and celebrate the gifts, talents, and resources of all of our members to build a church which is faithful to the mandate of God and working to bring about the fullness of God's reign.
- That we welcome gay, lesbian, and bisexual members to participate fully in the life, leadership, and employment of this church.

Finally, we present a Roman Catholic version of this third view, as articulated in *An Open Letter to Pope John Paul II*, by Thomas L. Leclerc, as it appeared in *Dignity/Boston Newsletter*, December 1986:

Your Holiness,

In a flock of eight hundred million, I am just one small sheep. I have no real hope that my voice will be heard, much less heeded. But sometimes it is more important to speak than to be heard. Sometimes, the words burn like fire in my heart, imprisoned in my bones, and I must cry out.

The publication by the Sacred Congregation of the Doctrine of the Faith of the letter addressing pastoral care to homosexuals leaves me asking, "Where is the shepherd?" The document represents one more impossible burden laid on people. It seems far easier to lay up burdens than to lighten the load. Will not the shepherd lighten the load? The flock in America, in this instance as in other recent instances, is being scattered, not gathered. Where is the shepherd? The document leaves me feeling like a bruised reed or a smoldering wick. And there is no one to heal my hurt, to fuel my hope. There is much in the letter that saddens me and that deserves responses, but I lack both the heart to undertake the task and the stature to be heard. One thing, however, demands a voice.

It is one thing to oppose justice for the oppressed, even to stand in complicity with others whose grudging tolerance of a group of people gives tacit approval to continued discrimination and violence; it is another thing altogether to promote actively, whether through ignorance or ill will, the scapegoating of the gay community in the matter of AIDS. A virus does not discriminate according to gender or orientation, any more than by class or economic standing. To add your voice to those who continue to blame falsely the gay community for the responsibility for the virus is the modern-day equivalent of standing with those who asked Jesus, "Whose sin is it that caused this man to be born blind?" Jesus, facing a man in need of healing, neither assigned responsibility nor sought causes. He did what is incumbent upon all people of compassion: He responded directly and immediately to the person standing before Him. That is the Good Shepherd in action. Where is the shepherd today?

This sheep is tired. I weary of the struggle to belong to a Church I experience as increasingly reactive and oppressive. My Shepherd once said, "Come to Me all you who are weary and find life burdensome and I will refresh you." It is His voice I now heed, for unlike other shepherds, His yoke is easy and His burden light. The burdens that are otherwise being laid up are impossible to bear. I trust in Jesus and in His promise to be with us always. In this dark hour, however, I find myself wondering, Where is the shepherd?

Respectfully,

Thomas L. Leclerc

Christianity: A Final Note

Several key points are important in Christianity:

- It was a minority religion, always in peril from competing religious and secular views.
- Originally it had no one authority on spiritual matters; it was not until 1546, for example, that the Roman Catholic Church in the Council of Trent established the Bible as we now know it; indeed, many books once venerated by Christians (e.g., the Epistle of Barnabus) are now regarded as apocryphal, while others once not recognized (e.g., the Revelation of St. John) now are venerated.
- It has a dualistic philosophy, in which flesh and spirit are irreconcilable.
- It originally viewed remaining life on earth as brief, and believed judgment would come in a matter of days.
- It evolved in a mixed culture, and so borrowed elements from both Judaism and Greek philosophy, in particular the monotheism of Judaism and the dualism of the Greeks.

It is in this context that a Christian ideology regarding sexual practices evolved. This chapter has suggested that the message of Christianity for homosexuality is not as clear-cut as one might suppose. Indeed, one can summarize this discussion by outlining several possible interpretations, all of which are consistent with Christianity:

- Some argue that the New Testament says nothing about homosexuality, that it was simply of no concern to Christian practitioners who had to face more immediate and urgent threats to their survival. This view maintains that the commonly cited passages which appear to condemn homosexuality are in fact mistranslations; what they *do* condemn are certain pagan practices, such as, for example, ritualized temple prostitution.

- Some argue that the New Testament does, at least by implication, condemn homosexuality, for it is generally a rather sex-negative picture. But to accept the condemnation of same-sex sexual practices is also to accept a host of other prohibitions, including oral sex, anal sex, birth control, masturbation, intercourse during menstruation, and many others. This view, then, holds that it would be completely arbitrary to accept pieces of the ideology and reject others with which one is more comfortable; this view sees Christianity as oriented toward spirituality, in opposition to the flesh, with sex as a means to the end of procreation. Hence, *any* sex for pleasure is immoral.

- Another view argues that there are scriptural condemnations of certain sexual practices, but that they refer not to specific acts themselves but rather to acts which either occur in a context of force, like homosexual rape, or are viewed to violate precepts of moderation. The Bible also condemns drunkenness; does this then condemn all use of alcohol? This would not impugn homosexuality *per se* but rather *any* sexual practices which violate principles of moderation and/or consent.

- Another position maintains that the New Testament may condemn homosexuality, but that when one looks at the contexts in which these condemnations appear, it becomes clear that it is viewed as a rather trivial offense. The word "abomination," for example, is also used to refer to eating pork and misusing incense. So, the argument claims, this hardly justifies the vehemence of some modern-day condemnations of homosexuality.

- A final argument accepts that the Bible condemns homosexuality, but also insists on the significance of the historical context in which this occurs. There are many other prohibitions in the Bible that are no longer taken seriously; some relate to sexual conduct, but others include shaving, growing flowers indoors, dietary rules, bans on divorce, and even the practice of usury or charging interest (viewed to be unnatural, since money does not naturally increase without labor). Further, the Bible permits certain practices most of us now find abhorrent. In particular there is the practice of slavery. In fact, prior to the Civil War, it was common for defenders of slavery to cite Scripture in their own behalf.

Conclusion

[C]areful analysis can almost always differentiate between conscientious application of religious ethics and the use of religious precepts as justification for personal animosity or prejudice. If religious structures are used to justify oppression by people who regularly disregard precepts of equal gravity from the same moral code, or if prohibitions which restrain a disliked minority are upheld in their most literal sense as absolutely inviolable while comparable precepts affecting the majority are relaxed or reinterpreted, one must suspect something other than religious belief as the motivating cause of the oppression. (Boswell, p. 7.)

To capture the essential principles of four major world religions in any sort of historical context is a task which could easily fill a work far longer than this entire text. To attempt to present some of these ideas in one chapter leaves one open to charges of misinterpretation, superficiality, and lack of attention to nuances in original texts. But this chapter does not claim to paint the definitive picture of religion and its connection to thinking about sexuality. Rather, it has only begun to explore the terrain. This terrain, as we have seen, is full of risks and surprises. We have, for example, seen that what we have generally taken for granted in our understanding of religion has not been so obvious. We have explored some of the historical underpinnings of the basic principles of these major religions, shedding some light on some of the possible reasons why certain guidelines rather than others are adopted. Indeed, we have rejected any historical treatment of theory or practice as unfair to the material in question.

We conclude this chapter, then, with some words of caution. It is essential to keep in mind that religious *ideology* may be (but is not necessarily) different from *practice*. We have seen that built into any ideology is a concept of deviance of acceptable and unacceptable behavior. But there is no "pure" society, nor is there any "pure" religion. Often there are contradictions within the religious doctrine, differences among practitioners in interpretation of dogma, and secular influences which modify certain religious practices. Stated norms may or may not be the actual norms of the group, and it is not always possible to know why certain policies are condemned. Finally, we have explored periods in time where very few people were even literate, and we generally know very little about the "deviants" themselves—including not only homosexuals, but also women, slaves, poor people, and children—other than what the doctrine states explicitly or by implication.

What we *do* know is that no religious ideology exists in a vacuum. Each experiences pressures from within and threats from without. Each responds to those forces in a variety of ways—including, for example, accommodation, assimilation, acculturation, division, stricter observance of and insistence on its own codes.

We have seen that some religions are *erotophilic*, some *erotophobic*, that some are mixed, and some have changed over time. Each religion claims to have found *the* truth, though each truth varies from one view to another. A certain degree of humility is no doubt requisite when one embarks on this journey. This chapter can only be the first step.

REFERENCES

Augustine. *Treatise on Marriage and Other Subjects.* Fathers of the Church Series, Vol. 27. Washington, D.C.: Catholic University Press, 1955.

Augustine. *Commentary on the Lord's Sermon on the Mount with Seventeen Related Sermons*, Fathers of the Church Series, Vol. 11. Washington, D.C.: Catholic University Press, 1951.

Bode, Janet. *View from Another Closet: Exploring Bisexuality in Women.* New York: Hawthorne Books, Inc., 1976.

Boswell, John. *Christianity, Social Tolerance, and Homosexuality: Gay People in Western Europe from the Beginning of the Christian Era to the Fourteenth Century.* Chicago: University of Chicago Press, 1980.

Bourke, Vernon J., eds. *The Essential Augustine.* Indianapolis: Hackett Publishing, 1964.

Bullough, Vern. *Homosexuality: A History from Ancient Greece to Gay Liberation.* New York: New American Library, 1979.

Chrysostom, St. John. *In Epistolam ad Romanus.* Homily 4. In *Patrologiae Cursus complaturs, Series Graeca,* 60: 415 ff. cited in Boswell (above), pp. 156-57.

Churchill, Wainwright. *Homosexuality in Males: A Cross-Cultural and Cross-Species Investigation.* Englewood Cliffs, N.J.: Prentice-Hall, 1967.

Coffin, William Sloane. *The Courage to Love.* New York: Harper & Row, 1982.

Commission of the Episcopal Diocese of Michigan. "Report," 1974. In *Homosexuality and Ethics*, edited by Edward Batchelor. New York: The Pilgrim Press, 1980.

Curran, Charles. "Homosexuality and Moral Theology." In *Homosexuality and Ethics*, edited by Edward Batchelor. New York: The Pilgrim Press, 1980.

Day, Donald. *The Evolution of Love.* New York: Dial Press, 1954.

Dover, K.J. *Greek Homosexuality.* New York: Vintage Books, 1980.

Gordis, Robert. "Homosexuality and the Homosexual." In *Homosexuality and Ethics*, edited by Edward Batchelor. New York: The Pilgrim Press, 1980.

Hamilton, Edith. *Mythology: Timeless Tales of Gods and Heroes.* New York: Mentor Books, 1940.

Hamilton, Edith. *The Greek Way.* New York: W.W. Norton, 1942.

Hoffman, Richard M. "Vices, Gods, and Viruses: Cosmology as a Mediating Factor in Attitudes Toward Male Homosexuality." In *Origins of Sexuality and Homosexuality*, edited by J.P. De Cecco and Michael G. Shively. New York: Harrington Park Press, 1984.

Homer. *Iliad*. Translated by Richard Lattimore. Chicago: University of Chicago Press, 1951.

Hopkins, John Henry. *A Scriptural, Ecclesiastical, and Historical View of Slavery*. New York: W.I. Pooley & Co., 1864.

Iskander, Kari Ka'us. *A Mirror for Princes*. London: Cresset, 1951.

Jerome. "Ep. ad Demetrias," 130, 10, in *Selected Letters*. Cambridge, Mass.: Harvard University Press, no date.

Jones, H. Kimball. "Toward a Christian Understanding of the Homosexual." In *Homosexuality and Ethics*, edited by Edward Batchelor. New York: The Pilgrim Press, 1980.

Knights of Columbus. "Pastoral Care and the Homosexual," pamphlet 85. Knights of Columbus, no date.

Matt, Hershel. "Sin, Crime, Sickness, or Alternative Lifestyle: A Jewish Approach to Homosexuality." In *Homosexuality and Ethics*, edited by Edward Batchelor. New York: The Pilgrim Press, 1980.

McNeill, John J. *The Church and the Homosexual*, 3d ed. Boston: Beacon Press, 1988.

Muehl, William. "Some Words of Caution." In *Homosexuality and Ethics*, edited by Edward Batchelor. New York: The Pilgrim Press, 1980.

Nasr, Seyyed Hossein. *Ideals and Realities of Islam*. Boston: Beacon Press, 1972.

Nelson, James. "Gay Christians: An Issue for the Church." *Theological Markings* (1975) 5:2.

Plato. *The Symposium*, edited by Irwin Edman. New York: Modern Library, 1958. (Also translated by W.H.D. Rouse. New York: New American Library, 1952.)

Plato. *Charmides*. Translated by Benjamin Jowett. New York: Bollingen Foundation, 1963.

Plotinus. *The Essential Plotinus: Representative Treatises from the Enneads*, trans. Elmer O'Brien, S.J. Indianapolis: Hackett Publishing Co., 1964.

Pomeroy, Sarah B. *Goddesses, Whores, Wives, and Slaves: Women in Classical Antiquity*. New York: Schocken, 1975.

Porphyry. *Abstinence from Animal Food*. I, 45; IV, 8, 20. Translated by Thomas Taylor. London: Thomas Rodd, 1823.

Ruether, Rosemary Radford. "Virginal Feminism in the Fathers of the Church," in *Religion and Sexism*, ed. Rosemary Radford Ruether. New York: Simon and Schuster, 1974, pp. 150-83.

Schlipp, P.A. *Albert Einstein, Philosopher-Scientist*. New York: Tudor, 1950.

Tavard, George. *Women in Christian Tradition*. London: University of Notre Dame Press, 1973.

Tertullian. *De Culti Fem*.

Thielicke, Helmut. "The Theologicoethical Aspect of Homosexuality." In *Homosexuality and Ethics*, edited by Edward Batchelor. New York: The Pilgrim Press, 1980.

Tillich, Paul. *The Courage to Be*. New Haven: Yale University Press, 1952.

Tripp, C.A. *The Homosexual Matrix*. Second Edition. New York: New American Library, 1987.

Veyne, Paul. "Homosexuality in Ancient Rome." In *Western Sexuality*, edited by Phillippe Aries and Andre Bejin. London: Blackwell, 1985.

Wheatly, Robert. "Where Love Is." Pamphlet. Boston: Unitarian Universalist Association, 1986.

Xenophon. *Memorabilia*. Translated by E.C. Marchant. London: William Heinemann, 1953.

Further Readings

Anon. "Must Homosexuals be Jewish Outcasts?" In *Homosexuality and Ethics*, edited by Edward Batchelor. New York: The Pilgrim Press, 1980.

Archdiocesan Gay/Lesbian Outreach. *Homosexuality: A Positive Catholic Perspective*. Baltimore: 1985.

Atkinson, Clarissa W., Buchanan, Constance H., and Miles, Margaret R., eds. *Immaculate and Powerful: The Female in Sacred Image and Social Reality*. Boston: Beacon Press, 1985.

Barth, Karl. "Church Dogmatics." In *Homosexuality and Ethics*, edited by Edward Batchelor. New York: The Pilgrim Press, 1980.

Bullough, Vern. *Sexual Variance in Society and History*. Chicago: University of Chicago Press, 1976.

Carmody, Denise L. and John T. *Western Ways to the Center: An Introduction to Religions of the West*. Belmont, Calif.: Wadsworth Publishing Co., 1983.

Curb, Rosemary, and Manahan, Nancy, eds. *Lesbian Nuns: Breaking Silence*. New York: Warner Books, 1985.

Daly, Mary. *Beyond God the Father*. Boston: Beacon Press, 1974.

Daly, Mary. *The Church and the Second Sex*. Boston: Beacon Press, 1985.

Eban, Abba. *Heritage—Civilization, and the Jews*. New York: Summit Books, 1984.

Goodrich, Michael. *The Unmentionable Vice: Homosexuality in the Later Medieval Period*. New York: Dorset/Marlboro Books, 1979.

Gordis, Robert. "Homosexuality and the Homosexual." In *Homosexuality and Ethics*, edited by Edward Batchelor. New York: The Pilgrim Press, 1980.

Leach, E. *Genesis as Myth and Other Essays*. London: Jonathan Cape, 1969.

Ochshorn, Judith. *The Female Experience and the Nature of the Divine*. Bloomington: Indiana University Press, 1981.

Pattison, Rev. Fred. *But Leviticus Says*. Phoenix, Arizona: Chisto Press, 1985.

Pennington, Rev. Sylvia. *Good News for Modern Gays*. Hawthorne, Calif.: Lambda Lite Productions, 1985.

Perry, Rev. Troy, and Lucas, Charles. *The Lord is My Shepherd and He Knows I'm Gay*. Austin, Tex.: Liberty Press, Inc., 1987.

Rowse, A.L. *Homosexuals in History*. New York: Carroll and Graf Publishers, Inc., 1977.

Ruether, Rosemary Radford. *Religion and Sexism: Images of Woman in the Jewish and Christian Traditions*. New York: Simon and Schuster, 1974.

Scanzoni, Letha, and Mollenkott, Virginia Ramez. *Is the Homosexual My Neighbor? Another Christian View*. New York: Harper and Row, 1978.

Sergent, Bernard. *Homosexuality in Greek Myth*. Boston: Beacon Press, 1984.

Siegel, Richard, Strassfeld, Michael, and Strassfeld, Sharon, eds. *The Jewish Catalogue*. Philadelphia: The Jewish Publication Society of America, 1973.

Chapter 5

Prejudice and Discrimination

In [Nazi] Germany they first came for the Communists, and I didn't speak up because I wasn't a Communist. Then they came for the Jews, and I didn't speak up because I wasn't a Jew. Then they came for the trade unionists, and I didn't speak up because I wasn't a trade unionist. Then they came for the Catholics, and I didn't speak up because I was a Protestant. Then they came for me—and by that time no one was left to speak up.

(Attributed to Pastor Martin Niemoeller, quoted in Bartlett, p. 824.)

When taking a walk through any of a number of major cities throughout the world, one will quickly discover enormous cultural diversity. In New York or London, for example, one will find a rich mixture of people from such places as China and Japan, Pakistan and Vietnam, Italy, and Greece; there are Jews, Catholics, and Moslems; people with dark and light skin, blondes and brunettes; people navigating in wheel-chairs, or with white canes; males and females; athletes, secretaries, and construction workers; the famous and those who are known only to their immediate circle.

In such cities one can sample French pastries, Japanese sushi, Cajun gumbo, Israeli falafel, and Indian curry, or hear the delightful sounds of Viennese waltzes, New Orleans jazz, Latin salsa, and Indonesia gamelan.

All these different people come together in a number of ways. Some have migrated voluntarily. Others may have been forced to leave their homeland because of unfavorable economic or political conditions or, like many black Africans, because they have been transported against their will.

218

The United States is one country which has prided itself in its acceptance of diversity and the Statue of Liberty in New York Harbor is a symbol of welcome. Within the United States, however, there is also a long tradition of denying equality of treatment to people on the basis of certain perceived characteristics.

This chapter focuses on the concept of homophobia which is prejudice and discrimination directed against lesbians, gays, and bisexuals. Homophobia, however, does not exist in isolation, for it shares many characteristics with other forms of prejudice. For this reason, we begin with a discussion of prejudice as a general concept.

Background

In many societies, there are groups of people who are denied access to the rights and privileges enjoyed by others on account of some physical, biological, social, or other trait. These segments of the population are sometimes called "minorities." There is, however, disagreement over the exact meaning of the term "minority." Some people define it strictly in terms of relative degrees of power irrespective of numbers. For example, black people under the system of apartheid in South Africa would constitute a minority. Though they vastly outnumber whites, they have little power to control the course of the country or their own lives. There are others, however, who argue that for a group to constitute a minority it must be placed in a lower position of power and must also be numerically smaller than more powerful groups. Though the term "minority" is used throughout this text, some members of these groups reject the term and it is possible that new terminology is developing.

There is evidence that virtually every society has in-groups and out-groups. Minority group members often receive negative treatment, ranging from negative beliefs (which may or may not be expressed), to exclusion, to denial of civil and legal protections, and in some cases to overt acts of violence directed against them. Though the reasons vary why certain groups are singled out for such treatment, some conditions remain constant.

Two related systems come into operation in keeping some groups on the fringe. The first is *prejudice*. Its Latin root means "pre-judgment," and to feel prejudice toward an individual or group is to hold an adverse opinion or belief without just ground or before acquiring sufficient knowledge. For example, a person is said to be prejudiced if he or she believes that all people within a given group—say, redheads—are inherently inferior.

When prejudiced feelings or beliefs move into the realm of behavior, the result is *discrimination*. Discrimination "denies to individuals or groups of people equality of treatment which they may wish." Therefore, it is discriminatory for parents not to allow their children to play with redhaired children, and for legislators to vote to deny redheaded people access to certain jobs, such as teaching.

It is sometimes the case that major social institutions—laws, customs, religion, education, and so forth—work to reinforce existing prejudice and discrimination. This is said to constitute *institutionalized discrimination*. (Eitzen.) It is obvious that the institutions of society can influence behavior and have enormous power to reward and penalize its members. They can, for example:

> ...reward by providing career opportunities for some people and foreclosing them on others. They reward as well by the way social goods and services are distributed—by deciding who receives training and skills, medical care, formal education, political influence, moral support and self-respect, productive employment, fair treatment by the law, decent housing, self-confidence, and the promise of a secure future for self and children. (Knowles and Prewitt.)

Where there exists widescale and deep-seated prejudice, often one of the byproducts is a condition known as *segregation*. This is the exclusion or separation of certain groups, usually minorities, by other groups, usually the dominant group. It has been most visible in the areas of neighborhood residences, schools, workplaces, and public accommodations.

There are two primary types of segregation: *de jure* and *de facto*. *De jure* segregation is a formalized system of segregation which exists by law. For example, the 1896 Supreme Court decision *Plessy v. Ferguson* ruled that segregated facilities did not constitute a violation of the United States Constitution. It was not until 1954, in *Brown v. Board of Education*, that this was overturned, and the Court decided that "separate but equal" was not truly equal.

De facto segregation exists more informally. For example, when a homeowner and real-estate agency refuse to show a residence to a member of a minority group, the result is that minority members do not attend certain neighborhood schools. Ultimately, there are segregated schools.

Though traditionally people with red hair as a group have not suffered from the effects of prejudice and discrimination, the same cannot be said about members of other groups, including racial and ethnic minorities. But how exactly are these groups defined?

Ethnicity and Race

Human beings have a propensity to categorize in an attempt to sort reality into neat and orderly arrangements. Since reality often does not fit this package, definitions may be arbitrary and inconsistent. Such tends to be the case when trying to provide adequate definitions of race and ethnicity.

Ethnic Groups. A standard definition of an ethnic group is one that is socially distinguishable from other groups, has developed its own sub-culture—which can include nationality, religion, and language—and has "a shared feeling of peoplehood." (Gordon.) If we return to our walk down the streets of New York City, we are apt to see many ethnic groups residing in various parts of the city. We might see Italian-Americans in the "Little Italy" section, Hispanics from a variety of Spanish-speaking countries living in "Spanish Harlem," Chinese-Americans in Chinatown, and so on. Often what distinguishes these groups is their shared culture, including their distinctive cuisine, music, and native language. However, there are also some ethnic groups that do not meet all these criteria. An example is the Jews, who, though they come from many different countries and different cultural backgrounds, constitute an ethnic group because of their shared sense of peoplehood, linking them through centuries of dispersion and migration.

Racial Groups. The concept of race is also problematic. Traditionally, social and physical scientists have used skin color, facial features (shape of the nose, eyes, and lips), and hair texture as immutable physical categories to define race. From this they arrived at four essential racial types: Caucasoid, Mongoloid, Negroid, and Australoid. (Krogmann.) However, there are groups of people who did not fit neatly into any of these divisions. For example, there are those who have dark skin and straight hair, such as members of Native American cultures and many people who reside on the subcontinent of India. Also, there was difficulty defining the race of native peoples of Alaska and the people of New Guinea.

Race has been defined as a distinct human type based on inherited physical characteristics. (Julian and Kornblum.) This definition implies that the concept is easily applied and that the categories we call "racial" are obvious and distinct. But today many sociologists and anthropologists maintain that race is a social or cultural concept rather than an inherent, observable characteristic, for all races are simply variations of a single human species of common prehistoric ancestry. Any differences in our species may have evolved to ensure the survival of people in varying geographic locales. For example, in the evolutionary process a greater amount of skin pigmentation (melanin) and thicker-textured hair developed in people in warmer, sun-drenched lands as a way to protect them from ultra-violet rays.

Often the concepts of ethnicity and race overlap and become confused:

> Black Americans and Asian Americans are relatively distinct racial groups in the United States and, for the most part, they are also ethnic groups. Yet some people belong to the groups racially but not ethnically. An example is a Japanese-American whose family has lived among Caucasians for two or three generations and who has few ties to Japanese culture and traditions. And many people—for instance, those who are mostly Caucasoid through intermarriage—may be blacks or Asians ethnically, but may not fit into these groups racially. Furthermore, an ethnic group may include more than one race. The people of India, for example, are called an ethnic group, even though they represent at least two racial groups. (Popenoe, pp. 270-71.)

Stereotypes

A great many traits go into the physical and psychological makeup of every person. How we look, behave, think, and relate affects the ways we are defined by ourselves and by others. The same is true for how groups are defined. Whether these groups are linked by race, ethnicity, sex, occupation, physical condition, age, nationality, social rank, or sexual orientation, a myriad of factors go into its essential composition.

Nevertheless, sometimes individuals and groups are defined by others in terms of one or a console of positive, though most often negative, characteristics called *stereotypes*. When this occurs, a network of belief develops around the group in question. The stereotypes may have originally contained some small grain of truth, but that element has since been exaggerated, distorted, or in some way taken out of context. So stereotypes may be based on false generalizations derived from very small samples or even on a unique case. Some stereotypes have no foundation in fact at all. When stereotyping occurs, people tend to overlook all other characteristics of the group. Individuals sometimes use stereotypes to justify the actions taken against members of that group.

Taking up once again our example of redhaired people, we can see more easily how stereotyping operates. Though every redhaired person is multifaceted, when we call them "hot-tempered," we make "redheadedness" reducible to a single trait. While some redhaired people may show their temper on occasion, it is not the case that all do. And besides, people with other hair shades, or for that matter, no hair at all, flare up sometimes. Further, stereotypes are self-perpetuating, for once a stereotype is in place, we tend to notice more the behavior consistent with the stereotype and miss that which is not. It is in this way that stereotypes are reinforced, regardless of the social realities.

Stereotyping is common in attitudes toward minority group members. Sometimes people stereotype by focusing on a positive quality of a group. However, in most cases, the stereotyping is negative. This can result in the singling out of individuals or groups of people as targets of hostility even though they may have little or nothing to do with the evils for which they stand accused. This is referred to as *scapegoating*. Hitler blamed Jews, Jehovah's Witnesses, Gypsies, homosexuals, and others for the collapse of the German economy prior to World War II. African Americans were scapegoated for the deplorable conditions of the Southern states following the American Civil War.

The origin of the scapegoat goes back to the Book of Leviticus (16: 20-22). On the Day of Atonement a live goat was selected by lot. The high priest placed both hands on the goat's head and confessed over it the sins of the people. In this way, the sins were symbolically transferred to the animal, which was then cast out into the wilderness. This process thus purged the people, for a time, of their feelings of guilt.

What conditions are necessary for certain people or groups to be chosen as scapegoats? First, prejudice must already exist against the particular groups or individuals before the scapegoating commences. Second, the individuals in question must appear to be too weak to fight back successfully when attacked. And finally, the society must sanction the scapegoating through its own institutional structures. (Saenger.)

With scapegoating, there is the tendency to view all members of the group as inferior and to assume that all members are alike in most respects. This attitude often leads to even further discrimination.

Exploring the "Isms"

As a black woman, a lesbian, a feminist, and an activist, I have little difficulty seeing how the systems of oppression interconnect, if for no other reason than that their meshings so frequently affect my life. (Smith, p. 7.)

Definitions.   There are as many names for the varieties of discrimination as there are minority groups. This in no way means to suggest that all groups experience the forms of discrimination similarly. The experiences of victims of racism, for example, are not identical to those who suffer the effects of homophobia. The many strands of discrimination, however, run parallel and at points intersect. All involve negative prejudgments whose purpose is to maintain control or power over others. Discrimination can be the result of a deliberate, conscious act; or it may be unconscious and unintentional, yet have discriminatory results nonetheless.

Typical names used for some of the many forms of discrimination are:

- *Racism*: discrimination on the basis of race;
- *Sexism*: discrimination on the basis of sex, most often by men;
- *Misogyny*: a hatred or distrust of women;
- *Ethnocentrism* or *Ethnic Prejudice*: the belief that one's own group is superior to all others resulting, at times, in discrimination toward those of different ethnic backgrounds or national origin;
- *Ageism*: discrimination on the basis of age, usually against the elderly and the young;
- *Ableism*: discrimination against the physically challenged (physically or mentally disabled);
- *Xenophobia*: fear and or hatred of strangers or foreigners or anything that appears strange or foreign;
- *Anti-Semitism*: discrimination against Jews (a traditional usage which does not include discrimination against Arabs, who are also Semites);
- *Religious Prejudice*: discrimination on the basis of a particular religious preference;
- *Chauvinism*: originally used to refer to jingoism or excessive patriotism, it has also come to be associated with sexist attitudes, most especially of men toward women;
- *Classism*: Prejudice and discrimination based on socio-economic level or class;
- *Heterosexism*: the system by which heterosexuality is assumed to be the only acceptable and viable life option;
- *Homophobia*: fear, dislike, or hatred of lesbians, gays, and bisexuals often resulting in acts of discrimination [Weinberg]. (Other terms have been coined to express this condition including "homophilephobia" [Rosen], literally meaning fear of persons of one's own sex; "homoerotophobia" [Churchill]; "homosexphobia" [Levitt & Klassen]; "homosexophobia" [Boswell]; "homosexism" [Lehne]; and "homonegativism" [Hudson & Ricketts]. Though the term "homophobia" has appeared in revised editions of some dictionaries since the mid-1970s, it is still absent from other standard lexicons.

Prejudice: Functions and Origins

Prejudice (along with its active component—discrimination) seems to be a universal phenomenon that has probably been around since the time of the first human grouping. One may ask: "Why do people hold on to their prejudices?" Beliefs, whether true or false, serve some function. And prejudice, like other beliefs, must meet some sort of need or fulfill a purpose. If this were not the case, prejudice itself would, in all likelihood, cease to exist and be replaced by more functional beliefs. In an attempt to understand what role prejudice plays in human interactions, social scientists have studied how it operates.

Functions

Jaime Wurzel has identified four basic functions of prejudice:

The Utilitarian Function. People maintain prejudicial attitudes to gain certain rewards and to avoid punishment. They generally want to be liked and, therefore, will take on the prejudices of others, including family members—namely parents—and peers outside the home environment. In doing so, they are consolidating their personal and social relationships, and in turn enhancing their own concept of self.

Also, when a leader exploits a prejudice widely held by her or his constituency, group members may experience a heightened sense of purpose and a stronger feeling of community while at the same time solidifying the leader's position.

Self-Esteem, the Protective Function. People often hate that which appears threatening or uncertain, as it reminds them of the fragility of the ego. All of us fail at times, and it is frightening to take responsibility for those failures. Prejudice protects one's sense of self-esteem against conflicts and weaknesses arising from one's limitations (whether internal or external). Thus, scapegoating certain groups shields people psychologically from their own inadequacies and fears.

> Holding the prejudice protects people from a harsh reality. For instance, a person who is unsuccessful in the business world may believe that members of a certain successful group are a scheming bunch of cheaters. (Breslin, p. 34.)

Value-Expressive Function. People prize their own particular sets of values and modes of living, and there may be some insecurity surrounding anything which is different from those standards. For any difference may be construed as a threat to those frameworks, a threat which would undermine the security which social norms provide. Consequently, any group which is perceived as challenging one's values is considered inferior and threatening. Prejudice against people who maintain values different from one's own tends to strengthen the values of those who hold the prejudice. Seeing even imaginary threats to one's shared values may not only increase animosity toward those who are perceived as threats but also make the values appear to be worth defending.

For example, a religious group may discriminate against members of another religion because their beliefs threaten their notion of God. Or people may engage in atrocities toward out-groups' members in order to retain their own supposed values of a pure social stock. (Wurzel.)

The Cognitive Function.   Cognition, by definition, is an act or process by which people come to know or understand. To comprehend a complex world, people tend to divide reality into distinct categories. In this process, the individual parts lose their uniqueness and are viewed in terms of their supposed similarity to others in the same category. This tendency toward homogeneity may be that which enables us to create concepts and make sense of a world which might otherwise seem overwhelming.

We may do the same with people. That is, we tend to evaluate others in terms of general categories. Stereotypes provide such categories and thus serve to order the world. Prejudice becomes a shortcut means of relating to others and digesting new information.

Origins

Prejudice and discrimination can be tools used by the dominant group to maintain its control or power. Unless and until a minority group challenges this, this treatment may be viewed as being a part of the natural order of things. The origins of prejudice are many and are extremely complex and include both the psychological makeup of the individual and the structural organization of the society.

Psychological Factors.   It is not uncommon for people to feel frustrated occasionally. They may want something but for some reason or another cannot get it. Anger and aggression may arise and find expression in a number of ways. One can, for example, strike out directly at the source of the irritation. But this is often difficult because the source is either unknown or else too dangerous to confront. Therefore, one must find another channel similar enough to the source of the frustration to provide satisfaction.

For instance, a parent may punish a child with a spanking. Unable to hit back at the parent, the child turns around and socks a younger sibling, who then runs outside and kicks the family dog. In an organizational setting, aggression may travel down from the president to the vice-president(s), then through the entire chain of command, eventually terminating with the worker with the lowest status. In terms of relative degrees of power, those lower down become the scapegoats in the social pecking order. In a social context, this leads to prejudice if the person transfers this aggression onto members of minority groups. Take, for example, the man who is interviewed for a desirable job but is passed over for the position by a woman who is better qualified. That night on a cab ride home the man may complain to the driver that "unless something is done soon, women will be taking over the country."

Personal insecurity can also give rise to prejudice, which in turn serves the function of building self-esteem and reducing feelings of guilt. People who are insecure about their social standing and expectations often have a great need for conformity. (Saenger; Weinberg.) By identifying with a dominant group, an insecure person gains a place in society and experiences a sense of importance. Because minorities are often seen as being nonconformist, they are easy targets of aggression.

Some people appear to be more prone than others to highly prejudiced beliefs. The psychologist Erich Fromm states that such people exhibit an "authoritarian personality." Unlike the "democratic personality," the authoritarian personality suffers from repressed feelings of weakness and rejection, where the world appears as a jungle in which everyone is the enemy of everyone else. Further, the authoritarian person values strength and toughness above all else; love and sympathy are signs of weakness; security can be obtained only through domination or submission, not love and cooperation. Distrust of others is coupled with the absence of secure emotional attachments. This person lacks a sense of belonging and is unsure of his or her role and place in society. She or he overrates the power of some people, while exaggerating the weakness of others. Because of insecurity, she or he gives up individuality, and is dependent on a strong person or conforms to the dictates of a group. This denial of self often results in frustration and hostility, which have to be displaced onto those perceived as weaker and noncomformist because the person cannot afford to attack those on whom she or he is dependent. (Saenger.)

Very often, highly prejudiced people are impervious to the sorts of logical arguments that could expose the fallacies in their beliefs. Using logic or facts does not usually succeed in changing the opinions of many prejudiced people because they do not play by common rules of reason. (Sartre.) This may be because their egos are threatened by contradictory evidence or because they recognize (perhaps unconsciously) that to change *one* belief might require changing a whole network of beliefs. Rather than sacrifice the prejudiced belief, prejudiced people may find clever rationalizations to accommodate what may be even blatant contradictions of their belief systems. "I don't care *what* you say, I still believe..." is a common response to inconsistent data. Anti-gay activist Anita Bryant showed clear signs of this form of reasoning in her "Save Our Children" campaign during the late 1970s. When directly pressed to give logical arguments for her position, she often would rise and sing *The*

Battle Hymn of the Republic in an attempt to play on the patriotic sympathies of her audience. Reason had no impact on her views.

Most people, from time to time, are either unwilling or unable to look at some of their own undesirable personality traits and may transfer these traits onto others. This process is referred to as *projection*. Allport describes three types of projection:

Direct projection involves the projection of attributes which lie *solely* within the person who projects them onto those who are blamed. Women, for example, may be blamed for being "seductive," when in reality it is their accusers who are denying their own sexual desires.

The *mote-beam mechanism* refers to the process of exaggerating a relatively minor negative trait or characteristic in other people which *both* they and we possess, though we may not realize we also possess this. All of us—men and women—are irrational at times. Yet one version of sexism singles out women as irrational and emotional, devalues emotion, and denies the existence of those qualities in men.

Complementary projection explains and justifies one's own state of mind in reference to the imagined intentions and behaviors of others. This has to do with finding *causes* for one's own troubled emotions in others ("I fear, therefore they threaten"). In the case of many so-called moral zealots, their self-righteousness may be the result of unconscious or even conscious feelings of guilt based on their own repressed sexual desires. (Saenger.) This point came to light dramatically in 1987 in separate incidents when two TV ministers, Jim Bakker and Jimmy Swaggart, were accused of engaging in "sexual indiscretions," the latter with a prostitute, and were forced to suspend their preaching.

Projection thus becomes another justification for aggression against minorities. Such aggression serves to cleanse the person of an undesirable trait. Projection onto an individual or group is used to free oneself of the forbidden thought while at the same time enjoying vicarious gratification of that desire. With respect to homophobia, prejudice against gays may serve to reduce the tension and anxiety aroused by unconscious doubts about one's own sexuality. Sigmund Freud termed this aversion *reaction formation*, which is the mechanism used to defend against an impulse in oneself by taking a firm stand against its expression in others.

The homophobic person is threatened by the mere existence of sexual minorities whom he or she sees as belittling or undervaluing the importance of his or her own personal qualities (e.g., sexual prowess and the ability to attract members of the other sex). (Weinberg.) Also, a person's negative feelings toward homosexuals of the other sex may stem from that person's feeling of rejection as a potential sexual partner. In addition, the person may experience a repressed envy of gays, lesbians, and bisexuals, who are often perceived as enjoying a greater degree of freedom by not accepting rigid gender roles. This can be extremely distressing for those who need to be rewarded for their conformity to rules. Such envy might be translated unconsciously into hostility.

Weinberg suggests the concept of *existence without vicarious immortality* as another psychological component of homophobia. Simply stated, homosexuals are generally regarded as people who either do not or cannot bear children. Though in fact this is often not the case, the thought of persons without children awakens in some people a fear of death, often unconscious, since children provide a continuation of the family line after the death of individual members. Any reminder of one's own mortality is threatening to the ego, and this fear translates into homophobia.

Those who have a solid sense of who they are and where they stand in the world are not only less likely to experience prejudice but are also more open to abandon prejudiced beliefs in the face of contrary evidence. Likewise, heterosexual males and females who are genuinely comfortable with their own sexual identities apparently feel far less threatened by homosexuality than those who are insecure. (Marmor.)

Psychological factors alone, however, do not completely explain the origins of prejudice. In particular, the psychological explanations do not make clear why some attributes are singled out over others, why some attributes are negatively valued, and why some groups and not others bear the brunt of social prejudice. Prejudice is not an individual phenomenon, hence it is important to look at the larger social context in which prejudice occurs and is reinforced.

Competition and Exploitation.

Racial prejudice is a social attitude propagated among the public by an exploiting class for the purpose of stigmatizing some group as inferior so that the exploitation of either the group itself or its resources may be justified. (Cox.)

Prejudice and discrimination are problems in societies where there are hierarchical structures. In social settings where some have more than others, a belief system develops which justifies the entitlement of those with economic power. In particular, people whose class status is somewhat tenuous may struggle to keep others from ascending the economic ladder. Furthermore, as goods and services become scarcer, there is increasing economic competition. Thus, "prejudice is reversely proportional to the economic climate of a society." (Saenger.) When economic times are good, there is more need of inexpensive immigrant labor, which tends to result in a decline of prejudice. However, in a bad economy, the reverse is usually true, and members of different groups may see others as competition for scarce resources.

The myth of inherent racial differences originally justified the institution of slavery and the exploitation of native populations by colonial powers. More recently, discrimination remains to buttress vested economic interests. Landlords can exact high rents and merchants can charge high prices from minorities forced to reside in segregated areas. Employers can get away with paying low wages to minority workers. Management has a stake in turning various groups of workers against each other so that they do not join together against their bosses to push for improved wages and working conditions.

Totalitarian regimes often whip up prejudice against minorities. In doing so, they divert popular attention from the real cause of the social conditions and prevent unity among diverse groups. In this way, they diffuse the power those groups together would have to create resistance.

Though economics seems not to be the primary reason for homophobia as it is in other forms of discrimination, it does at times play a role. Within many large urban areas, gays and lesbians may choose to reside in what have come to be called "gay ghettos" because there they may feel more comfortable being who they are. Within these areas, due to the law of supply and demand, they are often asked to pay higher rents and may be exploited by shop and bar owners. Also, women continue to earn 69 cents for every dollar earned by a man, so lesbians suffer from this double oppression. Lesbians are not only exploited as women, but also do not have access to the salary of a higher-earning male partner. Finally, in these times of a growing health-care crisis surrounding AIDS, homophobia has lent support to attempts to deny gay men health-care insurance and financial support for related care.

There are, of course, bona fide differences in the appearance, religion, social customs, and sexual orientation of various groups. However, many times the threatening nature of the differences is more imagined than real. People who look or sound different will actually appear to be threatening to some individuals. In most instances, however, the negative reputation of a given minority group is not so much earned as it is thrust upon them. Further, it is not clear why some differences appear to be more threatening than others. At times, competition for scarce resources or stressful or poor quality of contact between groups can also bring about hard feelings which can last for generations. This is true in many of our larger cities, where contact between people is often brief and impersonal. Allport terms the condition arising from this situation as "urban insecurity." In addition, prejudice often exists in populations of bordering countries where there is competition for land or natural resources, and where rapid change in population distribution occurs.

The rate at which a population changes its composition often determines how newly entering groups will be treated by the dominant group:

A slow, imperceptible change over years or decades is less likely to create a negative reaction than a sudden increase in minority populations over a short period of time. (Saenger.)

When individual minority members increase in number, are more visible, or when they begin to gain political or social advances, the dominant group may react unfavorably. Called *backlash*, this may result in increased and intensified incidents of discrimination against the minority group.

Short or unsustained positive experiences with minorities are often unlikely to alter prejudice if the negative stereotypes are strongly ingrained. Sometimes direct contact actually deepens prejudice because of the process of *selection* and *distortion*. (Saenger.) The prejudiced individual may select to focus on the negative contacts, thus distorting them to seem worse than they actually are. Prejudice then becomes circular, feeding off itself.

Once again, situational (or contact) theory is relevant to the existence of homophobia. Though homosexuals constitute a significant percentage of the population, most gay people are not visible. As a result, heterosexuals are not always aware of their contact with lesbians and gays. Thus, they may tend to focus on one isolated negative encounter or some lurid headline involving a gay person and generalize from that to all gay people. We frequently hear about murders on the evening news, for example. But when a gay man or lesbian is involved, homophobia encourages singling out this aspect of the case, reinforcing the already existing prejudice. Similarly, positive encounters which may contradict the stereotype are often dismissed as being atypical.

Social Norms and Values.

We prize our own mode of existence and correspondingly underprize (or actively attack) what seems to us to threaten it.... (Allport, p. 26.)

Through the process of socialization, people grow up learning the norms and values of their culture. Most social scientists assert that prejudice is not an innate human instinct, and that people learn over time the prejudices of those around them.

In this connection, prejudice is formed not so much by contact with a minority group, but rather by contact with the prevailing attitudes toward the group. (Horowitz.)

Most people are taught to distrust some groups when they are very young children. This "teaching" does not occur in the form of classroom "lessons," but is rather quite subtle and often unnoticed. Thus, we tend to forget specific instances when these attitudes were inculcated. Nevertheless, the attitudes tend to become ingrained. And, as members are taught to praise the values of their own group, they are likewise often taught to reject those of others. Consequently, the out-groups tend not simply to be thought of as different or unique, but rather as inferior and dangerous.

Allport outlines three stages in the process by which children acquire prejudice:

In the pregeneralized stage the child has not yet generalized after the fashion of adults and does not fully understand what attitudes toward others should be.

In the total rejection stage, if taught to reject members of a group, the child will reject all in that category in all circumstances and with considerable feeling. This stage reaches its peak in early puberty.

In the differentiation stage, as the child matures, she or he usually loses the tendency of total rejection and overgeneralization, and prejudice is less totalized.

Social systems, like individuals, seek ways to solidify power. When governments are torn by political, economic, or social strife, their minorities are often blamed for the problems. For example, prior to World War II, Germany was plagued by mounting rates of inflation and rising unemployment. The Nazis targeted blame on the Jews and other minorities, in order to consolidate their national power, leading to their eventual control of the government. Further, the Nazis created stereotypes of Jews as dirty and disease-ridden and as dangerous child molesters as a way to tap into people's already existing fears and to reinforce negative attitudes which then had currency.

Scapegoating individuals, groups, and governments then serves an ideological function. By keeping certain groups on the edge or fringe of society and branding them with such labels as "sick," "abnormal," "dirty," "oversexed," "heretical," "ignorant," etc., the dominant group can then define itself as normal. Subsequently, depending on the time and place, minorities have been welcome scapegoats. Not only is this true in the formulation of racial, religious, and other forms of prejudice, but also it is evident in the development of homophobia.

Most of us probably heard as children the negative labels and judgments about "effeminate" males and "masculine" females, and the stereotypes concerning the "predatory nature" of gays and lesbians and the lonely and unhappy lives they lead. Though some people may feel that they have transcended this early indoctrination, such conditioning is not easily tossed aside. Children today continue to call each other "faggot" before they even know about sex or what the term means, and many social institutions actively encourage such attitudes.

Whether conscious or not, the dominant group views homosexuality as essentially inconsistent with and therefore a fundamental threat to the concept of the family. Since the family is the basic unit of society, the belief is that whatever appears to threaten it eventually endangers the entire culture. This is especially distressing to the dominant group since it is primarily the family which passes on the values, customs, and norms of the dominant group.

This protective attitude toward the institution of the family has implications not only for gays and lesbians but also unmarried and childless heterosexuals.

As an adult beyond a certain age, not to be part of a nuclear family of one's own is to feel excluded from what is widely believed to be the only acceptable form of organizing one's sexual and social life. That homosexuals and single heterosexuals may live perfectly happily without marriage and children is rarely admitted—perhaps it cannot be admitted, for to do so would be to call into question the dominant ideology that forces most people into accepting marriage as inevitable and its perpetuation as highly desirable. (Altman, p. 57.)

The family serves as a model for the teaching of sex roles, with its own set of behavioral expectations for "mothers" and "fathers," "husbands" and "wives," and "daughters" and "sons." Traditional notions of "masculinity" and "femininity" spring from this model. Same-sex relationships obviously suggest different paradigms of behavior in which one can assume neither the automatic superiority of any one person based on sex nor the assignment of certain behaviors depending on sex.

Finally, another basic underpinning of this ideology concerns the purpose of sex itself. However much the sexual ethic has changed in the last fifty years, there still remains a prevailing belief that the proper and primary function of sex is procreative. This belief may stem not only from the biological imperative to continue the species, but also from the need for social order and control. The "Puritan Ethic" has led to the belief that pleasure for its own sake is immoral. Clearly, homosexual sex (and heterosexual birth control, child-free lifestyles, etc.) flies in the face of such beliefs. At a time when the family is undergoing change and many traditional values are being questioned, lesbians, gays, and bisexuals may serve as a convenient scapegoat for those who fear what those changes will mean.

A Brief History of Homophobia

In a number of ways the separate histories of Europe's minorities are the same story...[for example] the fate of Jews and gay people has been almost identical throughout European history, from early Christian hostility to extermination in concentration camps. The same laws which oppressed Jews oppressed gay people; the same groups bent on eliminating Jews tried to wipe out homosexuality; the same period of European history which could not make room for Jewish distinctiveness reacted violently against sexual nonconformity; the same countries which insisted on religious uniformity imposed majority standards of sexual conduct; and even the same methods of propaganda were used against Jews and gay people, picturing them as animals bent on the destruction of the children of the majority. (Boswell, p. 15.)

In July 1986 the United States Supreme Court, by a 5 to 4 vote in *Bowers v. Hardwick*, reaffirmed the constitutionality of a Georgia state anti-sodomy law dating back to 1816. This decision, which some people consider to be the gay equivalent of the Dred Scott decision for blacks, upheld the Georgia law which makes "any sexual act involving the sex organs of one person and the mouth or anus of another" a felony punishable by up to twenty years imprisonment. Although this law and similar laws in a number of other states could conceivably be applied to heterosexuals, they have primarily been used to intimidate and harass gays, lesbians, and bisexuals from participating in private consensual sexual activities.

Though the government of the United States is predicated on a policy of the separation of church and state, religious and historical justifications were cited in this decision. Adding his voice to the court's majority opinion, former Chief Justice Warren Burger wrote:

Decisions of individuals relating to homosexual conduct have been subject to State intervention throughout the history of Western Civilization. Condemnation of those practices is firmly rooted in Judaeo-Christian moral and ethical standards. Homosexual sodomy was a capital crime under Roman law.... To hold that the act of homosexual sodomy is somehow protected as a fundamental right would be to cast aside millennia of moral teaching. (Bowers v. Hardwick, 1986.)

History has shown that there exists a symbiotic relationship between religious and secular teachings on the issue of homosexuality, with one both influencing and used to justify the other. Religious, philosophical, social, and political attitudes set the groundwork for restrictive laws enacted toward the latter stages of imperial Roman civilization; Roman law was used as a basis for Medieval Canon Law (the law of the Catholic Church); Canon Law along with Roman law has been used as the cornerstone for punitive civil laws to the present day. Although not always strictly enforced, laws doling out punishments ranging from floggings to banishment to mutilation, to death have existed at various times in most Western countries. All of these statutes apply to males, though females have not always been exempt from their authority.

We know that homosexual love was an accepted practice between males during Classical Greek civilization. However, in the 9th century B.C.E., the Spartan lawmaker Lycurgus made it a felony punishable by banishment or death for a man to desire another man in mere lust. (Day.) Later, in 346 B.C.E., Greek law harshly forbade male prostitution, not out of any aversion to homosexuality *per se*, but rather out of concern that if a man or boy could sell his body, he might also sell out the interests of his community to any one of a number of warring states. (Dover.)

Though ancient Greece and Rome were tolerant of same-sex sexual practices, around the 4th century C.E. attitudes changed as Roman civilization became increasingly deurbanized with greater totalitarian controls over personal life. (Boswell.) During the declining years of imperial Rome, philosophical, political, and social forces merged, establishing a climate of intolerance. Christianity (with its pronouncements against homosexuality) became the official state religion under the rule of Constantine I. In this climate, laws were enacted which severely restricted same-sex eroticism. The edicts of Constantine and Constans of 342 C.E., and later the law of 390 C.E.—sponsored under the tripartite rule of Theodosius, Valentinian II, and Arcadius—prescribed death to men engaging in homosexual activity, especially in the case of prostitution:

> All persons who have the shameful custom of condemning a man's body, acting the part of a woman's, to the sufferance of an alien sex (for they appear not to be different from women) shall expiate a crime of this kind by avenging flames in the sight of the people. (The Theodosian Code.)

It seems, however, that these laws were rarely enforced, and male prostitution continued to be taxed into the 6th century. (Evagrius.)

These laws are important because they were incorporated into the *Corpus juris civilis*—the extensive collection of Roman law instituted under the sponsorship of Emperor Justinian in the 6th century C.E.—which later was used as the basis for canon and secular law in Europe, England, and America. (Bullough.) The *Institutes* is the name given to the section within the *Corpus juris civilis* which prescribes the death penalty for any person who is found guilty of adultery, or of engaging in "works of lewdness with their own sex."

To appreciate fully the character of the Roman system of values, it is useful to explore the context in which these anti-homosexual statements arise. Also found in the Institutes, under the title "The Rights of Persons," are laws designed to regulate and advance the accepted Roman practice of slavery:

> ...slavery is the constitution of the law of nations, by which the individual, contrary to nature, is subject to the mastery of another. Slaves are called [in Latin] *servi*, from *servare* [to save], because the generals were accustomed to sell their captives instead of killing them, and so saved them.... Slaves are in the power of their masters by the law of nations. For in almost all nations the power of life and death was exercised by the masters over their slaves, and whatsoever was acquired by the slave belonged to the master.... By the law of nations, those things which we take become ours. And therefore freemen are reduced to slavery.... (Institutes of Justinian, Title III, *Corpus juris civilis*, ed. Amstel, 1663.)

Slavery was thus part of a universal policy which, though initially the result of captivity in war, extended to the descendants of the vanquished, even when one of the parents was a "free" citizen. It is interesting to note that this section of the Institutes was later cited by a number of lawyers and clergymen to justify slavery in the United States, particularly when that institution was under attack during the 1850s and 1860s.

In addition to the Institutes of the *Corpus juris civilis*, Emperor Justinian issued two condemnations of his own against the practice of homosexuality. His Novella 77 of 538 C.E. called on men engaging in same-sex eroticism to change their ways and singled them out as the cause of the evils of society:

> For because of such crimes there are famines, earthquakes, and pestilences; wherefore we admonish men to abstain from the aforesaid unlawful acts, that they may not lose their souls. (Novella LXXVII.)

Six years later, in 544, following a devastating plague in Constantinople, Justinian issued Novella 141, demanding that his citizenry resist evil temptation. Homosexuality in particular was:

> ...that abominable and impious conduct deservedly hated by God. We speak of the defilement of males which some men sacrilegiously and impiously dare to attempt, perpetrating vile acts upon other men.... If, with eyes as if were blinded, we overlook such impious and forbidden conduct, we may provoke the good God to anger and bring ruin upon all—a fate which would be but deserved. (Novella CXLI, pp. 74-75.)

Novellas 77 and 141 were early edicts intended to scapegoat these males for general societal ills. Modern echoes of this attitude were sounded by Christian fundamentalists, led by Anita Bryant, in the late 1970s, when they placed blame for a lengthy and devastating drought in California on that state's municipal statutes protecting the rights of gay males and lesbians. Later, some people argued that the AIDS epidemic is God's punishment on homosexuals and on a society which condones homosexuality.

Though some modern Church leaders cite the early edicts of Justinian as justification for anti-gay laws, it does not appear that the early Church supported these rulings:

> There is no indication that any church official suggested or supported the emperor's action against gay people. On the contrary, the only persons known by name to have been punished for homosexual acts were prominent bishops. (Boswell, p. 172.)

Some of these include Isaiah of Rhodes, *prefectus vigilum* of Constantinople, who was tortured and exiled, and Alexander, bishop of Diospilis in Thrace, who was castrated and publicly ridiculed.

The fall of the Roman Empire signaled a change in the treatment of minorities. Though certainly not a golden age of pluralism, the 7th to the middle of the 12th centuries was an era (except in Spain) of relative calm and acceptance of same-sex acts, and minorities. Most Jews and people engaging in same-sex eroticism lived unmolested, and some even attained high social positions. The exception was Spain, which, around 650 C.E., was ruled by the Visigoths, who passed stringent laws prescribing castration for men found engaging in homosexual acts and denying basic rights to Jews.

However, the latter part of the 12th century ushered in a sustained period of universal intolerance throughout Europe. Minorities lost ground with the rise of new secular states and their powerful central governments and with the standardization of Catholic Church dogma. Both Church and State supported Justinian's law as the basis for widespread legislation and codes dictating conformity. (Boswell.)

The Camaldolese monk Gratian is generally considered the one who formulated and standardized Canon doctrine. In his *Decretum* of 1140 C.E., Gratian formalizes the concept of "Natural Law" and quotes the Roman Augustine in his condemnation of homosexuality:

> Acts contrary to nature are in truth always illicit, and without doubt more shameful and foul, which use the Holy Apostle has condemned both in women and in men, meaning them to be understood as more damnable than if they sinned through the natural use by adultery or fornication. (*Corpus iuris canonici*, 1144.)

The *Decretum* of Gratian became the fundamental and most widely accepted work of Canon law until the early 20th century, and it influenced many civil laws which were to come. One of the first of such laws to pay explicit attention to same-sex behavior in both males and females was included in the French code of 1270, in the section called *Li Livres di jostice et de plet* (Crompton 1980):

> 22. He who has been proved to be a sodomite must lose his testicles. And if he does it a second time, he must lose his member, and if he does it a third time, he must be burned.

> 23. A woman who does this shall lose her member each time and on the third must be burned. (Rapetti, ed., 1850.)

In the original French, *perdre membre* in these passages has come to be interpreted as loss of the penis, clitoris, and/or arms and legs.

In thirteenth century Spain, homosexuality carried a penalty of castration and "lapidation" (execution by stoning). This was changed under the rule of Ferdinand and Isabella in 1479, when people were burned alive.

The earliest civil law dealing specifically with homosexuality in England dates from 1533, under the rule of King Henry VIII, who stated that "there is not yet sufficient and condign punishment" for this "detestable and abominable vice." (Quoted in *The Challenge and Progress of Homosexual Law Reform*.) In that year the English Parliament classified buggery (a term which was used to denote same-sex activity, bestiality, and anal intercourse) as a felony. Penalties included loss of property and death. Then, in 1564, Queen Elizabeth declared the law a permanent part of English statutes; the death penalty for homosexual behavior in England was not repealed until 1861. The law was used as the basis for sending a number of men who frequented the "Molly Houses" (the first known residences in England where men met for sex and companionship) to their deaths around the early 1700s. (Bray.)

This English statute, like similar ones in Scotland, on the European continent, and in some Latin American countries, was drafted by lawyers who had backgrounds in both Roman law and Christian doctrine. Records show that such statutes resulted in the executions of a large number of men and women. Some of these include several dozen men burned by the Inquisition in Spain (Lea); sixteen young noblemen executed in Venice, Italy, in 1406-7 (Ruggiero); fourteen put to the torch in Mexico City in 1658 (Taylor); twenty-eight deaths recorded in Switzerland (Monter); sixty men executed in Holland in 1730-1 (Crompton); sixty hanged in Britain in 1806-35 (Crompton); forty-five hanged in the British navy from 1703-1829 (Gilbert); plus seventy-seven sentenced to death in France during the years 1565-1640 (Crompton).

GENEVAN SODOMY TRIALS, 1400–1800

#	Date	Reference	Judgment	Remarks about Suspects
1	1444	P.C. I/81	Hanged	Greek, episcopal cook
2	1444	P.C. I/105	Hanged	Genevan, partner of #1
3	1460	R.C. I/414-25	Unknown	Milanese, jurisdiction quarrel
4	1480	R.C. 3/128-35	Unknown	Physician, jurisdiction quarrel
5	1485	R.C. 3/427	Unknown	Genevan, tried by bishop
6	1513	R.C. 7/347-50	Unknown	Genevan, tried by bishop
7	1542	P.C. II/529	Banished	Genevan, also adultery
8	1555	P.C. I/517	Beheaded	Frenchman, journeyman printer
9	1555	P.C. II/1073	Whipped	Genevan schoolboy
10	1556	P.C. I/561	Hanged	Frenchman
11	1561	P.C. I/957	Banished	Frenchman
12	1561	P.C. I/957	Banished	Frenchman, partner of #11
13	1561	P.C. I/971	Banished	Frenchman
14	1561	P.C. I/971	Banished	Frenchman, partner of #13
15	1562	P.C. I/1078	Drowned	Frenchman
16	1562	P.C. I/1078	Drowned	Frenchman, partner of #15
17	1563	P.C. I/1167	Drowned	French student, age 20
18	1563	P.C. I/1168	Whipped	Three Genevan schoolboys
19	1565	P.C. I/1324	Banished	Frenchman
20	1565	P.C. II/1284	Unknown	Local peasant, bestiality
21	1566	P.C. I/1359	Drowned	Italian student, age 22
22	1567	P.C. I/1405	Banished	Frenchman
23	1568	P.C. I/1452	Drowned	Frenchman
24	1568	P.C. I/1465	Drowned	Genevan, lesbian
25	1569	P.C. I/1560	Banished	Italian
26	1569	P.C. I/1560	Banished	Frenchman, accuser of #25
27	1576	P.C. II/1433	Banished	Swiss, servant
28	1590	P.C. II/1634	Unknown	French galley slave, age 50
29	1590	P.C. II/1634	Burned	Turkish galley slave
30	1590	P.C. II/1634	Burned	Turkish galley slave
31	1590	P.C. II/1634	Burned	Turkish galley slave
32	1590	P.C. II/1634	Burned	French soldier, age 25
33	1590	P.C. II/1634	Burned	French valet of #32, age 18
34	1593	P.C. II/1751	Unknown	Genevan citizen
35	1593	P.C. II/1751	Unknown	German artisan, partner of #34
36	1595	P.C. II/1813	Unknown	French boy, age 12
37	1600	P.C. I/1818	Drowned	Genevan citizen
38	1600	P.C. I/1818	Drowned	Local peasant, partner of #37
39	1610	P.C. I/2013	Burned	Genevan official (P. Canal)
40	1610	P.C. I/2016	Fined	Genevan official, partner of #39
41	1610	P.C. I/2017	Drowned	Genevan gatekeeper, partner of #39
42	1610	P.C. I/2017	Drowned	Genevan, partner of #39

GENEVAN SODOMY TRIALS, 1400-1800

#	Date	Reference	Judgment	Remarks about Suspects
43	1610	P.C. I/2017	Drowned	Genevan, partner of #39
44	1610	P.C. I/2018	Banished	Genevan, accused by #39
45	1610	P.C. I/2018	Banished	Genevan, accused by #39
46	1610	P.C. I/2018	Banished	Genevan, accused by #39
47	1610	P.C. I/2018	Banished	Genevan, accused by #39
48	1610	P.C. I/2019	Banished	Genevan, accused by #39
49	1610	P.C. I/2019	Banished	Genevan, accused by #39
50	1610	P.C. I/2212	Banished	Genevan, accused by #39 (escaped)
51	1613	P.C. I/2212	Banished	Genevan, began as plaintiff
52	1614	P.C. I/2238	Drowned	Catholic stableboy, bestiality
53	1615	P.C. I/2297	Burned	French Catholic, bestiality and witchcraft
54	1617	P.C. I/2350	Burned	Swiss visitor, age 80
55	1617	P.C. I/2378	Burned	Catholic, age 46, bestiality
56	1621	P.C. I/2505	Burned	Catholic, age 50, Savoyard
57	1623	P.C. I/2579	Banished	Genevan citizen, age 83
58	1633	P.C. I/2948	Burned	Genevan citizen
59	1633	P.C. I/2948	Banished	Genevan boy, age 15, partner #58
60	1634	P.C. I/2981	Burned	Neapolitan
61	1634	P.C. I/2982	Banished	French valet, partner of #60
62	1636	P.C. II/2393	Banished	Frenchman, bestiality
63	1647	P.C. I/3330	Hanged	Italian
64	1647	P.C. I/3331	Burned	Italian, partner of #63
65	1660	P.C. I/3696	Released	Stableboy, age 17, bestiality
66	1662	P.C. I/3768	Burned	Italian officer, age 42
67	1662	P.C. I/3777	Banished	French valet, partner of #66
68	1663	P.C. I/3777	Banished	Genevan carpenter, bestiality
69	1672	P.C. I/4215	Unknown	Two Genevan schoolboys
70	1678	P.C. I/4405	Unknown	Local peasant age 18, bestiality
71	1721	P.C. I/6896	Unknown	Catholic stableboy, bestiality
72	1785	P.C. I/14478	Unknown	Genevan citizen, watchmaker
73	1786	P.C. I/14930	Banished	German, age 23, accused by guard
74	1787	P.C. I/15178	Banished	Genevan, accused by guard
75	1789	P.C. I/15711	Unknown	Genevan, billiard-parlor owner

Abbreviations

P.C.-Series of *Procès Criminels* at *Archives d'Etat*, Geneva
R.C.-*Registres du Conseil de Genève*, ed. Rivoire and van Berchem, 13 vols. (Geneva, 1900-1940). Series stops in 1536. (Compiled by Monter, 1980.)

Change was stirring in the air in the 18th century. "Liberty, Equality, Fraternity," the battle cry of those attempting to overturn the ruling French aristocracy, would carry over into the sexual realm as well. After the successful revolution of 1789, the death penalty was removed from all French laws dealing with sexuality. In 1810, after completion of a new criminal code—the Napoleonic Code—all penalties for consensual adult sexual activities were eliminated. Though homosexuality remained subject to social disapproval, the new French code was in many respects a watershed that was to have the effect of liberalizing legislation in other countries under French domination. This was particularly true in Belgium, much of Italy, Spain, Portugal, Romania, and Russia, as well as several Latin American countries. This did not, however, extend to countries outside the French sphere, including Prussia, the Scandinavian states, and, after 1871, Germany—which united under the Prussian realm. Russia, however, reinstituted laws punishing people engaging in homosexual acts with imprisonment for terms of up to five years. After 1866, when Denmark abolished the death penalty for same-sex activity, Germany and the English-speaking common-law countries remained virtually alone in retaining harsh penalties well into the 20th century. (Bullough.)

Though England abolished the death penalty for same-sex acts in 1861, under the reign of Queen Victoria in 1885, the Labouchiere Amendment was instituted. It created a totally new crime of "gross indecency with males in public or private" with punishments of imprisonment for up to two years. Oscar Wilde was convicted and imprisoned under the terms of this law which remained in force until July 27, 1967. In that year both houses of the English Parliament agreed to institute the recommendations of a select group appointed by the British Home Secretary in 1954. The committee was headed by Sir John Wolfenden of Reading University. What has since come to be known as the Wolfenden Report concluded that laws regulating sexual acts between consenting adults in private be removed from the criminal statutes.

In Germany, Paragraph 175 of the German Penal Code was the law Adolf Hitler and his Gestapo chief Heinrich Himmler eventually cited in their plan for the "relocation" and eventual extermination of thousands of homosexuals (see Chapter 6):

1. A male who indulges in criminally indecent activities with another male or who allows himself to participate in such activities will be punished with jail.
2. If one of the participants is under the age of twenty-one, and if the crime has not been grave, the court may dispense with the jail sentence.

The United States has inherited much from England, including its language, social customs, and many of its laws, particularly those concerning homosexuality and sodomy. Richard Cornish, a ship's master, was the first man to be executed in the British colony of Virginia in 1624 or 1625, for alleged homosexual acts with one of his stewards. (Katz.) Another early case involved John Alexander and Thomas Roberts of Plymouth in 1637, who were found "guilty of lude behavior and uncleane carriage one with another by often spendinge their seed one upon another." (Shurtleff.)

The earliest known case of a person put to death for homosexual acts in a territory which would become part of the United States was a Frenchman who was executed in St. Augustine, Florida, by Spanish military authorities in 1566. (Katz.)

Penalties were not restricted to homosexuality, but also applied to bestiality. For instance, one of the first of these cases dealt with William Hackett, an eighteen-year-old servant who was found copulating with a cow. After Hackett confessed, the cow was burned and Hackett was hanged. (Winthrop.) Another case involved a Thomas Granger, aged sixteen or seventeen, who confessed and was convicted of having sex with a mare, a cow, two goats, five sheep, and a turkey. The animals were burned and on September 8, 1642, Granger was executed.

The American Revolution in the late 18th century ended Britain's political and economic domination over her American colonies, but did not carry with it sweeping law reforms as would the revolution in France a few years later. Homosexuality and sodomy continued to carry harsh penalties, though executions became rarer. Between 1777 and 1779, the statesman and author of the Declaration of Independence Thomas Jefferson, along with other reformers, proposed that the death penalty be dropped for convictions of homosexuality in the colony of Virginia and replaced with the punishment of castration. (Katz.) Since that time individual states have created their own laws regulating such behavior. Though Wisconsin, Massachusetts, and some municipalities have passed legislation to protect the rights of gay males, lesbians, and bisexuals, in many others a person can be imprisoned or legally denied housing, employment, public accommodations, child custody, insurance, inheritance, and so forth, simply on the basis of sexual orientation. In addition, lesbians and gay males continue to be harassed and physically assaulted.

Homophobia and Heterosexism

It is difficult for anyone living in the United States in the 20th century to avoid internalizing homophobic attitudes. All around are messages which defame lesbians and gays.

A poll conducted by *Newsweek* magazine in 1983 estimated that 66 percent of the U.S. population feel that homosexuality is an unacceptable lifestyle. A Gallup poll (1982) found that 59 percent of those surveyed would exclude homosexuals from teaching grade school, while 51 percent would not permit them to enter the clergy. J.S. Simmons, in his book *Deviants*, states that homosexuals are considerably more disliked by the American public than ex-convicts, ex-mental patients, gamblers, and alcoholics.

A study of the sexual attitudes of over 1000 American teenagers (Coles & Stokes) found that 75 percent considered sex between two females to be "disgusting" and over 80 percent felt the same for sex between two males. Also, in this study, 32 percent of the males and 16 percent of the females said they would break off all ties with any same-sex friend discovered to be gay or lesbian.

In addition, *The Des Moines Register* found that an estimated 21 percent of Iowans eighteen years of age and older consider AIDS (Acquired Immune Deficiency Syndrome) to be God's punishment of gays.

Who Is Homophobic?

Who is most likely to have strong homophobic beliefs and reactions? Drawing from a large number of studies on this topic, Gregory Herek compiled a list of characteristics which appear to be common in people with such attitudes. Though there are of course scores of exceptions, Herek found that these people are generally:

1. less likely to have had personal contact with lesbians and gay men;
2. less likely to report having engaged in homosexual behaviors or to identify themselves as lesbian or gay;
3. more likely to perceive their peers as manifesting negative attitudes, especially if the respondents are males;
4. more likely to have resided in areas where negative attitudes are the norm (e.g., the Midwestern and Southern U.S., Canadian prairies, and in rural areas and small towns), especially during adolescence;
5. likely to be older and less well educated;
6. more likely to be religious, to attend church frequently, and to subscribe to a conservative religious ideology;
7. more likely to express traditional, restrictive attitudes about sex roles;
8. less permissive sexually or manifesting more guilt or negativity about sexuality;
9. more likely to manifest high levels of authoritarianism and related personality characteristics.

These studies also suggest that heterosexuals have more negative attitudes toward homosexuals of their own sex, with stronger and deeper negative attitudes in males.

Irwin and Thompson found in their study that Roman Catholics and Protestants are less tolerant of homosexuality than Jews, members of other religions, and nonaffiliates.

Further, studies reveal that homophobia is not an isolated phenomenon detached from other forms of prejudice and discrimination. In fact, a number of studies, including Minnergerode, and Henley and Pincus, for example, reported a strong correlation between respondents' negative attitudes toward lesbians and gays and negative attitudes toward women in general. In addition, Henley and Pincus found that respondents holding negative attitudes toward gays and lesbians also exhibited negative attitudes toward blacks.

Finally, Gregory Herek found that people who are most apt to be accepting or supportive of sexual minorities include city-dwellers, people from Northeastern and Pacific Coastal regions of the U.S., younger persons whose peers' values reflect the changes of the 1960s and 1970s, the more educated, and people whose parents demonstrated support for human sexual diversity.

Heterosexism

Homophobia has a close ally—*heterosexism*. This is the system by which heterosexuality is assumed to be the only acceptable and viable life option. Very often heterosexism is quite subtle or indirect and may not even be apparent. Because this norm is so pervasive, heterosexism is difficult to detect.

When parents automatically expect that their children will marry a person of the other sex at some future date and will rear children within this union; when the only positive and satisfying relationships portrayed by the media are heterosexual; when teachers presume all of their students are straight and teach only about the contributions of heterosexuals—these are examples of heterosexism. It also takes the form of pity—when the dominant group looks upon sexual minorities as poor unfortunates who "can't help being the way they are." All this amounts to, in the words of author Christopher Isherwood, a "heterosexual dictatorship."

Heterosexism forces lesbians, gays, and bisexuals to struggle constantly against their own invisibility, and makes it much more difficult for them to integrate a positive sexual identity. This is not unlike the feeling of a Jew or a Muslim in a predominantly Christian country during Christmas time; a wheelchair user in a town with only stepped entrances to buildings; or an English-speaking visitor in a country in which English is not spoken. It also occurs when African Americans and Asians see only white faces in the media; when elder citizens reside in a land that values youthfulness; and when the young are told continually by adults that they are "not old enough."

Though not direct or overt, heterosexism is a form of discrimination. Its subtlety makes it somehow even more insidious because it is harder to define and combat. Heterosexism is discrimination by neglect, omission, and/or distortion, whereas often its more active partner — homophobia — is discrimination by intent and design.

Forms of Homophobia

Macho men...need faggots. They've created faggots in order to act out a sexual fantasy on the body of another man and not take any responsibility for it.... The male homosexual...is a sexual target for other men and that is why he is despised and why he is called a faggot. (Baldwin in Goldstein.)

The Story of Charlie Howard
by Rev. Robert Wheatly

His name was Charles O. Howard, "Charlie" to most everyone, and described by his friends as a twenty-three-year-old gentle, flamboyant, happy sort of person.

In Bangor, Maine, Saturday night, July 7, 1984, he left a meeting of Interweave, a Unitarian-Universalist lesbian and gay support group that meets at the Unitarian Church, a little after 10:00 p.m., and was walking with a friend downtown, when the two of them were attacked by three youths, ages fifteen, sixteen, and seventeen.

His friend got away, but Charlie was not so lucky; he was kicked and beaten and thrown over the rail of a bridge over the Kendeskeag Stream canal, twenty feet down into ten-foot deep waters, despite his screams that he could not swim. His body was found the next day downstream.

Police said the teenagers charged with murdering Charlie bragged afterward to a friend that they "jumped a fag and beat the s--- out of him and then threw him into the stream."

Riding around town with two girl friends that night, they spotted Charlie and his friend, piled out of the car and chased them, beat Charlie and "picked him up and threw him over the railing." All three were released Monday, July 9, into the custody of their parents.

Lesbians and gay men in Bangor and throughout Maine were outraged at the treatment of those charged with Charlie's murder.

Thomas Goodwin, the assistant attorney general who will prosecute the case, said he recommended their release because they were "not a threat to the community," and that the youths did not necessarily intend to kill Charlie because "the evidence would suggest they didn't know he had drowned."

Sgt. Thomas Placella, the chief detective on the case, added, "I'm not trying to lessen the severity of the crime, but it's not like these were ax murderers. These people came from respectable families who own property in the city of Bangor."

That Monday night the Unitarian Church of Bangor was the setting of a memorial service led by its minister, the Rev. Richard Forcier, attended by some 200 persons who testified to their friendship with Charlie, expressed outrage at his murder, and marched to the police station for a candlelight vigil of protest.

Many told their own stories of harassment and violence at the hand of fag-bashers.

The same scene was repeated the following Friday night in the First Parish Society, Unitarian-Universalist, in Portland, Maine, in a service led by the Rev. Richard Hasty.

More than 400 persons memorialized Charlie Howard and participated in a protest march down Congress Street to the constant harassment of Bible-quoting fundamentalists who marched alongside.

Charlie was one of the effeminate ones—whose blond, soft looks, slender body, and graceful mannerisms could not hide the fact of his gayness, no matter how hard he tried to conceal them.

Christine Palmer, journalist with the *Bangor Daily News*, tells of watching him just six days before his death, at the morning worship service which he had begun attending regularly at the Unitarian Church, "Yes, he was bubbly and innocent and sweet and all those good things people said about him Monday night. But he was also a pain in the neck sometimes. He talked too much, listened too little, didn't do things *my* way.

"And isn't that exactly why, if we must find a reason, that he died? Charlie didn't do things the way others thought he should. He didn't conform."

He had learned to accept his gayness, had long since told his parents and family, and made "Glad to be Gay" his anthem, had moved beyond the shyness and self-doubt which haunted his childhood and, last week, told friends with a grin, "The fag-beaters were after me today, but they didn't get me."

Well, they did, they finally did. He was a sitting duck, a stereotypical target, the kind many love to hate. But as Christine Palmer said, "It doesn't make much sense that Charlie, whether he wanted to carry a purse or even if he had wanted to wear a dress, should be so hated."

I've known the embarrassment of which Christine speaks, for when the stereotypical gay male is envisioned, it is apt to be the swishy ones who come to mind—and that isn't me, I've convinced myself.

And yet, there it is—a Charlie Howard somewhere who carries the stigmata in my stead—and gets dumped over a bridge for it.

I am compelled once again to remember that it was the street queens in Greenwich Village who, in 1969, began the movement that resulted in my liberation, who shouted at the cops, "Hell, no, we won't go!" and locked up the police in Stonewall Bar: The Stonewall Rebellion. "Remind me, O Lord, of my debt to the street queens!"

...Members of the lesbian and gay group reached out in a supportive way to Charlie as did others, whose first reaction to him tended to be, "Oh no...!" but who came later to see and know more of his sweetness, his ingratiating ways, and thoughtful friendliness.

What the minister was saying, it seemed to me, was that the congregation had made an effort, intentionally, to become informed and knowledgeable about lesbian and gay people, had made them welcome users of its space, had taken time to know them as individuals, and were not locked into old stereotypes of who and what lesbians and gay men are like.

They had learned, as Rich Forcier put it, to become "extremely accepting." And all of this became evident when tragedy struck, when a time of need arose. (Wheatly.)

In large cities and small outlying villages, gays and lesbians continue to face harassment and physical abuse simply because of their sexual orientation, and Charlie Howard's case represents only one of a number of such assaults and murders each year. In this instance, as in the majority of cases involving anti-gay and lesbian violence, the assailants tend to be white males in their teens and early twenties who are acting out society's prejudices. The purpose of the assaults is not theft, though that sometimes is one by-product. Rather, some people choose to attack lesbians and gays simply because they do not like their lifestyles. Intimidation and humiliation are the means by which they make their beliefs known— beliefs which very often receive community sanction. There is a postscript to the Charlie Howard incident: the three teenagers accused of his murder did not go to trial. Instead, they accepted guilty pleas to reduced charges of manslaughter and were sent to the Maine Youth Center for a short time, after which they rejoined their families.

The town's only major newspaper is still opposing gay-rights legislation or any other measures that would foster tolerance of gays. The fundamentalist preachers who dominate the town's clergy are still taking every opportunity to tell their parishioners that homosexuality is a sin and a danger to society. Bars and discos in the city are still expelling couples of the same sex who try to dance together. And high-school students are still issuing death threats to various members of the town's gay community. (Canellos.)

Six months following Howard's murder, a high school teacher in the neighboring town of Madison, Maine organized "Tolerance Day" to educate students about discrimination against people of color, Jews, ex-prisoners, elderly people, poor people, the physically challenged, and gays and lesbians. Though the school's faculty committee approved the proposal, and though 300 of 400 of the school's students signed a petition in favor of Tolerance Day, the Madison School Board unanimously voted to cancel the program on January 21, 1985, claiming the appearance of Dale McCormick, president of the Maine Lesbian and Gay Political Alliance, would threaten "safety, order, and security of the high school." The Kennebec County Superior Court upheld the School Board's cancellation of Tolerance Day, saying that lesbians and gay men have no "judicially enforceable" right to be protected from discrimination.

For lesbians, as for heterosexual women, sexual assault is a common form of violence directed against them. Abby Tallmer notes, however, that it would be wrong to conclude that lesbians and heterosexual women always are assaulted in the same ways. She suggests a number of patterns of attack in anti-lesbian violence including: anti-lesbian verbal harassment sometimes as a prelude to assault; attack outside lesbian-identified establishments by a man or gang outside a lesbian bar, for example, or by a cabdriver who parks near a lesbian bar and waits for a potential victim—this frequently results in rape; attack by a man who may follow a lesbian couple home and, following a forced entry, ties up one of the women and in clear view rapes the other; assault by a male ex-lover, ex-husband, or acquaintance stemming from the man's feelings of anger or rejection; or sexual assault by a heterosexual man who poses as gay to gain the woman's trust.

There was a new twist to anti-gay violence in the mid-1980s as the AIDS epidemic was used to rationalize and justify such attacks. Take, for example, an interview of an admitted gay-basher on the nationally televised Oprah Winfrey Show:

Winfrey: So, you admit that you used to do gay bashing?
Guest: Yeah. Fag bashing. We used to go out driving in the car to [the] city—it has a strip of nightclubs, like go-go bars, and a strip of homosexual bars.
Winfrey: And why would you do this?
Guest: We were young and full of goofiness and we just—there was nothing to do on a Friday or Saturday night.
Winfrey: And so, did that give you pleasure, doing that?
Guest: At the time it was fun. Yes.
Winfrey: Where does this hostility, this hatred toward homosexuals come from?
Guest: I think it came from the area I grew up in and in the household.
Winfrey: In your house?
Guest: Yeah, in my household.
Winfrey: What does that mean?
Guest: Well, I mean, my father—I don't think anybody really cared for homosexuals in my house, and spoke highly against them.
Winfrey: So, if someone in your house were to say, or to admit that they were gay, what would happen in your house to them?
Guest: Well, I wouldn't talk to them no more.
Winfrey: So, you actually, you hate homosexuals.
Guest: Right.
Winfrey: Why, though? Why?
Guest: I think—

Winfrey: What has a homosexual ever done to you to cause you to have this kind of hatred? Where does it come from? I'm trying to understand.

Guest: If God wanted homosexuals he would have made all one sex. You know. Why'd he make men and women? If homosexuals had their way, about 100 years from now, where would we be? There would be no more children. We'd be extinct.

Winfrey: And so, that's why you hate them. And so, that hatred carries over into what other areas of your life?

Guest: I don't care to work—I won't work for them.

Winfrey: How do you know who is and who isn't?

Guest: Well, sometimes you don't, but I mean if he's obvious or open about it, I wouldn't work for them.

Winfrey: If you see one on the street or in a restaurant—

Guest: I'd get up and move to a different table.

Winfrey: See, in this society I think it's almost impossible not to encounter people who are homosexual...from the time you get up and leave your house and go to work and do whatever you do—if you ever go to a restaurant, if you ever go out—you encounter gay people all the time, male and female. So, you must be really troubled living in a society where you have to encounter them all the time.

Guest: Obviously, yes. I think, like, you go fishing, and you're fishing at the lake, and a mosquito bites a guy with AIDS, fishing down from you, and [the mosquito] comes and bites you.

Winfrey: (ironically) Yeah. I wonder how many times that's happened....

Guest: Yeah. Could you get the AIDS from them?

Winfrey: Does that concern you?

Guest: Yeah.

Winfrey: You fish a lot?

Guest: Yeah. I fish often. But I mean—

Winfrey: ...I think I understand what you're saying. And so, in your everyday—do you think about this a lot? Seriously. I mean, do you get up in the morning and think, "God, those gays. I'm out to get them."

Guest: No. I don't get up in the morning like that, but when you get up in the morning and read the papers there's something on gay rights, or you see the gay parade, or AIDS....

Winfrey: So, when you first heard about the AIDS virus what did you say?

Guest: Well, at first I thought it would be all right.

Winfrey: Why?

Guest: Because it was just affecting gays at that time. But now, you know, you see school children getting it from blood transfusions and now it's scary. It's very scary.

Winfrey: It's scary I think because a lot of people feel the way that you do. Do you have other friends who share this feeling?

Guest: Yes.

Winfrey: And you get together and you talk about it and you say—

Guest:	Yeah. And a lot of people are scared.
Winfrey:	So, does this fear come from you being afraid because of the AIDS virus or is it just a natural hatred that you have?
Guest:	I think it's some of both.
Winfrey:	It's amazing you admit it. That's really honest of you.

Direct violence against lesbians and gays is a nationwide phenomenon. The National Gay and Lesbian Task Force published a study involving over two thousand lesbians and gay males in eight major U.S. cities (Atlanta, Boston, Dallas, Denver, Los Angeles, New York, St. Louis, and Seattle). The results showed that over 90 percent of the respondents experienced some form of victimization on account of their sexual orientation— greater than one out of three had been threatened directly with violence:

> More than one in five males, and nearly one in ten females, say they were "punched, hit, kicked, or beaten," and approximately the same ratios suffered some form of police abuse. Assaults with weapons are reported by one in ten males and one in twenty females. Many of those who report having been harassed or assaulted further state that incidents occurred multiple times. (NGLTF.)

Victimization was reported to have occurred at home, at school, and at other community locales. Approximately one-third of the respondents were assaulted verbally, while more than one in fifteen was physically abused by members of their own family.

The most widely publicized instance of anti-gay violence in recent years occurred on November 27, 1978, in San Francisco. On that day, a former policeman and city supervisor, Dan White, left his home in San Francisco, a .38 Smith & Wesson gun in hand, and headed for City Hall. Once there, he crawled through a window to avoid metal detectors. He then proceeded to Mayor George Moscone's office, where he shot him four times at close range, twice directly into his brain. He then walked down a hallway to the offices of gay City Supervisor Harvey Milk, where he unloaded five bullets into his body, killing him too.

Harvey Milk was a visible spokesperson for the rights of gay people and other disenfranchised minorities—and the mayor, though not gay himself, was an ally.

Their murderer, Dan White, was, on the other hand, a long-time foe of the lesbian and gay community. He was deeply disturbed by the relative political gains of this community during the years leading up to his violent actions.

Shortly following the shooting, White was captured and tried. The police and fire departments reportedly raised over $100,000 for his defense. (Shilts.) Graffiti soon appeared across the city with such epithets as: "Kill Fags: Dan White for Mayor," and "Dan White Showed You Can Fight City Hall."

White was convicted of a reduced charge of voluntary manslaughter and sentenced to a prison term of six years. Though he was convicted of the deaths of two elected city officials, he received a relatively mild sentence. Many believe that homophobia played a major role in the trial itself. Former policeman, white, husband and father, regular churchgoer, one-time high school athlete, distinguished military service record—Dan White in many ways personified the archetype of the "all-American boy." His crime included the killing of a gay man and his friend. It is likely that the sentence would have been much harsher if the elements of the case had been different: for example, if Milk had shot White or if White had shot only Moscone.

On January 7, 1984, Dan White was released from jail, having served only 5½ years. On October 21, 1985 he committed suicide.

According to the National Gay and Lesbian Task Force, National Gay and Lesbian Anti-Gay/Lesbian Victimization Report, the number of reported incidents of violent acts is on the increase. Attacks included verbal harassment, intimidation, physical assault, vandalism, arson, rape, murder, and/or police abuse. In the year 1985 alone, the Task Force documented over two thousand such acts across the United States. That number increased to nearly five thousand in 1986, and a record 7,000 in 1987, and this is merely the tip of the iceberg because the majority of anti-gay/lesbian assaults are never reported due to victim's concern of "coming out" publicly, or lack of trust in the judicial system. Some reported incidents include:

In Jacksonville, Florida, arsonists twice set fire to the local Metropolitan Community Church, a Christian church serving the gay and lesbian community. Attacks against the church became so frequent that bullet-proof windows had to be installed.

Yelling "Sick Motherf-----," two men threw a beaker of acid at a lesbian employee of the Los Angeles Gay and Lesbian Community Services Center. The victim sustained serious burns on her face and torso.

In Vermont, a gay man was stabbed to death by a man who later said, "I killed him because he looked like a fag."

In Portland, Maine, an assailant called three women anti-lesbian epithets and assaulted them, leaving one of the victims with a fractured jaw, several broken teeth, and bruised ribs. The other victims also sustained injuries that required medical attention.

Direct violence is simply the most visible means by which homophobia is expressed. However, as with other forms of prejudice and discrimination, homophobia appears in many forms and affects people's lives in a great number of ways.

Institutional Homophobia

Major institutions such as government, schools, businesses, and religion create all sorts of policies which dictate codes of behavior and reinforce attitudes and values. Institutions have tremendous power and social status, and, through penalties and rewards, disapproval and approval, create incentives for conformity to norms. Few contemporary institutions have policies supportive of homosexuals, and many actively work against gays. In fact, homosexuals and bisexuals are adversely affected by existing laws, codes, rules, and procedures of established political, social, business, and religious institutions.

Government.   Though a number of communities have enacted laws protecting the rights of lesbians and gay males, no such statute exists on the national level. In fact, same-sex eroticism is still illegal in many states. The language used in such laws to describe homosexual acts includes "crimes against nature," "sodomy," "buggery," "perversion," "fellatio," "unnatural intercourse," "unnatural and lascivious acts," "unnatural or perverted practices," "indecent or immoral practices," "perverse acts," and "deviate sexual conduct." (*The Challenge and Progress of Homosexual Law Reform.*) Penalties range from fines to short prison terms to life imprisonment. As one state legislator in the Florida House put it: "The homosexual deserves no better treatment than any other criminal," and he proposed new laws to the legislature because "homosexuality must be eliminated." (Phoenix.) In many places, laws which spell out the limits of sexual behavior apply also to heterosexuals but in practice are used chiefly to harass gays, lesbians, and bisexuals.

Sexual minorities are, in many instances, excluded from protections regulating fair employment practices, housing discrimination, rights of child custody, immigration, inheritance, security clearances, public accommodations, and police protection.

In employment, a person can be denied or fired from a position solely on the basis of sexual orientation. In those locales where equal protection is in effect, other reasons for termination have been given (e.g., incompatibility with co-workers or sloppy performance) to get around the law when no just cause exists. In most instances, it is difficult to prove discrimination on the basis of sexual orientation.

In housing, gays and lesbians may be evicted from rented or leased spaces. Some landlords and realtors refuse to show one-bedroom apart-ments to same-sex couples.

Having little protection under the law, gays are often the target of police entrapment and harassment through periodic raids on their bars and other social meeting places; frequently police respond slowly to a request for aid from a gay person and often refuse to respond at all. In addition, police often do not carry on a follow-up investigation of a complaint.

> In order to catch persons engaged in homosexual acts, the police have chosen to rely on two major techniques—both very expensive in time and money: "clandestine observation" which means spying through peep-holes...or special mirrors, using hidden TV cameras, or secretly taking photographs; and trapping or "decoy operation," which means sending out plainclothesmen who dress, walk, talk and act as they think homosexu-als do for the sole purpose of enticing a homosexual solicitation. (*The Challenge and Progress of Homosexual Law Reform*, p. 21.)

Police have entered gay and lesbian bars under the guise of inspecting for possible code violations, but in actuality have done so to intimidate and harass patrons. Police have arrested people for jaywalking and for minor traffic violations as they leave a bar.

Police departments have also compiled lists of suspected and known homosexuals and have made arrests on the charge of solicitation, loiter-ing, disorderly conduct, lewd or indecent acts, indecent exposure, dis-turbing the peace, lewd vagrancy, assault, public nuisance, or being a lewd and wanton person. (*The Challenge and Progress of Homosexual Law Reform*.) Reports of the arrest of gays and lesbians have been sent to their employers and landlords. (Woetzel.)

One of the most famous cases involving police harassment of gays occurred in Boise, Idaho, in 1955. Police arrested sixteen gay men and charged five of them with committing homosexual acts with minors. The men were interrogated under questionable legal tactics and forced to give names of others. At the height of the scandal, the police collected over 500 names. Fear within the underground homosexual community ran rampant. Three men were convicted and handed prison sentences: one for seven years and two for five years each. It later came out that the "children" these men were alleged to have engaged in sex with were actually hardened street hustlers in their mid- to late teens—hardly the scenario of the older man seducing young innocent children as was portrayed in the press.

In the courts, gays and lesbians who have been victims of crime are often blamed for "provoking the crime." Perpetrators of anti-lesbian and-gay assault are often given light sentences or acquitted. In jails gays and lesbians are harassed, sexually assaulted, and sometimes murdered. Some states have castrated men for engaging in homosexual activity. Gays have been fair game to blackmailers, due to their illegal status.

There is no legal recognition of marriage vows taken by gay and lesbian couples, and hence they are not accorded the tax, medical, pension, and insurance breaks and other advantages accorded to heterosexual marriage partners. Rights of inheritance also do not extend to lesbians and gays.

In accordance with a widespread societal attitude that lesbians and gays should not have contact with children, many state and private child welfare agencies have stated or implied policies denying same-sex couples or individuals the right to adopt or serve as foster parents. In addition, gay fathers and lesbian mothers have repeatedly lost custody of their children in the courts primarily because of their sexual orientation.

Gay Foster Parenting: A Case Study

Donald Babets, age thirty-six, a senior investigator for the Boston Fair Housing Commission, and David Jean, age thirty-two, business manager of the Crittendon Hastings House, a multi-service women's health agency, applied to be foster parents. After spending twelve hours in training classes led by two social workers, having a routine police-record check and in-depth home study that included exhaustive interviews, they were approved for placement of children from two years nine months to nine years old. This whole process took almost a year, and involved the requisite four levels of approval from the home-finder to the area director. In addition, the application was sent to the regional office for review and then to the highest office—the central Department of Social Services—where it was finally approved.

Before these last two stages, this process was not so unlike other applications. But there was a key difference between Babets and Jean and other prospective foster parents: they were openly homosexual partners who had lived together for the past five years and were applying together to parent foster children.

Babets and Jean later received temporary custody of two children: a three-and-a-half-year-old boy and his twenty-two-month-old brother. Though the younger of the two was supposed to be placed in another foster home, the two men offered to keep them together, and later the social workers on the case agreed to the joint placement.

Soon after this, the Boston Globe newspaper ran a story about the case. Almost immediately after this story appeared, the children were removed from the home due in part to pressure from segments of the community.

Yet friends had commented on the improvements in the children after just two weeks with Babets and Jean. Says Jean:

> Whatever happened to us, we can deal with that. It's the pain I saw in the two kids that we felt was unforgivable.... The older child was really angry. He wouldn't even talk to me. How do you explain to a kid who thinks you as an adult have control over things, that you have nothing to say about this? I saw the pain in him. I knew the pain in me. What could I say? What could I do? Nothing. (Jean, quoted in Diament, p. 88.)

This episode resulted in a change in the DSS's policy regarding placement of foster children. A joint legislative committee, following the lead of Massachusetts Governor Michael Dukakis, voted to pass a law stating that DSS should place children in homes where sexual orientation "presents no threat to the well-being of the child." This was claimed to be "nonspecific" language, but its effect was to bar lesbians and gay men from being foster parents.

On May 24, 1985, Philip Johnston, Massachusetts Secretary of Human Services, announced the following policy:

> This administration [that of Governor Dukakis] believes that foster children are served best when placed in traditional family settings—that is, with relatives or in families with married couples, preferably with parenting experience and with time available to care for foster children.

"Nontraditional" is taken to mean families where both parents work, households headed by a single person, unmarried couples, and homosexuals. Johnston indicated that any future placements with gays or lesbians were "highly unlikely."

Since the removal of the children from the home of Babets and Jean, the children have been moved in and out of three more foster homes. They were sexually abused by the foster parents in the last home in which they lived.

Another form of governmental homophobia occurred in the United States Postal Service which has employed the tactic of "mail covers"—drawing up lists of names and addresses—on people known to receive lesbian and gay publications and has handed such lists over to employers. The Postmaster General, on request from the Congress, finally ordered his department to terminate this practice. (*Newsweek*, 1966.)

Immigration laws have also been used against gays and lesbians. The United States Immigration and Naturalization Service has been given the authority to exclude certain aliens from entry into the country or to deny them U.S. citizenship. Throughout the 20th century the Immigration and Nationality Act has been amended to extend such restrictions to anyone believed to engage in terrorism or who will attempt to overthrow the government, anyone with a "social psychopathic personality," "mental defect," or communicable disease, anyone whose political opinions or writings are deemed contrary to those of the government, or anyone suspected of engaging in "immoral sexual acts" (added to bar prostitutes).

In 1965 the law was further amended, under Section 212 (a) (4), adding the category of "sexual deviates" in an attempt to exclude homosexuals. The law has been used a number of times. Between 1971 and 1978 alone, thirty-one people were barred entry into the United States under the provisions of Section 212 (a) (4). (Sullivan.) Others have been denied citizenship and lesbians have been harassed by United States agents on the Canadian-U.S. border while trying to enter this country. Though the section has been challenged in the courts, it has been upheld as constitutional and remains in force.

Also on the governmental level, public schools and public libraries have limited or entirely restricted the purchasing of books, magazines, films, and recordings on lesbian, gay, and bisexual themes.

Military.

They gave me a medal for killing two men and a discharge for loving one. (Gay Vietnam veteran Leonard Matlovich)

Using the rationale that they would undermine effective operations and jeopardize security, the military bars homosexuals from enlisting in most branches of service. (In 1988, the Federal appeals court in San Francisco by a 2-to-1 vote ruled the Army's ban on homosexuals to be unconstitutional.) For those who remain silent about their sexual orientation and manage to get in, if discovered they can be placed in military stockades and/or given an undesirable discharge with all benefits suspended. In addition, students have been kicked out of college ROTC programs once their homosexuality becomes known.

Organized Religious Institutions.

As the [person] with Jewish religion was considered not fully human, because he was not Christian—so the homosexual is considered not fully human because he is not heterosexual. (Szasz, p. 244.)

For lesbians, gays, and bisexuals, the religious equivalent of illegitimacy is being branded as "heretic," "sinner," or "immoral." With these labels comes exclusion from many or all aspects of religious life. If discovered or admitting to be homosexual, priests, rabbis, ministers, and other officials are in many instances stripped of powers and licenses. Officials and parishioners alike have been excommunicated, ostracized, and denied ceremonial participation. Students and novices are often dismissed from parochial schools and orders. Sexual prohibitions handed down by religious institutions create fear and guilt in many religious people.

Though some religious denominations are beginning to change their negative views on homosexuality, most do not sanction gay and lesbian congregations, and many do not permit them use of their facilities. For example, the Vatican reiterated its position that gay and lesbian groups such as Dignity not be permitted to hold meetings on church property. Most religions do not recognize same-sex marriages.

Women as a group have also been excluded from full membership in some denominations. They have not had the right to conduct certain ceremonies, or to enter into the hierarchy. Some religious orders retain the practice of segregating males from females in services.

Medical and Psychiatric Professions.

...the physician replaced the priest, and the patient the witch, in the drama of society's perpetual struggle to destroy precisely those human characteristics that...identify persons as individuals rather than as members of the herd. (Szasz, p. 259.)

The medical profession is often insensitive to the needs of lesbian and gay patients. Most physicians make the assumption that their patients are heterosexual, and subsequently some needed medical tests may be overlooked. If the patients are known or thought to be homosexual, harsh examination procedures are frequently used, with accompanying negative moral judgments. The profession has also denied gays and lesbians licenses to practice medicine.

Policy dictates that only blood relatives or spouses are permitted visitation rights in certain medical situations such as hospital intensive-care units, so gays and lesbians are often denied access to severely ill lovers and friends.

A case in point involves a lesbian couple, Sharon Kowalski and Karen Thompson. While living together as lovers for over four years, Kowalski was severely injured in a November 1983 collision with a drunk driver causing injury to her brain which left her partially paralyzed. Her parents, upon hearing of the nature of her relationship with Thompson, forbade Thompson from visiting her in the hospital and filed a court suit for guardianship of their daughter. In April 1984, a Minnesota court appointed Sharon's father, Donald Kowalski, guardianship and following a lengthy court battle with Thompson, gained the right to move their daughter to a nursing facility completely barring Thompson from seeing her. Thompson has fought for many years, spending well over one-hundred-thousand dollars in legal expenses to be with her lover.

Though the American Psychological Association has taken homosexuality off its official list of psychological disorders, many practitioners still attempt to change their patients' orientations. To "convert" gays and lesbians to a heterosexual orientation, the psychiatric profession has used the ineffectual and often dangerous practice of what it refers to as "aversion therapy" or "shock therapy." Electrodes are connected to the patients' head, wrists, and genitals and pictures of people of the same sex and other sex are flashed on a screen. If the patient shows a positive response to same-sex images, an electric shock is discharged as a negative reinforcer, whereas a pleasurable sensation is released when other-sex images are projected.

At one time gays and lesbians were forced to have lobotomies to alter or diminish homosexual urges. The process involves the removal of a section of the brain (the frontal lobe) which controls emotions and affect.

Homosexuals have been committed to mental institutions by relatives or by the state for long periods of time solely on the basis of their sexual orientation. There they lose all civil rights and control over their lives. Some are never released.

Within the psychiatric and psychological communities, there are a number of counselors who are genuinely supportive of lesbians and gays and attempt to help clients adjust to their same-sex orientation. However, many therapists still consider homosexuality to be an unacceptable lifestyle and therefore aim treatment toward changing the client to a heterosexual orientation whether or not this is desired by the client.

Collective or Societal Homophobia

Legal sanctions directed against gays and lesbians are increasingly being acknowledged as visible and clear indications of homophobic actions. Less obvious and more difficult to change are the many social codes of behavior which, though not written into law, nonetheless work within a society to legitimize oppression.

The theologian James S. Tinney suggests five overlapping categories by which collective homophobia is manifested:

The Denial of Culture.   Gays and lesbians, as was true for many racial and ethnic minorities, grow up without an historical context in which to place their lives. They are fed the notion that they have no culture and no history.

From Europe in the Middle Ages to the present, there has been an active attempt to falsify historical accounts of same-sex love, making accurate reconstruction extremely difficult. Boswell has documented the various means by which this falsification has been enacted: through censorship, deletion, half-truths, and the changing of pronouns signifying gender.

Boswell cites as an example of censorship a manuscript of *The Art of Love* by the Roman author Ovid. A phrase which originally read, "A boy's love appealed to me less" (*Hoc est quod pueri tanger amore minus*) was altered by a Medieval moralist to read, "A boy's love appealed to me not at all" (*Hoc est quod pueri tanger amore nihil*), and an editor's note that appeared in the margin informed the reader, "Thus you may be sure that Ovid was not a sodomite" (*Ex hoc nota quod Ovidius non frerit Sodomita*).

One of the first instances of a change of gender pronouns occurred when "Michelangelo's grandnephew employed this means to render his uncle's sonnets more acceptable to the public." (Boswell, p. 18.) These sorts of strategies not only lead to the false conclusion that gays and lesbians made no significant contributions to culture, but also further the isolation and invisibility of gays and lesbians today.

The Denial of Popular Strength. No matter how many surveys are carried out concluding that a significant percentage of the population is lesbian, gay, or bisexual, and no matter how often these studies are confirmed, there still seems to be a general failure to acknowledge just how many gays or lesbians there really are. Though gays and lesbians are of all colors, come from all class backgrounds, and exist in every culture, many people assume heterosexuality as a matter of course.

> Society refuses to believe how many blacks there are in this country "passing" for white and how many lesbians and gays there are out there passing as heterosexuals. (Tinney, p. 5.)

The media generally refuse to acknowledge the impact and strength of liberation movements waged by sexual and other minorities and thus either trivialize or neglect to cover issues relevant to these communities.

Fear of Over-Visibility. A fear on the part of some heterosexuals is manifested each time they tell a gay male, lesbian, or bisexual that "it doesn't matter to me who you sleep with, you are just a person to me." Or: "People shouldn't label themselves in terms of the sex they are attracted to." The message that comes from these statements is that sexual minorities ought to keep their lives a secret, because it isn't very important. In fact, if it truly is not important, why do so many people get so upset about it? When people do discuss their same-sex attractions or when they express common signs of affection, they are often branded as being "blatant" or accused of "flaunting." The message is clear: keep quiet and remain invisible.

Many people who believe that they are "tolerant" of sexual diversity are actually homophobic in this sense. That is, they maintain a double standard with respect to similar expressions of affection, depending on whether the participants are of the same sex or differing sexes. Though their overt message conveys acceptance, in fact they fear homosexuality on a deeper level. Where heterosexual couples might kiss in public, embrace at the airport, walk arm in arm, wear wedding bands, and talk about their most recent "date," similar behavior in same-sex couples is judged quite differently. This form of discrimination has important repercussions for gays and lesbians who fear negative reactions from other members of society and as a result are made to think constantly about even the most casual forms of behavior.

Conspiracy to Silence.   Society attempts to prevent too many minority members from congregating in any one place. It tries to keep minority enrollment in any given school below a certain percentage. The same holds for minority representation in many neighborhoods and businesses. Therefore, though the dominant group may promote a "token" African American person, woman, or gay in order to justify its claim that it has "bent over backwards" to be equitable (Tinney), it does not tolerate truly open discussions of the subject or permit greater numbers of gays and lesbians to have a voice. Society may tolerate a "good gay" who is not vocal or open, but does not extend this tolerance to all gays.

Public discussion about sexual minorities has been severely curtailed:

From the Reverend Higgeson who referred in 1629 to sodomitical activity as "wickedness not to bee named" to the Illinois judge who in 1897 described the crime against nature as "not fit to be named among Christians"... To the general reticence of Victorian America, the purity crusades of the 1870s and later... Homosexuality continued to be a target of censorship forces.... (D'Emilio, p. 19.)

Creation of Defined Public Spaces.   Society tends to prefer the ghettoization of gays and lesbians as it does ethnic and racial minorities. Homosexuals often choose to reside in designated areas within larger cities (e.g., the Castro Street District in San Francisco, at one time the Christopher Street area in New York City, and parts of Boston's South End) to escape the battle-zone of homophobia on the outside.

Denial of Self-Labelling.   There is a general tendency to deny gays and lesbians the right to define and name themselves. Subsequently, there remains an almost inexhaustible array of derogatory labels thrown at them. It has taken a long time for African Americans and women to be referred to by the titles many have chosen for themselves, and it will probably take even longer for society to use words of respect when referring to lesbians and gays.

Negative Symbolism (Stereotyping). Negative stereotypes and myths about lesbians and gays abound while they remain the butt of many jokes. These instances of negative symbolism are also employed as a means of control and a further hindrance to understanding and to meaningful social change. But even "positive" stereotypes can be oppressive to the members of the stereotyped group. If a teacher, for example, has a stereotype that Asians are good at mathematics, she or he will resist the Asian student who wants to major in creative writing or art. Similarly, if we generalize that gay men are artistic or intuitive, or that lesbians are mechanical or strong, then we make those who are different invisible. Thus, all stereotypes—whether positive *or* negative—imprison individuals and erase diversity.

Tolerance, Acceptance and Homophobia. Psychologist Dorothy Riddle suggests two additional factors of collective prejudice. These are tolerance and acceptance.

> Most intelligent heterosexuals reject, intellectually, their hostility to homosexuality, while unable to conquer their emotional repugnance. The outward result is tolerance. (Altman.)

Many studies, including Sorenson and Sobel, report a conflict in cognitive and affective attitudes among a significant number of well-educated, young respondents who favor civil rights for lesbians and gays while finding homosexual sexual activity to be repugnant.

Though not as obvious as other forms of homophobia, tolerance can be a mask which hides a basic underlying fear or hatred. One is tolerant of a crying baby on a bus or a long line in a supermarket checkout counter. However, in these instances one tries to ignore a frustration or push aside a resentment.

Although many liberals support the idea of relaxing anti-homosexual statutes, and say that they accept lesbians and gays as people, they often do so without truly understanding lesbian and gay sexuality. A patronizing attitude often develops which author Christopher Isherwood has termed "annihilation by blandness." Lesbians and gays are considered less mature than straights and their movement for social change is considered naive or self-indulgent. Tolerance is extended to sexual minorities as toys to children. This type of manipulation is difficult to expose and eradicate because it is often so subtle and unclear.

However, one might ask: "How can acceptance be a form of prejudice?" or "Isn't acceptance by the dominant group the aim of the oppressed?" The answer is that within the very definition of "acceptance" there is an implication that there is indeed something to accept. Rather than considering acceptance a signal of reduced homophobia, Riddle suggests four positive levels of attitudes.

Support.   This is the basic civil-libertarian approach which works to safeguard the rights of minorities, including gays and lesbians. The people giving support may be uncomfortable with the issue of homosexuality, but they are aware of the homophobic climate which exists and the unfair ways in which sexual minorities are treated. Thus, they agree to work toward securing the rights of gay people in the same way that they would for any minority group.

Admiration.   This attitude is emphasized by an acknowledgment that being lesbian or gay in our society take an enormous amount of strength and courage. People with this attitude are willing to examine their own beliefs sincerely and work on their own homophobia.

Appreciation.   Appreciative people value the diversity of others and see lesbians and gays as an important part of that diversity. They are willing to combat homophobia in themselves and in others.

Nurturance.   People with this attitude assume that lesbians and gays are indispensable in our society. They view them with genuine affection and delight and are willing to be gay advocates.

Responses to Oppression

Suffering which falls to our lot in the course of nature, or by chance, or fate, does not seem so painful as suffering which is inflicted on us by the arbitrary will of another. (Schopenhauer, quoted in Allport, p. 138.)

Discrimination is the knife that cuts the world along lines of power, giving the dominant group a greater share while taking away from minorities full social acceptance. This lack of acceptance is commonly referred to as *stigmatization*.

The term originated with the ancient Greeks. A *stigma* was a physical sign, cut or burned into the skin of a person, to proclaim that the bearer was a slave, criminal, or traitor.

Today, the method by which some groups are stigmatized is usually not as crude, but its effects on the holder can be just as profound and devastating. Stigmas can have major repercussions—both negative and positive—on the personality development and behavior of minority group members.

People respond in a great variety of ways when confronting oppression. Allport terms these "traits due to victimization" or "persecution-produced traits." Some of these traits can be quite constructive and creative while others can be rather unpleasant or destructive. The way in which oppression is handled depends on the extent and degree to which it exists and on the personality of the individual:

> Every form of ego defense may be found among members of every persecuted group. Some will handle their minority-group membership easily, with surprisingly little evidence in their personalities that this membership is of any concern to them. Others will show a mixture of desirable and undesirable compensations. Some will be so rebellious...that they will develop many ugly defenses. (Allport, p. 140.)

Allport enumerates the varieties of negative responses to stigmatization including: 1) obsessive concern resulting in feelings of deep anxiety, suspicion, and insecurity; 2) denial (from both oneself and others) of actual membership in the minority group; 3) social withdrawal and passivity; 4) clowning, being the "court jester" in an effort to be accepted by the dominant group; 5) slyness and cunning—oftentimes for mere survival; 6) identification with the dominant group—a sign of self-hate; 7) aggression against and addressing blame to one's own group; 8) directing prejudice and discrimination against other minorities; 9) excessive neuroticism; 10) internalizing and acting out the negative social definitions and stereotypes—the self-fulfilling prophecy; and 11) excessive striving for status to compensate by substitution for the feelings of inferiority. Thus, many of the more undesirable characteristics often attributed to minorities are not intrinsic but are rather defenses and responses to discrimination. Yet, when these responses occur, they often lead to reinforcement of negative stereotypes and beliefs.

On the other side of the coin, some of the more positive things to come out of stigmatization include: 1) a strengthening of ties with minority-group members; 2) sympathy with and support for other minorities; 3) enhanced striving and assertiveness—seeing oppression as merely an obstacle or challenge to be surmounted; and 4) challenging the status quo in a variety of ways and refusing to "take it any longer," which often brings about progressive social change.

Responses to Homophobia

Internalized Homophobia.   Allport's "traits due to victimization" can be used to chart the possible responses used by any one of a great number of minority groups in the context of oppression. This is also true in the case of sexual minorities.

Bisexuals, lesbians, and gay males live in a world that teaches that same-sex activity is morally repulsive, psychologically damaging, or that it does not exist at all. No one is totally protected from internalizing these negative attitudes—neither straights nor sexual minorities.

This "internalized homophobia" manifests itself in a great number of ways among people with same-sex attractions. On the one hand, these responses may include total denial of one's sexual orientation, contempt for the more open and "obvious" members of the community, distrust of other gay people, projection of prejudice onto another minority group (reinforced by society's already existing prejudices), attempts to "pass" as heterosexual, sometimes marrying someone of the other sex to gain social approval, increased fear and withdrawal from friends and relatives, and in some instances suicide.

> We have been taught to hate ourselves and how thoroughly we have learned the lesson. (Hodges and Hutter.)

Some even attempt to change their sexuality. Groups have developed for just this purpose. They are organized and run by people calling themselves "former" or "recovered" homosexuals who promise that people who are "highly motivated" can fit into the heterosexual norm. Even for those who may be closer to the heterosexual end of the sexual spectrum and have the capacity to be exclusively heterosexual, their status as stigmatized individuals does not end:

> How does the stigmatized person respond to this situation? In some cases it will be possible for him to make a direct attempt to correct what he sees as the objective basis of his failing as when...a homosexual [undergoes] psychotherapy. Where such...is possible, what often results is not the acquisition of fully normal status, but a transformation of self from someone with a particular blemish into someone with a record of having corrected a particular blemish. (Goffman, p. 9.)

Goffman adds:

> ...the quest, often secret, that results provides a special indication of the extremes to which the stigmatized can be willing to go, and hence the painfulness of the situation that leads them to these extremes. (p. 9.)

Stigma Conversion.   Not all reactions to homophobia, however, are negative. Many lesbians and gays go through a *stigma conversion*, turning something negative into something positive. Many have worked hard to change discriminatory laws and attitudes and have served as positive role models for other gay people. Some have strengthened ties with other members of their own group and, since they are of every racial, ethnic, religious, social, and economic group, they have been the bridges of coalition between varying groups within the society. In fact, a part of this conversion occurs in the very act of claiming the terms "lesbian," "gay," and "bisexual" and thereby throwing off the negative labels attached to them.

> In converting his stigma, the oppressed person...emerges from a stigmatized cocoon as a transformed creature, one characterized by the spreading of political wings. At some point in the process, the politicized "deviant" gains a new identity, an heroic self-image as crusader in a political cause. (Humphries, p. 142.)

By understanding and integrating their sexuality and standing against intolerance in all its many forms, lesbians, bisexuals, and gay males can emerge emotionally stronger and personally secure.

Anti-Violence Organizing

Lesbian and gay people are actively working to reduce homophobia. Throughout the nation, organizations have formed to document anti-gay and lesbian violence and to assist victims. The Violence Project of the National Gay and Lesbian Task Force coordinates information and activities on the national level and local agencies provide direct services. Some of these agencies include Community United Against Violence in San Francisco, Anti-Violence Project of the Gay and Lesbian Community Center of Denver, Anti-Violence Project of Atlanta's Gay Center, Anti-Violence Project of Gay and Lesbian Horizons of Chicago, Gay and Lesbian Victim Recovery Program of Boston's Fenway Community Health Center, New York Gay and Lesbian Anti-Violence Project, Violence and Discrimination Hotline of the Philadelphia Lesbian and Gay Task Force. Other national groups include Committee on Lesbian and Gay Victims Concerns of the National Organization for Victims Assistance, Lesbian Task Force of the National Coalition Against Domestic Violence, and Lesbian Caucus of the National Coalition Against Sexual Assault.

Many of these agencies are working on a number of fronts. In the area of violence prevention, members are lobbying lawmakers to enact local and national laws to protect lesbian and gay people from discrimination. They are also undertaking community education programs: training sessions to sensitize police officers, and media education efforts for more accurate reporting. In addition, members of the numerous gay and lesbian speakers bureaus nationwide are leading discussions in schools, churches, businesses, and community organizations to personalize the issues and shatter the myths and fears surrounding homosexuality. Anti-violence organizations are also providing self-defense and "street-wise" training for people to better fend off attack.

These organizations are also documenting violence when it occurs and have established victim assistance programs to help people handle the bureaucratic and emotional aftermath of an attack. Some of these efforts include medical and counselling services, and if the client wishes to report the incident and pursue litigation, the agencies offer advocates who assist the clients to deal with the police, courts, and social service and other agencies. In addition, gay and lesbian anti-violence projects are networking with other organizations concerned with stopping violence and bias-motivated crime.

Conclusion

Virtually everyone has felt the effects of prejudice and discrimination in various forms sometime in life. From slavery, to the Black Codes and Jim Crow, to the Kerner Commission Report in 1968 stating that "...our nation is moving toward two societies, one black, one white—separate and unequal...," to the present, African Americans have been excluded from many of the social and economic spheres of this country. U.S. territorial governments waged wars to systematically eradicate American Indian populations, confiscated their ancestral lands, and attempted to force them to abandon their cultural traditions. Today, as a group, American Indians are the poorest in the country. Chinese people were legally excluded from entering this country, from marrying whites, and from becoming U.S. citizens. Japanese people were prevented from owning land, from attending schools with whites, and were eventually forced during World War II to enter guarded camps or reservations where all personal rights were suspended. The Irish got off the boat only to find signs announcing, "Irish Need Not Apply." Over six million Jews were put to death under the Nazi regime and in this country Jewish synagogues have been torched and Jews, along with Catholics, have been banned from certain professions, prevented from attending many colleges, and restricted from membership in social organizations. Latin Americans still find it hard to move into many neighborhoods or obtain certain desirable jobs because of the prejudice around them. Southeast Asian Americans have been threatened and challenged when attempting to operate shops or to practice their traditional occupation of fishing. America's elder citizens are often forced into retirement while they remain capable and productive in the workplace. The physically challenged are barred from a number of buildings by architectural barriers and are denied housing, employment, and public accommodations. On average the earning power of women workers remains far less than that of men. Tasteless jokes and slurs abound for virtually every group. And though certain conditions have improved, lesbians, gays, and bisexuals continue to remain a despised minority.

Homosexuality has been called many things. Fascists say it's a sign of racial impurity, Communists blame it on Western bourgeois decadence, Westerners say it's a sign of deviance, and parents around the world blame themselves. Religious leaders call it sin and perversion and try to purge it, psychiatrists have called it illness and disturbance and have tried to cure it. Governments attempt to isolate and sometimes eradicate it, and school children learn from their elders to fear and hate it. In the face of all the subtle and extreme means that have been used to control it, though some people have internalized society's attitudes, many have acknowledged their homosexuality and have developed a sense of pride.

Prejudice is not only learned but it also serves many purposes. Homophobia—like racism, sexism, anti-Semitism, etc.—is a form of prejudice. It may be deliberate and blatant or unconscious and unintentional. But in the final analysis it is harmful not only to those who are victims of it, but also to those who hold it.

REFERENCES

Altman, Dennis. *Coming Out in the Seventies*. Boston: Alyson Publications, Inc., 1979.

Allport, Gordon. *The Nature of Prejudice*. Reading, Mass.: Addison-Wesley, 1954.

Bartlett, John. *Bartlett's Familiar Quotations*. Boston: Little, Brown and Company, 1982 Edition.

Boswell, John. *Christianity, Social Tolerance, and Homosexuality: Gay People in Western Europe from the Beginning of the Christian Era to the Fourteenth Century*. Chicago: University of Chicago Press, 1980.

Bray, Alan. *Homosexuality in Renaissance England*. London: Gay Men's Press, 1982.

Breslin, R. "Structured Approaches to Dealing with Prejudice and Intercultural Misunderstanding." *Journal of Internalized Group Tensions*, (1978) 8.

Bullough, Vern, L. *Homosexuality: A History from Ancient Greece to Gay Liberation*. New York: New American Library, 1979.

Canellos, Peter. "A City and Its Sins: The Killing of a Gay Man in Bangor." *The Boston Phoenix*, November 13, 1984.

The Challenge and Progress of Homosexual Law Reform. San Francisco: Council on Religion and the Homosexual, Daughters of Bilitis, Society for Individual Rights, Tavern Guild of San Francisco, 1968.

Churchill, Wainwright. *Homosexuality in Males: A Cross-Cultural and Cross-Species Investigation*. Englewood Cliffs, N.J.: Prentice-Hall, Inc., 1967.

Coles, Robert, and Stokes, Jeffrey. *Sex and the American Teenager*. New York: Rolling Stone Press, 1985.

Cox, O.C. *Caste, Class and Race*. New York: Doubleday, 1948.

Crompton, Louis. "Gay Genocide: From Leviticus to Hitler." In *The Gay Academic*, edited by Louis Crew. Palm Springs: ETC Publications, 1978.

Crompton, Louis. "The Myth of Lesbian Impunity: Capital Laws from 1270-1791." In *The Gay Past: A Collection of Historical Essays*, edited by Salvatore J. Licata and Robert P. Peterson. New York: Harrington Park Press, 1980.

Day, Donald. *The Evolution of Love*. New York: Dial Press, 1980.

Des Moines Register. Des Moines, Iowa. November 9, 1986.

D'Emilio, John. *Sexual Politics, Sexual Communities: The Making of a Homosexual Minority in the United States, 1940-1970*. Chicago: University of Chicago Press, 1983.

Diamant, Anita. "In the Best Interests of Children." *Boston Globe Magazine*, September 8, 1985, pp. 86-100.

Dover, K.J. *Greek Homosexuality*. New York: Vintage Books, 1980.

Eitzen, D. Stanley. *Social Problems*. Boston: Allyn & Bacon, 1980.

Evagrius. *Ecclesiastical History*. London: Henry G. Bohn, III, 1854.

Fromm, Erich. *Escape from Freedom*. New York: Avon Books, 1969.

Gallup Report #205. "Political, Social and Economic Trends: Americans Pro Equal Rights for Gays...but Hedge in Some Areas." Princeton, N.J.: The Gallup Poll, October 1982.

Garraty, John A. *The American Nation: A History of the United States to 1877*. 2nd edition. New York: Harper & Row & *American Heritage*, 1971.

Gibbon, Edward. *The History of the Decline and Fall of the Roman Empire*, edited by Dean Milman, M. Guizot, and W. Smith. London, 1898.

Gilbert, Arthur. "Buggery and the British Navy, 1700-1861." *Journal of Social History* (1976) 10: 72-98.

Goldstein, Richard. "Go the Way Your Blood Beats: An Interview with James Baldwin," *Village Voice*, June 26, 1984.

Goffman, Erving. *Stigma: Notes on the Management of Spoiled Identity*. New York: Simon & Schuster, Inc., 1963.

Gratiani, Magistri. *Corpus iuris canonici: Decretum*. 2 vols., edited by Emil Friedberg and Emil Richter. Graz: Akademische Druk-U. Verlaganstalt, 1959.

Henley, N.M., and Pincus, F. "Interrelationship of Sexist, Racist, and Antihomosexual Attitudes," *Psychological Reports*, 42, 1978, pp. 83-90.

Herek, Gregory. "Beyond 'Homophobia': A Social Psychological Perspective on Attitudes toward Lesbians and Gay Men." In *Bashers, Baiters, and Bigots: Homophobia in American Society*. New York: Harrington Park Press, 1985.

Hodges, Andrew, and Hutter, David. *With Downcast Gays: Aspects of Homosexual Self-Oppression*. Toronto: Pink Triangles Press, 1977.

Horowitz, E.L. "The Development of Attitudes toward the Negro." *Archives of Psychology* (1936) 194.

Hudson, W.W., and Ricketts, W.A. "A Strategy for the Measurement of Homophobia." In *Journal of Homosexuality* (1980) 5(4).

Humphries, Laud. *Out of the Closets: The Sociology of Homosexual Liberation.* Englewood Cliffs, N.J.: Prentice-Hall, 1972.

Irwin, P., and Thompson, N.L. "Acceptance of the Rights of Homosexuals: A Social Profile," *Journal of Homosexuality*, 3(2) 1977, pp. 107-121.

Julian, Joseph, and Kornblum, William. *Social Problems.* 4th Edition, Englewood Cliffs, New Jersey: Prentice-Hall, Inc., 1983.

Katz, Jonathan. *Gay American History: Lesbians and Gay Men in the U.S.A.* New York: Avon Books, 1976.

Kerner, Otto (Chairperson). *Report of the National Advisory Commission on Civil Disorders.* Washington, D.C.: U.S. Government Printing Office, 1968.

Kinsey, Alfred, Pomeroy, W.B., and Martin, C.E. *Sexuality in the Human Male.* Philadelphia: W.B. Saunders, 1948.

Kinsey, Alfred, Pomeroy, W.B., Martin, C.E., and Gebhard, R.H. *Sexuality in the Human Female.* Philadelphia: W.B. Saunders, 1953.

Knowles, Louis L., and Prewith, Kenneth, eds. *Institutional Racism in America.* Englewood Cliffs, N.J.: Prentice-Hall Spectrum Books, 1969.

Krogman, W.M. "The Concept of Race." In *The Science of Man in the World Crisis,* edited by R. Linton. New York: Columbia University Press, 1945.

Lea, Henry Charles. *A History of the Inquisition of Spain.* 4 vols. New York: Macmillan, 1907.

Lehne, G.H. "Homophobia among Men." In *The Forty-Nine Percent Majority: The Male Sex Role,* edited by D. Davis and R. Brannon. Reading, Mass.: Addison-Wesley, 1976.

Levitt, E.E., and Klassen, A.D. "Public Attitudes toward Homosexuality: Part of the 1970 National Survey by the Institute for Sex Research." *Journal of Homosexuality* (1974) 1(1).

Marmor, Judd, ed. *Homosexual Behavior: A Modern Reappraisal.* New York: Basic Books, 1980.

Merton, Robert. "Discrimination and the American Creed." In *Discrimination and National Welfare,* edited by R.H. MacIver. New York: Harper & Row, 1949.

Minnergerode, F.A. "Attitudes toward Homosexuality: Feminist Attitudes and Social Conservatism." *Sex Roles,* 1, 1976, pp. 160-165.

Monter, E. William. "La Sodomie à l'époque moderne en Suisse romand," edited by R.H. MacIver. *Annales: E.S.C.* (1974) 29: 1023-33.

Monter, E. William. "Sodomy and Heresy in Early Modern Switzerland." In *The Gay Past: A Collection of Historical Essays,* edited by Salvatore J. Licata and Robert P. Peterson. New York: Harrington Park Press, 1980.

National Gay and Lesbian Task Force. National Anti-Gay/Lesbian Victimization Report. New York: 1984.

Newsweek, "The Watch on the Mails," 67:24, June 13, 1966.

"Newsweek Poll on Homosexuality." *Newsweek,* August 9, 1983, p. 33.

Phoenix, 1:13, Sept.-Oct. 1966—quoting from the *Sun-Sentinel.*

Rapetti, Pierre, ed. *Li Livres de jostice et de plet,* Paris: Didot Freres, 1850.

Riddle, Dorothy. From *Opening Doors to Understanding and Acceptance: A Facilitator's Guide for Presenting Workshops on Lesbian and Gay Issues,* organized by Kathy Obear and Amy Reynolds. Boston: 1985.

Robins, W. "Job Odds Are against Young Philadelphia Blacks." *New York Times*, Feb. 1, 1982, p. A-8.

Rosan, L.J. "Philosophies of Homophobia and Homophilia." In *The Gay Academic*. Palm Springs, Calif.: ETC Publications, 1978.

Ruggerio, G. "Sexual Criminality in the Early Renaissance." *Journal of Social History* (1975) 8: 18-37.

Saenger, Gerhart. *The Social Psychology of Prejudice*. New York: Harper, 1953.

Sartre, Jean-Paul. *Anti-Semite and Jew*. New York: Schocken, 1965.

Schopenhauer, Arthur, quoted in Allport, Gordon. *The Nature of Prejudice*. Reading, Mass.: Addison-Wesley, 1954, p. 138.

Shilts, Randy. *The Mayor of Castro Street: The Life and Times of Harvey Milk*. New York: St. Martin's Press, 1982.

Shurtleff, William, ed. *Records of the Colony on New Plymouth in New England*. Boston: William White, 1898.

Simmons, J.S. *Deviants*. Boston: Glandessry Press, 1969.

Sobel, H.J. "Adolescent Attitudes toward Homosexuality in Relation to Self Concept and Body Satisfaction." *Adolescence*, 11(43) pp. 443-453, 1976.

Smith, Barbara. "Homophobia: Why Bring It Up?" *Interracial Books for Children Bulletin* (1983), 14 (3-4). New York: Council on Interracial Books for Children.

Sorenson, R.C. *Adolescent Sexuality in Contemporary America*. New York: World, 1973.

Stencel, S. *Homosexual Legal Rights*. Editorial Research Reports (1974) 1, 181-200.

Sullivan, Gerard. "A Bibliographic Guide to Government Hearings and Reports, Legislative Action, and Speeches Made in the House and Senate of the United States Congress on the Subject of Homosexuality." In *Bashers, Baiters and Bigots: Homophobia in American Society*, edited by John P. De Cecco. New York: Harrington Park Press, 1985.

Szasz, Thomas S. *The Manufacture of Madness*. New York: Delta Books, 1970.

Tallmer, Abby. "Anti-Lesbian Violence." National Gay and Lesbian Task Force Monograph Series, Violence Project, Washington, D.C.

Taylor, Clark L., Jr. "El Ambiente: Male Homosexual Social Life in Mexico City." Ph.D. dissertation, University of California, Berkeley, 1978.

Tinney, James S. "Interconnections." In *Interracial Books for Children Bulletin* (1983) 14 (3-4). New York: Council on Interracial Books for Children.

United Nations. *Report on the Main Types and Causes of Discrimination*. Lake Success, N.Y.: 1949.

Weinberg, George. *Society and the Healthy Homosexual*. New York: St. Martin's Press, 1972.

Wheatly, Rev. Robert. "Candlelight Vigils Protest Killing of Gay Man." *Unitarian Universalist World*, August 15, 1984.

Oprah Winfrey Show. *Homophobia*, Transcript #8639. New York: Journal Graphics, Inc., Nov. 13, 1986.

Winthrop, John. *History of New England from 1630-1649*. Vol 2. Edited by James Savage. Boston: Little, Brown, 1853.

Woetzel, Robert K. "Do Our Homosexuality Laws Make Sense?" *Saturday Review of Literature*, 48, p. 23-25. Oct. 9, 1965.

Wurzel, Jaime. "The Functions and Forms of Prejudice." In *A World of Difference: Resource Guide for Reduction of Prejudice*. Boston: Anti-Defamation League of B'nai B'rith and Facing History and Ourselves National Foundation, Inc., 1986.

Chapter 6

History of Lesbian and Gay Movement Politics

The common image of the homosexual has been a figure divorced from any temporal-social context. The concept of homosexuality must be historicized. (Katz, p. 11.)

If we define politics, as some have, as the art of "who gets what, when, and why," then it becomes clear that the study of politics involves far more than the study of governmental structures and the laws that emanate from them. Rather, politics involves many layers of decision-making, influence, and differing power relations among individuals. In addition, political decisions are not merely technical, but rather involve critical value-claims and assumptions. These decisions do not, then, take place in a vacuum, but are mediated through their social setting.

This chapter presents and analyzes an overview of the history and politics of the gay and lesbian liberation/rights movement, and places it in a social setting. Rather than spotlighting individual personalities, the discussion focuses primarily on political trends and organizational activity. The three stages of the movement for lesbian and gay equality provide the organizational framework for this chapter. Though these stages interconnect and at times overlap, their evolution reflects major changes in the strategies and directions adopted by activists in this movement.

The first of these stages—the genesis of the movement—began in Germany as early as the 1860s with the emergence of a homosexual identity, and came to an abrupt end with the rise of European fascism and Soviet Stalinism in the 1930s. The second—the "homophile" stage— became visible in the United States in the early 1950s in the form of organizations such as the Mattachine Society and the Daughters of Bilitis, the emphasis of which was public education and legal reform. The third—the modern gay and lesbian liberation stage—is an activist movement, born of street riots at the Stonewall Inn in late June 1969 in New York City.

Though all of the different organizations discussed in this chapter seek "liberation," they frequently disagree not only on the particular strategies to achieve that goal, but also on their vision of the goal itself. This chapter examines some of the ideological underpinnings of those differences; but this is not to imply that that is all there is to politics. If politics is about gaining power over one's life, then, for a gay person, political actions can take many forms: fighting for custody rights, coming out to a parent or friend, taking a same-sex date to a high school prom, displaying affection publicly, purchasing a gay periodical, speaking out against a homophobic joke. Chapter 8 looks at some of these lifestyle decisions in greater depth.

Much of lesbian and gay political history has been lost to us, not only because of the invisibility of so many gays and lesbians but also because of the conscious efforts by those in power to erase or co-opt any signs of gay culture throughout history. But, even given such silencing, there is increasingly coming to light a wealth of information which affords us an opportunity to understand the historical roots of the gay and lesbian movement. This chapter can do no better than to summarize some of the highlights of that history, and to urge readers to explore the issues in greater depth by taking advantage of further readings.

Political Ideologies

All labels are shorthand summaries which convey ideas that are probably exceedingly complex. For that reason, labels can be convenient "markers" for those concepts, and can imply a longer message without a good deal of explanation. But a label can also become confused with the reality to which it refers, and its efficiency can mislead us into believing that the ideas they serve to capture are also simple and distinct. Political labels are no different. We say people are "liberals" or "conservatives," that policies are "reformist" or "radical," yet we seldom flesh out what those terms imply. Further, we mistakenly assume that there is no overlap in these terms, and that these theoretical models do adequately capture the complexity of the everyday world.

With this note of caution, the following outline may help to elucidate this chapter on the politics of the gay and lesbian movement. This framework is an unabashed simplification of the issues and views involved, and those who are interested in these topics are urged to explore them in more depth. This outline, then, is not meant to substitute for an adequate grounding in political theory, but rather to provide a context for understanding some of the key trends and ideas which served to motivate the lesbian and gay movement.

In the United States context, *conservatives* have generally been defenders of *laissez-faire* capitalism: an economic theory which believes in a minimum of governmental intervention in the marketplace. These theorists are sometimes termed *libertarians*. Conservative political theorists like Milton Friedman (see, for example, *Freedom to Choose*) and Robert Nozick (see, for example, *Anarchy, State and Utopia*) argue that the government's only legitimate purpose is defense—internal and external—and protection of property rights. Nozick, in fact, maintains that property rights are absolute, and they provide the basis for all other rights. Proponents of this political position—sometimes referred to as the "Old Right"—argue that business should be allowed to function unimpeded by any governmental interference. Governmental intervention, they maintain, serves only to create inefficiency and undermine motivation. Further, they view inequality itself as the result of differing capabilities, interests, and levels of motivation; thus, there is nothing intrinsically wrong with social inequality as long as it occurs within the rules of the system.

One should not confuse this view with a political perspective known as the "New Right," which is in fact not a "pure" political model but rather an amalgam of perspectives. These perspectives share the laissez-faire capitalist's interest in preserving the freedom of business to compete in the open market, but they add a conservative social-issues agenda to their framework, especially in the area of sexual politics. Thus the "New Right" (including the so-called Moral Majority, some fundamentalist religious groups, and conservative politicians) have launched an attack on sex education in the schools, legalized abortion, homosexuality, birth control, and pornography; often their campaigns focus on preserving the family (Anita Bryant's campaign against homosexuality went under the banner of "Save Our Children") and they insist that a split between the private (morality) and the public (law) is not really possible.

The *liberal* (or *moderate*) view is one which, similar to the conservative, essentially supports the capitalist system; but the liberal view differs in that it recognizes that the system does not always work perfectly and at times calls for some adjustments or revisions. Thus, though the liberal may not advocate any fundamental restructuring of the basic tenets of capitalism, he or she may defend some social and political programs designed to help out those who are worst off in society. Inequality, then, is justified, so long as there are not extreme disadvantages. People, so the moderate argues, do need competition to provide an incentive for hard work and creativity. But, they add, at times there occur circumstances beyond the individual's control—illness, death of a spouse, natural disasters—which are not one's fault but may have disastrous repercussions for one's life. This view—sometimes called "welfare capitalism"— advocates assistance for those who are unable to help themselves; programs like Medicare for the elderly, Aid to Families with Dependent Children (AFDC) for the temporarily poor, Social Security, low-interest loans for higher education, and so forth, are all consistent with the liberal's political agenda. Liberals, though, often disagree on the types of programs to be provided as well as the extent to which society should help its disadvantaged members.

Radicals believe that the basic system—capitalism—is essentially unjust and cannot be improved with minor changes and adjustments. Thus, radicals reject the "revisionism" of liberals and maintain that what is required is a basic or fundamental restructuring of society. The term "radical" is a very broad one and may also include the *anarchist* who believes that no government is justified.

Socialists maintain that cooperation, not competition, is the basis for human community, and that profit as the key motivation for human activity is ultimately a wedge which divides us all from one another. Instead, they argue that societies have an obligation to meet people's needs without regard to income. There are two major branches of socialist political theory: *democratic socialism*, which advances the notion that capitalism can be changed gradually (and peacefully) through the legal process; and *revolutionary socialism*, which maintains that radical change can only come about through class conflict and revolutionary struggle.

THE LESBIAN AND GAY MOVEMENT: A POLITICAL HISTORY

Suddenly the paddywagon arrived and the mood of the crowd changed. Three of the more blatant queens—in full drag—were loaded inside, along with the bartender and doorman, to a chorus of catcalls and boos from the crowd. A cry went up to push the paddywagon over, but it drove away before anything could happen. With its exit, the action waned momentarily. The next person to come out was a dyke, and she put up a struggle— from car to door to car again. It was at that moment that the scene became explosive. Limp wrists were forgotten. Beer cans and bottles were heaved at the window, and a rain of coins descended on the cops. At the height of the action, a bearded figure was plucked from the crowd and dragged inside.... Three cops were necessary to get [him] away from the crowd and into the Stonewall. The exit left no cops on the street, and almost by signal the crowd erupted into cobblestone and bottle heaving. The reaction was solid: they were pissed. The trashcan I was standing on was nearly yanked out from under me as a kid tried to grab it for use in the window-smashing melee. From nowhere came an uprooted parking meter—used as a battering ram on the Stonewall door. I heard several cries of "Let's get some gas," but the blaze of flame which soon appeared in the window of the Stonewall was still a shock. As the wood barrier behind the glass was beaten open, the cops inside turned a firehose on the crowd. Several kids took the opportunity to cavort in the spray, and their momentary glee served to stave off what was rapidly becoming a full-scale attack. By the time the fags were able to regroup forces and come up with another assault, several carloads of police reinforcements had arrived, and in minutes the streets were clear. (Truscott.)

Many present-day historians consider the beginning of the modern gay and lesbian liberation movement to be the Stonewall Riots on Christopher Street in New York City of June 1969 when gay people fought back against harassment. Yet at least one hundred years prior to the Stonewall Riots there was a healthy "homosexual rights movement" which was part of the growing social reform movement occurring in the 19th century in Germany, England, and the United States.

Definitions and concepts of sexuality differ with time and place. What is considered abhorrent in one society may fit the norm in another; a behavior of today may have carried very different social meanings in times long past.

Though records dating back to early antiquity document the universal existence of homosexual acts, it is not clear whether these people defined themselves in terms of their sexual behavior. Scholars who defend an essentialist viewpoint, such as Boswell, use the existence throughout the ages of anti-homosexual laws as evidence of a continuous homosexual culture.

Other social historians, however, argue that, though there have always been homosexual acts, homosexual identity has emerged in the West only since the latter part of the 19th century. Hence, a conceptual shift developed: some people do not merely engage in same-sex activity, but are themselves homosexual. Thus, constructivists like Foucault warn against automatically applying contemporary Western concepts and definitions of homosexuality to persons living in premodern and non-industrialized societies. Some constructivists concede that there were a few isolated and unsustained periods prior to modern times where aspects of a homosexual identity briefly surfaced. Examples include ancient China, the isle of Lesbos in ancient Greece, 17th-century Japan, and London in the early years of the 18th century in the underground male society of the "Molly Houses." (Bray.)

Constructivists provide a plausible explanation for the emergence of homosexual identity. It is probably no coincidence that the later 19th century was a period in human history when an intense struggle was occurring between rapidly advancing scientific discoveries and traditional ideology. This struggle had a major impact on traditional views about sexuality. Social conditions of this time were at least partly responsible for this change. This was a time, for example, when the developing capitalist system was pulling more men and women out of homes and into the marketplace. Products once produced and consumed in the home were now purchased on the market. Urbanization led to more impersonal, heavily populated living areas in contrast to the smaller communities of the past. Political theorists had begun to speak of privacy and personal choice. The family became smaller, birth rates declined, and sexuality and procreation could be viewed separately. (D'Emilio; Weeks.) Even some of the very concepts we now take for granted—"the child," "the housewife," and "the homosexual"—emerged during this period. (Weeks.)

This chapter begins with this period, though this approach is not meant to imply agreement with the constructivist view. Regardless of when a "homosexual identity" existed in time, it is in these last hundred or so years that there has been an organized and sustained political effort to protect the rights of people with same-sex attractions. The purpose of this chapter, then, is to present a coherent picture of those efforts and to look at some of the historical conditions leading to this change in ideology.

The Early Movement

Germany

In Germany in the 1860s, Karl Heinrich Ulrich, now called by many the "Grandfather of Gay Liberation," published his "social and juridical" studies of love between men. These works, entitled *Vindex* and *Inclusa*, were not only the largest body of literature on homosexuality at the time, but were also the first scientific treatments of the subject. In 1862, Ulrich coined the term "Uranian" to refer to this type of love. He borrowed the label from the *Symposium*, in which Plato describes love between two men as "the beautiful love, this Heavenly love, the love belonging to the Heavenly 'Muse Urania.'"

It was a Hungarian doctor by the name of Karoly Maria Benkert (who went by the pseudonym K.M. Kertbeny) who in 1869 coined the word "homosexual." He used the term in an attempt to provide a neutral label for the practice of same-sex eroticism. In response to the New Prussian Penal Code, Benkert called on authorities to reject its proposed Paragraph 175, which made sexual acts between men a criminal offense. In an open letter to the minister of justice, he argued for the right to privacy in areas relating to sexual conduct, maintained that homosexuality was no threat to heterosexuals (because it was innate), and even cited examples of famous homosexuals in history. He maintained that scientific knowledge rendered such laws unnecessary, and that religious fanaticism had already claimed "millions of innocent victims." His views represented the beginning of an effort to provide a rational understanding of homosexuality. Despite his efforts, however, the Paragraph was passed by the legislature in 1871. It was not until 1968 that East Germany abolished this law, and it remains in modified form in West Germany to this day.

The first gay emancipation organization, formed in part to combat the new Paragraph, was the Scientific Humanitarian Committee, which was organized in 1897, two years after Ulrich's death. The goals of the Committee were:

- to influence legislative bodies to abolish the anti-homosexual Paragraph 175 of the Penal Code,
- to enlighten public opinion on homosexuality,
- to "interest" the homosexual in himself and the struggle for rights.

To meet these goals, the Committee undertook a number of projects, including political activism, public speaking, and publication and distribution of literature. And though the law criminalized only male homosexuality, the Committee made an effort to include lesbians. "Uranian ladies," said one spokesperson, "have become an almost indispensable and prominent component of all our events." Though lesbianism was not outlawed, the lesbian "nevertheless suffers in the most varied ways because of the ignorance about her nature." (Magnus Hirschfeld, quoted in Lauritsen and Thorstad, p. 18.)

In addition, the Committee published a journal, the *Yearbook for Intermediate Sexual Types*, which appeared between 1899 and 1923. The journal contained reports, and literary, historical, anthropological, polemic, and scientific studies about homosexuality and other sex-related phenomena. By 1908, over 5,000 people had been contacted by or were members of the Committee. Many were prominent personalities and leading citizens who gave the movement credibility by coming forth publicly and acknowledging their homosexuality. (Later, however, this information was used against them by the Nazi regime.)

One of the founding members and most visible speakers for this organization throughout its thirty-five years of existence was Magnus Hirschfeld. Dr. Hirschfeld was a prominent sexologist who traveled extensively, conducting speaking engagments to enlighten the public on the issue of homosexuality and to make people more aware of the wide diversity of human sexuality. In Berlin, he founded the Institute of Sexology, later destroyed by the Nazis. Hirschfeld believed that homosexuality was an innate condition and even referred to homosexuals as constituting a "third sex."

A petition campaign calling for the abolition of Paragraph 175 was undertaken by the Committee in 1897, to gather as many signatures as possible from prominent individuals. The Committee stressed that, since the time of the Napoleonic Code of 1810, homosexual acts had had legal status in most countries in Europe. The petition campaign continued to be the Committee's central focus for many years.

In addition, the Committee published a pamphlet, "What You Should Know About the Third Sex," which, with nineteen printings in four years, developed and defended a positive view of "the nature of Uranianism."

By 1905, the Committee had made some progress toward its goal of increasing public discussion. The subject of homosexuality appeared with greater regularity in the press and in discussions in political campaigns. Candidates were regularly pressed for their stands on Paragraph 175. It was even rumored in the 1912 elections that close races were decided by the homosexual vote.

Other groups joined the Committee to oppose Paragraph 175. One such group, which was also working for homosexual rights, was the Community of the Special, founded in 1902 under the aegis of Benedict Friedlander. Though both of these groups agreed that the law should be overturned, they disagreed about the origins of homosexuality. In particular, Friedlander rejected Hirschfeld's claim that homosexuality was innate, maintaining instead that it was largely a result of environmental factors. Friedlander, once himself a member of the Committee, feared that labelling homosexuality as "inborn" would place it in the category of disease.

> Now with diseases, one can certainly have pity, one can behave humanely to the sick and indeed try to "heal" them; at no time does one acknowledge presumed physical inferiors as having equal rights. (Lauritsen and Thorstad, p. 50.)

A growing women's suffrage movement was developing at this time in much of Europe. Few early feminists, however, initially understood the connections between women's oppression and the special oppression of lesbians. Most feminist groups ignored the issue. However, with the new draft of the Penal Code in 1910—extending criminal status to sexual acts between women—many women's emancipation groups joined the struggle. In Berlin, on February 10, 1911, a meeting of the League for the Protection of Mothers adopted a resolution condemning the statute and calling any attempt to extend criminal status to female homosexuality "a serious mistake."

In the meantime, the Scientific Humanitarian Committee undertook several projects to advance the scientific and cultural life of the movement. One was the production of a film entitled *Anders als die Andern* ("Different from Other People") which was first shown to the press in 1919, but was banned by the government in 1920. Another was a scientifically dubious study which examined homosexual behavior among several thousand students and steel workers. The publication received wide distribution, but resulted in a 300-mark fine levied by the government against its coordinator, Hirschfeld, for influencing the "young and innocent."

Though the work of the Committee waned during the years of World War I, it resumed the struggle to fight and defeat Paragraph 175 after Germany's defeat in the war. Germany, however, was in the throes of economic disaster following its defeat in World War I, and world-wide depression soon followed. As a result, and despite signed petitions calling for the defeat of Paragraph 175, the issue languished in a German government committee and was never considered.

Despite this setback the Committee did succeed in 1919 in acquiring a building, which became an international center for sex research and for the study of homosexual literature. The Institute for Sexual Science, as it was called, was housed in a former palace purchased by Hirschfeld and endowed with his extensive scientific library.

> The Institute for Sexual Science was a repository for all kinds of biological, anthropological, statistical, and ethnological data and documentation relating to sexology. It became a kind of university for sex science, with regular classes on a variety of relevant subjects. It was the first institute of its kind anywhere in the world. It was truly a forerunner of the Kinsey Institute for Sex Research. (Ibid, p. 28.)

The Institute was the embodiment of the Committee's motto *"per scientiam ad justitiam"* (justice through science).

The Rise of Fascism.   The Institute became the intellectual center for the movement and a base for its political activities—a kind of forerunner of the gay and lesbian community services center we see in many cities today. By 1922, the Scientific Humanitarian Committee had about twenty-five branches throughout Germany, there was an increase in gay publications, and speaking and film engagements frequently had overflow audiences. The Committee urged the formation of a world-wide "Uranian community" and began to develop coalitions with homosexual rights groups in other countries. While these activities increased the movement's credibility, its heightened visibility also left it vulnerable to attacks from the growing Nazi movement. For example, Nazi supporters disrupted a 1920 meeting Hirschfeld was addressing and attacked some of the participants. The police did little to prevent the violence. Hirschfeld, himself a Jew, was brutalized and left for dead by anti-Semites in 1921 in the streets of Munich. During that same year, Nazi youth raided a lecture in Vienna and opened fire on the audience, wounding many.

The Nazis gained a majority in the German Reichstag in 1933. Soon afterward, Nazi storm troopers ransacked the Institute for Sexual Science, together with libraries containing other "un-German" material. More than 10,000 volumes were set ablaze in a street bonfire. A procession threw a bust of Hirschfeld into the pyre. Earlier, Hirschfeld had fled to Paris, where he died of heart failure on May 14, 1935, his sixty-seventh birthday.

The Nazis described the Institute as "the international center of the white-slave trade" and "an unparalleled breeding ground of dirt and filth." (Steakley, p. 104.) This was consistent with the Nazi party's view of homosexuality.

The fascist slogan "moral purity" led to an intense and violent campaign against homosexuals, beginning in June 1934 with the murder of gay German SA militia chief Ernst Röhm and his followers. The Nazi philosophy was one which emphasized racial and sexual "purity" and rigid sex roles. Adolf Hitler often used sexual metaphors in his attacks on Jews and other minorities. He said, for example, that the Jews were guilty of the "syphilitization of our people." (Plant.) Even before his rise to power, Hitler's official newspaper, *Völkischer Beobachter* had stated:

> ...among the many evil instincts that characterize the Jewish race, one that is especially pernicious has to do with sexual relations. The Jews are forever trying to propagandize sexual relations between siblings, men and animals, and men and men. We National Socialists [Nazis] will soon unmask and condemn them by law. (Rosenberg.)

It was, however, Heinrich Himmler, chief of the Gestapo (German secret police) who was the architect of the anti-homosexual campaign. He stated in a speech of 1936:

> As National Socialists we are not afraid to fight against this plague within our own ranks. Just as we have readopted the ancient Germanic approach to the question of marriage between alien races, so too, in our judgment of homosexuality—a symptom of racial degeneracy destructive to our race— we have returned to the guiding Nordic principle that degenerates should be exterminated. Germany stands or falls with the purity of its race.... (In Steakley, p. 112.)

Himmler believed that male homosexuals were like women, and to him would be unable to fight in the German war effort. Hence, they were considered a disgrace to and a contaminant of the State. Since women, he believed, were inferior, so too must be homosexual men.

It appears that lesbians were not persecuted in the same way as gays. Himmler and the Nazi leadership did not think that women were capable of having a sexual identity independent of marriage and child-bearing. Himmler developed the concept of a National Sexual Budget, which prescribed sexual rules and tasks for women. Aryan women were expected to breed blond-haired, blue-eyed children for the new Germany. For them abortion and birth control were unthinkable, and child production with an appropriately selected mate was their patriotic duty. Non-Aryan women were encouraged to abort rather than produce "inferior" children. Sexual contact between Jews and non-Jews was strictly forbidden. Himmler believed that if a woman had sex with a Jew (or a homosexual) and later had children, the children would carry the "contamination" of the first sexual encounter (even if that person were not the father).

In 1935 the Nazis extended Paragraph 175 to include kisses, embraces, and even homosexual fantasies in men. This became the rationale for the eventual incarceration of suspected homosexuals. Gay men and their friends were rounded up, questioned, and forced to give names of others. Each police interrogation led to more names and address books, and thousands more German gays and their friends were brought in for questioning and threatened with exposure, jail, and later concentration camps. Those gay men (and those who were suspected of being gay) who avoided the camps were frequently fired from their jobs and socially ostracized as a result of police harassment.

Himmler and his police forces concentrated their efforts mainly on German gays, plus those who resided in Holland and the Alsace region. Himmler decided to leave gays in Germany's other occupied territories unmolested during World War II because, since he considered homosexuality to be a form of contamination, he reasoned that, if left alone, it would contribute to the degeneracy and eventual demise of foreign populations. (Plant.) Jews in all occupied countries, however, were at risk of eventual extermination.

It is not certain exactly how many gays were arrested and murdered under the Third Reich since the Nazis did not thoroughly document the extent of its brutality. One estimate give the figures of 50,000 to 63,000 males convicted of homosexuality (many of whom were killed) plus 6 lesbians from the years 1933 to 1945. (Plant.) Most of the gays who did survive the prisons and concentration camps were sexually mutilated, some by castration.

In the Nazi camps, prisoners were classified by patches of different colors corresponding to their "crime." Jews were forced to wear a yellow star (two yellow triangles sewn together); political prisoners (liberals, socialists, communists) a red triangle; anti-socials (drunks, vagrants, etc.) a black triangle; hard-core criminals a green triangle; and Jehovah's

Witnesses a purple triangle. Gay men wore pink triangles placed point down on both the left shirt sleeve and right pant leg. (Although the pink triangle was not worn by lesbians, it is today a symbol for many gays and lesbians of the extremest forms of oppression which the community has endured. The pink triangle has also come to represent the ways in which gay men and lesbians continue to face prejudice and discrimination for being gay.)

Those few prisoners who did survive the camps remained in jeopardy after liberation. Since homosexuality remained an offense in postwar Germany, some of the more legally minded Allied military officers ordered gay prisoners returned to prison, where they were forced to sit out the remainder of their sentences. In addition, the German government refused to issue financial compensation to homosexual victims of Nazism though it did compensate other persecuted groups.

Stalinist Communism

Paralleling the anti-gay hysteria in Germany were the activities in the Soviet Union during the rule of Joseph Stalin, who had virtual control of the government from the death of Nikolai Lenin in 1924 until his own death in 1953. The Tsarist laws that forbade consensual homosexual acts, abolished under the new Communist leadership in 1917, were reinstated by Stalin in 1934. These laws prescribed sentences of up to eight years imprisonment or exile to Siberia for any male believed to be homosexual. Spying, denunciation, and Communist Party purges of homosexuals began in the early 1930s with mass arrests in Moscow, Leningrad, Kharkov, and Odessa. Homosexuals, whom Stalin termed the "product of decadence in the bourgeois sector of society," were eventually exterminated along with millions of other Soviet citizens. Even into the 1980s, *The Great Soviet Encyclopedia* defines "homosexuality" as "...a sexual perversion consisting in unnatural attraction to persons of the same sex..." The Stalinist laws against homosexuality remain in force today in the Soviet Union.

England

In England until 1861, homosexual acts between men were punishable by death, and until 1967 by imprisonment. There was, however, during this period an underground gay movement, which although influenced by the German movement, tended to take a more personal rather than legalistic approach. (The early anti-homosexual laws did not extend to women since Queen Victoria did not believe women capable of homosexual activity.)

The emphasis of the fledging homosexual emancipation movement in

England, as with other social movements, was on changing the attitudes of society and promoting a sense of pride among homosexuals. Such noteworthy writers and social reformers of the time as Edward Carpenter and John Addington Symonds described the wide-ranging benefits to humanity at large of the liberation of the homosexual spirit which they considered merely dormant in many men. Their interest lay mainly with male-male relations, and they suggested that by releasing the inhibitions society had placed on affectional and sexual relations between men, society would free itself from strict class barriers and advance true democracy.

When John Addington Symonds first read Walt Whitman's poems celebrating "manly attachment," he was introduced to what would become for him a life-long pursuit. For almost thirty years, he sought to prove that Whitman did in fact support homosexual emancipation and that this emancipation would provide the foundation for true democracy. For over nineteen years, Symonds corresponded with Whitman, asking the poet for clarification of his beliefs concerning male-male love and its social implications.

In 1883, Symonds privately and anonymously published ten copies of *A Problem in Greek Ethics*, an early defense of homosexuality which proposed that quiet legislation "without discussion" was the correct strategy for the legalization of homosexuality in England. He based much of his work in this and later writings on his extensive research into homosexuality in ancient Greece and Rome and his ongoing interest in Whitman and the meaning of his *Calamus*. Finally, in 1890, Symonds attempted to make Whitman an ally in the homosexual emancipation movement current in England by asking directly for the first time if Whitman supported such liberation:

> In your conception of Comradeship, do you contemplate the possible intrusion of those semi-sexual emotions and actions which no doubt occur between men? I do not ask, whether you approve of them, or regard them as a necessary part of the relation. But I should much like to know whether you are prepared to leave them to the inclinations and the conscience of the individuals concerned. (Symonds, p. 483.)

Though Whitman denied any homosexual theme in his writings, most historians believe that this denial was a result of negative social attitudes toward homosexuality at the time.

In addition to his *A Problem in Modern Ethics*, Symonds co-authored with Dr. Havelock Ellis the book *Sexual Inversion*. It contained many case histories of gay men and lesbians. In the first edition of the book, published in 1897, the authors included a letter from a "Professor X" giving powerful support of homosexuality:

I have considered and enquired into this question for many years; and it has long been my settled conviction that no breach of morality is involved in homosexual love; that, like every other passion, it tends, when duly understood and controlled by spiritual feeling, to the physical and moral health of the individual and the race, and that it is only its brutal perversions which are immoral. I have known many persons more or less the subjects of this passion, and I have found them a particularly high-minded, upright, refined, and (I must add) pure-minded class of men. In view of what everybody knows of the vile influence on society of the intersexual [heterosexual] passion, as it actually exists in the world, making men and women sensual, low-minded, false, every way unprincipled, and grossly selfish, and this especially in those nations which self-righteously reject homosexual love, it seems a travesty of morality to invest the one with divine attributes and denounce the other as infamous and unnatural. (Ellis and Symonds, pp. 273-74.)

The 1901 edition of *Sexual Inversion* includes a short history of a "Miss S" from the United States giving an early defense of lesbianism:

Inverts should have the courage and independence to be themselves, and to demand an investigation. If one strives to live honorably, and considers the greatest good to the greatest number, it is not a crime nor a disgrace to be an invert. I do not need the law to defend me, neither do I desire to have any concessions made for me, nor do I ask my friends to sacrifice their ideals for me. I too have ideals which I shall always hold. All that I desire—and I claim it as my right—is the freedom to exercise this divine gift of loving, which is not a menace to society nor a disgrace to me. Let it once be understood that the average invert is not a moral degenerate nor a mental degenerate, but simply a man or a woman who is less highly specialized, less completely differentiated, than other men and women, and I believe the prejudice against them will disappear, and if they live uprightly they will surely win the esteem and consideration of all thoughtful people. I know what it means to an invert—who feels himself set apart from the rest of mankind—to find one human heart who trusts him and understands him, and I know how almost impossible this is, and will be, until the world is made aware of these facts. (Ellis, p. 134.)

Edward Carpenter, another British homosexual emancipationist, socialist, and writer influenced by the works of Whitman, published in 1895 *Homogenic Love in a Free Society*, "a classic early defense of homosexuality." (Katz, p. 547.) Carpenter saw homosexual emancipation as a necessary step toward human emancipation. In his writings, Carpenter suggests some connections between the growing women's movement and lesbianism:

It is noticeable...that the movement among women for their own liberation and emancipation, which is taking place all over the civilized world, has been accompanied by a marked development of the homogenic [homosexual] passion among the female sex. It may be said that a certain strain in the relations between the opposite sexes which has come about owing to a growing consciousness among women that they have been oppressed and unfairly treated by men, and a growing unwillingness to ally themselves unequally in marriage—that this strain has caused womankind to draw more closely together and to cement alliances of their own...such comrade-alliances—and of a quite passionate kind—are becoming increasingly common, and especially perhaps among the more cultured classes of women, who are working out the great cause of their sex's liberation, nor is it difficult to see the importance of such alliances in such a campaign. In the United States where the battle of women's independence has been fought, more vehemently perhaps than here, the tendency mentioned is even more strongly marked. (Carpenter.)

By 1895 the movement was gaining a degree of intellectual momentum. However, about the same time, the British writer and known homosexual Oscar Wilde was arrested and tried for "gross indecency" and "sodomy" with a young nobleman, and sentenced to two years hard labor in prison. The trial and subsequent conviction were widely publicized and no doubt set back the movement in England. Carpenter wrote in his autobiography that "a sheer panic prevailed over *all* questions of sex, and especially of course questions of the intermediate sex." (Lauritsen and Thorstad, p. 33.) (For further discussion of Wilde and his trial, see Chapter 8.)

The United States

Unlike Germany and England, there seems to have been little organized political activity on the issue of homosexual emancipation in the United States in the late 19th century. It was not, however, completely ignored. For instance, Edward Prime-Stevenson is credited with publishing the first discourse in the United States on homosexuality. His 1908 book, *The Intersexes: A History of Similisexualism as a Problem in Social Life*, discussed the lives of homosexual men and women, whom he called "intersexes." In this work Stevenson attacked the social sanctions against homosexuality. (Licata.)

Feminist activist and anarchist Emma Goldman was the first prominent public supporter of homosexual rights in the United States at the beginning of the 20th century. Dr. Magnus Hirschfeld described her as "the first and only human being of importance in America to carry the issue of homosexual love to the broadest layers of the public." (Lauritsen, p. 37.) She was one of the first defenders of Oscar Wilde in the United States, despite the many taboos about women speaking on these topics. She wrote sensitively about the responses she received after a 1915 speaking tour:

The men and women who used to come to see me after my lectures on homosexuality, and who confided to me their anguish and their isolation, were often of finer grain than those who had cast them out. Most of them had reached an adequate understanding of their differentiation only after years of struggle to stifle what they had considered a disease and a shameful affliction. One young woman confessed to me that in the twenty-five years of her life she had never known a day when the nearness of a man, her own father and brothers even, did not make her ill. The more she tried to respond to sexual approach, the more repugnant men became to her. She had hated herself, she said, because she could not love her father and her brothers as she loved her mother. She suffered excruciating remorse, but her revulsion only increased. At the age of eighteen she accepted an offer of marriage in the hope that a long engagement might help her grow accustomed to a man and cure her of her "disease." It turned out a ghastly failure and nearly drove her insane. She could not face marriage and she dared not confide in her fiancé or friends. She had never met anyone, she told me, who suffered from a similar affliction, nor had she ever read books dealing with the subject. My lecture had set her free; I had given her back her self-respect.

This woman was only one of the many who sought me out. Their pitiful stories made the social ostracism of the invert seem more dreadful than I have ever realized before. To me anarchism was not a mere theory for a distant future; it was a living influence to free us from inhibitions, internal no less than external, and from the destructive barriers that separate man from man. (Goldman, pp. 555-56.)

Many representatives of the Scientific Humanitarian Committee came from Germany to spread the word in the U.S. For example, Otto Spengler spoke in 1906 to a group of professionals in New York City; this was probably the first speaking engagment in that city on the topic of homo-sexuality. Another spokesperson, Dr. Georg Merzbach, described his speaking experience in the following way:

The pictures and explanations I presented were received with tumultuous applause—an unusual thing, given the coolness of American scholars. A number of very distinguished doctors and legal scholars participated in the [almost two-hour] discussion, while Professor Beck, the surgeon, stood at my side as an interpreter to prevent misunderstandings in the heat of the exchange.... Naturally, rather naive questions were posed in the discussion, as well as some which were quite intelligent. I will mention a few: "Can homosexuality be eradicated by castration? What indications of homosex-ual tendencies does the animal kingdom provide? The names of historic or famous homosexuals, and the evidence thereof? Doesn't homosexuality lead ultimately to paranoia or other psychoses? Can homosexuals have children? Oscar Wilde, Shakespeare, Hamlet?" Some people spoke out forcefully against the penalization of homosexual acts.... The entire thing made such an overwhelming impression that Professor Beck, who had arranged the lecture, told me that he had never witnessed such success in presenting a scientific topic.... I had expected, and colleagues had predicted, a courteous but cool reception because of the subject matter; and now we have had this singular success in the very country where bigotry and prudishness are truly at home. Three ministers whom I had invited also attended the lecture and gave it their undivided attention. I can tell you, in the words of the dying messenger from Marathon who shouted to the Athenians:... "We have won a great battle." (Merzbach, pp. 76-77.)

An anonymous letter from Boston, Massachusetts, to the Committee spoke of the need for greater education on these issues in the United States:

I'm always delighted to hear about even the smallest success you have in vanquishing deep-rooted prejudices. And here in the United States we really need this kind of activity. In the face of Anglo-American hypocrisy, however, there is at present no chance that any man of science would have enough wisdom and courage to remove the veil which covers homosexuality in this country. And how many homosexuals I've come to know! Boston, this good old Puritan city, has them by the hundreds. The largest percentage, in my experience, comes from the Yankees of Massachusetts and Maine, or from New Hampshire. French Canadians are also well represented.

Here, as in Germany, homosexuality extends throughout all classes, from the slums of the North End to the highly fashionable Back Bay. Reliable homosexuals have told me names that reach into the highest circles of Boston, New York, and Washington, D.C., names which have left me speechless with astonishment. I have also noticed that bisexuality must be rather widespread. But I'll admit that I'm rather skeptical when homosexual friends say that they're far more attracted by the female sex. I'm often amused by someone assuring me of his bisexuality and later meeting him where there are no women.

There is astonishing ignorance among the Uranians I've come to know about their own true nature. This is probably a result of absolute silence and intolerance, which have never advanced real morality at any time or place. But with the growth of the population and the increase of intellectuals, the time is coming when America will finally be forced to confront the riddle of homosexuality. (*Ibid.*, pp. 98-99 taken from Katz, who added paragraphing and the ordering of the last two paragraphs to improve clarity.)

The first documented homosexual emancipation group in the United States was the Society for Human Rights (SHR) in Chicago, chartered in the state of Illinois on December 24, 1924. It was founded by Henry Gerber, a German-American immigrant. Gathering around him a number of working-class homosexual men, he attempted to fashion a group along the lines of the groups successful in Germany up to that time. According to its charter, SHR was formed:

> ...to promote and to protect the interests of people who by reasons of mental and physical abnormalities are abused and hindered in the legal pursuit of happiness which is guaranteed them by the Declaration of Independence, and to combat the public prejudices against them by dissemination of facts according to modern science among intellectuals of mature age. The Society stands only for law and order; it is in harmony with any and all general laws insofar as they protect the rights of others, and does in no manner recommend any act of violation of present laws nor advocates any matter inimical to the public welfare. (Taken from Katz, p. 581.)

Despite all Gerber's efforts, however, the organization never had more than ten members. They published a small newsletter, called *Friendship and Freedom*, which later got into the hands of local law-enforcement agencies. SHR officials were harassed by the police, jailed, and brought to trial. Though all charges were eventually dropped, Gerber lost his U.S. Post Office job and the group was disbanded.

Gerber wrote for many years, often using pseudonyms, in defense of law reform in the United States. His essay, "In Defense of Homosexuality," was published in *The Modern Thinker* in June 1932. In part, the essay criticizes the psychiatric profession for promoting myths dangerous to gay people. He suggested that the profession has wrongly diagnosed homosexuals as mentally ill when in fact, he asserts, it is societal oppression that creates the problems.

Chicago was a logical spot for the location of the first emancipation group in the United States, since it was the larger cities which attracted populations of gay people in the 1920s and 1930s. New York City's Riverside Drive and Lafayette Park in Washington, D.C., were well-known meeting places for homosexuals. New York, San Francisco, and New Orleans had the largest gay communities. A growing underground subculture was developing in Harlem, where homosexual men and women were a welcome part of black night club life. Many songs there even had homosexual sub-themes.

Numerous new lesbian and gay novels were being published in the 1920s. Most notable among these was the English lesbian classic *The Well of Loneliness* by Radclyffe Hall. It was written in an attempt to change negative views toward homosexuals and to emphasize to individual homosexuals that they were in no way unique or alone. Puddle, tutor of the book's protagonist in early 20th century Edwardian England, imagines what she would say to her agonized student if only she could speak the words:

> You're neither unnatural, nor abominable, nor mad; you're as much a part of what people call nature as anyone else; only you're unexplained as yet—you've not got your niche in creation. But some day that will come, and meanwhile don't shrink from yourself, but just face yourself calmly and bravely.... But above all be honorable. Cling to your honor for the sake of those others who share the same burden. For their sakes show the world that people like you and they can be quite as selfless and fine as the rest of mankind.... (Hall, p. 154.)

Shortly following its publication in 1928, the novel was declared obscene in both England and the United States and was banned for a time. But the very fact of its existence reflected the reality of an emerging homosexual identity and culture.

With the Great Depression of the 1930s, outward forms of discrimination against gay people and other minorities increased, and the move toward gay and lesbian visibility took a step backward. The movement in the United States, however, was soon to be advanced by a terrible historical phenomenon: war.

World War II.   From national mobilization and personal dislocation came a profound and irreversible advancement toward the creation of a true homosexual identity and community. The great Depression, followed by World War II, seriously rocked the stability of the American family. As the nation prepared for war, millions of women and men left their home towns and traveled to a variety of unfamiliar settings, many of which were segregated not only by race, but also by sex.

Men volunteered for or were drafted into the Armed Forces. Women too joined the military or entered the paid work-force for the first time in large numbers. This gave women not only a sense of independence from men, but also greater economic security.

Although the armed services refused to admit homosexuals into its ranks, few people willingly declared themselves. There were some cases of lesbians and gay men being purged from the military, but this was relatively rare. Most homosexuals were discreet and their behavior was generally tolerated in the Armed Forces, probably due to the country's enormous need for soldiers. Indeed, "the Women's Army Corps became the almost quintessential lesbian institution." (D'Emilio, p. 27.) As for the men:

> The sex-segregated nature of the Armed Forces raised homosexuality closer to the surface for all military personnel. Soldiers indulged in buffoonery, aping in exaggerated form the social stereotype of the homosexual, as a means of releasing the sexual tensions of life in the barracks. Such behavior was so common that a towel company used the image of a GI mincing with a towel draped around his waist to advertise its product. Army

canteens [clubs] witnessed men dancing with one another, an activity that in peacetime subjected homosexuals to arrest. Crowded into port cities, men on leave or those waiting to be shipped overseas shared beds in YMCAs and slept in each other's arms in parks or in the aisles of movie theaters that stayed open to house them.... In this setting, gay men could find one another without attracting undue attention, and perhaps even encounter sympathy and acceptance by their heterosexual fellows. (D'Emilio, pp. 25-26.)

Post War America.   Another element was tossed into the equation to produce an increasing sense of homosexual community immediately following the war. In their sweeping survey of the sexual habits of the American male in 1948, and in a similar study of the American female in 1953, sex researcher Alfred Kinsey and his associates shattered forever the myth that American adults followed a strict Puritanical code of sexual ethics. Evidence showed that a large percentage of young adults did not wait for marriage to become sexually active; married partners of both sexes had outside affairs more frequently than previously admitted; it was not uncommon for people to purchase pornography and erotica to enhance sex play; and not only had a large percentage of the population had sexual experience with someone of the same sex, but some people had homosexual experiences exclusively.

This study was released at a time of heightened Cold War tensions between the United States and the Soviet bloc countries. It was thought to be so potentially subversive that in 1954 a congressional committee accused Kinsey of aiding the cause of World Communism.

In this climate, a new stage in the political development of homosexual women and men began. This has come to be known as the *Homophile Movement*.

The Homophile Movement

The Rise of the Homophile

After the war, many "socially concerned" liberals organized around the goal of extending civil rights to members of minority groups. Groups such as the NAACP (National Association for the Advancement of Colored People) and the Urban League sponsored research on minority issues and to educate the public on prejudice. Their intention was primarily to show that blacks were the same as whites (except for the irrelevant difference of skin color) and to lobby for the abolition of all discriminatory laws.

This developing trend had an impact on many homosexuals. One was Donald Webster Cory, who, after attending some NAACP meetings in

New York City in 1944, saw many similarities between the problems faced by blacks and those faced by homosexuals. He was further encouraged by the findings of the Kinsey Report of 1948, which revealed the large percentage of American males who had had homosexual experiences. This led him to write his pioneering book, *The Homosexual in America* (1951), which argued that homosexuals constituted a minority deprived of rights and status by a prejudiced society. Further, he maintained that homosexuals shared a "caste-like status" with America's ethnic, religious, and racial minorities.

During this same time, other homosexuals saw the connection between homophobia and other forms of prejudice. One was Harry Hay of Los Angeles, a member of the Communist Party in the mid-1930s, who believed that political organizing was the key to self-protection and social change.

Unlike Cory who asserted that homosexuals were like anyone else, Hay saw a significant difference in the ways in which homosexuals and heterosexuals viewed the world—a difference in consciousness which extended far beyond sexuality. He believed that homosexuals possessed a special spiritual quality which, if fully realized, could be channeled for the betterment of humanity. With the tremendous rise in Cold-War tensions creating powerful anti-Communist sentiments in this country, Hay delayed formalizing a structure for a group. Instead, he proposed the formation of secret societies or autonomous guilds where men could come together for social and emotional support. One such guild was called The International Bachelors Fraternal Order for Peace and Social Dignity, sometimes known as Bachelors Anonymous. This guild eventually became a semi-public discussion group. Hay characterized the group as "a service and welfare organization devoted to the protection and improvement of society's androgynous minority." (Katz, p. 615.)

Attendance at these meetings began to swell, and some of the founding members organized their association of groups and guilds into what was to be called The Mattachine Society, founded in 1951 in Los Angeles. The name was taken from Les sociétés mattachines, a secret fraternal order of unmarried men who, in 13th- and 14th-century France and Spain, dressed as women and performed songs and spiritual rites for the peasantry.

A few months before the appearance of Cory's *The Homosexual in America*, Mattachine Society members wrote down a set of goals proposing to unify homosexuals "isolated from their own kind"; to educate homosexuals and heterosexuals alike to issues relating to identity and community "paralleling the emerging cultures of our fellow minorities— the Negro, Mexican, and Jewish People"; and to lead in the area of political action against discriminatory and oppressive legislation. Early leaders held the view that capitalism itself was responsible for the oppression of minorities. They believed that homosexuals must join with other minorities in defeating capitalism and replacing it with socialism.

A spiritual foundation for the group was also set. Members debated such fundamental questions as "Who are we?" "Where have we come from?" and "What are we here for?"—questions which would be posed many times by activists in succeeding decades.

A year after the founding of Mattachine, the homosexual group One, Inc., was formed in Los Angeles with a commitment to a liberal civil rights agenda. The group's name came from a line by the nineteenth-century essayist Thomas Carlyle: "A mystic bond of brotherhood makes all men one." The group began in January 1953 and published its journal *One*, which served until 1972 as a leading voice in the homosexual rights movement. Its goal was to bring to light the lack of civil rights protections for the homosexual and to bring homosexuals and heterosexuals together in closer communication. Thus, its agenda was more to the political center than Mattachine.

Although many of the leaders of the Mattachine Society tried to underplay their leftist affiliations, other members became concerned about the group's public image during a time of national conservatism. Senator Joseph McCarthy spearheaded a drive to purge Communists and homosexuals from the federal government. He and others preached that Communists corrupted the minds and homosexuals corrupted the bodies of "good Americans." McCarthy called, among others, Fred M. Snyder, Mattachine legal advisor, to testify before the House Un-American Activities Committee. McCarthy branded Snyder an unfriendly witness and led an attack to defame and publicly humiliate him.

President Truman issued an executive order in 1947 which established a loyalty program excluding Communists from obtaining government jobs. The witchhunts began, and a Senate report soon extended this to include homosexuals. The report asserted:

> Those who engage in overt acts of perversion lack the emotional stability of normal persons. Indulgence in acts of sex perversion weakens the moral fiber of the individual.

Even one "sex pervert in a Government agency," the Committee concluded:

> tends to have a corrosive influence upon his fellow employees. These perverts will frequently attempt to entice normal individuals to engage in perverted practices. This is particularly true in the case of young and impressionable people who might come under the influence of a pervert.... One homosexual can pollute a Government office. (U.S. Senate, Committee on Expenditures and Executive Departments.)

In 1953, Dwight D. Eisenhower issued Executive Order 10450, which extended and enlarged the Truman loyalty/security program to exclude explicitly those who engage in "sexual perversion" from obtaining government employment. The historian John D'Emilio estimates that slightly over 1,000 homosexuals per year were fired from federal jobs during the late 1940s. This number rose to 2,000 per year in the early 1950s, and to 3,000 by the beginning of the 1960s. This does not take into account the many thousands on the state and local level fired for alleged homosexuality.

Within this climate, the Mattachine Society held a convention in 1953 attended by over five hundred representatives from area homosexual organizations. At this convention a struggle for leadership took place between leftists who wanted to continue the course Mattachine had charted and those who were fearful of upcoming congressional investigations and did not want the group tarnished by a Marxist image. This latter group won out and, within one day, the Mattachine Foundation dissolved. Harry Hay then announced that the name Mattachine could be ceded to those who wanted to regroup into a national organization. Thus, a newly incarnated Mattachine Society was organized along liberal civil-rights lines. Its new charter explained that its "educational aim is directed toward the public at large, with a view to spreading accurate information about the nature and conditions of variation, and in this way eliminate discrimination, derision, prejudice, and bigotry" toward "the members of the variant minority, emphasizing the need for the definition and adoption of a personal behavior code which will...eliminate most—if not all—[of] the barriers to integrate." (Cutler, p. 44.) It is important to note here that during the 1950s the term "homophile" was used by many activists in preference to the word "homosexual" in order to dispel the common myth that homosexuality was only about sex. The label "homophile" was believed to connote emotional and not simply sexual attraction, and was also used to express a political outlook focusing on civil rights and social status.

While all of this activity was occurring on the West Coast, in New York City there was a small, informal group called The League, which was the remnant of a gay social club known as the Veterans' Benevolent Association that developed after World War II. Sparked by the activity occurring on the West Coast and by the publication of *The Homosexual in America*, two men—industrial psychiatrist Sam Morford and research chemist Tony Segura—formed a New York chapter of the Mattachine Society. They later founded and published *The Mattachine Review*, which was to become the organ of the Mattachine Society. Much of their political organizing had to be done cautiously, as homosexuality was a felony in New York State and was punishable by up to twenty years imprisonment.

The Mattachine Society soon became involved in a struggle with the New York Liquor Authority to overturn its ruling which forbade bars from serving liquor to homosexuals in New York.

Homophile Women

In San Francisco in the early 1950s, there was a small social club for lesbians. But in 1955, after hearing of Mattachine and its activities, two women—Del Martin and Phyllis Lyon—transformed this club into a women's organization to be called Daughters of Bilitis. Its stated purpose was to educate what they referred to as "the variant" to "understand herself and make her adjustment to society" by leading public discussion and "advocating a mode of behavior and dress acceptable to society," which they hoped would shatter negative myths and lead to the elimination of prejudicial laws. It also proposed the group's participation in research projects conducted by "duly authorized and responsible" experts in the fields of psychology and sociology to add "further knowledge of the homosexual." Nowhere in its initial charter did the word "lesbian" appear.

The group's name was taken from Pierre Louÿs's narrative "Song of Bilitis," in which Bilitis is a lesbian poet who lived in ancient Greece on the isle of Lesbos with Sappho. Its constitution provided for the establishment of other chapters throughout the country as well as a newsletter called *The Ladder*, which served as a resource for lesbians.

Lyon and Martin attended the Mattachine Society's fifth annual convention in the fall of 1958, where they persuaded another participant, Barbara Gittings, to found DOB-New York. Before long, DOB chapters were established in other cities: Los Angeles, Providence, Chicago, Boston, New Orleans, Reno, Portland (Oregon), San Diego, Cleveland, Denver, Detroit, Philadelphia, and Melbourne, Australia. For Martin, Lyon, Gittings, and others, DOB developed out of a need women had to find one another and end their own invisibility, often first steps toward improved self-image.

Looking back, Barbara Gittings remembers:

It never occurred to us in those early days that we could speak for ourselves, that we had the expert knowledge on ourselves. We were the ones explored, but we thought we needed the intervention of experts to do the exploring. Homosexuality had traditionally been the domain of people in law, religion, and the behavioral sciences.

At first we were so grateful just to have people—anybody—pay attention to us that we listened to and accepted everything they said, no matter how bad it was. That is how different the consciousness at the time was. But, I must emphasize, it was essential for us to go through this before we could arrive at what we now consider our much more sensible attitudes. You don't just spring full blown into an advanced consciousness. You do it step by step. Well, this was the important first step. We invited people who were willing to come to our meetings; obviously, it turned out to be those who had a vested interest in having us as penitents, clients, or patients. (Barbara Gittings, in Katz, 1976, p. 641.)

A Move Toward Militancy

Civil rights groups throughout the country during the 1950s and the 1960s were increasingly focused on direct political actions rather than simply educational efforts. These actions included marches, sit-ins, pickets, and other sorts of demonstrations. African Americans, for example, sat-in at lunch counters and other segregated public facilities in the South, protested laws which perpetuated discrimination, and organized effective economic boycotts. Gay activist groups at this time began to follow this trend.

One man, in particular, was to connect the earlier homophile philosophy with a more militant one. This was Franklin Kameny, a Harvard Ph.D. in astronomy, who was dismissed from his Army post in 1957 for being a known homosexual. Kameny appealed the decision and lost in both the federal courts and in the regular Army legal channels, leaving only the U.S. Supreme Court for redress. He wrote in a legal brief to the Supreme Court:

The Civil Service Commission policy on homosexuality is improperly discriminatory, in that it discriminates against an entire group not considered as individuals, in a manner in which other similar groups are not discriminated against, and in that this discrimination has no basis in reason.... (Tobin and Wicker, p. 94.)

Following his Army dismissal, Kameny developed a political strategy which would have long-range implications for future gay activists. He urged others to take a more active stance in pushing for homosexual rights rather than limit themselves to the narrower goal of educating the public on the issues. Taking the lead of African American militants like Stokely Carmichael in the 1960s, whose motto was "Black is Beautiful," Kameny coined the phrase "Gay is Good." This represented a radical departure from previous pleas for tolerance and more sympathetic treatment of homosexuals.

The *Mattachine Review* began to publish affirming literature on homophile themes. The poet Allen Ginsberg's controversial masterpiece *Howl* and Gore Vidal's pioneering novel dealing with same-sex attractions, *The*

City and the Pillar, are two examples. In addition, the ACLU (American Civil Liberties Union) became willing for the first time to fight for the constitutional rights of homosexuals, finally accepting them as another minority group. In 1967, the Columbia University student homophile group became the first gay or lesbian group to be granted an officially recognized campus charter; many others would soon follow.

By the end of the decade, most Mattachine Society chapters throughout the country were transformed from groups concerned mainly with education and research to organizations committed to changing discriminatory laws and ending police harassment of gay social clubs and bars. However, because of the ever-present fear of arrest or disclosure, only a small percentage of Society members actually took part in political actions. Through the actions which did occur were generally peaceful; the seeds for future militancy were planted.

The Lesbian and Gay Liberation/Rights Movement

The Stonewall Riots

There are points in history where conditions come together to create the beginnings of great social changes. The actions taken by Rosa Parks, a black woman who refused to give up her seat to a white on a Montgomery, Alabama municipal bus in 1955, signaled the start of a civil rights movement which would have profound and far-reaching consequences.

The incident credited with igniting the recent struggle for gay and lesbian liberation occurred at a small gay bar, the Stonewall Inn on Christopher Street, in New York's Greenwich Village, on June 27, 1969. On that Friday evening, Deputy Inspector Seymour Pine along with seven other officers from the Public Morals Section of the First Division of the New York City Police Department attempted to shut down a local bar frequented by gay street people, drag queens, and others. The charge was selling liquor without a license. This was a common event, for there were frequent police raids of gay bars in that city. Patrons usually accommodated the officials. This evening, however, was different. Feeling they had had enough of this treatment, people fought back by flinging bottles and rocks at police on this night and on successive nights.

It was no coincidence that the revolt began in a bar, for bars have been significant to gay culture long before Stonewall. Bars were places where people could meet others like themselves. They were also targets of longstanding state harassment. In New York City, for example, a law dating back to 1923 was used to arrest and fine any man who invited another man home for sex on grounds of "degenerate disorderly conduct." Behavior considered "campy," same-sex dancing, touching, and kissing were also classified as "degenerate." In the 1930s the Liquor Control Law was passed in New York City giving the State Liquor Authority the power to close bars it deemed "disorderly." "Homosexual" was often placed in this category and subsequently gay and lesbian bars were constantly threatened with closure and in many instances actually shut down. Though small pockets of resistance on the part of bars and bar patrons was in evidence, the Stonewall Riots marked a turning point in the struggle for equality. (Chauncey.)

The response by the Stonewall patrons was not unlike that of other groups at this time who were demanding social recognition: people of color, women, anti-war activists, students, Vietnam war veterans, people with physical disabilities, and others. Out of the ashes of the Stonewall Inn would rise a number of groups forming a new and highly visible movement. The next sections look at some of those groups in New York City to highlight some of the movement's activities. This is not to suggest that the new wave in the lesbian and gay movement was limited to the New York area—or even the East Coast of the U.S. In fact, the wave touched places as divergent as Lincoln, Nebraska; Sydney, Australia; London; and Mexico City.

The Gay Liberation Front

The homophile phase of the movement culminated in a greater sense of shared community and identity among gays and lesbians. This was a period when many groups of individuals were questioning traditional assumptions about power and authority, and this was no different for gays and lesbians. One of the first of these groups was the Gay Liberation Front (GLF). It had a vast and diverse pool of potential members from which to draw. There were, for example, gay and lesbian people from the ranks of the New Left. Some had been involved in the work of Students for a Democratic Society (SDS), a group offering revolutionary Marxist solutions to social, political, and economic inequalities. It was SDS's contention that the capitalist system was inherently unjust, racist, and dehumanizing and must be overthrown. Other GLF members came from the ranks of those who saw themselves as rejecting strict social norms. They proclaimed, "The personal is political," insisting on the freedom to explore alternative lifestyles as a part of a radical program. Pacifists and those who would come to be called "hippies" influenced many of the early GLFers with their concern for sexual freedom and a reevaluation of gender roles. A common belief held by both the revolutionaries and the social radicals was that a total transformation of society was necessary and that all oppressed minorities must link together in a common struggle.

The revolutionaries and social radicals were not the only ones to enter into this new movement. Carrying with them the notion that society could be "reformed" and that gays could one day become a respected segment of existing institutions, some people joined GLF after leaving more conservative homophile organizations such as the Mattachine Society and the Daughters of Bilitis.

On July 31, 1969, at a meeting at New York's Alternative University, the name "Gay Liberation Front" was very deliberately and consciously chosen:

"Gay"— a term self-chosen, not one which was imposed by society;
"Liberation"—suggesting freedom from constraint;
"Front"—a common radical term for a militant vanguard or coalition.

The name also suggested identification with the Viet Cong's National Liberation Front.

The concern became how to bring together people with disparate political and cultural philosophies (revolutionaries, social radicals, reformers, plus those who were politically indifferent) into a unified movement. From the outset, the radicals set the agenda for the group.

> The radicals rather than revolutionary homosexuals took the lead in forming and defining GLF because revolutionaries, lacking the radical eagerness to explore the personal in the name of the political, were little inclined to think of sexuality in political terms. (Marotta, p. 89.)

The group adopted a set of principles emphasizing coalition-building with other disenfranchised groups—women, ethnic minorities, blacks, working-class people, young people, elders, disabled people, all Third World peoples—as a means of dismantling the economic and social structures considered inherently oppressive.

As it turned out, GLF did not become a formalized organization *per se*, but rather it was a series of small groups in the U.S. and other Western countries. GLF meetings took place in people's living rooms, Unitarian and Episcopal church basements, and storefronts.

Believing that the "personal is political," GLF members adopted the technique of consciousness-raising popular at the time within the counterculture and most specifically within the women's movement. In these groups, people usually sat in a room, often in a circle, giving one another support in developing a strong and positive gay identity and helping one another to find avenues to express the anger they felt at a culture which had for so long made them feel isolated and guilty. These groups usually did not have a leader as a "traditional" therapy group might. Rather, the groups strived for the non-hierarchical structure they proposed for society at large.

New ways of thinking and living emerged from these sorts of groups. Lesbian feminists in GLF who had been dealing with many of these issues in the women's movement made important contributions to that discussion. In an attempt to spread the new message to as many people as possible, newspapers and other publications were published, including GLF-New York's *Come Out* and GLF-London's *Come Together*, and more popular commercial papers such as *Gay* and *Gay Power*. The new GLF publications made a number of claims: 1. personalized and emotion-filled sex is good; 2. role-playing is obsolete, while the violation of roles designated by gender is desirable; 3. professional recognition, status, and material rewards are bad, but unconventional emotional, sensual, spiritual, artistic, and interpersonal experience is salutary; 4. intuitive, expressive, genuine, gentle and cooperative behavior is good. (Marotta.) Along with these principles, radical men in GLF declared that many of the traditional patterns of gay male expression, such as the bar scene, the physical objectification of the body, and the emphasis on youth, were unliberating and must be challenged. Soon, collective gay male living centers were organized around non-sexist life styles.

GLF also organized protest demonstrations aimed at radicalizing other gays and lesbians while showing other movement groups that homosexuals were indeed an oppressed minority and thus part of the larger movement for social change. This latter point was often missed by many people in the New Left, who tended to trivialize the revolutionary potential of gays and lesbians. Cuba, which many on the Left viewed as a paradigm of socialist society, systematically incarcerated gays, seeing them as evil and as a threat to the culture. In May 1972, the Cuban government published a resolution on homosexuality in its official Communist party newspaper, *Granma*. It read, in part:

> The social and pathological character of homosexual deviations was recognized. It was resolved that all manifestations of homosexual deviations are to be firmly rejected and prevented from spreading. It was pointed out, however, that a study, investigations, and analysis of this complex problem should always determine the measures to be followed.... A study was made of the origin and evolution of this phenomenon and its present-day scope and anti-social character. An in-depth analysis was made of the preventive and educational measures that are to be put into effect against existing focuses, including the control and relocation of isolated cases, always with an educational and preventive purpose.... Finally it was agreed to demand that severe penalties be applied to those who corrupt the morals of minors, depraved repeat offenders, and irredeemable anti-social elements. Cultural institutions cannot serve as a platform for false intellectuals who try to make snobbery, extravagant conduct, homosexuality, and other social aberrations into expressions of revolutionary spirit and art, isolated from the masses and the spirit of the revolution. (Quoted in Jay & Young, 1972, pp. 246-47.)

Many Leftists in the United States accepted Cuba's anti-homosexual policies, which further alienated gays from those Leftist groups. Some New Left groups purged members who openly declared their homosexuality.

While gays and lesbians did have their own organizations on college campuses prior to the Stonewall riots, their numbers jumped enormously in the early 1970s. Many GLF chapters appeared on campuses throughout the country. These groups sponsored activities which were virtually unprecedented: college lesbian and gay dances. Gay reporter Basil O'Brien wrote about "the first gay dance on a campus in Pennsylvania" for the Philadelphia *Plain Dealer*, September 3, 1970:

> ...some straight heads were blown apart as we filled Temple's student center with the high that you feel when you contact with the rest of the alive world and it's all going your way...we'd turned off the bad trip of gay ghetto bars and street cruising and sitting on the wall in Rittenhouse Square...this dance floor full of freed-up people was the beginning of our community, us, people who could groove together without power roles and channeled sexual drive.

> We were feeling the high energy of the revolution based on love. Dancing together is a sharing thing. It's not the same as toking up, sitting inside ear-phones. It takes a lot of people.... It's an interpersonal thing that gay people do because we dig each other. Check out the straights some time as they sit on the benches at the Factory or on the Plateau. No energy. Everybody into their own thing, scared to open up to each other. But we're not scared of each other. We know that sisters dancing with sisters, brothers dancing with brothers, touching, kissing and balling people of the same sex is a far loving out expression of living. (Quoted in Teal, p. 59.)

Branching Off.   After a very short time, GLF began to feel severe growing pains. It soon became apparent that the ideological differences among the revolutionaries, social radicals, and reformers were too significant for all to remain in one organization. A handful of gay revolutionaries from GLF met separately to organize around principles fundamental to Marxism. One of these groups was the Red Butterfly cell in New York. A small contingent of GLF's Third World members also formed its own group. Some of the younger members regrouped, and by late 1970 gay youth organizations had formed in cities like Philadelphia, San Francisco, Chicago, Tampa, Detroit, and Ann Arbor.

The Gay Activists Alliance

Many gay reformers became disillusioned with some of the more radical political strategies of GLF, and subsequently left the ranks of GLF to push for political and cultural changes within the existing social order. These reformers formed a new organization: the Gay Activists Alliance (GAA). (Though GAA and the Mattachine Society had similar goals in reforming society, GAA was much more militant in its strategies.) Joined by some of the more activist members of the Mattachine Society's Action Committee, members of the new GAA created an organization which had a formalized structure; members concentrated chiefly on the single issue of ending the oppression of homosexuals. It presented itself as being a militant (though nonviolent) organization working for the civil rights of homosexuals, often through direct confrontation. Unlike GLF, GAA was a structured organization having elected officials who conducted meetings according to parliamentary law procedures. Though social activities were sponsored, the organization's primary focus was political. It took its logo from the Greek letter Lambda, a symbol for wavelength in quantum physics, suggesting dynamism. GAA organized petition drives to repeal laws against homosexual acts between consenting adults, demonstrated against newspaper and broadcast media accounts that were perceived to be inaccurate and derogatory, engaged in political "zaps" to confront elected officials and political candidates over the civil rights of homosexuals, and sent questionnaires to politicians polling them on their attitudes.

Political protest activities were a crucial strategy in pushing for gay rights, and GAA members viewed these actions as a useful way of politicizing large numbers of previously uninvolved gays and lesbians. To advance community-wide educational efforts, GAA published a newsletter, the *Gay Activist*, and established a speaker's bureau sending people to schools, media outlets, community groups, and various religious organizations. GAA chapters spread to most of the larger U.S. cities within a relatively short period of time.

While many pushed for political reforms, others in GAA were more concerned with changing negative societal attitudes. The reformers believed that as the number of proud and open gays increased, the public would begin to drop its fear and hatred, making it possible for gays to be accepted fully into all aspects of the social order. One strategy used to achieve this goal was "street theater," emphasizing open displays of affection on the street by same-sex couples, which included anything from holding hands and kissing to "gay-ins" in which large numbers of people picnicked and danced together in public parks and other open spaces. Some members wore buttons with slogans considered to be outrageous for the time, such as "Freaking Fag Revolutionary" and "Gay Love." GAA soon managed to raise funds to rent its own office space in a few cities around the U.S., including the "Gay Fire House" in New York's SoHo district and an old warehouse in Washington, D.C. Open community dances—social alternatives to the bars—were very popular in these spaces.

Gay Separatists

Comparable to the "Back to Africa" movement proposed by some black leaders in the first few decades of the 20th century, there were some gay "separatists" in the early 1970s who advocated separation from heterosexuals as a way to bring about true liberation. Many of these activists believed that gay consciousness is qualitatively different from the mainstream and that assimilation into a heterosexually dominated society leads to a cooptation of the spirit. A group of gay and lesbian activists in 1970 called for large numbers of homosexuals to move to the thinly populated rural area of California's Alpine County to gain the electoral power needed to guarantee their civil liberties.

Though the plan had no real chance of succeeding, organizers used it chiefly to focus media attention and to raise the political awareness of gays and lesbians.

This strategy did not gain widescale support, but some small rural communities were established: Golden, Oregon (1970); Elwha on Washington State's Olympic Peninsula (1973); Wolf Creek, Oregon (1975); Running Water and Short Mountain sanctuaries in North Carolina and Tennessee (late 1970s). Coming out of one such community, Grinnell, Iowa (1974), was *RFD*—a magazine focusing on gay country living and spirituality. (Thompson.)

The Lesbian Feminist Movement

Prior to the women's movement, women's sexuality was seen as dependent on male sexuality. Women were not encouraged to define what they wanted sexually or to take the initiative. The feminist movement began to change all that.

For many lesbians, the advent of this new wave in the women's movement in the 1960s signaled an affirmation of the ways in which they had already been living their lives. Lesbians had always been an integral part of the women's movement. For many years they had been in the forefront of the struggle for women's liberation, fighting against economic discrimination, male violence, sexism, and for reproductive rights. And with this new affirmation of female sexuality and the possibility of women's autonomy, many women were able to identify their experience as lesbian.

Although the presence of lesbians in the women's movement was a vital one, the response of the movement was mixed. In the case of the

National Organization for Women, which organized in 1966, the reaction was often initially negative. As NOW emerged as a national organization dedicated to defend the rights of women, the issue of lesbianism became a source of friction. The press and others hostile to NOW began using the assumed presence of lesbians as a reason to discredit and dismiss the entire movement. But a perceived anti-lesbian bias within NOW led many lesbians to resign from the organization after unsuccessful attempts to persuade the leadership to work for lesbian rights.

Triggered by the sexism in many of the male-dominated New Left organizations and by the anti-lesbian attitudes in parts of the feminist movement, lesbians joined together in 1969 to enunciate a new radical form of feminism, one which aspired to transform America into a society free of sexism. (Marotta.) Some former NOW members formed a women's caucus in organizations like the Gay Liberation Front. Some lesbians engaged in actions to challenge feminists' refusal to deal with lesbianism.

Lesbian Reformers. Women also worked among the ranks of the militant reformers in the Gay Activists Alliance. In New York what was originally called the "Women's Subcommittee," under the auspices of GAA's Community Relations Committee, became a full and separate committee in 1972, called the "Lesbian Liberation Committee." It then became a separate organization in 1973—Lesbian Feminist Liberation, Inc. (LFL)—to provide a place where lesbians could get together to explore the political implications of their sexuality and to socialize in places other than bars or small private circles.

Radicalesbians. While some lesbians remained in GLF and GAA, many women came to consider their issues and concerns different from those of gay men. They separated and formed groups along radical feminist lines stressing that traditional ideas of sex roles were inhibiting to all forms of female self-expression. They argued that the fight against sexism required all women to band together to challenge male privilege and heterosexual institutions. The following is from the concluding section of the Radicalesbian treatise "Women-Identified Women":

> Our energies must flow toward our sisters, not backwards towards our oppressors. As long as women's liberation tries to free women without facing the basic heterosexual structure that binds us in one-to-one relationship with our own oppressors, tremendous energies will continue to flow into trying to straighten up each particular relationship with a man, how to get better sex, how to turn his head around—into trying to make the "new man" out of him, in the delusion that this will allow us to be the "new woman." This obviously splits our energies and commitments, leaving us unable to be committed to the construction of the new patterns which will liberate us. (From Jay and Young, pp. 176-77.)

The evolution of groups to meet the specific needs of lesbians underscores the fact that though heterosexual feminists, gay men, and lesbians may all be working for an end to sexism, issues and philosophies often differ.

Christopher Street Liberation Day

In the fall of 1969 participants at the Eastern Regional Conference of Homophile Organizations (ERCHO) raised the idea of setting aside a day each year to commemorate the Stonewall Inn riots. A day of remembrance was not without precedent. The Mattachine Society had bussed people to Philadelphia for an "Annual Reminder" on July 4 from 1965 to 1969. The men and women wore conventional clothing, and all took part in peaceful picketing around Independence Hall.

After Stonewall, many of the newer members in the liberation movement wanted something more dynamic and festive. GLF radicals at the ERCHO conference successfully lobbied for the passage of a resolution which stated:

Resolved: That the Annual Reminder, in order to be more relevant, reach a greater number of people and encompass the ideas and ideals of the larger struggle in which we are engaged—that of our fundamental human rights—be moved both in time and location. We propose that a demonstration be held annually on the last Saturday in June in New York City to commemorate the 1969 spontaneous demonstrations on Christopher Street and that this demonstration be called CHRISTOPHER STREET LIBERATION DAY.... ("Gay Holiday," *New York Hymnal*.)

The resolution also proposed that homophile groups across the country be encouraged to hold parallel demonstrations on the same day.

A committee, The Christopher Street Liberation Day Umbrella Committee, formed, representing delegates from many of the East Coast groups. It planned a whole week of activities (including dances, art shows, theater, and political demonstrations), all culminating in a march on Sunday, June 28, 1970, up Sixth Avenue. Thousands marched, carrying posters reading: "Gay Liberation Front," "Lesbians Unite," "Homosexual Is Not a Four-Letter Word," "We Are the Dykes Your Mother Warned You About," "Everything You Think We Are, We Are," "Smash Sexism," "Sappho Was a Right-On Woman," "Free Oscar Wilde," "Gay Power," "I Am a Lesbian and I Am Beautiful."

The march ended with a "gay-in" in Central Park. One of the marchers saw it this way:

Wave on wave of gay brothers and sisters, multi-bannered, of all sizes and descriptions were advancing into the meadow, and a spontaneous applause seized the early marchers.... For all of us who have been slowly climbing for years toward our freedom, this one last hill which let us look across our dear brothers and sisters was a cup running over.... It was as if...now at last we had come to the clearing, on the way to the top of the mountain...and tho' we knew we still had far to go, we were moving, and knew it. (Liechti.)

From that first march in New York City in June 1970 grew others throughout the globe. The end of June each year is now reserved for local "Gay and Lesbian Pride" activities. Demonstrations on a national scale have also taken place, including the National Marches for Lesbian and Gay Rights held in October in Washington, D.C., in 1979 and again in 1987. Well over 100,000 participants attended the first and well over one-half a million the second to show their pride and solidarity and to lobby elected officials for support of anti-discriminatory legislation and funding for AIDS-related projects.

The Bisexual Liberation Movement

In part because of the increasing visibility and political power of the feminist and gay/lesbian movements, bisexuals began to organize in the late 1970s. For a number of reasons neither the homosexual rights movement nor mainstream political movements initially responded to the needs of bisexuals.

At first bisexual women organized themselves in same-sex groups for support and consciousness-raising; bisexual men later followed this example. Bisexual groups now march as contingents in gay/lesbian pride marches and, though differing on some concerns, share with many gay activists a desire to end homophobia and rigid definitions of gender roles. As one spokesperson notes:

A new movement is emerging and finding voice within the gay community. For years bisexuals have felt compelled to hide our true sexual identity in the gay community as well as in the straight world. Now many bisexuals have begun to organize. We are no longer willing to stay closeted within a community many of us view as our own. We have begun to speak out and to reach out to our gay brothers and lesbian sisters to discuss our similarities and our differences. We have begun to break down the walls of prejudice which separate us and to build new solidarity within the gay community so that we can fight collectively for the freedom to love whom we choose....

A major goal of the new bisexual networks is to dispel myths and stereotypes which are all too pervasive in the gay community. Bisexuality is often thought to be a mere transition stage between gay identification and a straight heterosexual privilege.

Bisexuality, however, is a valid sexual preference. While many gays have experienced bisexuality as a stage in reaching their present identity, this should not invalidate the experience of people for whom sexual and affectional desire is not limited by gender. For in fact many bisexuals experience lesbianism or homosexuality *as a stage* in reaching their sexual identification.

Since the question of gender in sexuality is fundamental to the gay movement, one would expect bisexuality to be of major interest. However, the gay community does not always differentiate between the institutionalized heterosexuality of society and the growing movement of bisexuals, whose struggles include the fight for sexual freedom of expression without regard for gender.

Bisexuals are people of every age, race, class, and gender. We may be celibate, monogamous, or involved with more than one person at a time. We choose our partners conscientiously and care for them as best we can. We are no more or less loyal, compassionate, or loving than the next person. We too experience homophobic discrimination and even violence in our lives. And now we are drawing together to share our common experiences, appreciate our differences and fight for our rights. (Morrison.)

The Men's Movement

Feminism had powerful effects not only on women, but on some men as well. In an attempt to create changes in their own behavior and more options in their lives, men in many locations borrowed the consciousness-raising model of the early days of the women's and gay movements and joined together to reexamine gender roles, to explore relations between the sexes, and to look at traditional conceptions of masculinity in general. In the process, they explored how homophobia affects both homosexuals and heterosexuals and the ways that narrowly defined male roles and expectations deny men the freedom to show emotion and vulnerability.

By 1974 there were hundreds of "Men's Awareness Networks." There were also a number of published newsletters and journals. As this movement developed, there was a growing recognition of two distinct streams within these groups. One was the "men's anti-sexist movement," which focused on feminist issues such as abortion, lesbian and gay rights, and gender-role transformation. The other was the "men's rights movement" (the "Free Men") which, though it too supported the Equal Rights Amendment, was in fact a reaction to women's demands for equality, focusing on revision of divorce and child custody laws to give men "equal rights" in alimony, child custody, and visitation.

Today, there are many men's centers around the country organized to serve as support networks for men who wish to transform the social conditions and expectations of what it means to be "masculine." Also, groups have formed at these centers to counsel men who have battered or emotionally abused women.

The Post-Stonewall Era

The Stonewall rebellion changed the entire complexion of a movement for social change as a volcanic eruption forever alters the face of a mountain. The rage that was smoldering for so long surfaced like molten lava burning away years of repression and denial. Also, like a volcano, though, the initial flurry of radical activity cooled substantially.

Though quite visible in relative terms, the number of people actively involved in lesbian and gay politics at this time was still small. The vast majority of lesbians, gays, and bisexuals had either not come out of the closet or were not willing to become politically involved. Some activists became less militant as modest goals were attained. In addition, as with all social movements, the gay and lesbian liberation movements were products of their time. In particular, as the political climate moved closer to the right by the mid-1970s, tactics and goals changed as well. Much of the militancy and radical activism of the late sixties and early seventies had moderated. Sociologist Dennis Altman talks about a "swing back to respectability" mid decade in which some of the visible leaders of the gay and lesbian movements, and similarly in the black movement, were no longer the "denim-clad radicals" but by the mid-1970s were men and women in suits. Though an oversimplification, this description does underscore a trend.

Many groups, such as the Gay Liberation Front and Gay Activist Alliance, either disbanded or scaled down their activities. Even the less militant groups, like the Mattachine Society and the Daughters of Bilitis, dissolved most of their chapters around the country. By the late 1980s the only remaining DOB chapter was in Boston.

Radical activity, however, did not cease altogether. Socialist discussion groups, direct action groups, and other informal political support networks formed to continue the advances of gay and lesbian politics. Some progressive organizations began to acknowledge the importance of sexual politics in their agendas for social change. In England, three National Gay Marxist Conferences were held between 1973 and 1974, and the journal *Gay Left* was launched in 1975 linking a Marxist analysis of gay and lesbian oppression to the struggle for socialism.

A profound change had occurred in the short span of time between

1969 and the middle of the following decade. Certainly, homosexuals were not universally loved, homophobia had not ceased, and the political system had not been significantly altered. There emerged, however, a radical new definition of homosexuality—from "sickness" and "perversion" to "alternative lifestyle." With increased visibility, the concepts of gay and lesbian identity and culture were strengthened though in somewhat different forms for men and women.

> The flowering of culture in the past decade has been especially true for lesbians. I think in part this has happened because, while gay men had more of a subculture because of "camp's" acceptance in the mainstream culture ...lesbians, since we are women, have been most subsumed and at the same time isolated in the straight culture. Therefore, theoretically, we started with a blank slate which, though it would appear to be a disadvantage, actually made it easier to build a new and different culture. (Jay, p. 51.)

By the mid-1970s, homosexuals constituted a bona fide and legitimate minority group sharing many commonalities with other disenfranchised groups, but unlike these other groups who for some time had a sense of their past and a feeling of community, the gay and lesbian minority was for the first time creating its own true feeling of identity and shared sense of community.

Community Organizations

This growing "new sense of community" extended farther than merely the bars, restaurants, and clubs, but was now beginning to include visible social, political, and business institutions. By the close of 1973, this proliferation of things lesbian and gay included over 1100 organizations and groups, and this list has continued to expand to the present time. Though many people now take these institutions for granted as mainstays of lesbian and gay culture, they are the result of long and hard-fought battles.

Such organizations and groups include informational organizations (e.g., speakers' bureaus, history/herstory projects, telephone hotlines); professional support groups for lawyers, scientists, schoolworkers, health-care providers, social workers, academics, business owners, artists; lesbian-and gay-owned businesses of all kinds; religious groups—Jewish, Lutheran, Unitarian, Catholic, Quaker, United Church of Christ; student organizations in virtually every state and on many campuses; support groups (e.g., Parents and Friends of Lesbians and Gays, Men of All Colors Together, groups for Asians, Latinos, bisexuals, physically challenged, gay and lesbian parents, elders, youth, men, women, etc.); recreational and artistic groups; media agencies (e.g., cable TV programs, radio programs, magazines, newspapers, journals, publishing houses, and media watchdog groups); legal agencies and prisoner projects; and local community service centers.

Community Service Centers.   Gay and lesbian community service centers began to develop in the early 1970s. Founded on the principle that lesbians and gays have unique and special needs that often go unmet, these centers were organized in such places as Los Angeles, San Francisco, and Orange County (California), Minneapolis, Chicago, New York City, Baltimore, Washington (D.C.), Albany, Philadelphia, Louisville, Boston, and Norfolk. They are funded by private donations and some by government and foundation grants and offer an array of services. One of the first and most successful of these organizations, Los Angeles' Gay and Lesbian Community Services Center, had an annual budget of over $2.5 million in 1986.

Some of the services provided by the centers include counseling and mental health programs, alcohol-abuse treatment, vocational services, lesbian advocacy, legal aid, medical services (including information, counselling, treatment, and advocacy in the wake of the AIDS crisis), youth and elders programs, information and referral, telephone hotlines, speakers' bureaus, newsletters, roommate referral, lending libraries, rap groups, coffeehouses, and other social activities such as community dances and potluck dinners.

Legal-Aid Agencies.   Though the political battleground was occasionally in the streets during the post-Stonewall era, more and more it came into the legislative arena, the voting booth, and the courts. Political organizing increasingly emphasized coalition-building with other minorities in an attempt to counter the growing influence of the so-called "New Right."

Civil rights strategies were winning favor, often to the dismay of movement radicals. Activists called for the repeal of repressive laws, many newly enacted out of a conservative backlash to lesbian and gay visibility. People increasingly began to challenge political inequalities in the courts related to housing and employment policies, police harassment and entrapment, assault and battery, child custody rulings, military dismissals, deportations, and so forth.

To assist in these battles, lesbian and gay legal-aid organizations were established. The oldest and largest of its kind is the nationally oriented Lambda Defense and Education Fund, Inc., founded in New York City in 1973 "to advance the rights of gay people and to educate the public at large about discrimination against gay men and lesbians." Other agencies include Boston's Gay and Lesbian Advocates and Defenders (GLAD), a regional agency serving the New England area; two national organizations in San Francisco: Lesbian Rights Project, and National Gay Rights

Advocates; plus two groups specializing in child custody cases: Philadelphia's Custody Action for Lesbian Mothers (CALM); and Seattle's Lesbian Mothers National Defense Fund. In the majority of these agencies, a network of volunteer attorneys file test-case litigation to establish legal precedents. Along with the numerous legal issues of concern to lesbian and gay people, these organizations now extend their services to deal with AIDS-related discrimination. Often these groups are allied with other legal rights agencies such as the American Civil Liberties Union, the National Conference of Black Lawyers, and the National Organization for Women's Legal Defense and Education Fund, among others.

The National Gay and Lesbian Task Force. The first gay and lesbian group coming from the new wave of gay liberation to take a national focus was the National Gay and Lesbian Task Force. It was founded in November 1973 as a professionally staffed organization which blended the old homophile and newer reformist gay and lesbian liberationist strategies. As originally stated, NGLTF's purpose is: "...to re-educate society, including its homosexual members, to esteem gay men and women at their full human worth and to accord them places in society which will allow them to attain and contribute according to their full human and social potential." (Bruce Voeller, in first *NGLTF Newsletter*.)

NGLTF originally opened its doors in New York City, but moved to Washington, D.C., in 1986. It serves as a clearinghouse to help facilitate communications among gay and lesbian organizations and other civil rights groups nationwide. It operates a national toll-free Crisisline which has taken tens of thousands of calls since it was installed in 1982.

NGLTF led the fight to have the American Psychiatric Association remove its "sickness" definition of homosexuality. (This goal was achieved on April 8, 1974, six months after the birth of NGLTF.) Shortly after this victory, the organization worked to have a gay rights bill introduced into the United States Congress. The bill (HR 5452) was introduced on March 23, 1975 to prohibit discrimination on the basis of affectional or sexual preference. Congressional sponsorship of the bill was spearheaded by Congresswoman Bella Abzug of New York and by a number of other members of Congress. Though it did not pass, it did raise the issue on a national scale.

In response to the 1977 anti-gay "Save Our Children" campaign by Anita Bryant, singer and spokesperson for the Florida Citrus Commission, NGLTF launched a nationwide education program which it called "We Are Your Children." The goals of the project were to educate the public on the issue of homosexuality and to lobby local and state lawmakers for the passage of civil rights legislation.

Ongoing NGLTF activities include a Media Project focusing media attention on gay and lesbian issues, a Violence Project documenting instances of violence directed against lesbians and gays while pushing for improvement of services to victims of such violence, and a Privacy Project working for the elimination of laws restricting sexual expression between consenting adults in the wake of a 1986 Supreme Court decision upholding Georgia's anti-sodomy law. NGLTF also works closely with other organizations, specifically those working around health issues, to lobby for greater funding for research on AIDS and to educate both the homosexual and heterosexual communities about the health crisis.

Partisan Politics

Many gay and lesbian activists began to work within the established political system of electoral politics (particularly within the Democratic Party), continuing the reformist or civil rights strategy for social change. People began to work for candidates sensitive to their personal issues and hoped for the time when more open lesbian and gay candidates could themselves run for public office. They also lobbied for statutes protecting individuals on the basis of sexual orientation. On the other side of the coin, they began to expose politicians whose policies were contrary to their collective interests and worked to overturn laws and ordinances denying them equal rights.

One form this new force would take was the gay and lesbian Democratic club. These clubs arose out of the need to channel and coordinate activities and to pull more people into the political process. The first of these was the Alice B. Toklas Gay Democratic Club of San Francisco in 1971. (Toklas was the longtime lover and companion of writer Gertrude Stein.) Members of this group and the many others soon to follow were keenly aware of the strong anti-gay forces in the country and worked to counter them within the established political process.

At the 1972 Democratic Party Convention held in Miami, Florida, Jim Foster, then chairperson of the Society for Individual Rights and founder of the Alice B. Toklas Gay Democratic Club, formally presented the first open gay rights address to that party. It was covered live on national TV and read, in part:

> We do not come to you pleading your understanding or begging your tolerance. We come to you affirming our pride in our lifestyle, affirming the validity to seek and maintain meaningful emotional relationships, and affirming our right to participate in the life of this country on an equal basis with every citizen...there are millions of gay brothers and sisters who will say to the Democratic Party, "We are here. We will not be still. We will not go away until the ultimate goal of gay liberation is realized, the goal that all people live in the peace, freedom, and dignity of who we are." (Foster, from Marotta, pp. 64-65.)

One of the leading forces who helped Foster gain a position at the 1972 convention was George McGovern, who was the Party's presidential candidate. Gays were instrumental in helping to secure McGovern's strong showing in the nationwide primary elections of 1972. For example, they collected over one-third of the northern California signatures needed to place McGovern's name atop that state's primary ballot. The technique was simple: gay civil rights activists went into the bars and registered everyone to vote, then had them sign a McGovern petition to have his name placed on the ballot. Gays also proved to be effective fundraisers to help fill McGovern's political coffers. (Marotta.)

Even with McGovern's support, though, the 1972 Democratic Party Presidential Platform did not include a gay rights agenda. Rumors abounded that backers of presidential hopeful Hubert Humphrey attempted to delay Foster's speech and were against a proposed Gay Rights plank.

(Jim Foster's address was actually the second time an openly gay person appeared in front of a political convention on the issue of gay and lesbian rights. The first occurred in February 1970 at the Peace and Freedom Party State Convention in Long Beach, California, where Harry Hay called from the floor for the creation of a gay caucus and helped to draft a seven-point gay rights plank which was read to the full membership of the party.)

At the 1976 Democratic Presidential Convention, no speaker was given permission to address the delegates on the issue of gay and lesbian rights, though there were three openly gay and lesbian delegates.

To insure that they had more clout at the next convention, the organization Gay Vote 1980 came into being with the goal of pushing for a gay and lesbian rights agenda during the national presidential conventions of 1980. Though having very little influence at the Republican Party Convention (helping to elect only two openly gay delegates, both of whom were committed to John Anderson's campaign), they fared much better at the Democratic Party Convention held in New York City. They were instrumental in the election of seventy-seven gay and lesbian delegates, alternatives, and permanent committee people, and also helped to establish the gay and lesbian caucus at the convention. Also, for the first time, a gay rights plank was included in the 1980 Democratic Presidential Platform and written into the Charter and By-Laws governing the National Democratic Party.

In the 1980 platform, the equal protection clause focused on ending discrimination, especially in the area of immigration. The language read:

> We must affirm the dignity of all people and the right of each individual to
> have equal access to and participation in the institutions and services of our
> society. All groups must be protected from discrimination based on race,

color, religion, national origin, language, age, sex, or sexual orientation. This includes specifically the right of foreign citizens to enter this country. Appropriate legislative and administrative actions to achieve these goals should be undertaken.

Another precedent was set at the 1980 Democratic Convention. As a purely symbolic action, the lesbian and gay caucus at the convention nominated a vice-presidential candidate. They chose Melvin Boozer, a thirty-five-year-old black gay activist who was at that time an alternative delegate from Washington, D.C., and president of the D.C. chapter of the Gay Activists Alliance. As millions of TV viewers watched, he addressed the Convention and raised the issue of lesbian and gay rights.

After the momentum gained during the 1980 political season, many gay and lesbian political activists felt that a national organization was needed to encourage communication between local gay Democratic clubs and maximize their impact. The National Association of Gay and Lesbian Democratic Clubs was established in Washington, D.C. in June 1982 to help make the gay and lesbian community a permanent part of the American electoral political process.

Not all gay activists are on the left of the political spectrum. For example, one group, Concerned Americans for Individual Rights (CAIR), was organized in the spring of 1984 to influence policy in the Republican Platform of the party's National Convention that year. Most of its small membership is made up of Republicans or Libertarians whose goal is to counteract the hostility toward homosexuality by that party's "New Right" wing and to provide a place for gays to organize. Their approach is not primarily legalistic or combative, but rather they use education to improve the "public image" of the homosexual. In part CAIR's *Statement of Purpose* reads:

> It has long been evident that moderate-to-conservative gays and lesbians need a national organization through which they can express their views. Despite the persistence of negative stereotypes, the vast majority of homosexual Americans are decent, productive, law-abiding citizens who contribute substantially to the betterment of their communities. In common with heterosexual Americans, we share the traditional values on which this country was founded, including patriotism, religious faith, personal and economic freedom, and hard work.

> Until now, we have been unrepresented by the gay extremists, and misrepresented by the religious right. It is time to speak for ourselves. We will present an accurate picture of gay Americans, reflecting the many positive contributions that we make to society. By this means we will break down the prejudices that oppress homosexuals in our nation today.

As pressure politics strategies increased, The Human Rights Campaign

Fund—a gay- and lesbian-organized and operated Political Action Committee (PAC)—was created to raise and distribute money for politicians sensitive to the needs of lesbians and gays and to help defeat candidates perceived as homophobic. In addition, the Fund supports lobbyists in Washington, D.C., to push the Congress on AIDS-related issues.

* * *

The first open lesbian or gay man to be elected to public office occurred in 1972. Since that time, many other lesbians and gay men have attained elected office. A partial list includes:

Mayors
West Hollywood, California
Santa Cruz, California
Key West, Florida
Bunston, Missouri

County Supervisors
San Francisco, California
Dane County, Wisconsin

City Council
Boston, Massachusetts
Madison, Wisconsin
Minneapolis, Minnesota
Laguna Beach, California
Santa Cruz, California
Rochester, New York
West Hollywood, California
Chapel Hill, North Carolina

State Senate
Minnesota

United States Congress
Massachusetts

Municipal Government
Lunenberg, Massachusetts
(City Clerk, Tax Collector, Treasurer) Republican

Numerous Judgeships Nationwide

Any substantial list of openly gay and lesbian elected officials would have been virtually impossible at the time of the Stonewall demonstrations. Due mainly to the grass-roots nature of the gay and lesbian movements, no nationally recognized leaders emerged, unlike other movements. There were and are, however, well-known personalities who wield a good deal of influence, including movement pioneers such as Harry Hay, Frank Kameny, Morris Kight, Del Martin, Phyllis Lyon, and Barbara Gittings; organization leaders such as Jean O'Leary and Bruce Voeller (first chairpersons of the National Gay and Lesbian Task Force) and Virginia (Ginny) Apuzzo (former NGLTF chairperson); elected officials such as Harry Britt and, before his assassination, Harvey Milk; Elaine Noble, Gerry Studds, and Barney Frank in Massachusetts, and Karen Clark in Minnesota; writers such as James Baldwin, Jane Rule, Arthur Bell, Rita Mae Brown, Sally Gearhart, Edmund White, Larry Kramer, and Armistead Maupin; poets like Allen Ginsberg, Audre Lourde, and Adrienne Rich; entertainers such as Robin Tyler and Holly Near; scholars such as John Boswell, John D'Emilio, and Jonathan Katz; and the founder of the Metropolitan Community Church, Reverend Troy Perry.

By the mid-1970s a grassroots network was tightly in place to facilitate communication and coordinate activities. Lesbians and gays had not only attained "minority" status, but also were well on their way to constituting a genuine political constituency. In the area of pressure politics, their voice was becoming louder. That voice would be sorely tested in the 1980s.

Conclusion

Gay historian and political theorist Dennis Altman tells the story of a San Francisco Gay Pride March in 1981 in which he overheard two gay men complaining about the presence of so many overtly political slogans. This story suggests that, though gay and lesbian people have been politically active in a variety of contexts, many others do not make political activity a high priority in their lives. Indeed, if it is true that one out of every ten people is gay, then it is likely that only a very small percentage of gay people are actively and visibly political.

But at the same time, one should note that this is probably true in all minority communities in which a small fraction of the members of the group are activist. Being politically active requires that one be able to undertake certain sorts of risks, for the political arena is first and foremost a public one. For many gay and lesbian people who lack job protections, rights to child custody, or are not "out" to their families, it is simply not possible to engage in political activism. Further, political activity should not be construed in an overly narrow way, that any open affirmation of homosexuality in a predominantly heterosexual society is a political act. Finally, the fact that there are so many openly lesbian and gay organizations, political groups, and service agencies testifies to the success of these political struggles. Indeed, the sense of identity and community which has grown out of this movement, though taken for granted today by some, is a radical change from the early days prior to the homophile movement where gay people felt alone, isolated, and starved for culture.

Though gay people may disagree about political strategies for liberation, there is nonetheless a gay and lesbian identity, or, as sociologists refer to it, a "consciousness of kind." Chapter 9 explores this concept of "culture" and the myriad ways in which it exhibits itself within the "gay community." The following chapter, though, looks at some of the political implications of the AIDS crisis and its impact on the gay and lesbian community of the 1980s.

REFERENCES

Altman, Dennis. *The Homosexualization of America*. Boston: Beacon Press, 1982.

Altman, Dennis. *Coming Out in the Seventies*. Boston: Alyson Publications, Inc., 1979.

Boswell, John. *Christianity, Social Tolerance, and Homosexuality: Gay People in Western Europe from the Beginning of the Christian Era to the Fourteenth Century*. Chicago: University of Chicago Press, 1980.

Bray, Alan. *Homosexuality in Renaissance England*. London: Gay Men's Press, 1982.

CAIR (Concerned Americans for Individual Rights). "Statement of Purpose," Washington, D.C., 1984.

Carpenter, Edward. *Homoerotic Love*. Manchester, England: Manchester Labour Press, 1894.

Chauncey, George, "From Prohibition to Stonewall: A History of Gay Bars and the State in New York City," a paper given at the conference "Lesbian/Gay Studies '87: Definition and Explorations", New Haven, Yale University, sponsored by the Center for Lesbian and Gay Studies at Yale University and the Whitney Humanities Center, October 30-31, 1987.

Cutler, Marvin, ed. *Homosexuals Today: A Handbook of Organizations and Publications*. Los Angeles: ONE, Inc., 1956.

D'Emilio, John. *Sexual Politics, Sexual Communities: The Making of a Homosexual Minority in the United States, 1940-1970*. Chicago: University of Chicago Press, 1983.

D'Emilio, John. "Capitalism and Gay Identity." In *Power of Desire: The Politics of Sexuality*, edited by Ann Snitow, Christine Stensell, and Sharon Thompson. New York: New Feminist Library, 1983.

Ellis, Havelock. *Studies in the Psychology of Sex: Sexual Inversion*. Philadelphia: F.A. Davis, 1901.

Ellis, Havelock and Symonds, John Addington. *Sexual Inversion*. 1st English ed. London; Wilson & Macmillan, 1897.

Friedman, Milton, and Friedman, Rose. *Freedom to Choose: A Personal Statement*. New York: Harcourt Brace Jovanovich, 1980.

Foucault, Michel. *The Use of Pleasure: The History of Sexuality*. Volume 2. New York: Vintage Books, 1985.

"Gay Holiday," *New York Hymnal*, January 1970, quoted in Teal, Donn, *The Gay Militants*. New York: Stein and Day, 1971, p. 322.

Gay Left Collective, ed. *Homosexuality: Power and Politics*. London and New York: Allison and Busby, 1980.

Goldman, Emma. *Living My Life*. Vol. 2. New York: Dover, 1971.

Hall, Radclyffe. *The Well of Loneliness*. New York: Pocket Books, 1928.

Jay, Karla. "No Man's Land." In *Lavender Culture*, edited by Karla Jay and Allen Young. New York: Jove/HB, 1979.

Jay, Karla, and Young, Allen. *Out of the Closets: Voices of Gay Liberation*. New York: Douglass/Links, 1972.

Katz, Jonathan. *Gay American History: Lesbian & Gay Men in the U.S.A.* New York: Avon Books, 1976.

Katz, Jonathan. *Gay/Lesbian Almanac: A New Documentary*. New York: Harper & Row, 1983.

Lauritsen, John, and Thorstad, David. *The Early Homosexual Rights Movement 1864-1935*. New York: Times Change Press, 1974.

Licata, Salvatore J. "The Homosexual Rights Movement in the United States: A Traditionally Overlooked Area of American History." In *The Gay Past: A Collection of Historical Essays*, edited by Salvatore J. Licata and Robert P. Peterson. New York: Harrington Park Press, 1985.

Liechti, Robert. "Of the Day That Was and the Glory of It." *Gay Scene* No. 3, 1970.

Marotta, Toby. *The Politics of Homosexuality*. Boston: Houghton-Mifflin, 1981.

Merzbach, Georg. *Monatsberichte des Wissenschaftlich-humanitären Komitees*. Vol. 6.

Morgan, Robin, ed. *Sisterhood is Powerful*. New York: Random House, 1970.

Morrison, Megan. "Loving Whom We Choose: Bisexuality and the Lesbian/Gay Community—What We are Doing." *Gay Community News*, Vol. 11, #31, February 25, 1984, p. 9.

National Democratic Party Presidential Platform, 1980.

Nozick, Robert. *Anarchy, State, & Utopia*. New York: Basic Books, 1974.

Plant, Richard. *The Pink Triangle: The Nazi War Against Homosexuals*. New York: Henry Holt, 1986.

Robinson, John. "Frank Discusses Being Gay," *The Boston Globe*, May 30, 1987.

Rosenberg, Alfred. *Völkischer Beobachter*, August 2, 1930.

Shilts, Randy. *The Mayor of Castro Street: The Life and Times of Harvey Milk*. New York: St. Martin's Press, 1982.

Steakley, James D. *The Homosexual Emancipation Movement in Germany*. New York: Arno Press, 1975.

Symonds, John Addington. *The Letters of John Addington Symonds*. Vol. 3. Edited by Herbert M. Schuller and Robert L. Peters. Detroit: Wayne State University Press, 1967-9.

Teal, Donn. *The Gay Militants*. New York: Stein and Day, 1971.

Thompson, Mark. *Gay Spirit: Myth and Meaning*. New York: St. Martin's Press, 1987.

Thorstad, David, ed. *Gay Liberation and Socialism: Documents from the Discussions on Gay Liberation Inside the Socialist Worker's Party* (1970-73).

Tobin, Kay, and Wicker, Randy. *The Gay Crusaders*. New York: Paperback Library, 1972.

Truscott, Lucian. "Gay Power Comes to Sheridan Square." *The Village Voice*, July 3, 1969.

United States Senate, 81st Congress, 2nd Session, 1950. Committee on Expenditures in Executive Departments. "Employment of Homosexuals and Other Sex Perverts in Government." Washington, D.C.

Voeller, Bruce, quoted in Coffey, A.L. "Growing Up: Some Thoughts." New York: National Gay and Lesbian Task Force Reprint Series, 1983.

Walter, Aubrey, ed. *Come Together: The Years of Gay Liberation 1970-73*. London: Gay Men's Press, 1980.

Weeks, Jeffrey. *Coming Out: Homosexual Politics in Britain, from the Nineteenth Century to the Present*. London: Quartet Books, 1977.

Further Readings

Abbott, Sidney, and Love, Barbara. *Sappho Was a Right-On Woman: A Liberated View of Lesbianism*. New York: Stein and Day, 1972.

Adam, Barry D. *The Rise of a Gay and Lesbian Movement*. Boston: Twayne Publishers, 1987.

Bailey, D.S. *Homosexuality and the Western Tradition*. London: Longmans, Green and Co., 1955.

Bauman, Robert. *The Gentleman from Maryland: The Conscience of a Gay Conservative*. New York: Arbor House, 1986.

Duberman, Martin Bauml. *About Time: Exploring the Gay Past*. New York: Gay Presses of New York, 1986.

Gerassi, John. *The Boys of Boise*. New York: Macmillan, 1968.

Gordon, Rebecca. *Letters from Nicaragua*. San Francisco: Spinsters/Aunt Lute, 1986.

Chapter 7

AIDS: Politics and Precautions

The decade of the 1970s was nearly at an end when a New York doctor discovered a patient with a number of unexplained maladies including an extremely rare form of cancer. Soon other doctors in large urban centers around the United States and some European countries began seeing patients exhibiting similar symptoms with the addition of a rare type of pneumonia. By the end of 1980 at least fifty patients had been identified—the overwhelming majority being gay men. It was apparent that something new and potentially devastating was on the horizon.

Medical researchers soon discovered that these patients were suffering from a whole range of infections brought about by a general breakdown in their bodies' immune system (the mechanism that helps to ward off diseases) leaving the body defenseless against a wide range of lethal, "opportunistic" infections and cancers.

As the number of cases increased, doctors were talking about a new "Gay Plague" that was sweeping the land. In fact, not knowing what else to call this constellation of diseases, medical researchers initially gave it the name Gay-related immune deficiency (GRID), but soon changed it to Acquired immune deficiency syndrome (AIDS) following objections from gay activists who argued against naming a syndrome of unknown origin after an already stigmatized group.

As more became known about this syndrome, it was apparent that it was not confined to gay men, but rather it was believed to have existed for some time in epidemic proportions among heterosexual populations in parts of the African continent. Its initial entry into the gay male community in the United States and other countries, however, seriously affected people's perceptions of homosexuality.

There have been grave misunderstandings in mainstream communities over the issue of AIDS. And there has been great controversy over treatment of people with AIDS (PWAs) and testing strategies for the HIV virus. What is not controversial is that this issue is not a purely medical one but is rather fraught with political implications.

Acquired Immune Deficiency Syndrome (AIDS)

AIDS is the term given to a physical condition brought about by a number of symptoms. Some include pneumocystis carinii pneumonia, Kaposi's sarcoma (a form of cancer), and cryptococcal meningitis. AIDS-Related Complex (ARC), which can also result in death, is a milder form and sometimes the precursor of AIDS. By the end of 1981, the Centers for Disease Control in Atlanta had classified AIDS as an epidemic. (By the summer of 1987, the Centers for Disease Control drew up a new definition of AIDS, adding several AIDS-related conditions—including emaciation, tuberculosis, and dementia—to the official definition. This action, in effect, statistically increased the number of AIDS cases by at least 10 percent.)

The syndrome is believed to be related to a special type of virus called a retrovirus. It invades the DNA of the human cell, taking it over and destroying the white-blood cells (T-lymphocytes), which are the body's immune system regulators. In many cases the virus also attacks the central nervous system, the brain (resulting in dementia and blindness), and the heart (causing the condition myocarditis).

Medical researchers isolated the deadly virus in the laboratory, giving it the name HIV (Human Immunodeficiency Virus) in the United States and LAV in France. It was originally called "Human T-Lymphotropic Virus Type III (HTLV-III in the U.S.). It is known as SIDA in Spanish—el Sindrome de Immuno-Deficiencia Adquirida—and French—Syndrome d'Immuno-Deficitaire Acquis.) (In some African countries, AIDS is referred to as "Slim's Disease" because a person with the disease often becomes extremely thin.)

A small number of medical professionals, however, suggest that to claim HIV as the primary cause of AIDS is unfounded. Peter Duesberg, professor of molecular biology at the University of California at Berkeley, in particular, believes that AIDS is caused by an as yet unidentified agent which may or may not be a virus. His conclusions have been vehemently denounced by most researchers.

Following the entry of any virus into the bloodstream, antibodies are produced in the blood to fight off infection. The HIV antibody, however, is believed to be ineffective in killing the virus. By 1985 blood-screening tests were developed to detect the presence of the antibody to determine exposure to the HIV virus. One of the first of these was the ELISA (Enzyme-Linked Immunosorbent Assay). If blood tests positively, another test—the "Western Blot"—is given. If this too comes out positive, the person is notified of an HIV exposure. The ELISA has some drawbacks. For one, it can give a high number of false positives, and some false negatives. It also can take upwards of four hours to produce results. Another test was developed in 1986, the Bioscience Test, which is less expensive, works in about two minutes, can be used directly in a doctor's office without the need of sending it out to a laboratory, and has been proven to be at least as effective as the ELISA. In addition to these antibody detecting and screening tools, tests have also been developed which directly detect the virus itself.

Researchers still are unable to determine the exact percentage of people who will eventually develop AIDS or ARC after exposure, but estimates range from 20 to 30 percent to over 50 percent.

The HIV virus is concentrated in the fluids of the body, primarily in blood, semen, and vaginal fluids, and to lesser degrees in saliva, tears, breast milk, urine, sweat, vomit, feces, cerebrospinal fluid, alveolar fluid, and pre-ejaculation fluid in males. The virus is certainly transmitted in the blood, semen, vaginal fluids, and possibly breast milk, but there is little evidence of transmission through other bodily fluids. There is some evidence to indicate that women who have been exposed to the virus have a greater chance of developing AIDS if they have taken birth control pills.

Many people have been exposed to the virus but are unaware of this because it may lay dormant in the body anywhere from one to fifteen years or more. Early symptoms of AIDS can include:

- rapid and extensive weight loss of more than ten pounds;
- recurring fever, night sweats, or chills,
- swollen and painful lymph nodes in the neck, armpits, or groin;
- extreme and persistent fatigue;
- chronic diarrhea;
- persistent sore throat, or white spots or patches in the mouth;
- painless pink or purple bumps or blotches on the skin;
- chronic cough;
- skin which bruises easily, or unexplained bleeding from anywhere on the body.

These symptoms, however, can also be indicators of other diseases as well, and people who have concerns should consult a physician.

The HIV virus is actually quite fragile. It cannot survive long outside body fluids. Therefore, it is believed that one cannot be infected through casual contact with a person in the workplace, in school, at home, or in other places of close proximity. A person does not get the virus by shaking hands, hugging, swimming in pools, sitting on toilet seats, eating off plates, or using public phones. To date, there are no known cases of AIDS occurring in family members of people with AIDS except in those members who have engaged in other recognized high-risk related behaviors.

The primary means of exposure to the HIV virus involves engaging in "unprotected" (without the use of a condom or dental dam) intimate sexual relations with a person infected with the virus; from blood or blood products; or by sharing infected drug needles. Basically, experts agree that the virus is most often transmitted through sexual contact in which the sperm, blood, or vaginal secretions of an infected partner come in contact with the blood of an uninfected partner. In addition, an infected woman can transmit the virus to her offspring by three possible routes: to the fetus *in utero* through the maternal circulation; to the infant during labor and delivery by inoculation or ingestion of blood and other infected fluids; and to the infant shortly after birth through infected breast milk.

Because the virus is carried in the blood, semen, and vaginal secretions, during sexual relations it may enter the partner's bloodstream through tiny tears in the vaginal walls, anal lining, penis, or mouth. Some researchers warn against deep kissing, in which the virus may enter through minute cuts in the mouth caused by tooth-brushing or dental-flossing, or by heavy kissing itself, even though the virus exists in low concentrations in saliva.

There is some speculation that possible environmental factors may also play a role in the transmission of the virus—factors other than the exchange of bodily fluids or the sharing of tainted needles. Belle Glade, Florida, is an example of a town where there is an enormously high rate of AIDS among the predominantly heterosexual residents.

Doctors first witnessed this syndrome in large numbers of heterosexual men, women, and children in the late 1970s in central Africa, where it existed in epidemic proportions. It is believed by some that it may have been transmitted to humans from the African Green Monkey, which had what was once a relatively harmless virus that somehow mutated to become the HIV virus. Others believe that the virus had existed for hundreds of years in remote areas on the African continent, but spread due to increases in mobility and changes in sexual attitudes.

A great many African leaders are upset with Western accounts of AIDS originating in Africa. There is now some doubt that the virus came from the Green Monkey since the prevalence of the virus among groups of Africans who commonly eat the animal is virtually non-existent. Some people are now blaming the spread of the virus in Africa on the smallpox vaccination program undertaken by the World Health Organization in which many people may have been injected with infected vaccine. (Shively.)

The earliest documented evidence of infection was found in Zaire in a blood sample taken in 1959. When the virus arrived in the United States, it hit hardest at gay males, intravenous blood users (people with hemophilia and others needing blood transfusions), and drug users who shared hypodermic needles. Evidence suggests that people were dying from the virus before the end of the 1970s. A sixteen-year-old from St. Louis died in 1969 from Kaposi's sarcoma and other complications. At the time of his death, his doctor did not know why he contracted this condition and froze his blood for screening to await the discovery of a new diagnostic tool. The blood was tested in 1987 and indeed showed the existence of the HIV virus.

It is generally accepted today that anyone—gay, lesbian, bisexual, and heterosexual—who is sexually active or who shares needles is at risk for contracting the HIV virus. Therefore, it does not matter who one is, but rather what one does—which is the significant variable in being infected. There are no longer any high-risk groups but rather high-risk activities. Tens of thousands of people in the United States alone have already been diagnosed as having AIDS, and the number doubles nearly every year. In 1985 virtually every country in the world reported cases. An estimated ten million people worldwide were believed to be carrying the virus in 1988.

With the advent of blood-screening tests, the country's blood supply became relatively free from the virus, though it is estimated that approximately fifty people each year will contract the HIV virus from blood transfusions or from receiving other blood products. It takes up to twelve weeks (some researchers estimate as long as fourteen months) following exposure to the virus for antibodies to develop. If an infected person donates blood before antibodies are produced, a false negative may result on the test.

Finding a cure for those who have been exposed and a vaccine for those who have not seems to be a number of years away. The problems are many, the major one being that the genetic structure of the virus itself is ever changing, resulting in a number of mutant strains. In fact, in May 1987 the New England Journal of Medicine announced a second strain of the virus discovered in west Africa, which has been given the name HIV-2. Less than a month later the discovery of yet a third strain was announced at the Third International AIDS Conference in Washington, D.C. The first patient diagnosed in the United States with the HIV-2 strain of the virus was found in January 1988. These other viruses do not show up on the earlier screening tests, but they do produce symptoms similar to the original HIV virus.

Another major problem in developing a solution is the dearth of available animals as reliable test models. Chimpanzees, though they do not become extremely ill, nonetheless do multiply the virus in their cells and macaques can develop antibodies. In addition, the fact that the incubation period of the virus is extremely long makes testing for a possible vaccine and cure difficult.

There is also another major hurdle for researchers to surmount. In theory, vaccines work to stimulate the body's natural immune system. When the body is infected by the HIV virus, however, is it this very system which is destroyed, making it extremely difficult for a vaccine to do its job.

There are a few drugs available and still others in the testing stages that have helped to prolong life and ease some of the symptoms in some AIDS patients. Any potential cure, to be effective, must interrupt the virus's life-cycle. One drug, Azidothymidine or AZT (commercial name Retrovir), has been shown to inhibit the course of the virus in some patients, though it is not a cure. It is, though, extremely expensive—costing as much as $8,000 to $10,000 per year—and often causes toxic side effects. In addition, when certain other drugs are taken in combination with AZT, such as acetaminophen—the active ingredient in Tylenol and some other pain killers—damage can result to the blood or blood-forming organs. Besides AZT, other drugs which have undergone experimentation go by the names ddI (Dideoxynosine), ribaviron (which has not proven effective), imuthiol (a drug which in some cases has been shown to postpone the onset of AIDS), and ampligen (a substance that behaves like an artificial virus, stimulating the immune system in some people). Others include AL-721 (a nutritional supplement), Dextran sulfate, Dideoxycytidine (ddC), DHPG (ganciclovir), Foscarnet, granulocytemacrophage colony-immunity stimulant (GM-CSF), HPA-23, Interferon alpha, Interleukin-2, trimetrexate with leucovorin, Peptide T, Compound Q, pentamidine, and more. In addition, researchers from Baylor University College of Medicine have discovered what they are calling "monoclonal antibody" which has been shown to prevent transmission of the virus from infected cells to healthy cells in the test tube. It has also been shown to attack the virus itself. Also under experimentation are certain enzymes to improve the immune system by increasing the white blood count of the patient.

A few preliminary vaccines have also been tested. Researchers theorize that a purified form of the virus' outer shell (or envelope) can trick the body into producing an effective antibody, which can kill off the virus. Some researchers are also experimenting with the virus' inner core. In addition, researchers at Massachusetts General Hospital and at the National Institutes of Health have discovered certain "killer cells" that locate and attack infected cells. Though these cells are not yet strong enough to overcome the virus entirely and it is not yet possible to grow these cells in the laboratory, this is another possible direction which may prove fruitful in developing a reliable vaccine.

The Federal Food and Drug Administration in May 1987 permitted people with extreme illnesses, including those related to AIDS, to use some of the more experimental drugs before they are given general approval if there is any chance that these drugs could help. By the end of the 1980s, HIV-related illnesses were increasingly seen as more manageable.

Societal Responses

In Puritan America, the "scarlet letter" was a stigma connected to adultery. Today it is connected to AIDS. In the United States and other countries, public fear undermines objective medical evidence which shows that the virus is not transmitted through casual contact.

Arcadia, Florida, is a case in point. In the late summer of 1987 the Ray brothers—Ricky, 10 years old, Robert, 9, and Randy, 8—who tested HIV positive following blood transfusions for hemophilia, attempted to attend their local grammar school. Despite assurances from medical professionals that the boys posed no threat to the health or safety of others, the DeSoto County school board voted to expel them from school. Clifford and Louise Ray, the boys' parents, won a federal court order allowing the boys back into school. Following this action, a parents' group organized a boycott of the school to protest the decision. The Rays' church pastor notified the family that they were no longer welcome at services. The family received numerous threatening phone calls and bomb threats ending in a fire (which Sheriff Joe Varnadore of DeSoto County said was deliberately set in several places), totally destroying their home. The Rays then moved to a local motel but were asked to vacate once the owners realized who they were. The family had no other choice but to move from the area.

In another incident, the mayor of Williamson, West Virginia, ordered the public swimming pool emptied, scrubbed, disinfected, and refilled after a person with AIDS swam in the pool, and forbade the person from returning to the pool.

Some immigration workers reportedly wore plastic gloves when processing Haitian applicants. In addition, reports surfaced of surgeons and dentists refusing to treat PWAs. These actions forced the American Medical Association to proclaim in 1987 that physicians have an ethical duty to treat AIDS patients.

Health insurance companies have sought ways of limiting liability for AIDS-related treatments thus increasing the difficulty for many businesses, most particularly gay-owned, from getting health coverage for their employees.

In addition, issues of personal privacy and anonymity have surfaced. HIV antibody testing is sometimes performed without good reason or without consent. A case in point occurred at Parkland Memorial Hospital in Dallas, Texas where an estimated seven hundred emergency room patients were tested without their knowledge.

Numerous airlines have been sued for refusing to allow people with AIDS to fly. The Minnesota Human Rights Commission, for example, filed charges of discrimination against Northwest Airlines in 1987 for refusing to bring home from China a person with AIDS who the airline argued would pose a threat of contamination to other passengers.

Results of a 1987 Gallup Poll reported in the *New York Times* revealed that 60 percent of the public agreed with the statement: "People with the AIDS virus should be made to carry a card to this effect." Only 24 percent disagreed, with the remainder undecided. And conservative commentator William F. Buckley wrote:

> Everyone detected with AIDS should be tattooed in the upper forearm, to protect common-needle users, and on the buttocks, to prevent the victimization of homosexuals.... Our society is generally threatened, and in order to fight AIDS, we need the civil equivalent of universal military training. (*New York Times*, March 18, 1986.)

Due to the anti-gay bias which exists in the media, mainstream newspapers and television networks virtually ignored the epidemic until heterosexuals were affected.

> The story of the first *Wall Street Journal* piece on the epidemic would later be cited in journalism reviews as emblematic of how the media handled AIDS in the first years of the epidemic. The reporter, it turned out, had long been pressuring editors to run a story on the homosexual disorder. He had even written a piece in 1981 that the editors refused to print.... With confirmation of bona fide heterosexuals, the story finally merited sixteen paragraphs deep in the largest-circulation daily newspaper in the United States, under the headline: "New, Often-Fatal Illness in Homosexuals Turns Up in Women, Heterosexual Males."
> The gay plague got covered only because it finally had struck people who counted, people who were not homosexual. (Shilts, p. 126.)

Capitalizing on the fear surrounding the virus, people on the political and religious right are using AIDS to reignite their anti-gay crusades. They charge gay men with causing the problem by overindulging in "immoral" sexual activity, calling AIDS "just retribution" and "God's punishment" for a sinful and despicable lifestyle. The AIDS epidemic, they claim, is proof of the correctness of so-called "traditional values" which emphasize abstinence or sexual monogamy within the institution of heterosexual marriage. They issued what are now known to be inaccurate explanations for the gay link to the disease: one hypothesis argued that gay men essentially wore out their bodies by engaging in fast-paced and drug-laden lifestyles. Another view charged that these men played a sort of Russian roulette by having large numbers of sexual partners.

The Moral Majority reported:

Over the last two decades, Americans have become increasingly tolerant of homosexuals and "homosexual practices." What consenting adults did in private was of no real concern at all to many of the last several generations.

Now it turns out that homosexuals and their practices can threaten our lives, our families, our children, can influence whether or not we have elective surgery, eat in certain restaurants, visit a given city or take up a certain profession or career—all because a tiny minority flaunts its lifestyle and demands that an entire nation tolerate its diseases and grant it status as a privileged minority. (Godwin, pp. 2 and 8.)

A conservative watchdog group calling itself "Morality in Media" called for the mandatory quarantining of all people with AIDS on Penik-ese Island, an abandoned colony off the Cape Cod coast where people with leprosy were once isolated.

People increasingly stigmatize anyone even suspected of being gay. (Though lesbians as a group have one of the lowest incidence of the syndrome, homophobic attacks continue to be directed against them as well.)

Reports of a gay backlash surfaced in the media, although gay activists generally claim that the health crisis merely highlights a longstanding climate of oppression. Thus, AIDS is now used to give credence to some people's deeply held revulsion toward people considered "other."

The belief in dirty individuals who leave germs in their wake creates a terror that anyone a little different harbors disease, and has the power to invade the human body. Honest concern about real illness blurs with the need to separate from people feared for racist, sexist, or homophobic reasons. Difference is experienced on a physical level as assault or pollution. On a social scale, the category of "disease" is manipulated to justify genocide, ghettoization, and quarantine: people said that Jews spread the plague, Irish immigrants spread typhoid, prostitutes spread syphilis, drug addicts spread hepatitis, Caribbean boat people spread God-knows-what exotic tropical disease. (Patton, pp. 11-12.)

The political right renewed its call for prohibiting gays and lesbians from serving as teachers and child care workers, and fought a heated and often times successful battle to close down gay public bathhouses.

This reaction occurred following documented medical and sociological evidence that AIDS did not originate within the gay male community, but rather existed previously in central Africa in an area stretching from the Congo to Tanzania. The syndrome in Africa differed in one significant respect from the United States—in Africa it spread mainly within the heterosexual population and affected an equal number of women and men. The precise reasons for gay and bisexual men being among the first affected in the United States is not yet understood. To date there is no adequate theory to explain why gay men in this country were among the first to contract the disease. It is possible that causation will never be established.

But as more and more knowledge of AIDS surfaces, medical researchers and gay and lesbian activists claim that it is inappropriate to link this or any other disease with any specific ethnic, regional, or cultural group. They make the point that Africans and gay and bisexual men are about as much to blame for causing AIDS as American Legionnaires are for causing legionellosis (so-called "Legionnaires' Disease"), blacks are for causing sickle-cell anemia, or women are for causing Toxic Shock Syndrome. Viruses have no sexual preference, and this holds true as well for the HIV virus. By 1986, heterosexual transmission of the disease increased faster than any other group.

In 1986, the number of AIDS cases attributed to heterosexual contact jumped 135 percent among Americans excluding those who came to the United States from countries where heterosexual spread of AIDS is prevalent. By comparison, AIDS cases among American homosexuals and bisexual men increased by 82 percent. (Knox, p. 14.)

This fact has not, however, been enough to halt AIDS-related discrimination directed against gays and lesbians and Africans.

Governmental Responses.

C. Everett Koop, who was bitterly denounced in 1981 by gay rights advocates for his previously-held anti-gay attitudes before his confirmation as Surgeon General in the Reagan Administration, was widely applauded by those same individuals for his courageous and consistent leadership in his public-education campaign. This campaign emphasized explicit, open, and nonmoralistic discussions of sexuality and safer sex practices as a means of preventing the spread of this lethal virus. Koop was often at odds with other conservatives and with religious fundamentalists, who felt that such discussions trivialized sex while encouraging promiscuity, particularly among the young.

Ronald Reagan, under whose presidency the AIDS epidemic originated and flourished, had not formally raised the issue until April 1, 1987 in a speech to a group of physicians in Philadelphia—a full seven years after the onset of AIDS in the United States. Long before this, however, when it was seen as a disease of gay men, Reagan's Chief of Communications, Patrick Buchanan, was quite outspoken, referring to it as "God's awful retribution" and saying it did not deserve a thorough and compassionate response. (Scondras, p. 5.)

As the disease spread, the government stood still by refusing to allocate sufficient funding to the National Institutes of Health to conduct research. While pressuring the government for funds, during the first years of the epidemic gay men in New York and other cities had no other alternative but to attempt to raise the needed funding privately.

According to Randy Shilts—the only reporter in America on a full-time AIDS beat since 1982 at the *San Francisco Chronicle*:

> No one cared because it was homosexuals who were dying. Nobody came out and said it was all right for gays to drop dead; it was just that homosexuals didn't seem to warrant the kind of urgent concern another set of victims would engender.... Scientists didn't care because there was little glory, fame, and funding to be had in this field.... (Shilts, p. 95.)

and:

> Nobody at the National Cancer Institute [a part of NIH] seemed to be in much of a hurry. The new syndrome clearly was a very low priority, even as it was becoming clear to more and more people that it threatened calamity. (Ibid., p. 120.)

Reagan's AIDS policy, which he outlined on June 1, 1987 at an AIDS benefit preceding the Third National Conference on AIDS, emphasized federal and state governments undertaking routine mandatory testing of selected groups for the virus to detect the extent to which it had spread throughout the population. The groups he singled out were people applying for marriage licenses, immigrants, aliens seeking permanent residence, federal prison inmates, and patients in veteran's hospitals. In the summer of 1987 the Reagan Administration added AIDS to the list of diseases—which include leprosy, tuberculosis, plus five other sexually transmitted diseases—that can be used legally to restrict immigrants entry into the United States.

Reagan was soundly criticized by medical experts and lesbian and gay activists. These critics claimed that his policy recommendations were punitive and would prove to be ineffective, would drain valuable resources, and would create greater stigmatization of people with AIDS and ARC.

In fact, a study undertaken by the Harvard School of Public Health concluded that if premarital screening were conducted for one year, fewer than one-tenth of one percent of people infected with the HIV virus would be detected at a cost of over $100 million. The study went on to recommend that the money would be better spent on public education, counselling, and voluntary testing. (*Harvard University Gazette*, p. 7.) Opponents of mandatory testing maintained that these measures would serve to drive underground the very people most needing treatment. The President's proposals also drew fire from civil libertarians, who were concerned about violations of personal privacy and AIDS-related prejudice.

Then, in July 1987, the President appointed a thirteen-member AIDS panel to make recommendations for government action. Most panel members, however, were criticized by respected AIDS specialists for their lack of expertise on the issue. The President, bowing to pressure, appointed one gay male doctor who was attacked by conservatives, including New Hampshire Senator Gordon Humphrey, who argued that "this appointment would legitimize homosexuality in the minds of Americans." Not long after the commission was established, its chairman and vice-chairman resigned, citing infighting and ideological differences among panel members which made their jobs impossible to carry out.

After months of bitter infighting, several membership changes, and sharp criticism from public health officials and AIDS activists, in 1988 the Commission came up with what many called a remarkably progressive report. Among its numerous recommendations, it proposed two billion dollars per year for treatment centers and education for IV drug users; the Food and Drug Administration (FDA) speed up the drug licensing process; a special FDA review process be used for medical foods, such as the egg-based AL-721; the number of full-time FDA drug application reviewers be "immediately doubled" to meet the number of new drug requests; the number of full-time employees working on federal clinical drug trials be immediately increased from 47 to 120"; a direct grant program be "immediately funded" to help support community-based drug trial initiatives; access to AZT and other experimental drugs be improved; and treatment on demand for all drug users who request it. The Commission also recommended vastly increased funding for medical services to PWAs, especially the "growing number of persons with AIDS who are poor and medically uninsured," and special AIDS training programs for medical professionals. Of particular importance was the Commission's strong recommendation for legislation to prevent discrimination against PWAs and people testing HIV positive.

Years before the President's restrictive policy, the United States military had already begun compulsory testing of recruits, and some government leaders called for widescale testing in the workplace. Some states passed laws mandating the reporting of names of those who tested HIV antibody positive to state departments of public health. A few states proposed what has come to be known as "mandatory contact tracing," in which people with AIDS are required to report the names of all their sexual partners to the government.

To combat the apparent inaction on the part of the Reagan Administration, the United States Congress consistently increased the President's relatively meager budgetary requests for AIDS research and education, and in April 1987 a group of Representatives from the House submitted a non-binding resolution urging television networks to run an advertisement for condoms during adult viewing hours. They called on Otis Bowen, Reagan's Secretary of the Department of Health and Human Services, to produce short public-service announcements suggesting preventative measures. Of particular poignancy to the House was the AIDS-related death in May 1987 of one of its members, Stewart McKinny of Connecticut. Original accounts reported him being infected through a blood transfusion, but it later came out that McKinny was gay and probably contracted the virus through unprotected sexual contact.

During the 1980s a number of United States Representatives publicly disclosed their same-sex orientation. The first to volunteer this information was Barney Frank, Democrat from Massachusetts, who, when asked by a *Boston Globe* reporter on May 30, 1987 if he were gay, simply responded, "Yes, so what...I don't think my sex life is relevant to my job. But on the other hand I don't want to leave the impression that I'm embarrassed about my life." [From Robinson, p. 1.] Other Representatives included Gerry Studds, also a Democrat from Massachusetts, who came out in 1983 following revelations of a consensual sexual relationship he had had ten years previously with a House page, and conservative Republican Maryland Representative Robert Bauman, who disclosed his sexual orientation following his arrest for solicitation of a male prosititute. (Studds retained his House seat in subsequent elections, while Bauman was voted out of office.)

Six months prior to the 1987 House resolution on the television networks' responsibilities in AIDS education, a scattering of stations across the country reversed a self-imposed ban and began to air condom ads and public-service announcements. This action was done over the protests of many local community groups and individuals, some of whom were on the religious right. On October 1, 1986, the Vatican added its voice by issuing an open letter to Catholic bishops restating its position on homosexuality, which it defines as "immoral" and as a "disordered sexual inclination which is essentially self-indulgent." It went further by blaming gay people for the AIDS epidemic by stating that "...the practice of homosexuality may seriously threaten the lives and well-being of a large number of people...." (See Chapter 4 for more extensive excerpts of the "Letter to the Bishops of the Catholic Church on the Pastoral Care of Homosexual Persons.")

In addition, on the eve of Pope John Paul II's 1987 pilgrimage to the

United States, Catholic archbishop John Foley proclaimed that AIDS is a "natural sanction on homosexual behavior."

The AIDS epidemic also affected local electoral politics. In communities throughout the nation, lawmakers cited their constituents' concern over the spread of the virus as a rationale for voting against lesbian and gay rights ordinances and for voting to overturn existing laws. This was most evident in the Houston mayoral campaign of 1985, when former five-term Mayor Louie Welch, who pledged if elected to work for the overturning of a gay rights bill passed a year before, was reported to have said that he would "shoot the queers" in order to stop the spread of AIDS. He later claimed, however, that this was an unthinking statement on his part. (Gaffney.)

Supporters of perennial presidential candidate Lyndon Larouche forced a 1986 California ballot referendum, Proposition 64, which would have required state public-health officials to quarantine some people with AIDS. This was viewed by many as an essentially anti-gay measure masked in a public-health disguise. Though it failed by a better than two-to-one margin, it set the stage for others like it in other states. In Colorado, for example, a prototype bill was passed in 1987 granting government health officials the power to quarantine persons who "endanger the public health." The measure gives the state the ability to take into custody for up to seventy-two hours any person who, after once being notified, does not "cease and desist" behaviors believed to be dangerous by public health officials.

In January 1988, Illinois passed a law requiring all couples planning on marriage to be tested for the HIV virus and, if positive, to be reported to state public health officials (repealed September 1989). Illinois also *mandates* its sex education teachers to emphasize sexual abstinence preceding marriage.

Due to the lack of any organized federal leadership in the Reagan years, the result was a patchwork of laws, regulations, health care efforts, and educational measures by government at all levels as well as by volunteers, self-help groups, hospitals, physicians, private groups, and businesses.

In the federal judiciary, the 1980s witnessed two apparently contradictory Supreme Court rulings which many see as being relevant to the AIDS epidemic. In *Bowers v. Hardwick* (July 1986), the court voted to sustain a 19th-century Georgia State anti-sodomy law which punishes "any sexual act involving the sex organs of one person and the mouth or anus of another"—protected or not. Though this law could conceivably be directed against heterosexual couples, it has mainly been applied to gays. Many legal observers believed this decision stemmed not only from an anti-gay bias on the part of a majority of justices, but also from the incorrect assumption that the statute would substantially reduce the chances for the spread of the HIV virus.

The other important decision, *Arline v. School Board of Nassau County*

[Florida] (1987) potentially provides a precedent for guaranteeing the civil liberties of people with AIDS, ARC, and those who test positive on the HIV screening test. The case involved a teacher who was dismissed from her teaching position by the school board because she had tuberculosis. In ordering the board to return her to her classroom, the justices, in effect, have placed tuberculosis—an infectious disease, as is the HIV virus—into a category of disabilities protected under law.

In a lower court, a precedent-setting case was decided in June 1987 by a Minneapolis jury. James V. Moore, a prison inmate who bit two guards after testing positive for the virus, was found guilty of assault with a deadly and dangerous weapon—his mouth and teeth—even though there is no conclusive evidence to prove transmission of the virus through saliva or through a bite.

International Responses

No other medical phenomenon has had as profound and far-reaching an impact as has AIDS, and countries throughout the world have dealt with the crisis in vastly different ways. Though the International Conference on AIDS began meeting annually in 1985, there was very little global coordination of strategies before the World Summit of Ministers of Health, sponsored by the British government and the World Health Organization in January 1988. At that summit, delegates from 146 countries drafted a resolution in part stating: "We are convinced that by promoting responsible behavior and through international cooperation we can slow the spread of the AIDS infection."

Rather than seeing a rational unified response, Dr. Jonathan Mann, director of the World Health Organization's AIDS program, speaking before the Third International Conference on AIDS in Washington, D.C., in June 1987, declared that the world had entered into the "third stage" of the disease—a stage of prejudice:

> We are witnessing a rising wave of stigmatization: against Westerners in Asia, against Africans in Europe, of homosexuals, of prostitutes, of hemophiliacs, of recipients of blood transfusions...[which is]...a direct threat to free travel between countries and, more generally, to open international exchange and communication. (Altman, p. 1.)

The first stage of AIDS he claimed is the period between the mid- to late-1970s, when AIDS was silently spreading but was generally unnoticed by the medical community. The second stage is the period when it began to receive greater attention.

Some European countries initially outdistanced the United States in their efforts at educating the public. In Britain, for example, government officials sent informational brochures to *every* household in the country (some 23 million). The U.S. followed suit in 1988. Also in Britain, the government produced full-page newspaper announcements, and conducted a "Don't Die of Ignorance" billboard campaign. In addition, the government-run British Broadcasting Company (BBC) produced a series of AIDS education specials on both radio and television. Also, the towns of Liverpool, England, as well as Amsterdam in the Netherlands, initiated a "clean needle exchange program" whereby drug addicts are encouraged to bring in used intravenous needles and syringes in exchange for sterile ones at drug treatment centers in an attempt to reduce the chances of spreading the virus within this population. Taking this lead, in 1988, New York became the first state in the U.S. to approve a similar program.

In Switzerland, which had the highest per capita incidence of AIDS of any Western country by the late 1980s, the government also distributed free sterilized hypodermic needles from drug-treatment centers, sent letters to all known prostitutes telling them to have their customers wear condoms, and used the public gay bathhouses as places for teaching safer sex education. And a rock group produced a chart-topping song extolling the use of condoms.

Spain and France also handed out sterile syringes, and in France condom-dispensing machines were installed on some college campuses. The Danish government provided coin-operated syringe machines in Copenhagen's "drug quarter" after treatment centers closed for the evening and, operating on the assumption that sex is essentially good, but that people must be protected, undertook its "Protect the One You Love" campaign. And Uganda conducted its "Love Carefully" program of public education.

West Germany, on the other hand, waged a concerted campaign (as did local governments in the United States) of shutting down gay bathhouses and of denying residency to immigrants suspected of carrying the virus. The Belgian government required all African students to be screened for the virus. South Korea banned suspected carriers from working in restaurants and hotels. And in a small town in southern Mexico, Catholic and parents' groups demanded the rounding up of all known gay men for AIDS testing and possible quarantining.

African countries were severely limited in their public education and medical research efforts because of an extreme scarcity of resources. Many of these countries blamed Western news media for overblowing the extent of the problem on the African continent.

Iraq proposed the deportation of people who test HIV-positive, and attempt to test all foreigners and returning Iraqis. The Iraqi government claims not to have a drug problem within its borders. The reason for this is that the state hangs suspected drug addicts.

Chinese officials moved to seal off its borders from the spread of the virus by demanding to test newly arrived foreigners. Business-people, students, and other non-Chinese who plan to reside in China for more than one year must either present certification that they are free from the virus, or undergo a blood test. If they refuse or fail the test, they are denied a residence permit. (Higgins.)

During most of the 1980s, many Communist-bloc countries claimed not to have been touched by the virus, insisting that it was a Western problem stemming from its "decadent sexual practices." Moscow posited a conspiracy theory of sorts to explain the origin of the virus:

On March 30, [1987] the Soviet news agency TASS repeated earlier reports of a study by two East German microbiologists, Jacob and Lilli Segal, concluding that AIDS was caused by a genetically engineered virus. The Segals argue that the virus may have been created and spread accidentally by the U.S. Army's Biological Warfare Laboratory at Fort Detrick, near Frederick, Maryland. According to his theory, the virus was experimentally injected around 1977 into "volunteer" prisoners, who, after several months with no symptoms, were released and unknowingly spread the disease. (Lederer, p. 3.)

Others charge that it was inadvertently developed in a laboratory when genetic engineering went awry.

The Communist world concedes having AIDS cases within its borders but the Kremlin blames this on foreigners, Westerners in particular. Anyone who knowingly infects another is sentenced to an eight-year prison term in the Soviet Union. In Yugoslavia, government officials cancelled the 1987 Fourth Gay and Lesbian Festival in that country on the pretext of preventing transmission of the virus. The Cuban government has instituted a policy of mass quarantine by isolating people who are known to carry the virus on a farm outside Havana.

There are reports from around the world of vigilante groups torturing and killing people perceived as being gay and suspected of carrying the virus. Several people have been beaten and killed, for example, in Rio de Janeiro, Brazil. Notes attached to some of the corpses announced: "Now I can no longer spread AIDS." (Rieder.)

Gay and Lesbian Organizing

This is not a gay disease. They didn't invent it, they didn't create it, they don't own it, and they are not going to take the blame for it. (Kessler.)

Hitting hardest as it did at gay males, the outbreak of AIDS set up a situation which heightened the sense of community under siege. People were assaulted by a perplexing and insidious virus from within and by homophobic attitudes and actions from without. As gay singer/song-writer Tom Wilson Weinberg put it, there are two diseases out there: AIDS and AFRAIDS.

The epidemic proved to have an enormous political and emotional impact, which tested the very nature and strength of a relatively young movement and forced people to take a hard look at the essential meaning of the concepts of identity and community.

Death and assault are not new or unique to the lesbian and gay communities. There is a longstanding tradition of police raids on their meeting places, and teenage street gangs have long engaged in "queer-bashing." Assaults by scientific, religious, and government institutions have been extreme. There have been witch hunts during the McCarthy era, exterminations by the Nazis, and censorship throughout time. The 1970s witnessed the anti-gay "Save Our Children" campaign led by Anita Bryant in Dade County, Florida, the brutal murder of gay San Francisco City Supervisor Harvey Milk, and organized opposition by the religious right led by the so-called Moral Majority.

The AIDS crisis highlighted the sexual aspect of gay lifestyles, placing it once again in the realm of disease—a focus activists had rejected during the previous decade. Once again lesbian and gay activists were placed in a position of negotiating with scientific and government officials from whom they have traditionally felt estranged. The straight radical left did not offer much support, at least during the initial stages of the crisis, and therefore lesbians and gays were left virtually alone. In fact, an editorial in the Spring 1987 issue of the progressive journal, *In These Times*, supported components of the Reagan administration's restrictive AIDS policy including mandatory testing.

By the time AIDS hit, a grassroots network of social, political, and informational organizations had already been put in place. Though liberation and civil rights organizing continued as before, the virus injected a new element into the political agenda.

> The AIDS organizing within the lesbian and gay community has grown into a curious mix of radical and traditional politics involving education, support, direct action, and coalition-building. But AIDS organizing, it was soon discovered, is significantly different from other projects. There are the usual conflicts about structure and process, about politics and support. But at no other time had I been involved in a project where one day I would learn that someone with whom I had planned meetings or argued a political point was suddenly and unalterably "one of them." A person with AIDS. (Patton, p. 16.)

This last point is a crucial one. People were stricken and died from a number of opportunistic diseases which could be triggered by a virus contracted through the intimate act of sex—an act which in some real sense defines gay identity and community. For some, this significantly increased the strain involved in coming out and, in some cases, delayed or prevented that decision. Others, though, who under other circumstances would probably not have entered into political organizing, were spurred by the crisis into activism.

AIDS put some gay men in the uncomfortable position of coming out to people who were previously unaware of their sexual orientation . Take the case of Ed:

> I have AIDS and I might die. My father doesn't know that I'm gay. My mother did, but she's dead so now I have to come out to the rest of my family. It's a double whammy. I don't need to be going through the emotional stuff of coming out to them at the same time that I'm in a hospital bed dealing with death and they're dealing with it. That's a very frightening issue...[but] things like coming out to my family are becoming increasingly important. (Quoted in Blumenfeld, p. 16.)

On a personal level, virtually everyone has been touched in some way by the effects of the epidemic. A community-wide bereavement process began as the number of AIDS-related deaths increased. Though at first there was much resistance, gay men in particular have altered their sexual practices, emphasizing safer-sex guidelines. In fact, they were the leaders in prevention education, organizing when AIDS was first recognized. Feminists, lesbian and heterosexual, who had a health-care agenda firmly in place, formed alliances with gay men early in the epidemic.

Lesbians and gays were also in the forefront of a coordinated effort to provide care and support for people with AIDS. Existing gay and lesbian community service centers expanded their services, while new centers dedicated to serving the needs of people with AIDS and their loved ones were established. These centers provide counseling, education, medical consultation and advocacy, legal and financial assistance, and guidance through the dizzying maze of local and national agencies. Volunteer "buddies" assist people with AIDS. AIDS telephone hotlines are staffed by volunteers who are equipped to answer questions and to refer people to the proper agencies. Some of these centers include the AIDS Action Committee of Boston, AID—Atlanta, the San Francisco AIDS Foundation, the Shanti Project (also in San Francisco), AIDS Project/ L.A., Austin AIDS Project, Howard Brown Memorial Clinic in Chicago, and the prototype Gay Men's Health Crisis of New York City—which opened its doors in September 1982.

As important as these efforts are, some of the more militant gay leaders claimed that gays and lesbians were not doing nearly enough. They chastised them for "contributing to their own genocide" by not directly challenging government inaction and systematic suppression of impor-

tant information. These leaders charged that government calls for mandatory testing and public education were merely stalling tactics to divert
discussion away from the real issues—namely, that the government was
virtually unconcerned with the epidemic because it killed primarily gay
men, blacks, and Hispanics. (At the first National Conference of AIDS and
Minorities held in Atlanta during August 1987, it was announced that
though blacks make up 12 percent of the U.S. population, 25 percent of
PWAs are black; 7 percent of the population is Hispanic but 15 percent of
PWAs are Hispanic. In addition, 80 percent of the babies born with the
virus are from minorities.)

The National Coalition of PWAs formed to give people with AIDS an
active voice over issues concerning their lives. Also, the National Minority
AIDS Council (NMAC) was established to help unite the efforts of educators around the country concerned with the disproportionate incidence
of AIDS among people of color.

By 1986, more militant groups organized around AIDS nationwide.
Under the banner "Silence=Death," a network of local groups called ACT
UP (AIDS Coalition to Unleash Power) formed in such cities as New York,
Los Angeles, Boston, Chicago, Philadelphia, Miami and others. These
groups, based on a philosophy of direct, grassroots action, conduct highly
visible demonstrations often involving civil disobedience in which participants are sometimes arrested. They demand substantial increases in
resources for AIDS education and research equivalent to the "Manhattan
Project" for the development of atomic technology in the 1940s. They
consistently fight calls by the federal government to require compulsory
HIV testing of certain groups, and demand the cutting of bureaucratic red
tape in the testing and distribution of experimental AIDS treatments.
They demand that research labs and pharmaceutical companies concern
themselves less with competition and the profit motive and more with
joint cooperation to arrive at solutions to the problem. In addition, they
fight for laws to prevent AIDS-related discrimination, demanded that
President Reagan's AIDS Commission arrive at realistic and appropriate
proposals to the problem, and push political candidates to become sensitive to the issue. Organizing also centers on legal issues such as protection
against mandatory testing, protection from quarantining people with
AIDS and ARC and those testing HIV-positive, plus issues related to
guaranteeing insurance and social security benefits, preventing job and
housing discrimination, issues related to immigration, and overall rights
concerning confidentiality and human dignity.

In addition to these direct action groups, legal service agencies such as
the Boston-based Gay and Lesbian Advocates and Defenders (GLAD) and
Lambda Legal Defense and Education Fund, Inc., of New York City, for
example, set up special units to deal specifically with AIDS-related cases.

Some organizers continued to stress coalition-building as a major polit-ical strategy. A number of gays and lesbians in the 1980s joined with others in their sustained efforts to end the system of apartheid in South Africa, to end U.S. military involvement in Central America, to counter the activi-ties of the Ku Klux Klan in this country, to lobby for reproductive free-dom, to push for labor and tenants' rights and the rights of the physically challenged, to end the arms race and terminate nuclear power installa-tions, and to provide equal educational opportunities for all who desire them. In addition, links between lesbians and gay males were strength-ened as a result of the AIDS crisis as many lesbians were on the frontlines of organizing alongside gay men around issues related to AIDS.

With the enormous media attention paid to all aspects of the epidemic, the general issue of homosexuality has come further out of the closet in dramatic fashion. AIDS has sparked discussions of homosexuality in class-rooms, workplaces, and homes in big cities, small town, and villages worldwide. Despite the hysteria surrounding AIDS, discussions have pro-vided numerous opportunities to expose many underlying myths and prejudices. And the deaths from AIDS-related diseases of celebrities such as Rock Hudson focused public attention on the double lives some gay people must lead to be accepted.

Some have said that the epidemic not only kills people but also that it has halted the so-called "sexual revolution" of the 1960s and '70s. Though agreement does not exist on whether such a revolution ever really occurred, it does appear certain that this health crisis has brought about a radical shift in the teaching of sexuality by forcing a more explicit and widespread discussion beginning at earlier stages in a child's education. Many local schools are now requiring AIDS education as part of the standard curriculum. Grants have been made available for development of curriculum and materials, and educational AIDS videos have been distributed to many high schools. Increasingly, authorities are recom-mending that information be made available and that such information be nonjudgmental. These kinds of strategies emphasize concerns for health and responsibility rather than focus on traditional value assump-tions about conduct. No doubt controversy will continue to rage over the merits of such an approach.

Other Sexually Transmitted Diseases

Sex with another person can be meaningful and enjoyable. With sexu-ality, however, come both responsibilities and risks. Of course, female and male partners who wish to avoid conception must be acquainted with birth control information, and every sexually active person should be familiar with the various diseases associated with sexuality and how to avoid contracting them.

Whenever people join together in sexual union there is always the possibility of transmitting or contracting a *sexually transmitted disease* (commonly referred to by the medical community as *STD*) or more popularly known as a "venereal disease." The word "venereal" comes from Venus, the Roman goddess of love. These diseases are almost always acquired by direct sexual contact. No one who is sexually active is immune from these—not heterosexuals, bisexuals, or homosexuals. Research, however, indicates that of all groups, lesbians are the least likely to contract sexually transmitted diseases.

In addition to AIDS which has been discussed previously, what follows are brief explanations of sexually transmitted diseases:

Gonorrhea

Gonorrhea is the most ancient and most prevalent of all sexually transmitted diseases, second only to the common cold in incidence of communicable disease in the United States. It is caused by the bacterium *Neisseria gonorrhea*. Penicillin has been effective in treating it in most cases, though new strains of gonorrhea have been more resistant to antibiotics. Gonorrhea's highest incidence is among those twenty to twenty-four years old. It can be contracted during sexual intercourse, with the *gonococcus* organism attacking the genito-urinary areas, though the rectum may also be affected. Women with gonorrhea are frequently (up to 80 percent of the time) asymptomatic. Both women and men may develop a yellowish discharge and experience a burning sensation during urination. Arthritis, skin infections, and kidney damage are complications of the disease. Women may develop an inflammation of the fallopian tubes. Samples of cervical and/or urethral secretions are examined for diagnostic purposes.

Syphilis

Caused by a bacterium known as *Treponema pallidum*, syphilis has existed in this country since at least 500 years before Columbus's voyage. It is treatable with penicillin, but it is also crucial to recognize the disease in its early stage (up to two years following infection) because it is most easily cured then; after the *primary stage*, irreversible tissue damage is likely to occur. This primary stage is also the period of greatest infectiousness. The primary stage is usually identified by a lesion or chancre (sore), usually appearing in the anal-genital area ten to fourteen days after contact with an infected person. Without treatment, the chancre heals in four to ten weeks, but the danger of internal damage remains. The secondary stage is usually characterized by a non-itching eruption, often with accompanying headache, throat infection, malaise, and fever. These symptoms usually disappear within a year if untreated. The *latent period* begins six months to two years after initial infection. It can last years, but is deceptive as it has no overt symptoms. Without treatment, the disease progresses to its final stage, *late syphilis* (or Tertiary syphilis) when it can manifest itself in any organ, in the central nervous and cardiovascular systems, and on the skin. These symptoms may appear as long as thirty years after initial infection. Very few people today reach this stage, though it was once termed "the great scourge." Improved prenatal care has also reduced the incidence of *congenital syphilis* (syphilis existing at birth). There are two blood tests for syphilis and a microscopic examination of the secretion of a sore.

Chancroid

This is a painful, contagious disease typically spread through sexual intercourse, characterized by ulcerations (usually at the point of physical contact) or by local lymph-gland swelling. It may be contracted in conjunction with other venereal diseases. Sulfonamides, the drug commonly chosen to combat chancroid infection, usually effect a cure in three to eight days.

Granuloma inguinale

This is a chronic infectious disease which causes extensive ulceration and scarring of skin and subcutaneous tissues. Genital and extragenital sites might be attacked. It can be cured by careful treatment with antibiotic drugs of the mycin family.

Lymphogranuloma venereum

This is a systemic disease, caused by the organism *Chlamydia trachomatis*. Some women with a chlamydia infection are asymptomatic while others have symptoms which may include vaginal discharge, burning sensation, more frequent urination, or lesions. It can lead to visible enlargement of the lymph nodes, and further complications such as elephantiasis of the penis, scrotum, or vulva. Tetracycline is a common treatment.

Venereal Warts

These are in fact benign tumors, usually soft and fleshy masses, the result of a viral infection *Condylomata accuminata*. In men, they usually appear around the base of the glans of the penis or the anal lining, and in women, on the labia. Venereal warts can be transmitted to other persons or to other parts of one's own body. Treatment is usually cauterization, topical application of medication, or application of liquid nitrogen.

Genital Herpes

This is an acute skin disease caused by the herpes simplex virus, which has two types, I and II. Type I typically appears as cold sores or fever blisters affecting the mouth, lips, or nose. Type II, or genital herpes, appears as a single sore or cluster of blisterlike sores located below the waistline, most frequently affecting the penis and urethra, or anal lining in men and the cervix, vagina, and vulva in women. Type II is usually sexually transmitted; Type I is not. Type II herpes now ranks second to gonorrhea in venereal incidence, accounting for 13 percent of all sexually transmitted or related diseases in the U.S. If a pregnant woman gives birth through a herpes-infected vagina, the baby may contract the infection and develop a form of meningitis. Genital herpes can be diagnosed through medical examination and viral culture. There is no really effective treatment as yet for herpes.

Viral Hepatitis

Two forms of hepatitis exist: hepatitis A and hepatitis B. They are caused by related viruses. Symptoms for type A generally appear fifteen to forty-five days following exposure, and forty-five to one hundred sixty days for type B. The symptoms are similar for both: fever, loss of appetite, and infection to the liver often resulting in a yellowing (jaundice) of the skin and eyes, darkening of the urine, and lightening of stools. A medical examination and blood tests are used to diagnose the illness. The hepatitis A virus can be transmitted in contaminated water and food and through unprotected anal-genital contact. Hepatitis B can also be transmitted during sexual activity through contact with infected body fluids including blood, saliva, semen, or urine and through exposure to infected drug needles. There is as yet no cure for hepatitis and, like other viral infections it must run its course. A hepatitis B vaccine to prevent the illness is available.

Nonvenereal Diseases

These are infections affecting the male and female sexual systems which are not necessarily related to sexual activity, though they can be.

Scabies (Crabs). This is a highly contagious skin disease of the genital area which can be sexually transmitted, caused by mites, the bites of which cause an itchy skin irritation. It is treated by topical medication.

Tinea cruris (Jock Itch). This is a fungus of the genital area which causes inflammation and painful itching.

Non-Specific Vaginitis. This can result from excessive douching, tampons, or sexual contact. It is caused by a bacterial organism: Gardnerella (Hemophilis vaginitis). It can also be caused by other organisms. Symptoms include burning or itching in the genital area often accompanied by an unpleasant smelling gray-colored discharge. A common treatment is the medication trademarked Flagyl and/or antiseptic douches. The bacteria can be transmitted to the urethra of a male sexual partner of an infected woman and simultaneous treatment of both partners may be necessary.

Trichomoniasis or "Trick". Another form of vaginitis, this is the most common of the minor gynecological diseases, afflicting 25 percent of all women. It is caused by a one-cell parasite. It can be sexually transmitted. It usually attacks the vagina and sometimes the cervix, causing inflammation and soreness of the vulva often resulting in a yellowish discharge. A microscopic examination of the discharge can often diagnose the illness. The drug metronidazole has a success rate of over 85 percent.

Cystitis. This is an inflammation of the bladder which causes a severe burning sensation during urination. Treatment includes high fluid intake and cleaning of the external genitalia.

Leukorrhea. This refers to excessive vaginal mucous discharge caused by a chemical, physical, or infectious agent.

Moniliasis. This is a fungus infection of the genital area primarily affecting women, and which can cause acute discomfort.

Epididymitis. Affecting over 600,000 men per year in the U.S., it is an inflammation of the epididymis, closely attached to each testicle. Mild cases involve only slight swelling and tenderness, more severe cases can result in major swelling and pain. It can be treated with antibiotics.

Prostatitis. This is an inflammation of the prostate gland, and it may be either acute or chronic. Since the discovery of antibiotics, however, acute prostatitis is rare. Chronic cases are caused by infection of bacteria invading the prostate.

Yeast. A yeast infection is another form of vaginitis. It is characterized by a cottage cheese-like discharge, itching, and swelling of the vaginal opening. Though microscopic tests of discharge secretions are available, a medical examination is usually all that is necessary for diagnosis. Treatment may include medicated vaginal creams or suppositories. Yeast is not officially termed an STD, but male sexual partners may develop irritation of the penis and may require treatment.

Intestinal Disorders (Enteric Diseases). The most common intestinal disorders are amebiasis and giardiasis (caused by parasites) and shighellosis and salmonellosis (bacterial infections). They are transmitted through contaminated water and food and through oral-anal contact. Symptoms include low-grade fever, abdominal cramps, weight-loss, vomiting, and diarrhea which may contain mucus or blood. The condition may, in some cases, be asymptomatic. Stool specimens are analyzed for diagnosis. Blood tests are also available to detect the presence of amebiasis and giardiasis. Treatment includes the intake of ten to twenty glasses of fluids daily to flush out the organisms from the body, and, on occasion, antibiotics are prescribed.

"Safer Sex" Guidelines

Each time one has sex with someone, one is, in essence, having sex with all of his or her past partners. Unless one practices complete sexual abstinence or is in a relationship where both partners have had and continue to have sex only with one another, it is important to follow guidelines designed to reduce the chances of contracting the HIV virus and other sexually transmitted diseases. Some of these guidelines include:

- Limit the number of partners you have sex with. It is safer to have sex with only one person—the one who only has sex with you.
- Know your sexual partners as well as you can. It is perfectly acceptable to ask them the details of their medical histories as it is for you to tell them about yours. Also, talk about safety precautions *before* having sex. If they refuse to use such precautions, you may consider not having them as partners.
- Figure out your own sexual history. You need to be able to tell your partners what you have done in the past.
- Avoid exchanging bodily fluids and waste materials (especially blood, semen, and vaginal fluids, but also saliva, urine, and feces, and pre-ejaculation fluid.) The use of condoms and dental dams can reduce the chances of this exchange of fluids, but they do not eliminate the risk entirely.
- Try to avoid injuring body tissues during sex, and try not to allow any of your partner's body fluids to enter an existing cut or bruise.

This also includes any tiny, undetected cuts in the mouth, penis, and vagina.

- For extra safety, do not place fingers in anus or vagina without rubber gloves or finger cots (gloves for a single finger).
- Do not mix sex with alcohol or drugs (such as "poppers," marijuana, cocaine, etc.) Drugs tend to impair one's judgment and lessen one's ability to make important decisions. When one is "high," caution is often tossed to the wind. Besides, many drugs have been shown to inhibit the body's immune system, leaving it vulnerable to infection.
- *Never* share sexual aids such as dildoes or vibrators. If you do, put a fresh condom on them each time a different person uses them, or disinfect them by dipping them into a solution of one part chlorine bleach to ten parts water and rinse them off with running water.
- Never share intravenous drug needles or other drug paraphernalia. This is one of the primary means of transmission for the HIV virus, along with other infectious diseases. (A 100 percent solution of bleach followed by a complete rinse with clean water can sterilize drug needles and drug "works" or "cookers." Nevertheless, IV drug users are strongly urged to enroll in drug treatment programs.)

How to Use a Condom

A condom ("rubber") is a thin, pliable cover placed over the penis to reduce the chance of transmitting semen and pre-ejaculation fluid to a sexual partner. It can be purchased at virtually any drugstore and is reasonably priced. It can be found in a number of styles and materials (ribbed and unribbed, latex and natural fiber, lubricated and unlubricated). It is also produced in a variety of different colors and flavors. Though there is no guarantee that condoms will offer complete protection against pregnancy or the transmission of STDs, latex condoms have been shown to be more reliable than natural fibers.

To apply a condom, first remove it from its protective seal. Before unrolling it, gently squeeze the tip with one hand to expel any air from the tip. This provides space for semen to collect during ejaculation, and also pushes out tiny air bubbles which can break the condom.

While still holding the tip, place the condom over the head of the erect penis. Gently and slowly unroll the condom down the shaft to the hair at the base, taking care not to allow any air to enter.

To help prevent bruising to a partner and to lessen the chances of breakage or slippage of the condom during sex, it is wise to use a lubricant. The best type is a water-base lubricant such a KY jelly, For-Play,

PrePair, or Probe. Purchase one that is sold in a sealed tube or package because these do not spread viruses or dirt as easily as open jars or containers. Never use saliva as a lubricant or oil- or petroleum-base products such as Crisco, Vaseline, hand lotions, mineral or baby oil, or butter. These can weaken the condom, increasing the risk of breakage.

Immediately following ejaculation, hold the base of the condom with one hand to make sure it remains on your penis. Slowly withdraw your penis from your partner, trying not to allow any leakage or spillage. Then throw the used condom away. Never use a condom more than once. Only use fresh condoms and do not stretch them or blow them up or place them in wallets—because this can also increase chances of breakage.

Along with condoms, some people prefer the added protection of the spermicide Nonoxynol-9, which has been shown to kill the HIV virus in laboratory test tubes. Effectiveness within the human body, however, has not been established. The spermicide can be used *along* with a condom, but never alone as a substitute. Since some people get skin irritations with spermicides, it is wise to test them first.

When condoms are used during anal intercourse, use extra amounts of water-based lubrication because of the tightness of the anus, which increases the chances of slippage or breakage. It is not wise to engage in unprotected anal intercourse due to the high concentration of blood vessels in that area which can easily rupture upon contact with the penis.

How to Use a Dental Dam

Dental dams, sometimes called oral dams, should be used in oral-vaginal and oral-anal sex. They are six-inch latex squares available at dental- and medical-supply stores. If you cannot find a dental dam, you can also use a kitchen plastic wrap such as Saran Wrap, Handi-Wrap, or Reynolds Plastic Wrap as a substitute, but these materials should be used in a double layer to provide maximum protection. Do not use materials such as plastic garbage bags which can contain harmful toxins.

Always use a fresh dam. Never reuse an old one. Rinse it first to remove any powder or lint that might be clinging to it. Dry it by gently patting with a low-lint towel or simply allow it to dry in the air ahead of time.

Holding two edges with your hands, place the dam over the entire vulva, making sure to cover both the vaginal opening and clitoris. Or, using the same procedure, place the dam over the entire anal lining. Make sure to use separate dams if you engage both in oral-vaginal and oral-anal contact to avoid harmful anal organisms entering the vagina.

Once the dam is in place, you may use your mouth and tongue to stimulate your partner. When finished, throw the dam away.

To date, no reliable data is available on the effectiveness of dental dams in preventing the spread of disease.

Other Activities

Upon first glance, it may appear that safer-sex guidelines reduce all sexual enjoyment. In actuality, the reverse is true. First of all, when consistently used, these guidelines not only reduce your chances of contracting sexually transmitted diseases, but can also reduce some of the fear and anxiety one may have about these diseases. Furthermore, there are numerous activities in addition to those already mentioned. Some of these include: massaging the body, hugging, fondling, caressing, stroking; combing or playing with one another's hair; watching sexy movies, looking at pictures, or mirrors; kissing dry and unbroken areas of the body; talking sexy and sharing fantasies; mutual or simultaneous masturbation with your hands without direct contact of semen or vaginal fluid to the skin; "dry humping," undressing your partner, or dressing up in sexy clothing; showering together; reading erotic literature; rubbing body lotion on each other; licking whipped cream or other foods off your partner's body (except for unprotected body openings); talking, sleeping, and dreaming together; eating in bed together; putting a condom or dental dam on your partner; having telephone sex. The list is limited only by one's imagination.

Conclusion

By the faint light of a cool October dawn, blocks of cloth were unfurled and hooked together and laid to rest upon the Mall of the U.S. Capitol. Complete, it formed an immense patchwork quilt larger than two football fields made up of panels created by friends, lovers, and family members of people who died of AIDS-related diseases. Individual panels included objects and images special to those who were memorialized: articles of clothing, favorite poems, silk flowers, feather boas, buttons. People took turns reading aloud the nearly two-thousand names from virtually every state. Most of the names were of men, but there were also names of women and even infant children. It was a somber occasion, a time of reflection, of remembrance, of grief, but also one of solace and pride. Some people sobbed, embraced. Some remained silent, alone.

The quilt is the realization of the "Names Project" conceived by Cleve Jones of San Francisco with the assistance of numerous volunteers to humanize the enormity of the epidemic and to provide a way for people to see beyond the mere statistics in an attempt to mobilize the country's efforts in fighting this disease.

Though we are learning more about AIDS every day, there is much that we may never know. Theories abound to explain its development: from a primate bite to a Pentagon plot, from an ancient virus coming out of isolation, to faulty genetic engineering, to environmental factors. It is clear, however, that governmental and societal responses have been slow in coming and resources remain scarce while discrimination against people with AIDS continues. The fact that some of the quilt panels were anonymous brings home this point. One panel reads:

> I have decorated this banner to honor my brother. Our parents did not want his name used publicly. The omission of his name represents the fear of oppression that AIDS victims and their families feel.

REFERENCES

Altman, Lawrence K. "Key World Health Official Warns of Epidemic of Prejudice on AIDS." *New York Times*, June 3, 1987.

Blumenfeld, Warren J., "Do Not Go Gently into That Good Night. " *Gay Community News*, Vol. 11, No. 16, Boston, November 5, 1983.

Boston Globe. "Patients Weren't Told of Dallas AIDS Test," Feb. 7, 1988, p. 28.

Buckley, William F, Jr. *New York Times*, March 18, 1986.

Duesberg, Peter. "Retroviruses as Carcinogens and Pathogens: Expectations and Realities." In *Cancer Research*, March 1, 1987.

Gaffney, Dennis. "Fear and Politics." *The Tab*, Cambridge, Mass., Dec. 10, 1985.

Godwin, Dr. Ronald. "AIDS: A Moral and Political Time Bomb." *Moral Majority Report* 2, July 1982.

Harvard University Gazette. "SPH Says Premarital AIDS Screening Not Effective," Vol. LXXXIII, No. 5, Cambridge, Mass., October 2, 1987.

Higgins, Andrew. "Beijing Moves to Prevent AIDS Import." *Boston Globe*, March 13, 1988.

Kessler, Larry. Quoted in "Congress Calls for AIDS Education Campaign." *The Boston Globe*, Sept. 22, 1985.

Knox, Richard. "Drugs Cited in Fast Rise of Heterosexual AIDS." *The Boston Globe*, June 3, 1987.

Lederer, Bob. "U.S. Denies AIDS Bio War with Contradictions." *Gay Community News*, Vol. 14, No. 40, Boston, April 26-May 9, 1987.

New York Times. "Public is Polled on AIDS," August 30, 1987.

Patton, Cindy. *Sex and Germs: The Politics of AIDS*. Boston: South End Press, 1985.

Rieder, Inez. "Gay Murders in Brazil." *Gay Community News*, Vol. 15, No. 29, Feb. 7-13, 1988.

Robinson, John. "Frank Discusses Being Gay." *The Boston Globe*, May 30, 1987.

Shilts, Randy. *And the Band Played On: Politics, People, and the AIDS Epidemic*. New York: St. Martin's Press, 1987.

Shively, Charley. "AIDS and Genes: Part I." *Gay Community News*, Vol. 15, No. 12, Oct. 4-10, 1987.

Further Readings

Altman, Dennis. *AIDS in the Mind of America*. New York: Anchor Press/Doubleday, 1986.

Cerullo, Margaret, et al. editors. *Radical America: A Special Issue—Facing AIDS*, Vol. 20, No. 6, Somerville, Mass.: Alternative Education Project, Inc., Nov.-Dec. 1986.

_____*Radical America: AIDS—Communities Respond*, Vol. 21, Nos. 2–3, Somerville, Mass.: Alternative Education Project, Inc., March–Apr. 1987.

Crimp, Douglas, ed. *AIDS: Cultural Analysis, Cultural Activism*. Cambridge, Mass.: MIT Press, 1988.

Hunt, Morton. *Gay: What Teenagers Should Know about Homosexuality and the AIDS Crisis*. New York: Farrar/Straus/Giroux, 1987.

Liebowitch, Dr. Jacques. *A Strange Virus of Unknown Origin*. New York: Doubleday, 1986.

Nungasser, Lon G. *Epidemic of Courage: Facing AIDS in America*. New York: St. Martin's Press, 1986.

Peabody, Barbara. *The Screaming Room*. San Diego: Oak Tree Publications, 1986.

Watney, Simon. *Policing Desire: Pornography, AIDS, and the Media*. University of Minnesota Press, 1988.

Chapter 8

Lifestyles and Culture

Difference is that new and powerful connection from which our personal power is forged. (Lorde, p. 99.)

We are named by others and we are named by ourselves. (Cameron, p. 52.)

Previous chapters have explored, each from its own perspective, some of the history that gay males and lesbians share. These chapters have assumed a "group sensibility" to emphasize the characteristics—attitude, history, values, and so forth—that lesbians and gays have in common. But gay people are of all classes, races, ethnic groups, physical types, religions, and ages. They possess different abilities, talents, virtues, and interests. This chapter—through theoretical background materials as well as more personal anecdotes—uncovers some of that diversity. It does not claim to give a complete picture, as one is not possible. There is no universal "gay type" or "gay lifestyle" or "gay characteristic." And in exploring these differences, we can reassess some of the common stereotypes we have learned about gays and lesbians.

Culture: Historical Roots

The Stonewall Riots of June 1969 (see Chapter 6) brought to the attention of the American public the reality of a homosexual militancy that had not existed before. Up to that time, mainstream America had its images of gay people as girls' gym teachers, hairdressers, and interior decorators; they were aberrations, parodies of heterosexuality, products of disastrous family constellations, emotionally undeveloped; and they were a threat to the family, particularly younger children.

Though it is almost a cliché that this country is a "melting pot," the popular media around this time constructed a picture of American life that was uniform and homogeneous. Television, for example, portrayed the typical American family as being white, solidly middle-class, and heterosexual; Mother rarely worked outside the home, and Father "knew best."

The reality of American life, however, is that it has its roots in diverse racial, religious, ethnic, class, and gender variations. The image of the "melting pot" may, then, be misleading, if we assume from the analogy that all the parts become a homogeneous whole. Rather, the diverse groups in this country have tended to maintain their own unique identities, at times not "blending" by choice, at other times not "blending" because the dominant groups did not allow it. (See Chapter 5.)

The 1960s were a time when many were questioning some of the assumptions—the "unconscious ideology"—that pervaded American culture. This was the time of the second wave of feminism, the black civil rights movement, and growing organized opposition to the war in Vietnam. These movements increasingly called into question social norms, authority relations, and many of the traditional values of American ideology.

Any given society probably has a number of cultures present at any given time. If we construe culture as "the set of definitions of reality held in common by people who share a distinctive way of life" (Kluckhohn), then it is probably true that there is no society in which there is one "pure," homogeneous culture. In fact, more complex societies often have a number of cultures, often in conflict with one another. Popular (or "mainstream") culture may have to compete with alternative cultures. Though writers disagree about the precise characteristics of these alternative cultures or subcultures, all agree that a subculture is a "normative system of some group or groups smaller than the whole society." (Wolfgang and Ferracuti, p. 139.)

Who is included (the "in-group") and who is excluded (the "out-group") from a prevailing ideology depends on many variables. Subcultures exist within the doiminant culture and they seek to discover ways to preserve their own cultural identity. At the same time, though, mainstream culture may actively exclude those aspects of the subculture which it perceives to be threatening. In the process of doing so, however, a dynamic emerges; just as the dominant culture affects the subcultures, so too does the alternative culture begin to change prevailing norms.

This may be a reasonably friendly dynamic, or it may be overtly hostile. The dominant culture may assimilate the out-groups' norms, or it may fight tenaciously against them. Regardless, though, individuals and groups form *identity* in this process. Such identity formation is a lifelong task for everyone, but it is often all the more difficult for those out-group members who lack a supportive social environment. If, as the psychologist Erik Erikson argues, identity is formed through the "raw materials" the individuals provide *and* the values and norms of the collective culture, then the ideal is one in which the individual finds congruence between one's subjective feelings about oneself and the culture's "objective" view of him or her. Culture, then, provides patterns that serve as the basis for the development of personal identity. But if the culture prescribes limited roles for certain groups (for example, blacks or women), individuals within those groups may lack self-worth or may feel incapacitated by the society's restrictive models for them. Some cultures, then, nourish and support differences in personality, others restrict and stigmatize those outside the norm.

The process of creating a "gay culture" is no different from that described above. All cultures—gay culture included—have certain characteristics. These include social networks through which individuals interact; a sense of group identity (in this case based on sexual preference); subcultural values derived from the main culture (in contrast with a *counterculture*, whose norms are in almost total opposition to those of the overall culture); and a set of organizations and settings for those individuals' interactions, even including specific vocabulary, dress, and folkways. One might also term such a grouping a "community," which as one author puts it, is "a way of organizing and stabilizing relationships between members, implicitly establishing and enforcing rules for behavior." In fact, the community may be seen as "a partial alternative form of family unit for community members." (Barnhart, p. 93.)

Mainstream culture, then, struggles to minimize non-conformity; in addition, the openness of a gay subculture brings to the fore all of the negative connotations which our society carries about sex and sexuality. Prior to Stonewall, mainstream society characterized the homosexual as sick, unhappy, pathetic, on the fringe, and few in number. But, as gays began to proclaim "we are everywhere," those assumptions began to be challenged.

Furthermore, lesbians and gay males sought increasingly to gain civil rights—Lieutenant Leonard Matlovich who in 1975 fought to keep his position in the U.S. Air Force; Mary Jo Risher, a lesbian mother who battled in 1974 for custody of her son; Jack Baker, who became in 1970 the first openly gay elected university student-body president—and in doing so made media headlines, creating new visibility for gay people. This increasing visibility made it possible for more gays to accept themselves, while at the same time making already existing homophobia more acute. Conservative groups assailed homosexuality as a threat to the family and traditional social norms. The issue, then, was no longer simply an affectional preference of a fringe group, but rather a political question of power and social priorities. *Harper's Bazaar* ran a feature entitled "How to Spot Homosexuality in Children." *Time* Magazine began one story with: "The love that once dared not speak its name now can't seem to keep its mouth shut." (Oct. 31, 1969.)

It is important to acknowledge, as Chapter 6 makes clear, that the homosexual civil rights movement dates back at least 100 years before the Stonewall rebellion. In this country in the early 1950s the gay male Matta-chine Society and the lesbian Daughters of Bilitis formed to promote a better understanding of gay people and to push for an end to discrimina-tory laws. Later, gay liberationists adopted more militant strategies, chal-lenging the distinction between the public and the private with the feminist slogan "the personal is the political." This was a challenge even for the most liberal of intellectuals, who tended to see homosexuality as a matter of private choice, a "bedroom issue." A "minority" exists not just because of the existence of a difference, but because of a difference that social groups make *relevant*. Thus, there exists an uneasy relationship between the dominant culture and a subculture. With respect to sexual-ity, the dominant culture has sought in various ways to reinforce hetero-sexuality as a norm. Homosexuality, as previous chapters have shown, has been characterized as a "sin" in a religious context; as a "violation of the social order"; as a "sickness," whether psychological or physiological. Being "outside" mainstream culture, homosexuality challenges tradi-tional norms and gender arrangements; it challenges the status quo.

Attempts to suppress alternative expressions of sexuality have led not only to the development of a homosexual counterculture, but also to the emergence of a positive gay identity. As previous chapters have shown, though same-sex sexual acts have probably always existed, homosexuality itself (with perhaps some exceptions) did not appear as a separate sexual category until fairly recently. This change in thinking may have produced "gay culture," but it may also have reinforced stereotypes and generaliza-tions about gay men and lesbians.

Is There a "Gay Sensibility"?

Culture is not really something a person has a choice in keeping or discard-ing. It is in me and of me. Without it a person would be an empty shell. There was a psychological experiment carried out once in which someone was hypnotized and first told they had no future; the subject became happy and careless as a child. When they were told they had no past, they became catatonic. (Moschkovich, p. 83.)

Men

The early 18th century in England saw the existence of "Molly Houses," meeting places for gay men which were in "sharp contrast to the socially amorphous forms homosexuality had taken a century earlier." (Bray, p. 85.) But it was not until the middle of the 19th century that a solid homosexual identity developed. For the first time, reputable scientists and political theorists urged sympathy and acknowledgment for the "Uranian." Also, this identity evolved through the liberal and radical reformers whose social criticism challenged existing conceptions of sexuality and gender.

Indeed, popular thinking during this time tended to be anti-sex and heavily moralistic in tone. Austrian sex researcher Richard Krafft-Ebing, in his massive *Psychopathia Sexualis,* details sex as a "nauseous disease," while viewing homosexuality as a fundamental sign of "degeneration" and a product of vice. Though Britain abolished the death penalty for sodomy in 1861, a clause in the 1885 Criminal Law Amendment made all sexual activities between men (in public or private) acts of "gross indecency" punishable by up to two years hard labor. This law (the original intent of which was to raise the age of consent for girls to sixteen) had the effect of sharpening the division between "legitimate" and "illegitimate" sex, focusing on the importance of the family and socially sanctioned sex roles.

In this climate, political theorists and writers such as Edward Carpenter, scientists such as Havelock Ellis, and writers such as John Addington Symonds (see Chapter 6) all criticized prevailing norms. Though their writings were heavily theoretical, they were widely read and heatedly criticized by the lay public; Havelock Ellis's book *Sexual Inversion,* for example, was labeled scandalous and obscene. In fact, as a result of this response, he took the book out of print, and to this day no full British edition of Ellis's most important work has appeared. He himself was reluctant to put himself in such a sensitive position. He wrote:

> The pursuit of the martyr's crown is not favorable to the critical and dispassionate investigation of complicated problems. I must leave to others the task of obtaining the reasonable freedoms that I am unable to obtain. (Quoted in Calder-Marshall, p. 218.)

Others did accept Ellis's call to action. But there were very real dangers in doing so, including social ostracism, blackmail, and even imprisonment. Ellis's withdrawal of his book resulted in even more publicity, and many homosexuals wrote to him with their problems, stories, and viewpoints. Some of these writers he reassured; others he referred to gay friends like Carpenter. Many of these stories found their way into his books. This was the beginning of the growth of a "homosexual self-consciousness."

Some view Walt Whitman's concept of homoeroticism (see Chapter 6), glorifying male "adhesiveness," as a forerunner of a gay male sensibility. His sexuality was "without name...it is a word unsaid, it is not in any dictionary or utterance or symbol." (Whitman, p. 95.) Whitman's personal vision of sexuality was inextricably linked with a political vision of egalitarianism and he saw in sexuality the possibility for progressive social change. "I am large, I contain multitudes." (Ibid.) The popular culture viewed such a stance as subversive. His Leaves of Grass was removed from the library shelves at Harvard, and was placed under lock and key with other books thought to undermine student's morals. About that book, the Boston District Attorney wrote to Whitman's publishers:

> We are of the opinion that this book is such a book as brings it within the provisions of the Public Statutes respecting obscene literature and suggest the propriety of withdrawing the same from circulation and suppressing the editions thereof. (Kaplan, p. 20.)

Whitman's writings, then, were exceptional for their time, not only for their homoerotic content, but also for the unabashed joy which he expressed about his own sexuality:

> I mind how we lay such a transparent summer morning,
> How you settled your head athwart my hips and gently turned over upon me,
> And parted the shirt from my bosom-bone, and plunged your tongue to my
>   bare-stript heart,
> And reached till you felt my beard, and reached till you held my feet.
>   (Whitman, p. 52.)

Edward Carpenter was a political theorist who, because of his homosexuality and his feminism, not only extolled the value of same-sex relationships such as were found between males in ancient Greek society (he insisted, for example, on rejecting the "arbitrary notion that the function of life is limited to childbearing"), but also criticized that very society for its misogyny. Carpenter stressed the importance of sexual pleasure in and of itself, a most radical idea for its time. And he linked that vision, like Whitman, to one of social change:

> The love of men for each other—so tender, heroic, constant;
> That has come all down the ages, in every clime, in every nation,
> Always so true, as well assured of itself, overleaping barriers of age,
>   or rank, or distance.
> Flag of the camp of Freedom;

The love of women for each other—so rapt, intense, so confiding, so
  close, so burning passionate,
To unheard deeds of sacrifice, of daring and devotion, prompting,
  and (not less) the love of men for women, and of women for men—On a
  newer greater scale than has hitherto been conceived.
Grand, free and equal—gracious yet never incommensurable—The soul of
  Comradeship glides on. (Coote, p. 228.)

In the scientific community, Havelock Ellis was one of the first
researchers to attempt to take discussions of homosexuality out of the
realm of disease. In Germany, Karl Heinrich Ulrichs had argued that the
male homosexual was a product of abnormal development in the human
embryo. He coined the term "Uranian" in preference to terms like
"sodomite" or "pederast," which were popular in his day. He borrowed
the term from Plato's *Symposium*, in which those who worship Aphrodite
Urania (Heavenly Love) "are attracted toward the male sex, and value it as
being naturally the stronger and more intelligent...their intention is to
form a lasting attachment and partnership for life." Later, in 1869, a
Hungarian doctor, Karoly Maria Benkert, coined the term "homosexual."
    Ellis struggled in his writings to escape the language of disease, suggest-
ing that instead people think of homosexuality as an "anomaly" or "sport
of nature." His collaborator, John Addington Symonds, thought Ellis still
too inclined to "neuropathological jargon," and urged instead an analogy to color-blindness, a harmless variation. Ellis, though, decided even
this sounded too much like a deficiency, and so suggested "color-
hearing"—the ability to assimilate sounds with particular colors—as an
analogue.
    Ellis, like many liberals of today, proposed an agenda primarily in
support of tolerance and civil rights for homosexuals. His argument relied
on two major claims. First, he stressed the importance of the diversity
among cultures, suggesting that norms are neither absolute nor innate.
Second, he maintained that the phenomenon of homosexuality is biologically determined, implying that neither civil penalties nor medical treatments could change the behavior. (He later distinguished "homosexuality," as any sexual and physical relation between two people of the same
sex, from "inversion," defined as a congenital condition.)
    Such an analysis, though progressive for its time, is limited in its goals
and somewhat defensive. Ellis, like Carpenter and Magnus Hirschfeld in
Germany, played down the sexual aspects of homosexuality for fear of
jeopardizing reform efforts. They denied stereotypes (like "effeminacy"),
doctored some of their cases in order to put them in a favorable light, and
maintained that "inverts" were completely ordinary in all but sexual
behavior (hence their penchant for lists of "famous gays"). Ultimately,
this approach does not challenge social assumptions about sex roles. It

presupposes that male sexuality is active and female passive (Ellis, for example, explains lesbians as essentially masculine, though he denies that the opposite is true for gay men). Further, this defense supports the view that masculinity and femininity are deeply rooted biological qualities, as opposed to fluid social constructs; Ellis rejected, for example, Freud's theory of bisexuality, as it allowed for the influence of environmental factors.

Ellis's writings are essentially a plea for tolerance, much like the "Wolfenden Report" in Britain sixty years later. He argued that the law should stick to addressing issues of violence and the protection of minors, and stay out of private lives. His case studies suggest that homosexuals (but for the disapprobation of society) are healthy, productive individuals. And, since the condition is characteristic of a fixed minority and is incurable, the costs of enforcement far outweigh any possible benefits.

These writers all helped to contribute to the development of a gay male sensibility. In addition, the trial of Oscar Wilde—condemned for "posing as a sodomite"—brought the issue of homosexuality to public attention. "If one tells the truth," wrote Wilde, "one is sure, sooner or later, to be found out." The court's sentence of Wilde to two years hard labor resulted in a societal swing back to conformity, strict gender roles, and class divisions. For Wilde was not only openly homosexual, he was also a social critic and an aesthete. He advocated art for art's sake, insisting "there is no such thing as a moral or an immoral book. Books are either well written or badly written. That is all." This signaled to mainstream Britain "the return of the Philistine," and the moral was clear.

> England has tolerated the man Wilde and others of his kind too long. Before he broke the law of his country and outraged human decency, he was a social pest, a center of intellectual corruption. He was one of the high priests of a school which attacks all the wholesome, manly, simple ideals of English life, and sets up false gods of decadent culture and intellectual debauchery. (Hyde, p. 18.)

Thus, as a "gay identity" was developing, the battle lines between culture and subculture were drawn.

It is important to look at culture and sexuality in this context. And, just as males have been socialized differently from females in their consideration of their sexuality throughout history, so too are there historical differences in the evolution of definitions of gay and lesbian sexuality and sensibility.

Women

For women, prior to the late 19th century, contradictory images of "femininity" existed. One the one hand, commentators viewed the "normal" woman as without sexual desire:

> The majority of women (happily for society) are not very much troubled by sexual feelings of any kind.... Here is one perfect example: she assured me that she felt no sexual passions whatsoever; that if she was capable of them, they were dormant. Her passion for her husband was of a platonic kind, and far from wishing to stimulate his frigid feelings, she doubted whether it would be right or not. She loved him as he was and would not desire him to be otherwise except for the hope of having a family. I believe this lady is the perfect ideal of an English wife and mother, kind, considerate, self-sacrificing, and sensible, so pure-hearted as to be utterly ignorant of and adverse to any sensual indulgence, but so unselfishly attached to the man she loves as to be willing to give up her own wishes and feelings for his sake. (Acton, quoted in Comfort, pp. 61-62.)

Yet, on the other hand:

> There was also...a repeated male complaint about the sexual insatiability of women. "Of woman's unnatural insatiable lust, what country, what village does not complain?" declared Robert Burton in his *Anatomy* in 1621.... Apparently old beliefs of feminine sexual evil combined with a popular view that the active vagina and insistent clitora were too much for any man to cope with. (Rowbotham, pp. 6-7.)

Many feminist writers have criticized this dichotomization of women's sexuality: from Eve the temptress to the holy Madonna; from frigid wives to dangerous prostitutes; from "patient Griselde" to witches burned at the stake—these images have found their way into much of our culture. In the 19th century, prostitution flourished alongside middle-class monogamy with its insistence on premarital chastity, marital fidelity, and the asexuality of the bourgeois woman. Seldom were women's own voices heard or recorded. Women had little or no say in their choice of partners; marriages were often made without consideration of the parties' affections. Marriage between equals was impossible. And women's sexuality could only be seen as pathological, a source of venereal diseases in working-class women, a source of hysteria in upper-class women. The Victorian "cult of true womanhood" emphasized for white bourgeois women the values of piety, purity, submissiveness, and domesticity; man was the patriarchal, benevolent ruler whose authority was linked to his ownership of property. So strong was this ideology that the 19th-century feminists Frances Wright, Mary Wollstonecraft, and Harriet Martineau were condemned as "mental hermaphrodites"; and references to "unsexed" women were common antifeminist epithets. Men were dominant in the bedroom as well as the workplace. And an ideology of sexuality developed based on male sexual needs and female passivity, with strict sanctions imposed on women who strayed too far from these prescribed roles. Such sanctions included divorce (without alimony), loss of children, imprisonment, and institutionalization.

How does lesbianism fit into this historical context? Though male homosexuality was becoming a more and more explicit concern for bourgeois 19th-century society, lesbian sexuality was, for the most part, invisible. (Even Havelock Ellis, whose wife Edith was a lesbian, includes only six lesbians in his pioneering case study of homosexuality.) This ideology precluded the possibility of an active female sexuality; women without reference to men were sexless. Since this view did not conceive of sexual relations outside of a model of dominance and submission, it followed that males were initiators and females responders. Lesbians had no place in this sexual ideology, except perhaps as part of male pornography, in which "true" sexual satisfaction is still attainable only with men. Two women, then, could live together, sleep together, even kiss passionately, but mainstream society did not label it sexual. Also, since men's power over women was so established, how could any woman threaten that stronghold? Indeed, two women probably could not survive together financially. "Romantic friendships" or "Boston marriages" between women were, in fact, encouraged as a kind of prelude to heterosexual marriage. Men and women at this time lived in almost entirely separate domains. Lady Anne Halkert of the 17th century, for example, notes in her autobiography that she could not remember three times when as a young woman she was in the company of any man other than her brothers. This continued to be true well into the 18th century. (Nichols, p. 3.) A woman's chastity was her "purse," making her marriageable; this presented a real double bind for women, as they were pursued by men whose sexual appetites were viewed to be insatiable and unremitting. So, the separation of the sexes may have arisen out of the social need to preserve virginity.

Thus, in the framework of this ideology, two women together were ignorant of and indifferent to sexual activity. In fact, women were not even mentioned in the 1885 Criminal Amendment Act in Britain, not simply because Queen Victoria would not understand such a reference to her own sex, but also because women's sexuality was not acknowledged. One myth had it that lesbians had enlarged clitorises so that sex between women always involved penetration of one by the other; clearly, anything other than a phallocentric model of sexuality was unthinkable. Further, it seems that punishments were meted out mostly for such acts between women as cross-dressing and/or using a dildo, acts which must have seemed threatening, not for their sexual overtones, but rather for the implied usurping of male privilege. Stereotypes about lesbians as male posers abound toward the end of the 19th century. Dr. Allan McLane Hamilton, for example, wrote in 1896 that the lesbian was "usually of a masculine type, or if she presented none of the 'characteristics' of the male, was a subject of pelvic disorder, with scanty menstruation, and was more or less hysterical and insane." (Quoted in Federman, p. 155.)

Some feminists of that time responded to this ideology by arguing that men should become as "spiritual" as women and that sexuality should become an insignificant part of human relationships. Many feminists upheld a kind of sexual puritanism—in part a response to the very real dangers of pregnancy and childbirth, in part a reflection of their acceptance of the prevailing ideology about women's lack of sexual appetite—as a solution to these problems. For example, Harriet Taylor and John Stuart Mill (feminists of their time and leading defenders of women's suffrage) did not in their twenty-year-plus marriage engage in sexual relations, congratulating each other in their letters on the "purity" of a connection which transcended physical needs.

Changes occurring in the later 19th and early 20th centuries led to a questioning of this ideology of women's sexual and social passivity. For one, some women, especially working-class women, had always left homes to work; and in this century ever greater numbers of women were drawn into the labor force. Second, with families smaller and infant mortality lower, a woman's active reproductive years became a much smaller part of her life. Third, some feminists such as Emma Goldman and Victoria Claflin challenged the family, characterizing it as the locus of female oppression. Such radical feminists went so far as to extol the virtues of "free love." Such love was not unbridled promiscuity, but rather a love freely chosen and between equals. Such relationships, they maintained, could only occur in a society where women's sexuality was acknowledged and women's economic independence fostered. Finally, changes in technology, including contraception and legalized abortion (though this is still not a reality for many women), made it possible to rethink traditional assumptions about sexual practices. Sex could be sex for pleasure, as it was now technically possible to separate sex and procreation.

Culture Today

Whereas straight people have a vested interest in being dull literalists, and unimaginative to keep their world going, gay people are, I have learned, in the truest sense of the word *fabulous*. More than any other people in the macroscopic society, we've broken down the rules that are used for validating the difference between real/true and unreal/false. The controlling agents of the status quo may know the *power* of lies. Dissident subcultures, however, are closer to knowing their *value*. (Mitzel, p. 12.)

The middle to late 19th century saw the development of a distinct homosexual community, particularly for men. This may have been due in part to the decriminalization of homosexual acts in countries influenced by the French Napoleonic Code (1810). Organizations formed to educate the public on the issue of same-sex attraction. Though the vast majority of the scientific community considered homosexuality a disease and a form of degeneracy, this was nonetheless the first time that researchers sought empirical data on the subject and applied scientific method to its analysis. One police official in Paris in the 1880s estimated that 7,242 male homosexuals had come to the attention of the police. In the ten years between 1898 and 1908, over 1000 titles on homosexuality appeared in Germany alone. (Bullough, p. 8.) Repressive laws in other countries independent of France's influence, though, pushed this growing gay subculture further underground. Gay males and lesbians, as a result, had to develop unique manners and styles as a means of survival and protection. Consequently, many of the characteristics of the "gay sensibility" are linked to concealment. Signals emerge, varying by geography and time, which exist to communicate a subtle message of membership in the "community." At one time, for example, gay males in large cities in the early part of the 20th century wore red ties as a sign to others who understood the code.

> Homosexuals have had a hard time organizing as a political and cultural force, owing to the centuries of social stigma (still legally enforced in many parts of the U.S.) that obliged them to communicate indirectly, by signs. Cultural objects, items of dress, changing fashions in speech and gesture and even cologne became protective measures, ways of conveying a man's predilection that didn't put him in legal jeopardy or destroy his status in the eyes of the straight world. (Feingold, p. 77.)

Even the word "gay" probably arose from a need for ambiguity.

These codes abounded in written materials as well. Many writers consciously changed pronouns of love-objects to conceal their preference. Some writers—E.M. Forster, for example—could not find publishers for their work with gay themes or deliberately withheld publication of such works during their lifetimes. The poet Edward Lear and the authors James Barrie (of *Peter Pan*) and Gertrude Stein all developed styles to mask homosexual subthemes.

Another development in gay culture is the evolution of camp. *Gay Talk*, a gay slang dictionary, defines the word "camp" as coming from a 16th century theatrical term, "camping," meaning "young men wearing the costume of women in a play." And camp can be a form of humor as well as social commentary. Camp can criticize as well as exaggerate and stylize what is usually thought to be normal.

> The homosexual fondness for such sexual/gender stereotypes as Mae West, Hedy Lamarr, or Victor Mature comes from the fact that they are parodies ...of what is thought to be normal. (Bronski, p. 42.)

In her "Notes on Camp," Susan Sontag has written that "homosexuals have pinned their integration into society on promoting the aesthetic sense." (p. 290.) This aesthetic sense, perhaps inherited from Wilde, carries with it a degree of definition and acceptability, respectability. It can be a way to attain upward mobility. The stress on "style," Sontag maintains, is aimed at "neutralizing indignation, sponsoring playfulness." (p. 292.)

Another example is dressing in drag, which can be a way to comment on the usual gender arrangements as well as to act out one's own feelings, something not permitted by traditional gender roles. "Camptalk"—when gays refer to one another by the other-sex pronouns—similarly may have evolved as a coded way to speak about one's sexual life without fear of reprisal. Thus, though camp may at times be self-denigrating, it can also serve as a defense against a society which forces concealment.

Film, too, may provide a vehicle for escape from terrifying realities. Parody, fantasy, and ambiguity are key elements for much of homosexual culture, and they find an appropriate means of expression in film. Gay men have turned to film as a way of envisioning an alternative world.

> Deprived of the ability to "act" in real life, gay men identified with the ability to "feel" portrayed by female movie stars. The emotion might be "love" with Greta Garbo or "strength" with Bette Davis or "wit" with Eve Arden or perhaps simply "beauty" with Elizabeth Taylor. But in each case, gay men experienced the vicarious pleasure of entering a safe world where they could experience emotions and fantasies without threat. (Bronski, p. 108.)

The lesbian "pulp fiction" of the later 20th century may serve a similar function for women who could live vicariously through the novels of writers like Jane Rule and Anne Bannon. Though these early lesbian novels often had tragic endings, they nonetheless provided lesbians with an opportunity for identification with other "women-loving-women."

Though few mainstream films have portrayed gay men and lesbians accurately, Hollywood has at least begun to acknowledge the presence of homosexuals, owing largely to the cultural inroads made by the gay liberation movement. The careers of Judy Garland, Barbra Streisand, and Bette Midler all owe much to the influence of gay sensibility on mainstream culture. Recent films about role reversal (for example, *Victor/Victoria, Tootsie, Liquid Sky, La Cage Aux Folles, The Rocky Horror Picture Show, Torch Song Trilogy,* etc.) are all, whatever their weaknesses, responses to dissatisfaction with traditional gender arrangements.

The stress on "style" in gay male culture has led to a valuing of certain forms of high culture such as opera and ballet.

> Given the concealment involved it was natural for male homosexual audiences to be attracted to art with a certain degree of flamboyance—repressed impulses return in a distorted or exaggerated form. What has happened with the dropping of many sexual barriers and public taboos over the last two decades is that these signs have been worn as badges of homosexuality instead of masks for it, like a fascist prison system taken over by revolutionaries for emergency housing. (Feingold, p. 77.)

Thus, the drama and "larger-than-life" quality of both opera and ballet have long appealed to gay men, leading one commentator to describe opera as the "upper-class closeted equivalent of drag shows." (Altman, p. 154.)

> The opera offers gay men a social experience in which they can be openly gay. The sensibility of the art—especially the triumph of form over content and the permission which opera gives to the expression of sexuality and feeling—also attracts a gay male following. Because gay men were attracted to opera, and because opera itself was perceived as corresponding to certain stereotypes of gay men, it became a haven—or ghetto—in which gay men could be open about their lives. Historic associations between high culture and wealth reinforced other traditional associations between wealth and sexual non-conformity. Both before and after Stonewall, opera has offered gay men a space where they could listen to the love which might sin—but dared not speak its name. (Bronski, p. 143.)

The number of gays involved in the arts has consistently been far larger than what has been visible in front of the camera and on stage. Also, untold numbers of actors and actresses whose careers were built upon their romantic heterosexual personae lived secretly as homosexuals. Further, it is probably not a coincidence that many of our best love songs were written by homosexuals: Cole Porter, Ivor Novello, Lawrence Hart, and many others.

Lesbian culture has developed in a direction somewhat different from gay male culture. In part this is due to socially constructed differences between men and women, in part because lesbian culture has been, to a great extent, a component of feminist culture. Novelists like Marge Piercy, novels like *Rubyfruit Jungle* by Rita Mae Brown, writers like Audre

Lorde, and singers like Holly Near and Cris Williamson emphasize self-reflection and authenticity, in contrast to the emphasis on style by gay men.

The existence of mainstream "gay culture" signals the presence of gay expression within the wider culture. Heterosexual artistic forms which convey gay content are now common: the detective novels of Joseph Hansen, romantic/sentimental novels such as *The Front Runner* and *The Color Purple*, movie thrillers like *Dog Day Afternoon*, television programs such as "Soap" and "Brothers," and musical groups like The Village People. *Time* Magazine (December 4, 1976, p. 68) even attributed the late 1970s phenomenon of disco music to the "gay subculture." It is difficult, though, to assess the effects of this culture on society as a whole.

One should not minimize the importance to gay identity of the bars. Though criticized by opponents as dens of hedonism and unbridled sexuality, gay bars have provided gays and lesbians with what in many communities has been the only meeting place available to them. Further, for many gay men and lesbians, going to a gay bar has been an admission of being different, and the ever-present possibility of police raids and the fear of disclosure have made these visits akin to a political act.

Whatever the form, though—opera, ballet, fiction, song—these aspects of culture have come to provide a basis for gay people to feel connections with others like them. Because of the invisiblity of gay people, art has become a crucial tool for teaching the life-styles and attitudes ordinarily taught by families, schools, and religious organizations. For many gays isolated by time or geography this has been the only chance to learn about the "gay experience" and to compare it to their own.

> The culture that has grown since the Stonewall rebellion has been an important contribution (perhaps the most important) of the current gay and lesbian movements. Legislative gains have been minimal. We have merely chipped away at silences and at social prejudice; we have gained but a few token open representatives in prestigious positions (although thousands more lurk in the closets!). But in the almost twenty years since the Stonewall uprising we have created a culture and put fruitful energy into unearthing our heritage. That's a major achievement. Even if all the laws turn against us, if the so-called backlash of heterosexuals against "permissiveness" increases (although I personally don't believe there is a backlash, since I don't believe I've ever seen a frontlash—that is, any true acceptance), we will still have our songs to sing, our books to keep with us, our [history] to treasure in our hearts, and the knowledge that there is a common core uniting us as a people. We are a people who have always survived and always will survive. (Jay, pp. 50-51.)

Diversity within Subculture

In order to feel fully safe I need to feel known. (Beck, p. xvi.)

Man, like all the other animals, fears and is repelled by that which he does not understand, and mere difference is apt to connote something malign. (Walker, p. 169.)

Most people have viewed the existence of gay men and lesbians through a lens filtered by certain stereotypes. In truth, there are no known patterns of homosexuality which correlate to race, class, religion, or ethnicity. The 1948 publication of Alfred Kinsey's *Sexual Behavior in the Human Male*, and *Sexual Behavior in the Human Female* in 1953 provided empirical data that homosexuality was pervasive in all strata of American life and that homosexuals could not be identified by stereotypes. In addition, the Second World War brought about major upheavals in American life—women were encouraged to work in factories; there was increasing urbanization, bringing gay men and lesbians into contact more than ever before. Life outside the traditional nuclear family became possible. Try as it might to return to its antebellum ways, the country could not turn back the clock.

Gay men and lesbians exist in all socioeconomic classes, all age groups, all ethnic groups, all races, all religions, in all geographical settings. Yet it is also important to acknowledge that there may well be places (e.g., San Francisco and New York City) more hospitable to gays, and even occupations in which they can be less fearful of discovery.

Unlike blacks, for example, gays are not an easily identifiable minority. Often, then, those who are more visible are assumed to be representative of all or the majority of gay men and lesbians. Today's popular imagination seems to have two very different images of "the gay man." One is that he is a white, middle-class, male professional urban dweller with what is considered good taste and a good deal of discretionary income. Some advertisers now even try to cater to this stereotypical gay man, and popular media, when it wants the viewer to feel friendly toward a gay male character, makes use of this stereotype. This image has also, to some extent, been accepted by many gay men to promote their own acceptance into society as well as to heighten their own feelings of respectability.

On the other hand, there still remains the popular image of the flamboyant, "swishy" gay male who is probably an interior decorator or hairdresser, loves color, dresses wildly, and probably talks with a lisp. Interestingly, the cable TV show *Brothers* has one of each of these "types," and the two characters are used as counterpoint.

Lesbians fare even less well in the media and the popular imagination.

Though programs like *Kate and Allie* and *The Golden Girls* have had episodes which featured lesbian characters, lesbians are, for the most part, invisible. Or they are pathetic, asexual women who have missed out on family; or men-haters who, ironically, behave and look just like men.

Although lack of visibility makes it impossible to collect accurate statistics about gay people, there are probably similar proportions of gay people in all classes and racial and ethnic communities. Individual subgroups may have different attitudes about homosexuality and so some groups may *appear* to have fewer or more homosexuals, but the actual numbers are probably about the same in every group. Similarly, many gay people may seek the security, social networks, and cultural activities of well-organized gay communities in cities, but gay people exist in all geographical locations around the globe.

Gay people are also economically diverse. Those gays who are members of ethnic groups may suffer not only because they are gay but also because of their membership in those ethnic groups. Lesbians as women still earn, on the average, sixty-nine cents for every dollar earned by a man; lesbians of color on the average earn even less. But it is also true that some gay men, both because they are male and because they may have no dependents, may be better off financially than some others. And, though it is true that money may help to buy one an entry into society, financial security should not be confused with social acceptance.

The well-off as well as the poor get queer-bashed when leaving gay bars. Money and fine clothes do little to soften the hearts of those who hate "queers." (Bronski, p. 179.)

Gay men and lesbians are as varied in their dress, mannerisms, and styles as their heterosexual counterparts. There are many gay male football players and other athletes, just as there are lesbians who fit a traditional feminine image. Similarly, there are many people who define themselves as heterosexual who appear to be gay or lesbian. This is particularly true with respect to transvestites. The vast majority of men who wear "women's" clothes define themselves as heterosexual. It is perhaps more obvious that the vast majority of women who wear "men's" clothes are not making a statement about their sexual orientation. And "dressing like a man" (whether it is said in reference to a lesbian or heterosexual woman) may be less about "trying to be a man" and more about wanting to have the comfort and enhanced social mobility that traditional male clothing affords.

In the recent past many gay commercial ventures have blossomed. These include bars, travel agencies, restaurants, and publications. These enterprises surely have the making of money as one purpose; but they also have a commitment to the gay community and probably could not exist without the identity which has come as the result of social and political change. Some gay business people see their lifestyles as an integration of both the professional and the social aspects of their lives. These businesses may even serve the function for gays that families serve for ethnic minorities.

There are also many gay people who identify with a particular religion, though traditional religion has not always been especially sympathetic toward homosexuality. (See Chapter 4.) However, Quakers, Unitarians, and the Disciples of Christ have all moved toward acceptance of homosexuality. The Metropolitan Community Church (MCC), founded by a charismatic gay minister, Rev. Troy Perry, in Los Angeles, California, has over 30,000 members in 170 churches around the world. The United Church of Christ was the first church in the United States to ordain an openly gay clergyman, William Johnson, in 1972. And groups such as Dignity for Catholics and Integrity for Episcopals and similar groups for gay Jews have many members all of whom believe that their sexual orientation is compatible with the teachings of their faith.

The stereotypes of the "swishy faggot" or the "diesel dyke" are just that: stereotypes. This means that there are some lesbians who dress in masculine clothes and appear to be very tough and threatening to the heterosexual community, and there are some gay men with very effeminate mannerisms who may appear to be mimicking women. However, according to Kinsey Institute associate Wardell Pomeroy, though approximately 15 percent of gay men are effeminate, the same percentage holds for heterosexual men as well. (Cited by Voeller, in Marmor, p. 234.) And it is probably true that "effeminate" mannerisms were standard among gay men in other times, in particular in the 1920s in this country. Such a public stereotype also provided a way to pass in the straight world, by not being *obviously* effeminate. (Chauncey, pp. 29-32.) Nevertheless, society seems to focus on these members of the gay and lesbian community as models of all gay people. Obviously, though, if a significant percentage of the population is gay and lesbian, then there are many who are successfully "passing" as straight.

> Visibility is important, psychologically, because of the profound role played by its opposite in the life of every homosexual—that is, secretiveness. (Robinson, p. 10.)

We are all given the message that we are not supposed to act counter to our assigned gender roles. (See Chapter 1.) Deviating from these roles means that one is "queer" and therefore not acceptable. People—straight *and* gay—may go to great lengths to "prove" that they are not homosexual. One college gay group, for example, announced that on a certain day homosexuals should wear jeans. It turned out that many students who unwittingly wore jeans to school that day went home to change.

Often gay people employ "passing strategies" to present a convincing front to straight people. Some, for example, change the pronouns they use to refer to their lovers when speaking with heterosexuals. Others are secretive about their personal lives; in other cases, which author Barbara Ponse (p. 165) refers to as "counterfeit secrecy," lesbians and gays cooperate with heterosexual friends and family members in not making explicit what is implicitly known.

Families

Homosexuality has been assailed throughout history as a threat to the traditional nuclear family and the values it represents. Gays and lesbians—in a concrete, daily way—must deal with the issue of *family*, both in terms of the biological families into which they are born as well as in terms of the sorts of families they wish to create.

Families of Origin

As children, we need and seek the approval of our families; adulthood does not erase those needs. And gay men and lesbians are products of all the same parenting and family constellations as their heterosexual brothers and sisters. (See Chapter 3.) Gay men and lesbians who value their relationships with their families of origin must, at some point in their lives, make a decision: if they "come out" to their families, they may jeopardize those ties, even dissolve them irrevocably; or they may never "come out" and withhold a fundamental truth about who they are from others about whom they care deeply. This fact makes homosexuals different from other minority group members. Obviously, most often African American children have African American parents, Jews have Jewish parents, Chinese people have Chinese parents; but, statistically, the vast majority of homosexuals have parents who are heterosexual. Thus, unlike other oppressed groups, gay people cannot always count on the family structure as a basis for support; indeed, in some cases, the family may be the locus of the greatest hostility.

In the process of "coming out," lesbians and gays meet with a variety of responses from their families. For some, there is acceptance, but for many, the news is received as calamitous, akin to the feelings associated with a death in the family. Others respond with anger or denial or guilt in that perhaps they themselves were somehow responsible. Family members may seek to find an explanation for a daughter's or son's homosexuality, but this is usually an attempt to ascribe blame. In some families, understanding grows over time; in others, reconciliation never occurs. In still others, the knowledge is never shared.

When a son or daughter announces his or her homosexuality, for many families that proclamation signals the death of expectations. Marriage and raising children, "carrying on the family name" (for sons), traditional "in-law" relationships—all such values and dreams are thrown into doubt with the announcement of a child's homosexuality. Social events, holidays, and family gatherings may take on a wholly different meaning. One's lover may not be welcome, or if he or she is invited, it might be on the condition that there be no overt affection or a denial of the real relationship ("We're just roommates"). For some more traditional, ethnic families this can be especially disturbing, particularly for lesbians. Since women are often expected to be more involved in family traditions than are men, many lesbians, even those in long-term relationships, talk with sadness of spending holidays fulfilling their family responsibilities apart from their lovers. Some families manage to adjust well to the changes brought on by homosexuality; for others, conformity to conventional values is such a priority that they are never able to accept any divergence from them. Groups such as Parents and Friends of Lesbians and Gays now exist to serve as resources for families dealing with this issue.

These conflicts within families are not unique to the late 20th century. The following was written by Sigmund Freud to a mother concerned about her son's homosexuality:

Dear Mrs._____:

I gather from your letter that your son is a homosexual. I am most impressed by the fact that you do not mention this term yourself in your information about him. May I question you, why you avoid it? Homosexuality is assuredly no advantage but it is nothing to be ashamed of, no vice, no degradation, it cannot be classified as an illness; we consider it to be a variation of the sexual function produced by a certain arrest of sexual development. Many highly respectable individuals of ancient and modern times have been homosexuals, several of the greatest men among them (Plato, Michelangelo, Leonardo da Vinci, etc.). It is a great injustice to persecute homosexuality as a crime and a cruelty too. If you do not believe me, read the books of Havelock Ellis.

By asking me if I can help, you mean, I suppose, if I can abolish homosexuality and make normal heterosexuality take its place. The answer is, in a general way, we cannot promise to achieve it. In a certain number of cases we succeed in developing the blighted germs of heterosexual tendencies, which are present in every homosexual; in the majority of cases it is no more possible. It is a question of the quality and the age of the individual. The result of treatment cannot be predicted.

What analysis can do for your son runs in a different line. If he is unhappy, neurotic, torn by conflicts, inhibited in his social life, analysis may bring him harmony, peace of mind, full efficiency, whether he remains a homosexual or gets changed. If you make up your mind he should have analysis with me—I don't expect you will—he has to come over to Vienna. I have no intention of leaving here. However, don't neglect to give me your answer.

Sincerely yours with kind wishes,

Freud

Creating Families

Humans are social animals, created by and through their interactions with others. Families are obviously key mechanisms for transferring values and social norms. But families can also be repressive or even abusive. Recent statistics, for example, state that at least one million children a year are abused. Most of this abuse occurs within the biological family.

The family as it is portrayed in the media most of us grew up with is, in reality, a myth. In fact, few families meet traditional norms. For example, according to recent studies, 16 percent of American homes are single-parent households, 23 percent are child-free or past the age of childrearing, 16 percent are dual-career families, and 4 percent are cohabitors. (Ramey.) In addition, nearly one-third of all children under six have working mothers. (Moroney.)

Lesbians and gays are helping to redefine the family. Some seek more traditional family arrangements, even "marriage," though such bonds are not legally recognized. Others may live singly or in groups. But a family need not be seen as narrowly as traditionally defined—family can be a support network. People in the family need not be biologically related, sexually interacting, or even live in the same place. (See, for example, Lindsey.)

Families often serve as support systems for people as they grow older in a society that tends to be youth-oriented and production-focused. The older gay person shares in the difficulties that accompany aging in this society, but may suffer even more if isolated from family. In one study on aging in the gay male community, a majority of gay men interviewed expressed concern about certain aspects of aging, including hospital visitation rights, insurance company policies, housing, and retirement homes. (Kelly.) At the same time, however, many older gay men and lesbians have developed lifelong friendships, relationships, and communities that are more stable than the heterosexual counterpart of marriage. Many gay and lesbian "families" include people of all ages living together. Some gay people without children have planned group living arrangements so that the aging experience can be enriching rather than lonely.

There are difficulties unique to the experience of older lesbians and gay men that are probably a result of society's attitudes and the lack of legal protection. For example, since there is no legal validation of gay and lesbian relationships, when a partner dies, the other is often left without any benefits from inheritance, insurance, or property which had been shared previously. Blood or "legal" relatives of the deceased can have wills contested. There is no legal assurance for any gay person that his or her wishes will be respected after death. There have even been examples in which the surviving partner of a relationship has been barred from the funeral because the relatives would not acknowledge the relationship.

Many gay men and lesbians already have children from previous or existing heterosexual relationships. Some seek to have children after they have "come out," through alternative insemination (by a known or unknown donor) or adoption. In all such arrangements, there are associated legal problems. Lesbians and gay men have had to fight ex-spouses for custody of their biological children. Many placement agencies are reluctant to place children with known gay men or lesbians. Some places that provide alternative insemination services insist that eligible candidates show evidence of a long-term heterosexual relationship.

Thus far, there is no evidence that the children of such arrangements suffer any more psychic damage than children raised in other sorts of homes. One study (Miller) showed that, in a comparison of lesbian and heterosexual mothers, lesbians were more nurturing and more child-centered. Nor is there any evidence to suggest that gay parents produce gay kids in any greater numbers than in the total population, though there is some reason to believe that children of gay or lesbian parents are more aware of options and more tolerant of others' differences. Many of the problems gay parents face are similar to those with which single heterosexual parents have to deal. For lesbians and especially lesbians of color, who as women still earn significantly less than men, economic survival can be a major struggle.

One fear that many people express is that homosexuals molest young children. The singer Anita Bryant, in her campaign in Dade County, Florida, in the late 1970s to prevent gays from teaching in the schools, exploited this fear to win voters over to her side. Yet studies consistently show that most child sexual abuse is by a family member and most often involves men who abuse young girls. One study, for example (Jaffe, et al.) reported that 88 percent of the victims were female, while the vast majority of the abusers are male. This evidence has led researcher Sarafino to conclude that 92 percent of all child sexual abuse cases are heterosexual. Further, another study notes that a review of all available evidence "provides no basis for associating child molestation with homosexual behavior." (Newton, p. 40.) Although the data are sparse, the evidence suggests that a great many of the men who victimize young boys do not identify themselves as homosexuals. In fact, many abusers of boys appear to be married and to have had lengthy heterosexual histories. (Gebhard, *et al.*) Others are exclusive pedophiles who have no interest at all in adult partners and do not consider themselves gay. (Groth and Birnbaum.) According to the Gay Teacher's Caucus of New York, while there are many complaints on file about male teachers making sexual advances to female students, there have been no complaints about teachers making advances to students of the same sex. And women, including lesbians, almost never sexually molest children.

Relationships: Exposing the Myths

> It is in the knowledge of the genuine condition of our lives that we must draw our strength to live and our reasons for acting. (de Beauvoir.)

Long-term Relationships

One common stereotype is that gay men and lesbians do not have long-term committed relationships. Yet, according to the *New York Times*:

> A major new study on homosexuality concludes that many homosexual men and women lead stable lives without frenetic sexual activity and that some are considerably happier and better adjusted than heterosexuals as a whole. (Brody in *NYT*.)

This study of 979 gays and lesbians examined a highly diverse group and its authors, Dr. Alan P. Bell and Martin S. Weinberg, concluded:

> [H]omosexual adults who have come to terms with their homosexuality, who do not regret their sexual orientation, and who can function effectively sexually and socially, are no more depressed psychologically than are heterosexual men and women. (*Ibid.*)

Indeed, this study found that gay "closed couples" were happier than their heterosexual counterparts. Further evidence suggests that gay relationships can be psychologically rewarding. One test, for example, the

Locke-Wallace scale, a standardized test of marital adjustment, compared homosexual and heterosexual couples and revealed that they were indistinguishable, with the same numbers scoring in the "well-adjusted" range (Peplau, p. 205.) In fact, sex researchers and other social analysts have used same-sex relationships as a vehicle to try to gain insight into heterosexuality. For example, researchers have discovered from studies of lesbian relationships, that female sexuality is most easily disturbed by momentary interruptions many men make without even being aware of it. Similarly, researchers have studied male-male relationships as a way to understand what terminates a man's sexual interest and what reactivates it.

Further, another study shows that approximately 60 percent of lesbians and 40 percent of gay men are involved in a long-term relationship. This statistic does not tell us what percentage of the community would like to be in a relationship, nor does it reflect the numbers of gay people who define themselves as gay but are not interested in having a sexual involvement with another person. It does, however, suggest that the desire for long-term intimacy has no correlation with a particular sexual orientation. Indeed, researchers have consistently observed that it is gender and not sexual preference that exerts the greater influence on relationships. (Peplau.) For example, women are socialized to be monogamous, committed, "other-oriented," and less aggressive sexually. Men, in contrast, learn different values: independence, responsibility, separation from others, and sexual initiative. These contrasts have obvious and important implications for same-sex relationships.

Further to equate emotional maturity with the ability to sustain a long-term relationship would also make many heterosexuals emotionally immature. With many heterosexual marriages ending in divorce, it seems clear that, for whatever reason (including, for example, increasing life expectancy), relationships are ending long before "death us do part."

One might wonder why it is that we tend to value longevity in relationships. There are of course economic and social reasons which support remaining in long-term living arrangements, in addition to the "natural" human resistance to change itself. But that does not imply any moral value or even necessary personal benefit from longevity per se. Indeed, one could argue that there are competing values in long- and short-term relationships: the former may provide stability, security, and the possibility for heightened intimacy; the latter may offer diversity, excitement, and a chance to savor different individuals' styles. Some sociologists now refer to "serial monogamy" as the lifestyle which characterizes many contemporary relationships. Gay relationships appear to be no different.

In addition, gay relationships generally do not receive many of the social sanctions which often come to heterosexual relationships. For one, gay relationships do not receive the institutional support of legal marriage. Families may intervene to "save" a heterosexual union, but lend no emotional support to a gay couple. Sometimes, even gay and lesbian friends, socialized to these same attitudes, may fail to provide support for the continuance of a relationship. Such relationships, then, are not openly validated, nor are there external constraints (joint property, for example) to keep a relationship together.

Roles

Before the new wave of women's and gay liberation movements in the 1960s, there were very few options available other than the traditional heterosexual model in which men and women knew what was expected of them in terms of attitude, behavior, and dress. Socialized in these same ways, gays and lesbians also had limited options and often chose to copy this heterosexual model. Often one member of a couple, then, played the "butch" or masculine role, the other the "femme" or feminine role.

However, with the advent of the new wave in the women's and gay liberation movements, these roles have been called into question. Women, in particular, have struggled against many aspects of the feminine role: passivity, servitude, uncomfortable and impractical dress, limited job opportunities, and the like. Women have also asked men to change and begin to relinquish the strictly masculine role (aggressiveness, goal orientation, emotional control, etc.), which sacrifices feelings for rationality. Some men have also begun to ask for more freedom to express different parts of themselves and to want closer relationships with their lovers and children. These changing attitudes are touching all parts of society.

At the same time, the very nature of gay relationships—man loving man, woman loving woman—challenges the old structures and provides an impetus for further change. Lesbians, for example, cannot count on men to support them or take care of them. Out of survival, they may widen their own experiences and develop their potential—for example, learning to do the kinds of home and auto repairs that most boys learn as teenagers. Similarly, lesbians are often in the forefront of movements for equal pay and increased employment opportunities. Similarly, gay men usually don't have a woman around the house to do the housework or take care of their emotional needs. Because of these direct experiences, lesbians and gay men cannot make assumptions about "proper" conduct for each sex. In fact, though there has not been much research on lesbian and gay couples, one study did reveal that lesbians are less bound by traditional gender divisions of labor (Tanner) and another that lesbian relationships tend to be more egalitarian. (Taylor.)

One gay man, for example, told researchers:

> My lover and I have constantly shifting roles, depending on the needs of the moment. If ever I felt we were getting locked into any roles...I would run to escape this relationship. (Peplau, quoted from Jay and Young, p. 203.)

And a lesbian comments:

> I don't like role playing because it copies the traditional male/female relationship. I'm proud to be a woman. And I love women, not pseudomen. (*Ibid.*)

Likewise, many heterosexuals are questioning traditional views about relationships and the values associated with them. No matter what else is true about them, gay relationships are outside the mainstream. So it makes sense that gay men and lesbians, lacking social legitimacy, have felt freer to question other commonly held assumptions about relationships. Is monogamy, *per se*, for example, preferable to open relationships? Why do we tend to value longevity in relationships?

Though it is important to acknowledge that gay men and lesbians have been in the forefront of attempts to restructure models for relationships, it is also true that there are still many gay men and lesbians committed to adhering as closely as possible to traditional norms and roles, and that this questioning occurs at a time in our history when heterosexuals are also questioning many of the more rigid codes which govern social relationships. (See, for example, Wasserstrom, O'Neill, Elliston, and others.) In addition, the problem of AIDS has led many gay men to put renewed emphasis on monogamy and longevity in relationships.

Promiscuity

There is a common misconception that all gay men and only gay men engage in promiscuous sexual behavior. What is true is that while some gay men choose to have a variety of partners, many others don't. The word "promiscuous" is a value-laden term and seems to carry a negative connotation when applied to gay men. Indeed, similar behavior which is condoned or approved in heterosexual men is frequently condemned when it is part of a gay male lifestyle. This double standard becomes clear when we consider terms which our culture uses to refer to promiscuous heterosexual men: "Don Juan," "lady-killer," or "stud," to name just a few. The term "promiscuous" is not simply descriptive of a behavior pattern, but heavily moralistic. To say that someone is promiscuous, then, is usually to imply a critical judgment. Yet, to have a variety of partners does not necessarily preclude the possibility of having truly loving, intimate, and stable relationships.

Sexuality and values within relationships also reflect our socialization. Males in general, gay or straight, are taught to express their sexuality differently from females. Males are trained in this society to be sexually aggressive. The argument certainly can be made that "promiscuity" among gay men is more a function of socialization than gayness. If gay men are more "promiscuous" than heterosexual men, that fact might reflect the nature of male conditioning rather than gayness *per se*.

This question of gay male promiscuity has become increasingly important due largely to publicity about Acquired immune deficiency syndrome (AIDS), a condition in which the body's immune system becomes suppressed, leaving one vulnerable to a number of rare diseases (see Chapter 7). Thus, many gay men have altered their sexual behavior because of AIDS.

Originally, AIDS struck the heterosexual community in west central Africa. When it later spread to the United States, approximately three-quarters of all persons known to have AIDS were homosexual or bisexual men (hemophiliacs, and intravenous drug users were other groups with a disproportionate representation). As with other diseases or disasters which affect the gay male community, there is a "blame the victim" mentality that is not applied to other groups. For example, society does not generally place blame on children for getting measles, nor did people blame members of the American Legion for Legionnaire's disease.

Many people assume that all manner of diseases of a sexual nature are rampant among gay people. While there is an obvious connection between increased sexually transmitted diseases and having many sexual partners, it is important to point out that this phenomenon transcends sexual preference. Lesbians, as a group, have among the lowest rates of sexually transmitted diseases of any identifiable group in the population at large. Further, more and more gay men, as they became aware of the problem of AIDS, are exploring what are sometimes called "safer sex options" (see Chapter 7), which allow one to engage in sex while reducing the possibility of exchanging bodily fluids.

Safe sex doesn't mean you have to cut out everything, or even very much. The important thing is to educate yourself and your friends so you're not alone. Decide with your lovers what makes health sense and what makes nonsense. Talk in concrete terms. Set clear limits that you both respect. Then do it. You've got a team effort to find hot options for sexual expression. (Pamphlet by AIDS Action Committee, Boston.)

Historical Figures

Throughout history there have always been men and women who have experienced and acted on attractions to members of their own sex. Some theorists, therefore, maintain that there has always been "a gay culture," while others argue that sex acts are not synonymous with sexual identity. Regardless, however, of what stand one takes on this theoretical issue, we do know that, despite all manner of penalties up to and including loss of life, individuals have acted on their romantic inclinations toward others of the same sex. The following list, compiled from a number of sources, gives at best only the most incomplete sense of just how many such individuals there have been and probably how many more will never be known to us.

Sappho (c. 600 B.C.E.), Greek poet
Christina (1626-1689), Swedish queen
Madame de Stael (1766-1817), French author
Charlotte Cushman (1816-1876), U.S. actress
Gertrude Stein (1874-1946), U.S. author
Alice B. Toklas (1877-1967), U.S. author
Virginia Woolf (1882-1941), British author
Vita Sackville-West (1892-1962), British author
Bessie Smith (1894-1937), U.S. singer
Kate Millett (b. 1934), U.S. author
Janis Joplin (1943-1970), U.S. singer
Zeno of Elea (fifth century B.C.E.), Greek philosopher
Sophocles (496?-406 B.C.E.), Greek playwright
Euripedes (480?-406? B.C.E.), Greek dramatist
Socrates (470?-399 B.C.E.), Greek philosopher
Aristotle (384-322 B.C.E.), Greek philosopher
Alexander the Great (356-323 B.C.E.), Macedonian ruler
Julius Caesar (100-44 B.C.E.), Roman emperor
Hadrian (76-138 C.E.), Roman emperor
Richard the Lion-Hearted (1157-1199), British king
Richard II (1367-1400), British king
Sandro Botticelli (1444?-1510), Italian painter
Leonardo da Vinci (1452-1519), Italian painter, scientist
Julius III (1487-1555), Italian pope
Benvenuto Cellini (1500-1571), Italian goldsmith and sculptor
Francis Bacon (1561-1626), British philosopher, statesman
Christopher Marlowe (1564-1593), British playwright
James I (1566-1625), British king (commissioned *King James Bible*)
John Milton (1566-1625), British author

Jean-Baptiste Lully (1632-1687), French composer
Peter the Great (1672-1725), Russian czar
Frederick the Great (1712-1786), Prussian king
Gustavus III (1746-1792), Swedish king
Alexander von Humboldt (1769-1859), German naturalist
George Gordon, Lord Byron (1788-1824), British poet
Hans Christian Andersen (1805-1875), Danish author
Walt Whitman (1819-1892), U.S. poet
Horatio Alger (1832-1899), U.S. author
Samuel Butler (1835-1902), British author
Algernon Swinburne (1837-1909), British author
Peter Illich Tchaikovsky (1840-1893), Russian composer
Paul Verlaine (1844-1896), French poet
Arthur Rimbaud (1854-1891), French poet
Oscar Wilde (1854-1900), British playwright and author
Frederick Rolfe (Baron Corvo) (1860-1913), British author
Andre Gide (1869-1951), French author
Marcel Proust (1871-1922), French author
E.M. Forster (1879-1970), British author
John Maynard Keynes (1883-1946), British economist
Harold Nicholson (1886-1968), British author, diplomat
Ernst Rohm (1887-1934), German Nazi leader
T.E. Lawrence ("Lawrence of Arabia") (1888-1935), British soldier, author
Jean Cocteau (1889-1963), French author
Waslaw Nijinsky (1890-1950), Russian ballet dancer
Bill Tilden (1893-1953), U.S. tennis player
Christopher Isherwood (1904-1986), British author
Dag Hammarskjöld (1905-1961), Swedish U.N. secretary-general
W.H. Auden (1907-1973), British-U.S. poet
Jean Genet (1910-1986), French playwright
Tennessee Williams (1911-1983), U.S. playwright
Merle Miller (1919-1986), U.S. author
  (Wallechinsky, Wallace, and Wallace, 1977.)

Gaius Valerius Catullus (c. 84-85 B.C.E.), Roman poet
Virgil (70-19 B.C.E.), Roman poet
Horace (65-8 B.C.E.), Roman lyric poet
Albius Tibullus (55-19 B.C.E.), Roman poet
Edward II (of Caernarvon) (1284-1327), British king
Henry III (1551-1589), French king
Philip, Duc d'Orleans (1640-1701), brother of Louis XIV
Eugene of Savoy (1663-1736), Franco-Italo-Austrian general
Prince Henry of Prussia (1726-1802)

Friedrich Krupp (1854-1902), German industrialist
A.E. Housman (1859-1936), British poet
George Santayana (1863-1952), essayist, novelist
Serge Diaghileff (1872-1929), founder of modern Russian ballet
Somerset Maugham (1874-1965), British writer, playwright
Rainer Maria Rilke (1875-1926), Austro-German poet
Radclyffe Hall (1880-1943), British author
Hugh Walpole (1884-1941), New Zealand writer
Ludwig Wittgenstein (1899-1951), Austrian mathematician
   (Vern Bullough, *Homosexuality: A History*.)

Tiberius (42 B.C.E.-37 C.E.), Roman emperor
Caligula (12-41 C.E.), Roman emperor
Nero (37-68 C.E.), Roman emperor
Henry IV of Castile (1425-1472), Castilian king
Louis XIII (1601-1643), French king
   (Mitch Walker, *Men Loving Men*.)

Plato (427?-347 B.C.E.), Greek philosopher
Pope Sixtus IV (1414-1484), Italian pope
Michelangelo Buonarroti (1475-1564), Italian artist, poet
Montezuma II (1480-1520), Aztec emperor of Mexico
Nikolai Gogol (1809-1852), Russian dramatist, novelist
Camille Saint-Saens (1835-1921), French composer
Federico Garcia Lorca (1894-1936), Spanish poet, dramatist
   (Erwin J. Haeberle, *Sex Atlas*.)

Alexander Hamilton (1758-1804), U.S. statesman
Ralph Waldo Emerson (1803-1882), U.S. poet, philosopher
Margaret Fuller (1810-1850), U.S. feminist, writer, educator
Henry David Thoreau (1817-1862), U.S. writer
Herman Melville (1819-1891), U.S. novelist
Edward Carpenter (1844-1929), British author, gay rights pioneer
Magnus Hirschfeld (1868-1935), German sexologist, gay rights pioneer
Willa Cather (1873-1947), U.S. novelist
   (Jonathan Katz, *Gay American History*.)

Colette (1873-1954), French author, actress
Romaine Brooks (1874-1970), U.S. painter
Renee Vivien (1877-1909), British poet
Natalie Clifford Barney (1878-1972), U.S. author
   (Dolores Klaich, *Woman + Woman: Attitudes Towards Lesbianism*.)
All the above names were taken from Human Rights Foundation, Inc.

James Baldwin, U.S. writer
Rock Hudson, U.S. actor
Rita Mae Brown, U.S. writer
Martina Navratilova, U.S. tennis player
Leonard Bernstein, U.S. conductor, composer
Barney Frank, U.S congressman
Gerry Studds, U.S. congressman
Elaine Noble, U.S. state legislator

Conclusion

Sex becomes a means of access both to the life of the body and the life of the species. (Foucault.)

The requirement that there shall be a single kind of sexual life for everyone disregards the dissimilarities, whether innate or acquired, in the sexual constitution of human beings; it cuts off a fair number of them from sexual enjoyment, and so becomes the source of serious injustice. (Freud, p. 51.)

Homosexuality did not come to be considered a separate category until the 1860s and as a term had very little general usage before the 1880s. It was types of behavior, not persons, that were punishable by law. Beginning in the 19th century, however, we begin to see the evolution of the concept of a *condition*, a state of mind distinct from individual activities.

There is no question that the appearance in nineteenth-century psychiatry, jurisprudence, and literature of a whole series of discourses on the species and sub-species of homosexuality, inversion, pederasty, and "psychic hermaphrodism" made possible a strong advance of social controls into this area of "personality"; but it also made possible the formation of a "reverse" discourse: that its legitimacy or "naturality" be acknowledged, often in the same vocabulary, using the same categories by which it was radically disqualified. (Foucault.)

Thus, "where there is power, there is also resistance." This is true not just for that group which defines itself as homosexual, but also for women who began during this period to struggle within a context established by the newly emerging women's movement in opposition to how their husbands and doctors were defining them. This was the era of new sexual categorizations, not simply for the homosexual, but also for the "masturbating child," the "hysterical woman," the "perverse adult," the "congenital prostitute," the "degenerate," the "innate criminal." And with the explosion of these new sexual categories arose the field of sex research which attempted to explore them.

Our culture has, as we have seen, developed a concept of sexuality that is linked to reproduction and genitality but these notions are neither innate nor universal from one culture to another. Thus, sex and sexuality are the products of certain historical circumstances and part of an ideology which seeks to organize and unify the various possibilities for sexual pleasure. Such categories serve not ony to delineate appropriate behavior from inappropriate and to separate people from each other, but also to control the behavior in question.

This concept of sexuality has significant ramifications for all people, not just homosexuals. In particular, to reject the "essentialist" view of sex (that is, believing that sexuality has only one essential character) is to challenge the orthodox model of the nuclear family as necessary and sufficient to any appropriate sexual model. It is also to reject strict definitions of masculinity and femininity. In addition, it is to reject the notion (defended by Freud and others) that sexual repression is essential in preserving social order and stability. It is instead to argue, as does Jeffrey Weeks:

> The struggle for sexual self-definition is a struggle in the end for control over our bodies. To establish this control we must escape from those ideologies and categorizations which imprison us within the existing social order. (Weeks, p. 20.)

This chapter can only begin to scratch the surface in its picture of the tremendous diversity in gay people's lives. We have seen that lesbians and gays are single and in every sort of relationship, parents and non-parents, political and apolitical, old and young, of all races, classes, and ethnic groups. We have seen that, though many of the stereotypes people hold about lesbians and gay males may contain some grain of truth, none of them gives an accurate picture of the enormous variety of gay lifestyles. In fact, some commentators have suggested that the *only* thing gays have in common is an attraction for their own sex.

Homosexuality as a cultural phenomenon is not simply a behavior, but rather a way of being. As such, it is produced by historical circumstances. Gay life prior to the Stonewall Riots was primarily organized around the need for survival; after Stonewall, however, gay "liberation" became the catchword, involving self-affirmation and assertion rather than mere survival.

It is sometimes said that we fear that which we do not understand, that it is the mysteriousness of what is "other than" that provokes our fear of it. If this is the case, then social taboos about homosexuality can only serve to increase homophobia and to deepen people's fears about it. But:

> It requires something more than personal experience to gain a philosophy

or point of view from any specific event. It is the quality of our response to the event and our capacity to enter into the lives of others that help to make their lives and experiences our own. (Goldman, p. 386.)

To enter into those lives requires that we look at the lives of actual gays and lesbians, hear their stories, and look at the context in which those lives occur. Or, as Jonathan Katz has noted:

All homosexuality is situational, influenced and given meaning and character by its location in time and social space. Future research and analysis must focus as much on this conditioning situation as on the same-sex relations occurring within it. (Katz, p. 11.)

REFERENCES

Altman, Dennis. *The Homosexualization of America*. N.Y.: St. Martin's Press, 1982.

Barnhart, E. "Friends and Lovers in a Lesbian Counterculture Community." In *Old Family/New Family*, N. Glazer Malbin, ed. N.Y.: Van Nostrand Press, 1975.

de Beauvoir, Simone. *The Second Sex*. New York: Alfred A. Knopf, 1953.

Beck, Evelyn Torton. "Why Is This Book Different From All Other Books." In *Nice Jewish Girls*, Evelyn Torton Beck, ed., new edition. Boston: Beacon Press, 1989.

Brody, Jane. "Study Finds Some Homosexuals are Happier than Heterosexuals." *New York Times*, July 9, 1978, p. 22.

Bronski, Michael. *Culture Clash: The Making of Gay Sensibility*. Boston: South End Press, 1984.

Calder-Marshall, Arthur. *Havelock Ellis*. London: Rupert Hart-Davis, 1959.

Cameron, Barbara, "We Are Named by Others and We Are Named by Ourselves," in *This Bridge Called My Back: Writings by Radical Women of Color*. Cherrie Moraga, and Gloria Anzaldua, eds. Watertown, Massachusetts: Persephone Press, 1981.

Chauncey, George, Jr. "The Way We Were." *The Village Voice*, July 1, 1986.

Comfort, Alex. *The Anxiety Makers*. London 1968.

Cooper, Kenneth J. "Some Oppose Foster Placement with Gay Couple." *Boston Globe*, May 8, 1985.

Coote, Stephen. *The Penguin Book of Homosexual Verse*. New York: Viking Penguin, Inc., 1983.

Cruikshank, Margaret, ed. *The Lesbian Path*. Monterey, CA: Angel Press, 1980.

Feingold, Michael. *The Village Voice*, June 14, 1980.

Federman, Lillian. *Surpassing the Love of Men*. N.Y.: William Morrow, 1981.

Ferguson, Caroline. "A Long Struggle." In *Lesbian Path*, ed. Margaret Cruikshank, Monterey, California: Angel Press, 1980.

Finkelhon, David. *Child Sexual Abuse: New Theory and Research*. New York: The Free Press, 1984.

Foucault, Michel. *A History of Sexuality* Vol. I. London: Vintage, 1979.

Freud, Sigmund. *Civilization and Its Discontents*, James Strachey, trans. N.Y.: W.W. Norton, 1961.

Gay Left Collective, ed. *Homosexuality: Power and Politics*. London: Alison & Busby, 1980.

Grahn, Judy. *Another Mother Tongue*. Boston: Beacon, 1984.

Goldman, Emma. *Red Emma Speaks*, N.Y.: Random House, 1972.

Gebhard, P., et al. *Sex Offenders: An Analysis of Types*. N.Y.: Harper and Row, 1965.

Groth, N., and Birnbaum, J. "Adult Sexual Orientation and the Attraction to Underage Persons." *Archives of Sexual Behavior* (1978).

Hollibaugh, Amber. "Right to Rebel." In *Homosexuality: Power and Politics*. H. Montgomery, Gay Left Collective, ed. London: Allison and Busby, 1980, pp. 205-215.

Human Rights Foundation, Inc., *Demystifying Homosexuality: A Teaching Guide About Lesbians and Gay Men*, New York: Irvington Publishers, Inc., 1984.

Humphries, Laud, and Miller, Brian. "Identities in the Emerging Gay Culture." In *Homosexual Behavior: A Modern Reappraisal*, Judd Marmor, ed., N.Y.: Basic Books, pp. 142-156.

Hyde. *Famous Trials: Oscar Wilde*. Baltimore, Md.: Penguin Books, 1962.

Jaffa, A.C. et al. "Sexual Abuse of Children: An Epidemiologic Study." *American Journal of Disabled Children* 129 (6) 1975, pp. 689-692.

Jay, Karla. "No Man's Land." In *Lavender Culture*. Karla Jay and Allen Young, eds. N.Y.: Jove, 1979

Kaplan, Justin. *Walt Whitman: A Life*. N.Y.: Simon and Schuster, 1980.

Katz, Jonathan. *Gay American History: Lesbians and Gay Men in the U.S.A.* New York: Avon Books, 1976.

Katz, Jonathan. *Gay/Lesbian Almanac: A New Documentary*. New York: Colophon Books, 1983.

Kelly, James. "Homosexuality and Aging." In *Homosexual Behavior: A Modern Reappraisal*, Judd Marmor, ed. N.Y.: Basic Books, 1980, pp. 176-193.

Kluckhohn, C. *Culture and Behavior*. N. Y.: Free Press, 1962.

Lindsey, Karen. *Friends as Family*. Boston: Beacon Press, 1981.

Lorde, Audre. "The Master's Tools Will Never Dismantle the Master's House." In *This Bridge Called My Back: Writings by Radical Women of Color*, edited by Cherrie Moraga and Gloria Anzaldua. Watertown, Mass.: Persephone Press, 1981

Miller, Judith Ann, Jacobsen, R. Brooke, and Bigner, Jerry J. *Journal of Homosexuality* (1981) 7 (1): 49-56.

Mitzel, John. *Fag Rag*. No. 20. Boston.

Moraga, Cherrie, and Anzaldua, Gloria, eds. *This Bridge Called My Back: Writings by Radical Women of Color*. Watertown, Mass.: Persephone Press, 1981.

Moroney, R. "Note from the Editor." *Urban and Social Change Review* (1978) 2.

Moschkovich, Judith. "But I Know You American Woman." In *This Bridge Called My Back: Writings by Radical Women of Color*, edited by Cherrie Moraga and Gloria Anzaldua. Watertown, Mass.: Persephone Press, 1981.

Newton, David E. "Homosexual Behavior and Child Molestation: *A Journal of Adolescence*, Vol. XIII, No. 49, Spring 1978, pp. 29-43.

Nichols, John. *The Journals of Lady Anne Halkert*. New York: Johnson Reprint Co., 1965.

Peplau, Letita Anne. "What Homosexuals Want," In *Human Sexuality*. Dushkin Publishing Co., 1983/1984, pp. 201-207.

Peplau, Letita Anne, *The Gay Report: Lesbians and Gay Men Speak Out about Sexual Experiences and Lifestyles*, Karla Jay and Allen Young, eds. N.Y.: Simon and Schuster, 1979.

Ponse, Barbara. "Lesbians and Their Worlds." In *Homosexual Behavior: A Modern Reappraisal*, Judd Marmor, ed. N.Y.: Basic Books, 1980, pp. 157-175.

Rainwater, L. *Behind Ghetto Walls: Black Families in a Federal Slum*. Chicago: Aldine Publishing, 1970.

Ramey, J. "Experimental Family Forms—The Family of the Future." *Marriage and Family* (1978) 1: 1-9.

Robinson, Paul. "Invisible Man." *New Republic*, June 3, 1978.

Rowbotham, Sheila. *Hidden from History*. London: Pluto Press, 1973.

Sarafino, E.P. "An Estimate of Nationwide Incidence of Sexual Offenses Against Children." *Child Welfare* 57 (2) 127-134, 1979.

Sontag, Susan. *Against Interpretation*. New York: Dell, 1969.

Tanner, D.M. *The Lesbian Couple*. Lexington, Mass.: Lexington Books, 1978.

Taylor, V. "Review Essays of Four Books on Lesbianism." *Journal of Marriage and the Family* (1980) 42: 224-228.

Voeller, Bruce. "Society and the Gay Movement." In *Homosexual Behavior: A Modern Reappraisal*, Judd Marmor, ed. N.Y.: Basic Books, 1980, pp. 232-252.

Walker, Alice, ed. "What White Publishers Won't Print." In *I Love Myself When I Am Laughing: A Zora Neale Hurston Reader*. New York: The Feminist Press, 1979.

Wasserstrom, Richard. "Is Adultery Immoral?" In *Philosophy and Sex*, Robert Baker and Frederick Elliston, eds. Buffalo, N.Y.: Prometheus Books, 1984, pp. 93-106.

Weeks, Jeffrey. "Capitalism and the Organization of Sex." In *Homosexuality: Power and Politics*. Gay Left Collective, ed. London: Allison and Busby, 1980, pp. 11-20.

Whitman, Walt. "Song of Myself." In *Leaves of Grass*, edited by Gay Wilson. Allen, NY: Signet Books, 1955.

Wolfgang, M.E., and Ferracuti, F. *The Subculture of Violence*. London: Tavistock, 1967.

Further Readings

Ackland, Valentine. *For Sylvia: An Honest Account*. New York: Norton Books, 1986.

Adelman, Marcy, ed. *Long Time Passing: Lives of Older Lesbians*. Boston: Alyson Publications, 1986.

Alpert, Harriet, editor. *We Are Everywhere: Writings by and about Lesbian Parents*. Freedom, Calif.: The Crossing Press, 1988.

Baker, Michael. *Our Three Selves: The Life of Radclyffe Hall*. New York: William Morrow and Company, 1985.

Baldwin, James. *The Price of the Ticket: Collected Non-Fiction 1947-1985*. New York: St. Martin's Press, 1985.

Carpenter, Humphrey. *W.H. Auden: A Biography*. New York: Houghton-Mifflin, 1983.

Cavitch, David. *My Soul and I: The Inner Life of Walt Whitman*. Boston: Beacon Press, 1985.

Christian, Barbara. *Black Feminist Criticism: Perspective on Black Women Writers*. New York: Pergamon Press, 1985.

Cruikshank, Margaret. *Lesbian Studies: Present and Future*. Old Westbury, N.Y.: The Feminist Press, 1982.

Deacon, Richard. *The Cambridge Apostles: A History of Cambridge University's Elite Intellectual Secret Society*. New York: Farrar, Straus, and Giroux, 1986.

De-la Noy, Michael, ed. *The Journal of Denton Welch*. New York: Dutton, 1985

Dynes, Wayne R. *Homosexuality: A Research Guide*. New York: Garland Publishing, 1987.

Farnan, Dorothy J. *Auden in Love*. New York: Simon and Schuster, 1984.

Fido, Martin. *Oscar Wilde: An Illustrated Biography*. New York: Peter Bedrick Books, 1985.

Fone, Byrne R.S., ed. *Hidden Heritage: History and the Gay Imagination*. New York: Irvington Publishers, 1981.

Foster, Jeanette H. *Sex Variant Women in Literature*. Tallahassee, Fla.: Naiad Press, 1985.

Foucault, Michel. *Death and the Labyrinth: The World of Raymond Roussel*. New York: Doubleday, 1986.

Galloway, David, and Sabisch, Christian. *Calamus: Male Homosexuality in Twentieth-Century Literature, an International Anthology*. New York: Quill, 1982.

Gill, John, trans. *Erotic Poems from the Greek Anthology*. Trumansburg, N.Y.: The Crossing Press, 1986.

Grier, Barbara. *The Lesbian in Literature*. Tallahassee, Fla.: Naiad Press, 1981.

Grobel, Lawrence. *Conversations with Capote*. New York: New American Library, 1985.

Hart-Davis, Rupert, ed. *More Letters of Oscar Wilde*. New York: The Vanguard Press, 1985.

Hemmings, Susan. *A Wealth of Experience: The Lives of Older Women*. London: Pandora Press, 1985.

Hession, Charles. *John Maynard Keynes: A Personal Biography of the Man Who Revolutionized Capitalism and the Way We Live*. New York: Macmillan Publishing Co., 1984.

Hodges, Andrew. *Alan Turing: The Enigma*. New York: Simon and Schuster, 1983.

Hudson, Rock, and Davidson, Sara. *Rock Hudson: His Story*. New York: William Morrow and Company, 1986.

Hyde, H. Montgomery. *Lord Alfred Douglas*. New York: Dodd, Mead and Company, 1985.

Hyde, Mary, ed. *Bernard Shaw and Alfred Douglas: A Correspondence*. New York: Ticknor and Field, 1982.

Jullion, Jeanne. *Long Way Home: The Odyssey of a Lesbian Mother and Her Children*. Pittsburgh: Cleis Press, 1985.

Kellogg, Stuart, ed. *Essays on Gay Literature*. New York: Harrington Park, 1985.

Kirk, Kris, and Heath, Ed. *Men in Frocks*. London: Gay Men's Press, 1984.

Lewis, Sasha Gregory. *Sunday's Women: A Report on Lesbian Lifestyles Today*. Boston: Beacon Press, 1979.

Martin, Robert K. *The Homosexual Tradition in American Poetry*. Austin: University of Texas Press, 1979.

Martin, Del, and Lyon, Phyllis. *Lesbian Woman*. New York: Bantam, 1972.

Miller, Neil. *In Search of Gay America: Women and Men in a Time of Change*. New York: Atlantic Monthly Press, 1989.

Ormrod, Richard. *Una Troubridge: The Friend of Radclyffe Hall*. New York: Carroll and Graf Publishers, 1985.

Pollack, Sandra, and Vaugh, Jeanne. *Politics of the Heart: A Lesbian Parenting Anthology*. Ithaca, N.Y.: Doubleday and Co., Inc., 1986.

Rader, Dotson. *Tennessee: Cry of the Heart*. New York: Doubleday, 1985.

Richardson, Major-General Frank M. *Mars without Venus: A Study of Some Homosexual Generals*. Edinburgh: William Blackwood, 1982.

Rofes, Eric, ed. *Gay Life: Leisure, Love, and Living for the Contemporary Gay Man*. Garden City, N.Y.: Doubleday and Co., Inc., 1986.

Rorem, Ned. *The Paris and New York Diaries of Ned Rorem*. San Francisco: North Point Press, 1984.

Rule, Jane. *Lesbian Images*. New York: Doubleday, 1975.

Russo, Vito. *The Celluloid Closet: Homosexuality in the Movies*. New York: Harper and Row, 1981.

Sarotte, Georges-Michel. *Like a Brother, Like a Lover: Male Homosexuality in the American Novel and Theater from Herman Melville to James Baldwin*. Garden City, N.Y.: Anchor Press, Doubleday, 1978.

Sedgwick, Eve Kosofsky. *Between Men: English Literature and Male Homosocial Desire*. New York: Columbia University Press, 1985.

Skidelsky, Robert. *John Maynard Keynes: Hopes Betrayed 1883-1920*. New York: Viking, 1986.

Smith, Jane S. *Elsie de Wolfe: A Life in the High Style*. New York: Atheneum, 1982.

Spoto, Donald. *The Kindness of Strangers: The Life of Tennessee Williams*. Boston: Little, Brown and Company, 1985.

Stein, Gertrude, and Toklas, Alice B. *Dear Sammy: Letters from Gertrude Stein and Alice B. Toklas*, Samuel M. Steward, ed. Boston: Houghton-Mifflin, 1977.

Troubridge, Una. *The Life and Death of Radclyffe Hall*. London: Hammond, 1961.

Tyler, Parker. *Screening the Sexes: Homosexuality in the Movies*. New York: Holt, Rinehart, and Winston, 1972.

Uhrig, Larry. *The Two of Us: Affirming, Celebrating and Symbolizing Gay and Lesbian Relationships*. Boston: Alyson Publications, 1985.

White, Edmund. *States of Desire: Travels in Gay America*. New York: E.P. Dutton, 1980.

Wolff, Cynthia Griffin. *Emily Dickinson*. New York: Alfred A. Knopf, 1986.

Woolf, Virginia. *The Letters of Virginia Woolf*. Vols. 1-5. New York: Harcourt Brace Jovanovich, 1975-1979.

Chapter 9

Literature

There is no way that a chapter, particularly one so brief, could do justice to the amazing richness and tremendous diversity of gay and lesbian literature. This tradition extends back more than 4500 years in references on papyrus to same-sex practices in Egypt. The ancient Sumerians' epic poem "The Story of Gilgamesh" is a love story between the hero Gilgamesh and his male friend Enkidu. The literature of the ancient Greeks is full of many overt references to homosexual relationships between gods as well as mortals, including the king of all the gods, Zeus, and his young lover Ganymede. There are also stories of Apollo and Hyacinthus, Dionysius and Achilles, Pan and Daphnis, Hermes and Perseus, and Heracles and Eurystheus. Poets such as Ovid, Homer, and Hesiod wrote formally of male same-sex relationships. The philosopher Plato in the *Symposium* glorifies love between men. The writings of Greek poet Sappho, one of the finest lyric poets in Western literature, contain many references to her love for women. In addition, Middle Eastern, Indian, and Asian sources have also recognized and honored homosexual love, even at times above heterosexual.

But it wasn't until the latter part of the 19th century that literature that was self-consciously homosexual emerged. Up until that time there was no unified and extensive "homosexual identity" and views about homosexual "practices" varied greatly. Christopher Marlowe's *Edward II*, Mary Wollstonecraft Shelley's *Mary, A Fiction*, poems of Lord Byron, Alfred Lord Tennyson, and scattered other readings of the early modern period do deal with homosexuality as a theme but such works are rare.

What follows is an outline of some of this literature of the last two centuries. But even within this restricted time period, there is still far too much to be covered in so short a space. Those readers interested in pursuing these sources more earnestly should consult the list of further readings or one or more of the excellent bibliographies devoted to this topic. We suggest several:

Grier, Barbara. *The Lesbian in Literature*, an outgrowth of *The Ladder*, a lesbian magazine published from 1956-1972. This book contains over 7000 entries and is regularly updated for new or newly discovered entries.

Galloway, David and Christian Sabisch. *Calamus: Male Homosexuals in 20th-Century Literature*.

Martin, Robert, *The Homosexual Tradition in American Poetry*.

Coote, Stephen. *The Penguin Book of Homosexual Verse*.

Rule, Jane. *Lesbian Images*.

Levin, James. *The Gay Novel*.

The problems in compiling a list of "gay literature" are not limited to space constraints. If that were the case, it would be easy to mention a few titles, and urge interested readers to pursue the rest independently. There is, in addition, the deeper theoretical question of what selections should "count" as part of the gay and lesbian tradition in literature. Should we include works by lesbian and gay authors if their content does not include any homosexual characters or themes? Some might argue, for example, that being gay or lesbian is automatically to participate in "gay culture" or a "gay sensibility," so any text written by a lesbian or gay man—no matter what its content—will offer a different perspective from that of mainstream authors. Others will maintain that being gay or lesbian is different only in the fact of one's choice of love object, and thus there is no *a priori* difference in (or even meaning to) a "homosexual" or "heterosexual" perspective.

Further, should we include works with minor homosexual characters? Should we include only works whose portrayals of gay characters and gay lifestyles are positive? Should we include works which may have "homoerotic" themes though there are no overtly homosexual sexual relationships between the characters? The previous chapter, for example, discussed the phenomenon of "Boston marriages" or "romantic friendships" which existed between women in the 18th and 19th centuries. These friendships were probably not sexual though the women involved in them may have been lifelong partners. Should stories of these couplings be part of a lesbian or gay tradition in literature? What about the poetry of Walt Whitman to which the author explicitly denied any homoerotic content?

Surely we cannot date gay literature with the dawn of gay liberation. To do so would not only dismiss an enormous body of material relevant to our interests but also treat events as occurring in a vacuum. And to limit our survey to positive portrayals of gay life would also ignore much of the literature of the late 19th and early 20th centuries, where it was common for protagonists to end in suicide or self-hatred. For example, one of the classics of lesbian literature, Radclyffe Hall's *The Well of Loneliness* (1928), ends with its lesbian hero Stephen manipulating her lover into the arms of an adoring male suitor. Thus, insofar as literature is as much a part of its time as is anything else, we cannot divorce our understanding of it from general attitudes—both popular and scientific—toward homosexuality at a given period of history.

Given these words of caution, our survey begins in earnest in the 19th century. There were many more works dealing with male homosexuality than lesbianism, and this imbalance is largely due to the invisibility of lesbianism and the general ignorance of and disregard for women's sexuality. Today, there are many more literary works dealing with lesbian themes. But because these two traditions have developed independently, this survey deals separately with literature for gay men and for lesbians.

For the most part, 19th-century literature contains only the most veiled and indirect references to sexuality; sexual indiscretions of any sort were severely punished as "sinful," for example, Nathaniel Hawthorne's Hester Prynne in *The Scarlet Letter*, and Tess in Thomas Hardy's *Tess of the D'Urbervilles*.

> In 19th century British and American writings, it is almost impossible to find a single direct description of male homosexual behavior. (Levin, p. 8.)

Oddly enough, this was less so a century earlier.

Gay Male Literature

In 1899, the first American novel to mention overt sexual relations between males appeared. *A Marriage Below Zero*, written by Alfred J. Cohen under the pseudonym of Chester Allan Dale, is a cautionary tale written as a first person narrative. In it, Elsie Bouverie Ravener warns her female readers to beware of marrying men with homosexual tendencies. The book ends with its homosexual protagonist dead of a drug overdose, the first of many such deaths in novels with gay characters.

Imre: A Memorandum, written and privately published in 1908 by Edward I. Prime-Stevenson under the pseudonym of Xavier Mayne, was the first in an opposite genre of gay fiction, that of seeking to justify homosexual behavior. Though it suffers from awkward fiction, it did seek to mention famous gays, rejected stereotypes, and saw homosexuality as congenital and hence no danger to society. In this sense, it mouthed many of the same arguments for civil rights of homosexuals that were current in supporters like Ulrichs and Ellis.

Homosexuality is a central theme in Henry Blake Fuller's *Bertram Cope's Year*. But despite greater acceptance in the 1920s of sexuality as a theme in novels, still there is little mention of homosexuality. Controversy developed over the "homoerotic" content in Sherwood Anderson's *Winesburg, Ohio* and Carl van Vechter's *The Blind Bat*.

In the 1930s, there was less reticence about sexuality, but still little appeared dealing with homosexuality. One reason may have been that writers chose to focus on social themes (e.g., poverty) during the depression era. But several novelists did produce works with clear homosexual themes: Blair Niles's panorama of gay life of New York, *Stranger Brother* (1931); Andre Tellier's *Twilight Men* (1931); Myron Brinig's *This Man is My Brother* (1932); Richard Meeker's *Better Angel* (1932); Charles Henri Ford and Parker Tyler's *The Young and the Evil* (1933); Kennilworth Bruce's *Goldie* (1933); Lew Levinson's *Butterfly Man* (1934); Daphne Greenwood's *Apollo Sleeps* (1937); James Cain's *Serenade* (1937); and one of the best-known of this period, Djuna Barnes's *Nightwood* (1937) which dealt with lesbianism as a main theme. Few of these works portrayed homosexuality uncritically. There is a tragic ending for the protagonist in *This Man is My Brother*, and in *Better Angel* we get a negative picture of gay social life. Yet in both *The Young and the Evil* and *Goldie*, in particular, there is less stress on gender confusion (a popular theme at the time) and a discussion of the importance of civil liberties for gays.

The late 1930s were preoccupied with wartime activities and from 1939-1945 only one novel appears in which homosexuality is the central theme: Harlan D. McIntosh, *This Finer Shadow*. Its treatment of the topic is typical of this period: it warns of the decadence of public gay life, views homosexuality as a confusion of gender identity, recommends sexual abstinence for those with homosexual tendencies, and presents death as the usual end to a homosexual lifestyle.

During the postwar period, some homosexual rights groups were forming. Though most were small and secretive, this was a signal of some change in awareness. Further, the *Kinsey Report* of 1948 described sexual practices in the United States in a nonjudgmental fashion. The report also maintained that homosexuality was not a "condition" *per se* but rather part of a sexual continuum. In addition, the post-war economic boom and increased mobility enabled more lesbians and gay men to find each other. Novels of this period are more accurate in their treatment of homosexuality and in their portrayal of gay social life. Richard Brooks's *The Brick Foxhole* (1945) was the first to link homophobia with racism and anti-Semitism. In it an interior decorator is murdered and the reader feels sympathy toward the victim. Charles Jackson's *Fall of Valour* (1946) chronicles the gradually dawning homosexual awareness of a married man in his 40s.

There were important novels in 1947: Vance Bourjailly's *The End of My Life*, John Horne Burns' *The Gallery*, Calder Willingham's *End as a Man*, and Stuart Engstrand's *The Sling and the Arrow*.

In 1948, Gore Vidal's *The City and the Pillar* received the widest public circulation of the time, and the novel is still widely read today. Although depressing in tone, his men are not confused about their gender identity. In 1948, Norman Mailer's *The Naked and the Dead* and Truman Capote's *Other Voices, Other Rooms* appeared. Ward Thomas's *Stranger in the Land* (1949) stressed the effects of oppression on the homosexual, connecting it to other forms of oppression ("the invert must copy from the Negro and the Jew all their tricks of survival in the stronghold of white Nordic supremacy.") [pp. 188-89.] Less positive portraits are Nial Kent's *The Divided Path* and Michael de Forrest's *The Gay Year*.

Eugene MacGown's *The Siege of Innocence* (1950) has several homosexual characters and presents a casual, nonjudgmental treatment of homosexuality. James Barr's *Quatrefoil* has become a "classic" in the homosexual subculture, though initially it received very little general attention.

With the 1950s came a decline in social tolerance, the Cold War, and "McCarthyism." Novels about homosexuality that appeared during this time reflect these more repressive changes. More specifically, out of the nine homosexual protagonists in the novels that appeared in 1951, there were 3 suicides, 1 untimely death, and 3 desperately unhappy lives. There were also historical novels about homosexuality including Mary Renault's *The Last of the Wine* which dealt with the Greece of Socrates and Plato, and Norah Loft's *The Lute Player* whose focus is Richard I of England. Two books, Loren Wahl's *The Invisible Glass* (1951) and Ralph Leveridge's *Walk on the Water* (1951) used the war as background for their treatment of homosexuality. Fritz Peters's *Finistere* was the most widely read novel within the gay community that year.

Wilma Prezzi's *Dark Desires*, Vin Packer's *Whisper His Sin*, and Jean Evan's *Three Men* all appeared in 1953 and were all uniformly negative in their portrayals. Margaret Millar's *Beast in View* (1955) is an almost unbelievably negative picture of a gay man.

In 1956, at least 5 works by homosexual authors appeared in print. Though far less negative than others, they still tended to be defensive rather than affirming. They were: James Baldwin's *Giovanni's Room*, James Barr's *The Occasional Man*, Jay Little's *Somewhere Between the Two*, Gerald Tesch's, *Never the Same Again*, and Gore Vidal's *The Judgment of Paris*. The decade ended with a more positive picture, 1959's *Sam*, by Lonnie Coleman.

In the late 1940s and 1950s a literary counterpoint to the social conservatism occurred among a small group of poets and novelists in San Francisco's North Beach section. Called the "beats," they rebelled against middle-class values and experimented sexually. Poet Allen Ginsberg's *Howl* (1955) gave this movement a decidedly gay voice with its joyous celebration of homosexuality, taking it out of the realm of deviance.

Early novels of 1960 and 1961 continued the generally negative, heavily psychoanalytic perspective of the 1950s (e.g., Alexander Federoff's *This Side of the Angels*). There were a few exceptions like, for example, Christopher Isherwood's *Down There on a Visit*, set in Europe and Hollywood, which gave a positive treatment of homosexuality. But the 1960s could not long fail to be affected by the activism (particularly from the Women's and Black Liberation movements) of this time. In particular, James Baldwin's *Another Country* (1962) was way ahead of his time for its positive portrayal of homosexual relationships. Indeed, so positive was the picture of same-sex love that critics were furious. John Rechy's *City of Night* (1963) made the best-seller list for that year and dealt with street hustlers. Christopher Isherwood's *A Single Man* "arguably one of the very finest books ever written about male homosexuality in the U.S." (Levin, p. 240) appeared in 1964. In addition, Sanford Friedman's *Totempole*, Donald Nindham's *Two People*, Gore Vidal's *Myra Breckinridge*, and John Toriolan's *A Sand Fortress*, all in 1965, were frank in their treatments of sex, and progress in their questioning of sex roles and stereotypes.

In the early 1970s, directly following the Stonewall rebellion, there was less focus on fiction. But major works still appeared. The detective novels of Joseph Hansen including *Fadeout* featured a gay detective, David Brandsetter. Isabel Holland's *The Man Without a Face* is a very positive account of homosexual life written for adolescents.

Patricia Nell Warren's *The Front Runner* (1974) and Laura Hobson's *Consenting Adult* (1975) are both more openly political, dealing with the effects of homophobia.

1978's *Dancer from the Dance* by Andrew Holleran and *Faggots* by Larry Kramer are both dismal pictures of gay social life.

Lesbian Literature

Lesbian literature has evolved in very different ways from literature for gay males. Specifically, it has been more recent, partly because women's sexuality was unacknowledged until fairly recently, partly because fiction has tended to focus on men's lives with women playing subordinate roles. In addition, the existence of lesbian literature, like other forms of lesbian culture, has been very much a part of the women's movement of the 1960s.

Jane Rule tells the story of critics' reaction to her first novel in 1964. "Perhaps a little too frank," one wrote. "[It] almost makes it [lesbianism] seem desirable," said another. "But all the time you keep turning to the photograph of the author on the jacket and wondering how such a nice looking woman could ever have chosen so distasteful a subject." (Quoted in *Lesbian Images*, p. 1.)

Radclyffe Hall's (1886-1943) *The Well of Loneliness*, a classic lesbian novel, was published in 1928. A lesbian herself, she wanted to educate the public about lesbianism to show that "inversion was as natural an orientation as left-handedness." The first printing included a sympathetic introduction written by sexologist Havelock Ellis. Yet, despite its sympathetic treatment, the book defends rigid sex roles, never questions men's right to power, and portrays women as silly and inferior.

Other writers dealing with lesbianism include Gertrude Stein (1874-1946), Willa Cather (1876-1947), Vita Sackville-West (1892-1962), Ivy Compton-Burnett (1892-1969), Colette (1873-1954), Violette Leduc (1907-1972), and May Sarton (1912-   ).

In 1971, Alma Routsong, whose reputation as a novelist was already established under her own name, published *Patience and Sarah* (original title: *A Place for Us*) under the name Isabel Miller and it became a major lesbian novel. This work, dealing with the eventual relationship and "marriage" of two women, is a graceful love story which assumes that the only impediments to lesbian love are social prejudices.

Charlotte Wolff's *Love Between Women* (1972) is lauded as the first really sympathetic and fair treatment of lesbians.

Author Jane Rule has written many lesbian novels, including *Against the Season* (1971), *Contract with the World* (1980), *The Desert of the Heart* (1964), and *This is Not for You* (1982).

Valerie Taylor is another highly published lesbian author. Her works include *The Girls in 3-B* (1963), *Journey to Fulfillment* (1964), *Love Image* (1977), *Return to Lesbos* (1964), *Stranger on Lesbos* (1960), *Unlike Others* (1963), *Whisper Their Love* (1957), *A World Without Men* (1963).

Today fiction dealing with the lives of gays and lesbians abounds. This brief outline can only suggest some of the history out of which these novels have evolved. Following is a list of some of the fiction dealing with these topics.

BIBLIOGRAPHY

Fiction

(Code: L = Lesbian, G = Gay Male, LG = Lesbian/Gay, Y = Younger Readers, I = Issues of Gender Without Specifically Being Gay or Lesbian, M = Mystery, S = Science Fiction, F = General Fiction, N = Non-Fiction)

Ackroyd, Peter, *The Last Testament of Oscar Wilde*, New York, Harper and Row, 1983 (GF)

Aldridge, Sarah, *Misfortune's Friend*, Tallahassee, FL, Naiad Press, 1985 (LF)

————, *The Late Corner*, Tallahassee, FL, Naiad Press, 1982 (LF)

————, *Tottie: The Tale of the Sixties*, Tallahassee, FL, Naiad Press, 1980 (LF)

————, *Cytherea's Breath*, Tallahassee, FL, Naiad Press, 1982 (LF)

————, *All True Lovers*, Tallahassee, FL, Naiad Press, 1978 (LF)

Aldyne, Nathan, *Vermillion*, New York, Avon, 1980 (GF)

————, *Slate*, New York, Ballantine, 1985 (GF)

————, *Cobalt*, New York, Ballantine, 1986 (GF)

Allard, Jeannine, *The Legend*, Boston, Alyson Publications, 1984, (LF)

Alther, Lisa, *Other Women*, New York, Alfred A. Knopf, 1984

————, *Kin Flicks*, New York, New American Library, 1977

————, *Original Sins*, New York, Alfred A. Knopf, 1981

Anzaldua, Gloria, *Borderlands/La Frontera*, New York, Inland (LF)

Arnold, Jane, *Sister Gin*, London, The Women's Press, 1987 (LF)

————, *The Cook and the Carpenter*, (LF)

Baldwin, James, *Giovanni's Room*, New York, Dial Press, 1956 (GF)

————, *Another Country*, New York, Dell, 1985 (GF)

————, *Evidence of Things Not Seen*, New York, Holt, Rinehart and Winston, 1985 (GN)

Bannon, Anne, *Beebo Brinker*, Tallahassee, FL, Naiad Press, 1983 (LF)

————, *I Am a Woman*, Tallahassee, FL, Naiad Press, 1983 (LF)

————, *Odd Girl Out*, Tallahassee, FL, Naiad Press, 1983 (LF)

————, *Journey to a Woman*, Tallahassee, FL, Naiad Press, 1983 (LF)

————, *Woman in the Shadows*, Tallahassee, FL, Naiad Press, 1983 (LF)

Barger, Gary W., *What Happened to Mr. Forster?*, New York, Clarion, 1981 (YGF)

Barnes, Djuna, *Nightwood*, New York, New Directions, 1946 (LF)

Barr, James, *Quatrefoil*, Boston, Alyson Publications, 1984 (GF)

Beam, Joseph, ed., *In the Life: A Black Gay Anthology*, Boston, Alyson Publications, 1986 (GF/N)

Bell, Arthur, *Dancing the Gay Lib Blues*, New York, Simon & Schuster, 1971 (GF)

————, *Kings Don't Mean a Thing*, New York, William Morrow, 1978 (GF)

Bernard, Robert, *A Catholic Education*, New York, Holt, Rinehart, and Winston, 1982 (GF)

Bowen, Elizabeth, *Eva Trout*, New York, Avon, 1968 (LF)

————, *A World of Love*, New York, Avon, 1954 (LF)

————, *The Heat of the Day*, New York, Buccaneer Books, 1981 (LF)

_____, *Death of the Heart*, New York, Modern Library, 1984 (LF)

_____, *The House in Paris*, New York, Avon, 1979 (LF)

_____, *The Last September*, New York, Avon, 1952 (LF)

_____, *The Hotel*, New York, Avon, 1956 (LF)

Bowles, Jane, *Two Serious Ladies*, New York, Dutton, 1984 (LF)

_____, *My Sister's Hand in Mine: The Collected Works of Jane Bowles*, New York, Ecco Press, 1978 (LF)

Bowles, Paul, *Collected Stories*, Santa Rosa, Calif., Black Sparrow Press, 1983 (GF)

_____, *Let It Come Down*, Santa Rosa, Calif., Black Sparrow Press, 1980 (GF)

_____, *Up Above the World*, New York, Ecco Press, 1982 (GF)

Brady, Maureen, *Folly*, Trumansburg, New York, The Crossing Press, 1982 (GF)

Brown, Rita Mae, *Rubyfruit Jungle*, Plainfield, VT, Daughters, Inc., 1973 (LF)

_____, *A Plain Brown Rapper*, Oakland, Calif., Diana Press, 1976 (LF)

_____, *Sudden Death*, New York, Bantam, 1984 (LF)

_____, *Six of One*, New York, Bantam, 1978 (LF)

Bryant, Dorothy, *Miss Giardino*, Berkeley, Calif., Ata Books, 1978 (LF)

_____, *The Garden of Eros*, Berkeley, Calif., Ata Books, 1979 (LF)

_____, *Prisoners*, Berkeley, Calif., Ata Books, 1980 (LF)

_____, *Ella Price's Journal*, Berkeley, Calif., Ata Books, 1982 (LF)

_____, *Myths to Lie By*, Berkeley, Calif., Ata Books, 1984 (LF)

_____, *Confessions to Madame Psyche*, Berkeley, Calif., Ata Books, 1986 (LF)

Burroughs, William S., *Cities of the Red Night*, New York, Holt, Rinehart & Winston, 1981 (GF)

_____, *The Wild Boys*, Grove Press, 1981 (GF)

_____, *Queer*, New York, Viking/Penguin, 1985 (GF)

Cameron, Anne, *How the Loon Lost Her Voice*, Madeira Park, Canada, Harbour (LF)

_____, *How Raven Freed the Moon*, Madeira Park, Canada, Harbour (LF)

_____, *Dzelarhons: Mythology*, Madeira Park, Canada, Harbour, 1986 (LF)

Capote, Truman, *Other Voices, Other Rooms*, New York, Random House, 1968 (GF)

_____, *Music for Chameleons*, New York, Random House, 1980 (GF)

_____, *Breakfast at Tiffany's*, New York, New American Library, 1959 (IF)

_____, *The Grass Harp and Other Short Stories*, New York, New American Library, 1945 (GF)

_____, *The Dogs Bark and Other Stories*, New York, New American Library, 1977 (GF)

Christian, Paula, *The Cruise*, New Milford, CT, Timely Books, 1982 (LF)

_____, *Edge of Twilight*, New Milford, CT, Timely Books, 1978 (LF)

_____, *This Side of Love*, New Milford, CT, Timely Books, 1978 (LF)

_____, *Love is Where You Find It*, New Milford, CT, Timely Books, 1978 (LF)

_____, *Another Kind of Love*, New Milford, CT, Timely Books, 1980 (LF)

_____, *Amanda*, New Milford, CT, Timely Books, 1981 (LF)

_____, *The Other Side of Desire*, New Milford, CT, Timely Books, 1981 (LF)

Clark, Cheryl, *Living as a Lesbian*, Ithaca, New York, Firebrand Books, 1986 (LF)

Clausen, Jan, *Sinking/Stealing*, Trumansburg, New York, Crossing Press, 1985 (LF)

————, *Mother, Sister, Daughter, Lover*, New York, Crossing Press, 1980 (LF)

Colette, *The Pure and the Impure*, New York, Farrar, Straus & Giroux, 1978 (LF)

Conlon, Faith, Rachel da Silva, and Barbara Wilson, eds., *The Things That Divide Us*, Seattle, The Seal Press, 1985 (LF)

Covina, Gina, *City of Hermits*, Berkeley, Calif., Brown Owl Books, 1983 (LF)

Curry, Gerard, *Tangled Sheets and Other Stories*, Austin, Texas, Banned Books, 1986 (GF)

David, Christopher, *Joseph and the Old Man*, New York, St. Martin's Press, 1986 (GF)

Denneny, Michael, *Lovers: The Story of Two Men*, New York, Avon Books, (GN)

————, *Decent Passions: A Book of Real Love Stories*, Boston, Alyson Publications, 1984 (GN)

————, et al. *First Love/Last Love*, New York, Putnam, 1985 (GF)

————, et al. *The Christopher Street Reader*, New York, Putnam, 1984 (GN)

deVries, Rachel Guido, *Tender Warriors*, Ithaca, New York, Firebrand Books, 1986 (LF)

Dick, Kay, *The Shelf*, London, Gay Men's Press, 1984 (GF)

Douglas, Anne Carol, *To the Cleveland Station*, Tallahassee, FL, Naiad Press, 1982 (LF)

Duffy, Maureen, *That's How It Was*, Hutchinson, Great Britain, 1962, reprint, Dial Press, 1983 (LF)

Decarnin, Camilla, Eric Garber, and Lyn Paleo, eds., *Worlds Apart: An Anthology of Lesbian and Gay Science Fiction and Fantasy*, Boston, Alyson Publications, 1986 (LGS)

Duplechan, Larry, *Eight Days a Week*, Boston, Alyson Publications, 1985 (GF)

Elliot, Jeffrey M., ed., *Kindred Spirits*, Boston, Alyson Publications, 1984 (LGS)

Ferro, Robert, *The Family of Max Desir*, New York, Dutton, 1985 (GF)

Findley, Timothy, *The Butterfly Plague*, New York, Penguin, 1969 (GF)

————, *Not Wanted on the Voyage*, New York, Penguin, 1984 (GF)

Firbank, Ronald, *Flower Beneath the Foot*, New York, New Directions, 1981 (GF)

Fisher, Pete, *Dreamlovers*, New York, Sea Horse Press, 1982 (GF)

Fisher, Peter, and Marc Rubin, *Special Teachers, Special Boys*, New York, St. Martin's Press, 1979 (GF)

Forrest, Katherine, *Curious Wine*, Tallahassee, FL, Naiad Press, 1983 (LF)

————, *Daughters of a Coral Dawn*, Tallahassee, FL, Naiad Press, 1984 (LF)

————, *Amateur City*, Tallahassee, FL, Naiad Press, 1984 (LF)

————, *Murder at the Nightwood Bar*, Tallahassee, FL, Naiad Press (LF)

Friedel, Richard, *The Movie Lover*, Boston, Alyson Publications, 1983 (GF)

Forster, E.M., *Maurice*, New York, W.W. Norton, 1971 (GF)

————, *The Life to Come and Other Stories*, New York, W.W. Norton, 1973 (GF)

Fox, John, *The Boys on the Rock*, New York, St. Martin's Press, 1984 (GF)

Gapen, Jane, *Something Not Yet Ended*, Tallahassee, FL, Naiad Press, (LF)

Garden, Nancy, *Annie on My Mind*, New York, Farrar, Straus & Giroux, 1982 (YlF)

Gearhart, Sally, *The Wanderground*, Watertown, Mass., Perspehone Press, 1978 (LSF)

Geller, Ruth, *Triangles*, New York, Crossing Press, 1984 (LF)

Genet, Jean, *Our Lady of the Flowers*, New York, Bantam Books, 1963 (GF)

————, *The Miracle of the Rose*, New York, Grove Press, 1968 (GF)

————, *Funeral Rites*, New York, Grove Press, 1969 (GF)

————, *Querelle*, New York, Grove Press, 1975 (GF)

Gide, André, *The Immoralist*, New York, Random House, 1970 (GF)

————, *If It Die*, New York, Penguin, 1957 (GF)

Gilman, Charlotte Perkins, *HerLand: A Lost Feminist Utopian Novel*, New York, Pantheon, 1979 (LF)

Gluck, Robert, *Jack the Modernist*, New York, Gay Presses of New York, 1985 (GF)

Gomez, Alma, Cherrie Moraga, and Mariana Romo-Carmona, eds., *Cuentos: Stories by Latinas*, New York, Kitchen Table Press, (LF)

Grae, Camarin, *The Winged Dancer*, Chicago, Blazon Books, 1983 (LF)

Greene, Graham, *May We Borrow Your Husband? and Other Comedies of the Sexual Life*, New York, Penguin (GF)

Grumbach, Doris, *Chamber Music*, New York, Dutton, 1979 (GF)

————, *The Ladies*, New York, Dutton, 1984 (LF)

————, *Magician's Girl*, New York, Macmillan, 1987 (LF)

Hale, Keith, *Cody*, Boston, Alyson Publications, 1986 (GF)

Hall, Lynn, *Sticks and Stones*, Chicago, Follett, 1972 (YGF)

Hall, Radclyffe, *The Well of Loneliness*, New York, Pocket Books, 1928 (LF)

————, *The Unlit Lamp*, New York, Doubleday, 1981 (LF)

————, *Adam's Breed*, New York, Penguin, 1986 (LF)

Hall, Richard, *The Butterscotch Prince*, New York, Pyramid Books, 1975 (GM)

————, *Letter from a Great-Uncle & Other Stories*, Eugene, Oregon, Grey Fox Press, 1985 (GF)

Hamilton, Wallace, *Kevin: A Moving and Revealing Novel About Love Between a Teenage Boy and an Older Man*, New York, St. Martin's Press, 1980 (GF)

Hanscombe, Gillian E., *Between Friends*, Boston, Alyson Publications, 1982 (LF)

Hansen, Joseph, *A Smile in His Lifetime*, New York, Holt, Rinehart & Winston, 1981 (GM)

————, *Nightwork*, New York, Holt, Rinehart & Winston, 1984 (GM)

————, *Death Claims*, New York, Holt, Rinehart & Winston, 1983 (GM)

————, *Troublemaker*, New York, Holt, Rinehart & Winston, 1975 (GM)

————, *Skinflick*, New York, Holt, Rinehart, & Winston, (GM)

————, *The Man Everybody Was Afraid Of*, New York, Holt, Rinehart & Winston, (GM)

————, *Job's Year*, New York, New American Library, 1983 (GM)

Harrison, Donald, *The Spartan*, Boston, Alyson Publications, 1982 (GF)

Harrison, William, *Burton and Speke*, New York, St. Martin's Press, 1982 (GF)

Harvey, Andrew, *Burning Houses*, Boston, Houghton-Mifflin, 1986 (GF)

————, *The Web*, Boston, Houghton-Mifflin, 1987 (GF)

Hautzig, Deborah, *Hey Doll Face*, New York, Bantam Books, 1978 (YLF)

Hobson, Laura, *Consenting Adult*, New York, Doubleday & Co., 1975 (GF)

Holland, Isabelle, *The Man Without a Face*, New York, Dell, 1972 (YGF)

Holleran, Andrew, *Dancer from the Dance*, New York, William Morrow, 1978 (GF)

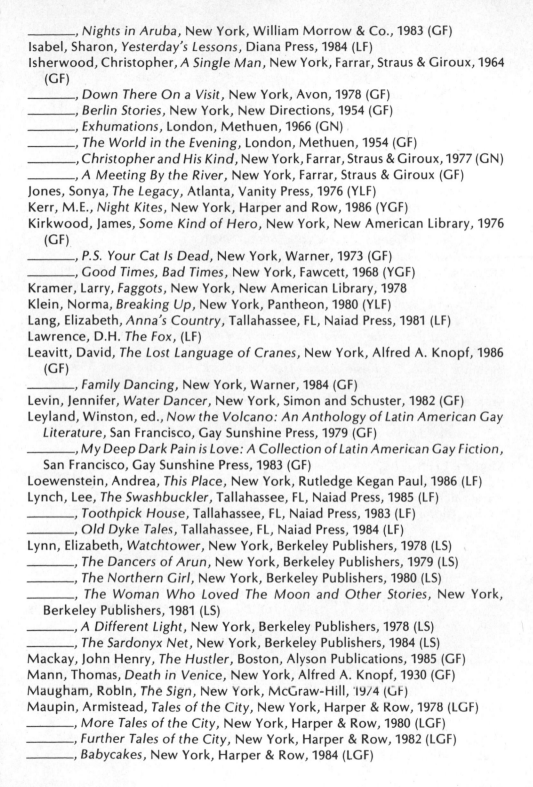

————, *Nights in Aruba*, New York, William Morrow & Co., 1983 (GF)

Isabel, Sharon, *Yesterday's Lessons*, Diana Press, 1984 (LF)

Isherwood, Christopher, *A Single Man*, New York, Farrar, Straus & Giroux, 1964 (GF)

————, *Down There On a Visit*, New York, Avon, 1978 (GF)

————, *Berlin Stories*, New York, New Directions, 1954 (GF)

————, *Exhumations*, London, Methuen, 1966 (GN)

————, *The World in the Evening*, London, Methuen, 1954 (GF)

————, *Christopher and His Kind*, New York, Farrar, Straus & Giroux, 1977 (GN)

————, *A Meeting By the River*, New York, Farrar, Straus & Giroux (GF)

Jones, Sonya, *The Legacy*, Atlanta, Vanity Press, 1976 (YLF)

Kerr, M.E., *Night Kites*, New York, Harper and Row, 1986 (YGF)

Kirkwood, James, *Some Kind of Hero*, New York, New American Library, 1976 (GF)

————, *P.S. Your Cat Is Dead*, New York, Warner, 1973 (GF)

————, *Good Times, Bad Times*, New York, Fawcett, 1968 (YGF)

Kramer, Larry, *Faggots*, New York, New American Library, 1978

Klein, Norma, *Breaking Up*, New York, Pantheon, 1980 (YLF)

Lang, Elizabeth, *Anna's Country*, Tallahassee, FL, Naiad Press, 1981 (LF)

Lawrence, D.H. *The Fox*, (LF)

Leavitt, David, *The Lost Language of Cranes*, New York, Alfred A. Knopf, 1986 (GF)

————, *Family Dancing*, New York, Warner, 1984 (GF)

Levin, Jennifer, *Water Dancer*, New York, Simon and Schuster, 1982 (GF)

Leyland, Winston, ed., *Now the Volcano: An Anthology of Latin American Gay Literature*, San Francisco, Gay Sunshine Press, 1979 (GF)

————, *My Deep Dark Pain is Love: A Collection of Latin American Gay Fiction*, San Francisco, Gay Sunshine Press, 1983 (GF)

Loewenstein, Andrea, *This Place*, New York, Rutledge Kegan Paul, 1986 (LF)

Lynch, Lee, *The Swashbuckler*, Tallahassee, FL, Naiad Press, 1985 (LF)

————, *Toothpick House*, Tallahassee, FL, Naiad Press, 1983 (LF)

————, *Old Dyke Tales*, Tallahassee, FL, Naiad Press, 1984 (LF)

Lynn, Elizabeth, *Watchtower*, New York, Berkeley Publishers, 1978 (LS)

————, *The Dancers of Arun*, New York, Berkeley Publishers, 1979 (LS)

————, *The Northern Girl*, New York, Berkeley Publishers, 1980 (LS)

————, *The Woman Who Loved The Moon and Other Stories*, New York, Berkeley Publishers, 1981 (LS)

————, *A Different Light*, New York, Berkeley Publishers, 1978 (LS)

————, *The Sardonyx Net*, New York, Berkeley Publishers, 1984 (LS)

Mackay, John Henry, *The Hustler*, Boston, Alyson Publications, 1985 (GF)

Mann, Thomas, *Death in Venice*, New York, Alfred A. Knopf, 1930 (GF)

Maugham, Robin, *The Sign*, New York, McGraw-Hill, 1974 (GF)

Maupin, Armistead, *Tales of the City*, New York, Harper & Row, 1978 (LGF)

————, *More Tales of the City*, New York, Harper & Row, 1980 (LGF)

————, *Further Tales of the City*, New York, Harper & Row, 1982 (LGF)

————, *Babycakes*, New York, Harper & Row, 1984 (LGF)

_____, *Significant Others*, New York, Harper & Row, 1987 (LGF)

McCauley, Stephen, *The Object of My Affection*, New York, Simon and Schuster, 1987 (LGF)

McConnell, Vicki P., *Mrs. Porter's Letter*, Tallahassee, FL, Naiad Press, 1982 (LF)

_____, *The Burnton Windows*, Tallahassee, FL, Naiad Press, 1983 (LF)

McCullers, Carson, *The Ballad of the Sad Cafe*, New York, Bantam, 1969 (IF)

McGehee, Peter, *Beyond Happiness*, Toronto, Stubblejumper Press, 1985 (GF)

Merrick, Gordon, *An Idol for Others*, New York, Avon, 1977 (GF)

_____, *Forth Into Light*, New York, Avon, 1974 (GF)

_____, *The Lord Won't Mind*, New York, Avon, 1971 (GF)

_____, *One for the Gods*, New York, Avon, 1972 (GF)

_____, *The Quirk*, New York, Avon, 1978 (GF)

_____, *Now Let's Talk About Music*, New York, Avon, 1981 (GF)

_____, *Perfect Freedom*, New York, Avon, 1982 (GF)

_____, *A Measure of Madness*, New York, Warner, 1986 (GF)

Miller, Isabel, *Patience and Sarah*, Greenwich, CT, Fawcett Crest, 1973 (LF)

_____, *The Love of Good Women*, Tallahassee, FL, Naiad Press, 1986 (LF)

Miller, Merle, *What Happened*, New York, St. Martin's Press, (GF)

Miner, Valerie, *Blood Sisters*, New York, St. Martin's Press, 1982 (LF)

_____, *Murder in the English Department*, New York, St. Martin's Press, 1983 (LF)

Mishima, Yukio, *Confessions of a Mask*, New York, New Directions, 1958 (GF)

_____, *Forbidden Colors*, New York, Putnam, 1968 (GF)

Morden, Ethan, *I've a Feeling We're Not in Kansas Anymore: Tales from Gay Manhattan*, New York, St. Martin's Press, 1985 (GF)

_____, *Buddies*, New York, St. Martin's Press, 1986 (GF)

_____, *One Last Waltz*, New York, St. Martin's Press, 1986 (GF)

Morgan, Claire, *The Price of Salt*, Tallahassee, FL, Naiad Press, 1986 (LF)

Nachman, Elana, *Riverfinger Woman*, Plainfield, VT, Daughters, 1974 (YLF)

Nava, Michael, *The Little Death*, Boston, Alyson Publications, 1986 (GF)

Naylor, Gloria, *The Women of Brewster Place*, New York, Penguin Books, 1983 (LF)

_____, *Linden Hills*, New York, Ticknor & Fields, 1985 (LGF)

Orton, Joe, *Head to Toe*, New York, St. Martin's Press, 1971 (GF)

Peters, Fritz, *Finistere*, New York, New American Library, (GF)

Picano, Felice, *The Lure*, New York, Delacorte Press, 1979 (GF)

_____, *Slashed to Ribbons in Defense of Love and Other Stories*, New York, Gay Presses of New York, 1983 (GF)

_____, ed. *A True Likeness: Lesbian and Gay Writing Today*, New York, The Sea Horse Press, 1980 (GF)

_____, *Ambidextrous: The Secret Lives of Children*, New York, Gay Presses of New York, 1985 (GF)

Piercy, Marge, *Small Changes*, New York, Fawcett, 1978 (LF)

_____, *Women on the Edge of Time*, New York, Fawcett, 1981 (IS)

Pintauro, Joseph, *Cold Hands*, New York, New American Library, 1979 (GF)

Preston, John, *Sweet Dreams*, Boston, Alyson Publications, 1984 (GF)

_____, *The Golden Years*, Boston, Alyson Publications, 1984 (GF)

_____, *Deadly Lies*, Boston, Alyson Publications, 1985 (GF)

_____, *Stolen Moments*, Boston, Alyson Publications, 1985 (GF)

_____, *Franny: The Queen of Provincetown*, Boston, Alyson Publications, 1983 (GF)

_____, ed., *Hot Living*, Boston, Alyson Publications, 1985 (GF)

Puig, Manuel, *Kiss of the Spider Woman*, New York, Alfred A. Knopf, 1979 (GF)

_____, *The Buenos Aires Affair*, New York, Random House, 1980 (GF)

_____, *Betrayed by Rita Hayworth*, New York, Random House, 1981 (GF)

_____, *Heartbreak Tango*, New York, Random House, 1981 (GF)

Purdy, James, *The Mourners Below*, New York, Penguin, 1981 (GF)

_____, *I Am Elijah Thrush*, London, Gay Men's Press, 1986

_____, *Narrow Rooms*, London, Gay Men's Press, 1985 (GF)

_____, *In the Hollow of His Hands*, London, Weidenfeld and Nicolson, 1987 (GF)

_____, *In a Shallow Grave*, New York, Arbor House, 1975 (GF)

_____, *The Nephew*, New York, Penguin, 1960 (GF)

Reading, J.P., *Bouquets for Brimbal*, New York, Harper and Row, 1980 (YFL)

Rechy, John, *City of Night*, New York, Grove Press, 1964 (GF)

_____, *The Sexual Outlaw*, New York, Grove Press, 1977 (GF)

_____, *Rushes*, New York, Grove Press, 1979 (GF)

_____, *Numbers*, New York, Grove Press, 1967 (GF)

_____, *Bodies and Souls*, New York, Carroll & Graf Publishers, 1983 (GF)

_____, *The Vampires*, New York, Grove Press, 1971 (GF)

_____, *The Fourth Angel*, New York, Grove Press, 1975 (GF)

Reed, Paul, *Facing It: a Novel of A.I.D.S.*, San Francisco, Gay Sunshine Press, 1984 (GF)

Rees, David, *In the Tent*, Boston, Alyson Publications, 1979 (GF)

_____, *The Estuary*, Boston, Alyson Publications, 1983 (GF)

_____, *The Milkman's on His Way*, Boston, Alyson Publications, 1982 (GF)

Reid, John, *The Best Little Boy in the World*, New York, Ballantine, 1977 (GF)

Renault, Mary, *The Charioteer*, London, Longmans, 1953 (GF)

_____, *The Last of the Wine*, New York, Random House, 1975 (GF)

_____, *Fire From Heaven*, New York, Pantheon, 1969 (GF)

_____, *The Persian Boy*, New York, Pantheon, 1972 (GF)

Rice, Ann, *Cry to Heaven*, New York, Alfred A. Knopf, 1982 (GF)

Rivkin, J.F., *Silverglass*, New York, Ace Fantasy Books, 1986 (LS)

Robinson, Jack, *Teardrops On My Drum*, London, Gay Men's Press, 1986 (GF)

Rogers, Paul T., *Saul's Book*, New York, Penguin Books, 1983 (GF)

Rossner, Judith, *August*, New York, Warner Books, 1984 (LF)

Rule, Jane, *The Desert of the Heart*, Tallahassee, FL, Naiad Press, 1983 (LF)

_____, *This Is Not For You*, Tallahassee, FL, Naiad Press, 1982 (LF)

_____, *Against the Season*, Tallahassee, FL, Naiad Press, 1984 (LF)

_____, *Inland Passage and Other Stories*, Tallahassee, FL, Naiad Press, 1985 (LF)

_____, *Contract With the World*, Tallahassee, FL, Naiad Press, 1980 (LF)

_____, *Hot-Eyed Moderate*, Tallahassee, FL, Naiad Press, 1985 (LF)

_____, *The Young in One Another's Arms*, Tallahassee, FL, Naiad Press, 1984 (LF)

————, *The Outlander*, Tallahassee, FL, Naiad Press, 1981 (LF)

————, *Memory Board*, Tallahassee, FL, Naiad Press, 1987 (LF)

Russ, Joanna, *The Female Man*, Boston, Beacon Press, 1987 (LF)

————, *On Strike Against God*, Crossing Press, 1985 (LF)

————, *Extra (Ordinary) People*, NY, St. Martin's Press, 1984 (LF)

Sarton, May, *Mrs. Stevens Hears the Mermaids Singing*, New York, W.W. Norton, 1974 (LF)

————, *A Reckoning*, New York, W.W. Norton, 1978 (LF)

————, *The Magnificent Spinster*, New York, W.W. Norton, 1985 (LF)

————, *Faithful are the Wounds*, New York, W.W. Norton, 1972 (LF)

Scoppettone, Sandra, *Happy Endings Are All Alike*, New York, Bantam, 1974 (YGF)

Shockley, Ann, *Loving Her*, Tallahassee, FL, Naiad Press, 1978 (LF)

————, *The Black and the White of It*, Tallahassee, FL, Naiad Press, 1980 (LF)

Sinclair, Jo, (Ruth Seid), *The Changelings*, Old Westbury, New York, Feminist Press, 1985 (LF)

Sitkin, Patricia, *The Alexandros Expedition*, Boston, Alyson Publications, 1984 (GF)

Snyder, Anne, *The Truth About Alex*, New York, New American Library, (YGF)

Stambolian, George, ed., *Men on Men: Best New Gay Fiction*, New York, New American Library, 1986 (GF)

Stein, Gertrude, *Three Lives*, New York, New American Library, 1985 (LF)

————, *Ida*, NY, Random House, 1972 (LF)

Stimpson, Kate, *Class Notes*, New York, Avon, 1979 (YLF)

Taylor, Sheila Ortiz, *Faultline*, Tallahassee, FL, Naiad Press, 1981 (LF)

————, *Spring Forward/Fall Back*, Tallahassee, FL, Naiad Press, 1985 (LF)

Taylor, Valerie, *Journey to Fulfillment*, Tallahassee, FL, Naiad Press, 1982 (LF)

————, *Return to Lesbos*, Tallahassee, FL, Naiad Press, 1982 (LF)

————, *A World Without Men*, Tallahassee, FL, Naiad Press, 1982 (LF)

————, *Prism*, Tallahassee, FL, Naiad Press, 1981 (LF)

Toder, Nancy, *Choices*, Boston, Alyson Publications, 1984 (LF)

Torchia, Joseph, *Kryptonite Kid*, New York, Holt, Rinehart and Winston, 1980 (GF)

Tournier, Michel, *Gemini*, Garden City, NY, Doubleday 1981 (GF)

Vidal, Gore, *The City and the Pillar*, New York, Ballantine, 1948 (GF)

————, *Myra Breckinridge*, New York, Ballantine, 1968 (GF)

————, *Homage to Daniel Shays*, New York, Random House, 1973 (GF)

Vivian, Jean, *The Love of Two Women*, Galena, Kansas, Woman Prints, 1982 (LF)

Vivien, Renee, *A Woman Appeared to Me*, Tallahassee, FL, Naiad Press, 1979 (LF)

————, *The Woman of the Wolf*, New York, Gay Presses of New York, 1983 (LF)

Walker, Alice, *The Color Purple*, New York, Washington Square Press, 1983 (LF)

————, *You Can't Keep a Good Woman Down: Stories*, Harcourt, Brace, Jovanovich, 1980 (LF)

Warren, Patricia Nell, *The Front Runner*, New York, William Morrow, 1974 (GF)

————, *The Fancy Dancer*, New York, William Morrow, 1976 (GF)

————, *The Beauty Queen*, New York, William Morrow, 1978 (GF)

Welch, Denton, *Maiden Voyage*, New York, Dutton, 1943 (GF)

_____, *In Youth is Pleasure*, New York, Dutton, 1945 (GF)

_____, *A Voice Through a Cloud*, New York, Dutton, 1950 (GF)

_____, *The Stories of Denton Welch*, ed. Robert Philips, New York, E.P. Dutton, 1985 (GF)

White, Edmund, *Nocturnes for the King of Naples*, New York, St. Martin's Press, 1978 (GF)

_____, *A Boy's Own Story*, New York, Dutton, 1982 (GF)

_____, *Caracole*, New York, Dutton, 1985 (GF)

_____, *The Beautiful Room is Empty*, New York, Random House, 1988 (GF)

Whitmore, George, *The Confessions of Danny Slocum*, Oakland, Calif., Grey Fox Press, 1980 (GF)

Wilde, Oscar, *The Picture of Dorian Gray*, New York, Bantam, 1982 (GF)

_____, *The Happy Prince*, Oxford University Press, 1980 (YIF)

Wilhelm, Gale, *We Too Are Drifting*, Tallahassee, FL, Naiad Press, 1985 (LF)

_____, *Torchlight to Valhalla*, Ayer Co. Publishers, 1975 (LF)

Williams, Tennessee, *Tennessee Williams: Collected Stories*, New York, Ballantine, 1985 (GF)

Wilson, Barbara, *Sisters of the Road*, Seattle, The Seal Press, 1986 (LF)

_____, *Murder in the Collective*, Seattle, The Seal Press, 1984 (LF)

Wittig, Monique, *Les Guerilleres*, Boston, Beacon Press, 1986 (LF)

Wolitzer, Meg, *Hidden Pictures*, Boston, Houghton-Mifflin Co., 1986 (LF)

Wood, Roy F., *Restless Rednecks: Gay Tales of a Changing South*, Oakland, Calif., Grey Fox Press, 1985 (GF)

Woolf, Virginia, *Orlando*, NY, Harcourt, Brace, Jovanovich, 1973 (IF)

Worsley, T.C., *Fellow Travellers*, London, Gay Men's Press, 1984 (GF)

Yourcenar, Marguerite, *Memories of Hadrian*, New York, Modern Library, 1984 (GF)

Index

405